PRAISE FOR NEXT WAVE

● ● ●

"Some mighty great journalism here. I just wish I had assigned more of it."
Graydon Carter, Editor, *Vanity Fair*

"When young editors (or aspiring editors) ask me where we find writers and reporters at *Esquire,* I tell them that all you have to do is look. There is a wealth of young men and women doing ambitious journalism. *Next Wave* is both proof of that assertion and a blueprint for the generation that will follow these writers."
David Granger, Editor-in-Chief, *Esquire*

"And literary journalism was supposed to be dying? This collection is proof positive that ambitious, inspired non-fiction storytelling has life in it yet."
Adam Moss, Editor, *New York*

"Even more than journalism as literature, it rips (and soars) as the truth about the way we live and tell each other who we are."
Terry McDonell, Editor, *Sports Illustrated*

"The work in this anthology has all the heft and ambition, and all the literary fireworks, of the great anthologies of American journalism like *Smiling Through the Apocalypse,* which was sort of a bright and shining *New Testament* to me and ought to be in every reporter's crusty-ass backpack. It's still an apocalypse out there. Thank God we have gifted writers like these to show us how to grin and bear it."

Jim Nelson, Editor-in-chief, *GQ*

"The collection of young writers in this anthology have the kind of talent that inspires the next generation to tell great stories. They have ambition and brains and, thankfully, many, many years left of finding the kinds of gems that make us stop what we are doing for the sake of a good read."

Chad Millman, Editor-in-Chief,
ESPN The Magazine

NEXT WAVE

America's New Generation of
Great Literary Journalists

Edited by
Walt Harrington and Mike Sager

THE SAGER GROUP

Artifex Te Adiuva

NEXT WAVE: America's New Generation of Great Literary Journalists,
Edited by Walt Harrington and Mike Sager

Cover Designed by: Siori Kitajima, Sf AppWorks LLC. http://www.sfappworks.com
Formatting by Siori Kitajima and Ovidiu Vlad for SF AppWorks LLC
E-Book Formatted by: Smashwords
Cataloging-in-Publication data for this book is available from the Library of Congress.
ISBN-13: 978-1481160896   ISBN-10: 1481160893
E-book published by The Sager Group at Smashwords.
info@TheSagerGroup.net   info@MikeSager.com

Dedication

●●●

For all the great editors who hire and mentor and edit and give us stories to write and put up with our crazy outbursts and idiosyncrasies and long sentences in the name of raising journalism to art.

For all the great magazines and newspapers and other institutions that have spent precious resources on outlandish capers and dogged pursuits, allowing our form to flourish, even in difficult times.

Contents

• • •

Dedication / v

Introduction / xi

Walt Harrington and Mike Sager, The New Masters

Pamela Colloff, "Hannah and Andrew" / 1

When a four-year-old dies mysteriously of salt poisoning, his foster mother is charged with capital murder, vilified from all quarters, and sent to prison for life. But is this churchgoing young woman really a vicious child killer? *Texas Monthly*

Luke Dittrich, "Tonight on *Dateline* This Man Will Die" / 31

As a SWAT team stormed his house and NBC's "To Catch A Predator" crew waited on his front lawn, a Texas prosecutor— who'd been having an explicit, on-line flirtation with an actor posing as a 13-year-old— takes his own life. *Esquire*

Todd C. Frankel, "The $1 Million Bill" / 63

Out of work, out of luck, living with his wife in his daughter's cramped public housing apartment, he finds a peculiar piece of money in a pay phone outside a gas station in St. Louis. One man's hopeful odyssey. *St. Louis Post-Dispatch*

Vanessa Grigoriadis, "The Tragedy of Britney Spears" / 75

A pop star at the mall is an eternal cause for pandemonium, especially on a Sunday afternoon in the Valley. She's 26 now, a mother of two. She has been in and out of hospitals, rehab and court. How Britney lost it all. *Rolling Stone*

Justin Heckert, "Lost in the Waves" / 95

Swept out to sea by a riptide, a father and his 12-year-old autistic son struggle to stay alive. As night falls miles from shore, with no rescue imminent, the dad comes to a devastating realization: If they remain together, they'll drown together. *Men's Journal*

Wil S. Hylton, "The Unspeakable Choice" / 111

After the state of Nebraska makes it legal to abandon a child, the floodgates open—eleven a day at one point, from all over the country. Are there more bad parents or monstrous kids than anyone knew? How can a mother abandon her child? *GQ*

Chris Jones, "Roger Ebert: The Essential Man" / 129

It has been years since Roger Ebert lost his lower jaw and his ability to speak. Now television's most famous movie critic is rarely seen and never heard, but his words have never stopped. One man's triumph over silence. *Esquire*

Michael Kruse, "A Brevard Woman Disappeared" / 147

When a man buys a run-down house at a foreclosure auction, he finds dirty dishes stacked high, plates of mold-covered cat food and... the body of the former owner. How a woman went missing inside her own home. *St. Petersburg Times*

Thomas Lake, "The Boy Who Died of Football" / 157

Three days after he collapsed from heatstroke at practice, 15-year-old Max Gilpin became one of at least 665 boys since 1931 to die playing high school football. This time, the Commonwealth of Kentucky decided to prosecute his coach. *Sports Illustrated*

Dan P. Lee, "Travis the Menace" / 179

He was a newborn when Travis first came to live with Sandy and Jerry, a tiny diapered chimpanzee with a pink face and two Dumbo ears that jutted from the top of his head. In time, he was the most famous ape in America. Then things went horribly wrong. *New York*

Ariel Levy, "Either/Or" / 195

Growing up in rural South Africa, 800-meter running champion Caster Semenya became accustomed to visiting the bathroom with competing coaches in order to prove her sex. One individual's very public struggle with the parameters and stereotypes of gender. *New Yorker*

Brian Mockenhaupt, "Sgt. Wells' New Skull" / 221

One minute he's on patrol. The next he's crumbled in the dirt with a bullet in his head. A soldier's long, slow and miraculous triumph over his traumatic brain injury, an often baffling injury that has become epidemic in the Iraq and Afghanistan wars. *Esquire*

Maximillian Potter, "The Assassin in the Vineyard" / 241

Who would poison the vines of La Romanée-Conti, the tiny, centuries-old vineyard that produces what most agree is Burgundy's finest, rarest, and most expensive wine? *Vanity Fair*

Tony Rehagen, "The Last Trawlers" / 257

For generations, shrimp boats like Michael Boone's *Little Man* have plied the waters along the coast of Georgia, supporting families and honoring traditions. But as foreign seafood floods the market and gas prices soar, a way of life is threatened. *Atlanta*

Robert Sanchez, "The Education of Ms. Barsallo" / 269

Fresh out of college, Millie Barsallo becomes a teacher in one of Denver's most challenging public schools. Can she change the lives of 40 boys and girls? Or will these profoundly needy children leave her forever transformed? *5280*

Eli Saslow, "Three Minutes to Fort Totten" / 291

In one terrifying rush-hour instant, two subway trains crash. Nine people die. Many more are injured. The lives of a chaplain, a doctor, a hair salon owner, and an architect become forever entwined. What happened in Car 1079. *Washington Post*

Wright Thompson, "The Last Days of Tony Harris" / 301

The Charlton Hotel in Brasilia is a most unlikely place to go insane. A former college basketball star faces mortality in the jungle far from home. He knows he sounds crazy, but something—or someone—is after him. *ESPN The Magazine*

Seth Wickersham, "The Final Furlong" / 319

The lethal liquid injected into the jugular of a broken down racehorse is always colored pink—no time for fumbling when a 1,200-pound animal has suffered a catastrophic injury. Facing death every day with a track veterinarian. *ESPN The Magazine*

Jason Zengerle, "Going Under" / 331

Two years into his anesthesiology specialty, Dr. Brent Cambron had great promise. Then one day he stuck a needle full of morphine into his thigh muscle and he was never the same again. Was his spiraling drug addiction a function of his personal demons? Or was it his high-pressure job itself that was dragging him down? *The New Republic*

Notables: More great writers from the Next Wave / 347

Walt Harrington's Suggested Readings / 348

Acknowledgments / 351

Permissions / 352

About the Editors / 354

About the Publisher / 354

Introduction: The New Masters

●●●

"The report of my death was an exaggeration." Mark Twain

We're here to prove that the naysayers who predicted the end of literary journalism—compelling, long-form, nonfiction stories distinguished by in-depth reporting, artful writing and unique authorial point of view—were greatly mistaken.

Next Wave is a collection of articles written in recent years by literary journalists under forty, members of a new generation who have come of age during the Internet boom. Despite the changes wrought by digital media, and the widespread fear that fine and lively nonfiction writing was in eclipse, these journalists are still pursuing the genre Tom Wolfe dubbed "The New Journalism." Building on work by the likes of Wolfe, Joseph Mitchell, John Hersey, Lillian Ross, Gay Talese, David Halberstam, Jane Kramer, John McPhee, Robert Caro, Susan Sheehan and Hunter S. Thompson... and on the later work by the likes of Tracy Kidder, Richard Ben Cramer, Ted Conover, Jon Franklin, Susan Orlean, Adrian Nicole LeBlanc, Gary Smith, Tom Junod, David Remnick, Katherine Boo and David Finkel... this new generation of masters continues the lineage into the present.

In their hands, the craft of journalism is raised to art.

It's not as if we weren't worried. For the last decade, publishers have been wringing their hands, trying to figure out ways to harness their new mistress Internet—and having a rough go of it. All thoughts—and budgets—turned to websites, Facebook, smartphone apps, crowd-sourcing, and data, data, data. Editorial ranks were thinned and thinned again; budgets for reporting, photography and art were slashed. The almighty freelancer's dollar-a-word fee plunged to five cents a word for writing website news. Nobody seemed to care anymore about actual content. It was as if the suits couldn't wrap their minds around the idea that something substantive needed to be placed between the ads. Hell, they couldn't even figure out how to get paid for the ads. Everything became a chase for page hits: How many unique eyes? With whom can we partner to get more unique eyes?

Meanwhile, we were sitting at our respective keyboards—Walt in his professor's office at the University of Illinois in Urbana-Champaign and Mike in his converted pool house office in San Diego. We had met in the *Washington Post* newsroom in 1980 and remained friends and colleagues. Between us we have seventy-three years in the trenches pursuing what has been variously called feature writing, narrative journalism, literary journalism, creative nonfiction, narrative nonfiction, and intimate journalism. Whatever the label, we're talking about a journalism rooted in scene, setting, characters, dialogue and point of view.

Was it really possible that we were witnessing the death rattle of our beloved calling?

Thankfully, the answer is no.

Even as the business of journalism contracted, we kept hearing from people devoted to the literary journalism form. A veteran of the *Post, Rolling Stone* and *Esquire*, Mike continued to hear from college students, alternative weekly and newspaper staffers, and magazine freelancers who tracked him down for advice. At Illinois, Walt continued to find a strong cadre of students who wanted to take his literary journalism class. Bored with journalism's daily diet of news and superficial features, they yearned to do deeply human, complex, textured stories written with personal flair and voice, as Mike and Walt had yearned to do when they were kids. Around the country, Walt's book, *Intimate Journalism*, continued to be used liberally in college classes.

Surprisingly, as it stands today, more opportunities exist for young writers to study and learn the craft of literary journalism than ever before. The country's fine journalism schools and writing programs—many with respected nonfiction writers on their faculties—continue to graduate talented hopefuls. *Niemanstoryboard.org*, maintained by Harvard University's prestigious Nieman Foundation for Journalism, is collecting fine narrative articles from newspapers and magazines and conducting regular author interviews, giving sophisticated guidance to aspiring narrative journalists nationwide. The International Association for Literary Journalism Studies has established the form as a subject for academic study and launched annual conferences in exotic locales such as London, Paris and Brussels. Literary Journalism has even taken off in Scandinavia, Slovenia, Romania, Argentina, Spain and Belgium.

And a funny thing happened on the way to the funeral for long-form journalism: The source of its supposed demise—the Internet—may well turn out to save it by bringing an unexpected renaissance of opportunity for practitioners and readers alike. New websites such as *Byliner.com*, *Longform. org*, *Atavist.com*, and *LongStories.net* are collecting literary journalism from all around the world, making it more easily available to readers than ever. Some of these sites are taking on the role of traditional publications— assigning original stories for pay. (And sharing the back-end profits with the writers, who have to ante up their own expenses.) The *Huffington Post* Web operation even won a Pulitzer Prize for its 10-part series on wounded war veterans. The websites of individual magazines are just a net search away. And eBooks give anyone the ability to become a publisher. Just ask Mike. *Next Wave* is being released as an eBook (with on-demand paper publishing available) by The Sager Group, a boutique cooperative of artists and writers who want more creative control over the disposition of their work.

Given this dichotomy—an army of aspiring young reporter-writers in contracting economic times—it has been hard to know what to tell the hopeful. Weeklies, dailies, glossies, book publishing: They're all under duress. How does a young man or woman begin to tell Mom and Dad, who are spending the cost of a house on a college degree, that he or she wants to be a ... literary journalist?

As it happened, without consulting, we were both giving the same advice.

Becoming a writer—any kind of writer—has always been a long shot. It defies all cost-benefit analyses. You have to be willing to hear no and keep going back. You often have to do it on the side around your day job. There never has been a defined career path for doing this kind of work—there's no exit on the occupational highway of life marked "Literary Journalist." To become one you have to want it more than anything. More than job security or predictable career trajectory. More than always being home for your partner's birthdays. More than your fear of personal bodily harm or the threat of arrest in some cases. More than great wealth in almost all cases—although there's always the small chance that honest hard work will pay off with a lucrative book contract or movie deal.

For all the uncertainties, there is beauty in our writers' meritocracy: Good work speaks for itself.

As they like to say in our field: Show it, don't tell it.

That's what *Next Wave* does.

The stories here are the result of more than a year of searching, reading, culling, and mild argument between Walt and Mike, with the help of enthusiastic students from the University of Illinois and Goucher College. Notices were posted on nonfiction websites, writers nominated themselves and their peers. Our student researchers pored through the last decade of National Magazine Award, Pulitzer Prize and Society of Professional Journalists feature award winners, as well as the Nieman Storyboard collection. The stories come from glossy New York magazines, city and regional magazines, and newspapers. Some are award winners; others are secret gems that got little attention, except from other writers. Some of these amazing stories seemingly tell themselves—meaning that a good writer was crafty enough to get him or herself out of the way. Some stories are what folks in the country call a silk purse from a sow's ear—stories that wouldn't exist without the artful execution of the writer.

We have collected only stories written fundamentally in third person. Mike believes that deeply first-person journalism is a different genre; Walt believes it less so. Following the example of Walt's previous anthology of first person journalism, *The Beholder's Eye*, we plan to collect a second volume dedicated to the amazing first-person work of this new generation, which is flourishing in this age of self-confession. The other arbitrary factor in this effort is the age limit—people under age forty in 2011, when we started assembling the potential selectees. As a result, we missed the work of some excellent literary journalists born a bit too soon. For that we are sorry, but we had to cut it off somewhere. In the end, our choices came down to taste—our taste. If we missed someone deserving, we are sorry. It was nothing personal. But we do promise that what we've chosen is some really amazing work.

It's heartening that a few of the stories included in this collection come from grubby old newspapers, where the art of storytelling—and the medium itself—seems comatose. Yet if you look around the country at the papers still working hard to stay alive, many are moving toward more feature or news feature coverage because they know they can't compete with the breaking news advantages of the Web. We hope so. Newspapers were our training ground. We also believe quality storytelling is one of the keys to newspaper survival. At the end of the daisy chain of cross marketing and linking of brands, maybe the answer is this: Giving people something beautifully enjoyable to read.

That's what we hope we've done here. A poor man who discovers a $1 million bill and his quest to have it authenticated. The tragedy of a beloved pet chimp run amok. The sad yet hopeful tale of a first-year teacher in an impoverished school. The Florida woman who died in her house—and nobody noticed. The confusing issues over the genetic sex of one of the world's greatest athletes. The minutes before and after the Washington, D.C., subway crash that took nine lives. The prosecutor, caught in a sting by *Dateline's* "To Catch a Predator," who takes his own life. A father and his autistic son, enjoying a swim, swept out to sea. The brilliant doctor who succumbed tragically to the temptations of his own occupation. A woman who legally abandons her child. An unthinkable crime in the French vineyard that produces Burgundy's finest wine. The last days of a mentally ill basketball player alone in a distant land. The horse-track veterinarian who ends the lives of beautiful creatures. The fortitude of a shrimp boat captain trying to maintain his family's long tradition in a changing world. A reluctant high-school football player who died on the practice field. A good woman who may have been wrongly convicted of killing her adopted, troubled child. A wounded soldier given a new skull. And profiles of movie critic Roger Ebert and pop diva Britney Spears that offer rare and substantial glimpses behind the curtain of celebrity.

The common denominators these stories share are humanity, compassion and poignancy. They take us beyond accepted wisdom and inside human experience in a way that often feels like a movie, short story or novel—in a way that feels real. They blend deep reporting of hard facts with the reporting of sensation, emotion and, importantly, ambiguity. In a world where it seems everybody has a strong opinion about everything, these stories remind us to be humble about what we think we know. They illustrate how literary journalism can unlock the inner workings of human experience in ways that traditional news, investigative and feature journalism can't. As in all journalism, the work demands literal, verifiable fact. That's the heart of the craft, the start of the art. Yet the form also honors the facts of human frailty and failing, human emotion, struggle, hope, confusion, fear and wisdom. It is factual storytelling with head, heart and soul. Like no other form of journalism, it allows us to go behind the exterior world around us and explore the interior of real lives in all their complexity.

The journalists who do this work love it and it shows: The deep time spent with real people, the weird places they visit, the joy of practicing junk-yard anthropology, the chance to leave their own heads and enter the psyches of their subjects and come away wiser, the time spent mastering the turning of a good phrase or a nice simile, collecting the telling details others miss, finding meaning in the jumble of facts, quotes and events they have witnessed. As you will see when you read their personal essays, they have a lot in common; though their styles are different, their hearts are very much the same. One thing writers agree about: we love to share our work. Especially with discerning readers, people who love the form as much as we do. We write for ourselves, dear readers, but we are nothing without you.

Walt Harrington and Mike Sager

Pamela Colloff

Pamela Colloff is an executive editor at *Texas Monthly*, and has been writing for the magazine since 1997. Her work has also appeared in the *New Yorker* and has been anthologized in *Best American Magazine Writing, Best American Crime Reporting,* and *Best American Sports Writing*. Colloff has been a finalist for two National Magazine Awards, first in 2001 for her article on school prayer, and again in 2011 for her two-part series, "Innocence Lost" and "Innocence Found," on wrongly convicted death row inmate Anthony Graves. "Innocence Lost" was credited with helping Graves win his freedom after eighteen years behind bars. Colloff holds a bachelor's degree in English literature from Brown University and was raised in New York City. She lives in Austin with her husband and their two children.

Hannah and Andrew

W hat little is known about Andrew Burd's early life is contained in a slim Child Protective Services case file that chronicles the boy's descent into the child welfare system. His mother was just sixteen, the file shows, when she gave birth to him in Corpus Christi on July 28, 2002. She would later admit, according to one report, "to using alcohol, methamphetamines, cocaine and crack cocaine, LSD, marijuana, cigarettes, and taking prescription Xanax." His father was seventeen and worked for a traveling carnival. CPS launched its initial investigation into Andrew's well-being shortly after his first birthday, when his mother took him to a local hospital with a broken arm. Four subsequent investigations were triggered by reports of abuse or neglect, including one allegation that both his mother and maternal grandmother were incapable of properly caring for him because they used methamphetamines. When Andrew was two-and-a-half years old, CPS determined that he was in "immediate danger," according to an affidavit, and he was put in foster care. His mother's and father's parental rights were terminated soon after he turned three.

If not for a Corpus Christi couple named Larry and Hannah Overton, Andrew might have lingered in state custody, shuffled from one foster home to another. The Overtons already had four children, and Larry's income—he installed landscape lighting—was barely enough to make ends meet. But as devoted Christians, their desire to adopt a foster child was rooted in faith more than in practicality. Both Larry and Hannah had done missionary work, and as a teenager, Hannah had spent holidays volunteering at an orphanage across the border, in Reynosa, where she had fed, bathed, and ministered to kids who had been living on the streets. The experience had affected her deeply, and she told Larry that she was willing to adopt a child with disabilities or an older child who had been unable to find a permanent home. As a former private-duty nurse, Hannah felt equipped to handle the challenges of a foster child; she had spent several years caring for special-needs children, some of whom were profoundly disabled. In 2005 the Overtons began to pursue the idea seriously. They considered adopting a nine-year-old girl who was deaf, but when, after much prayer and deliberation, they decided to move forward with the adoption, they learned that the girl had been placed with another family.

Not long afterward, Larry and Hannah heard about Andrew at their church, Calvary Chapel of the Coastlands, which Andrew's foster mother also attended. The non-denominational church, on the south side of Corpus Christi, drew many young evangelicals with its emphasis on a verse-by-verse understanding of the Bible, and Larry and Hannah were well-regarded members. Larry taught Sunday school, Hannah led a Bible study, and their children, whom Hannah homeschooled, attended youth group and socialized with other members' kids. Andrew accompanied his foster mother to services every Sunday, and with his thatch of blond hair and beaming grin, he was hard to miss. He had a speech delay and spoke haltingly, sometimes with a stutter, but every week, when his Sunday school classmates went around in a circle to say their prayer requests, he made the same wish aloud: that he would be adopted. The Overtons' daughters, four-year-old Isabel and three-year-old Ally, reported back to their parents that the new boy in their class needed a family. "Can Andrew be our brother?" the girls pleaded.

A church elder, who was himself an adoptive parent, invited the Overtons to dinner one night and encouraged them to consider bringing Andrew into their home. Andrew's foster mother, who had provided refuge to roughly three hundred children over three decades, was also supportive. But others at Calvary Chapel expressed their concern. The church's pastor, Rod Carver, and his wife, Noreen, had initially considered taking in Andrew but ultimately decided he was more than they could handle. More outspoken was Andrew's Sunday school teacher, who sat Hannah and Larry down and told them that he was a troubled kid. He hoarded food and sometimes ate from the trash, she warned, and he threw intense temper tantrums, which could be tamed only by holding and rocking him. On several occasions his fits had grown so extreme that she had resorted to asking a male parishioner to physically remove him from the classroom until he could regain self-control. "Think of your other children," she urged the couple.

Yet if anyone was up to the task, most everyone agreed, it was the Overtons, and Hannah in particular. She was unflappable and unfailingly patient with children. Hannah shrugged off the teacher's warnings, certain that Andrew would improve once he had the stability of a permanent home. "All he needs is lots of love and attention," she told Larry.

The Overtons moved forward with the adoption process, and in the spring of 2006, they received word that Andrew would be coming to live with them for a six-month trial period before the adoption was finalized. In anticipation of his arrival, Larry built a three-tiered bunk bed for Andrew and the two Overton boys: Isaac, who was seven years old, and Sebastian, who was two. Larry and Hannah knew that Andrew loved Spider-Man, so they made sure to have all manner of Spider-Man-themed necessities for him: sheets, pajamas, a toothbrush, a towel, a swimsuit, and even a plate embossed with the superhero's image.

Andrew spent his first night at the Overtons' modest ranch-style house on Mother's Day, when he was two months shy of his fourth birthday, and he seemed to quickly grow attached to his new family. He called Hannah and Larry "Mommy" and "Daddy," and he followed Larry everywhere he went, often stepping on Larry's heels as he trailed after him. At Sunday school, he became more expressive, stringing words into sentences and holding hands with his new sister Ally. "The Overtons are nurturing, loving, patient, and very family-oriented," an adoption supervisor noted in her paperwork. "Andrew seems very happy in this home."

Four months later, on October 2, 2006, Andrew fell suddenly and acutely ill while he was alone with Hannah. Larry hurried home to help, but Andrew, who had been vomiting, only grew worse. The Overtons rushed him to a nearby urgent care clinic after his breathing became labored and he stopped responding to their questions, but by the time they arrived, he had fallen unconscious. The following evening, Andrew was dead. The cause of death was determined to be salt poisoning, an extremely rare occurrence that, in children, results from either a child inadvertently ingesting too much salt or a caretaker deliberately forcing the child to do so. People who knew the Overtons were certain that Andrew's bewildering death was accidental. But law enforcement and emergency medical personnel who treated Andrew thought otherwise. The following week, Hannah—who had no history with CPS and no previous arrests, and had never had so much as a parking ticket—was charged with capital murder.

Before Hannah got married, when she was still Hannah Saenz, she knew she wanted a large family—"at least six kids," she used to tell people. Standing just five feet tall, with wide-set brown eyes, a girlish laugh, and a warm, easy manner, Hannah was almost childlike herself. The daughter of a pastor and a homemaker, she had grown up longing for the companionship and boisterous energy of the big, churchgoing families she saw around her. She had only one sibling, a brother who was seven years her junior, and a father who was largely absent from her life.

Hannah's father was the Reverend Bennie Saenz, an evangelical preacher in Corpus Christi whose fall from grace profoundly altered the course of her childhood. Hannah was seven when Saenz was arrested in 1984 and charged with a singularly horrific crime: the bludgeoning death of a sixteen-year-old girl whose nude body was discovered at the water's edge on Padre Island. Until his arrest, Saenz had led a seemingly normal life: In addition to leading his non-denominational congregation, he worked as an office-machine mechanic while his wife, Lane, stayed home with their two children. He delivered sermons to a small but devoted following that met every Sunday, and during services he also played guitar. (Larry's parents, who were friends of the Saenzes, were parishioners.) But Saenz's account of his whereabouts on the evening of the murder did not jibe with the evidence, and blood that matched the victim's type was discovered inside his van. After a week-long trial, he was convicted of murder and sentenced to twenty-three years in prison. The congregation quickly dissolved. Hannah understood little of what had taken place except that she, her mother, and her brother had to leave Corpus Christi behind.

Lane and her children moved to the East Texas town of Lindale, where a missionary organization, the Calvary Commission, allowed them to live in a modest apartment on its grounds free of charge. Lane earned her college degree and became an elementary school teacher, while Hannah played with, and later babysat, the children of missionaries who used the campus as a home base between trips abroad. "She looked after dozens of children, including my grandchildren, and in all the years she was here, I can't recall one negative thing being said about her," the commission's founder, Joe Fauss, told me. "Kids loved her. She was always smiling, always laughing." As a teenager, she was captivated by missionaries' stories of serving in far-flung places, and she began going on group mission trips herself, once venturing as far as Romania. Every Easter and Christmas holiday was spent at the Reynosa orphanage, whose wards were primarily the unwanted children of prostitutes who worked the nearby red-light district. Though the kids were in poor health, Hannah was unreserved in her affection. She hugged them and let them climb onto her lap, often returning to Lindale with head lice. "Some people love stray animals," remembered her mother, now remarried. "Hannah was always drawn to stray people."

When she was fifteen, Hannah returned to Corpus Christi with her family to visit, and Larry, who had not seen her since they were kids, was immediately smitten. Hannah was less impressed, given that Larry—who, at sixteen, was an enthusiastic fan of Christian punk rock—was sporting a nose ring and a blue mohawk. Despite appearances, however, he was hardly a reprobate. A committed Christian, he had gone on mission trips with his family since he was a child, including a fourteen-month stint in Papua New Guinea and several treks across Mexico. He didn't drink or smoke, and the bands he listened to sang about glorifying God. He struck up a correspondence with Hannah, but she did not warm up to him until their paths crossed again at a year-long missionary training school outside Tyler, when she was nineteen and he was a more clean-cut twenty. Hannah liked the tall, serious-minded student who shared the same hopes she had of creating a life centered on children and Christian outreach. They wed a year later and moved to Corpus Christi. On their honeymoon, they stopped at the orphanage in Reynosa, where Hannah wanted Larry to meet some of the children she had told him so much about.

Before they started a family, Hannah worked as a private-duty nurse for disabled children, and her longest assignment—with a four-year-old named Michael Subialdea—became as absorbing to her as her time in Reynosa. Michael, who had been born prematurely, was severely impaired; he had cerebral palsy, was blind, and could not walk or talk. Rather than let him remain in his wheelchair most of the day, as previous caretakers had done, Hannah kept him moving; she took him into his family's pool to stretch and used massage to loosen his contracted muscles. He felt at ease around her; his favorite thing to do was sit on her lap and rest his mouth on her cheek, and she gladly obliged. "She had a way with Michael that even my wife and I didn't completely understand," his father, Richard, told me. He recalled how Michael used to chew on his fingers, a chronic problem that left his skin bloody and raw. Richard and his wife had tried all sorts of tactics to deter him: redirecting his attention, putting gloves on him, even restraining his hands. Only Hannah had been able to break through. "When Michael put his fingers in his mouth, she would call his name softly—there was no anger in her voice—and he would smile and slowly slide his fingers out," Richard said. "We were in awe."

Hannah went into labor with her first child, Isaac, at the Subialdeas' house, and though she had planned to come back to work after her son's birth, she found the separation from him too wrenching. She left nursing behind, channeling her energy instead into raising the large family she had always wanted. "I'm a pretty easygoing guy, but I remember thinking, 'Six kids?'" Larry told me. "Hannah was sure I would eventually come around. I figured, 'Well, we've got to start with one, so let's see how far we get.'" Isabel, and then Ally, followed. Each pregnancy felt extraordinarily fortunate; after Isaac, Hannah had suffered two miscarriages and been advised that she might not be able to have more children. But after the girls, the Overtons conceived their fourth child, Sebastian. Early in the pregnancy, Hannah and Larry were informed that the boy would likely have Down syndrome. They declined to do any further chromosomal testing and turned to prayer instead. "If he had Down's, that was the blessing that God had chosen to give us," Larry said. Not until Sebastian was born did doctors discover that his only impairment was a hole in his heart, which healed on its own.

Two years later, the Overtons learned that their adoption application had been approved and that Andrew would be joining their family. They also discovered that Hannah was pregnant again. Just as she had hoped, they would have six children. It was, Hannah and Larry would later remember, one of the happiest times in their lives.

At first, the transition with Andrew went smoothly. He seemed to enjoy having brothers and sisters to play with, and the Overton kids—especially the girls, who doted on him—were enthralled by the new arrival. Although he hung back when his siblings embraced their parents in group hugs, Larry and Hannah learned that if they asked Andrew to join in, he would do so enthusiastically, throwing his arms around them. Whenever he got scared—and there was a long list of things that petrified him, from swimming to large crowds to the sound of balloons popping—the Overtons worked to help him overcome his fears, reassuring him that they loved him and that he was in safe surroundings. "I can do all things through Christ who strengthens me," Hannah would remind him, quoting Philippians.

Andrew's standard answer whenever he was asked to perform a simple task was "Sorry, I can't," but Hannah was heartened one day that summer when he deviated from the script. "Sorry, I—" he began, when she asked him to put on his shoes. Then he corrected himself. Reaching for his shoes, he announced, "I can do all things." Larry remembered, "We felt like we were really making headway with him."

Although the adoption agency that had worked with CPS to find Andrew a home had described him as "developmentally on target" except for his speech delay, Larry and Hannah observed otherwise. He acted more like a toddler than a preschooler, they noted; if he wanted an object, he pointed to it and grunted. At four, he spent most of his time playing with Sebastian, who was two, rather than Ally, who was his own age, and his motor skills lagged far behind those of his peers. He moved unsteadily, and he was so clumsy that Hannah had him wear a life jacket whenever he splashed around in their inflatable kiddie pool. Most striking to the Overtons, and to their neighbors and friends, was his preoccupation with eating. Regardless of how much food he consumed, he complained that he was hungry. If he was denied a second or third helping, he would routinely throw a tantrum or get down on his hands and knees to scavenge the floor for crumbs. Larry and Hannah caught him trying to eat cat food, crayons, toothpaste, glow sticks, tufts of carpeting—anything he could get his hands on. When they took him along on errands, they had to keep him from eating the old gum and cigarette butts he found on the ground.

Yet the Overtons were not too concerned. In the classes they had been required to take by CPS to become adoptive parents, they had been warned that foster children often hoarded food and were more likely to have eating disorders. And given that abuse and neglect during the first year of life can profoundly affect behavioral development, they were not surprised that Andrew was different. "We had been told to expect a lot of the things we were seeing with Andrew," Larry told me. His foster mother had taken him to a pediatrician for an adoption screening shortly before he had come to live with them, and the checkup had raised no red flags. "We truly thought his obsession with food was a behavioral issue, not a medical one," Larry said. "We thought that he would stop turning to food for comfort when he learned that he could trust us." To try and curtail Andrew's compulsive eating, they put him in time-outs, though to little effect. Other couples they knew who had adopted foster children assured them that their kids had outgrown similar eating issues, and the Overtons assumed that, with time, Andrew would outgrow his as well.

Andrew's behavior worsened that September, after the family was involved in a car accident. The Overtons were returning from a visit to the obstetrician's office, where they had brought the children to find out whether the baby they were expecting was a boy or a girl. The mood in the car was giddy; the kids were excitedly discussing the news that they would have a baby sister when Larry, distracted, ran a stop sign and collided with another car. The passenger side of their old Ford van was not equipped with an air bag, and Hannah, who had pulled down her seat belt so she could turn to talk to the kids, was jolted forward, her face hitting the dashboard. Afterward, she instinctively looked back to check on the children, not realizing that her face was covered in blood. In the midst of the chaos that followed, no one recognized how distressed Andrew was by the sight of Hannah's bloodied face. Hannah and the girls, who complained of feeling achy, were taken to the hospital in an ambulance while Larry's parents picked up the rest of the family and, after dropping Larry off at the hospital, took the boys to a nearby Whataburger. Throughout the meal, Andrew repeatedly asked, "Is my mom okay?" He also kept requesting more food.

Hannah, who was left with whiplash and a severely swollen jaw, spent the next several weeks immobilized by a neck brace, mostly confined to bed. Financially, the accident had come at a precarious time; Larry had recently purchased his boss's landscape lighting business, and he needed to put in long hours just to make ends meet. Relatives, neighbors, and members of the Overtons' church pitched in to look after the kids during Hannah's recovery, but the revolving door of caregivers proved to be difficult for Andrew, who began acting out on a scale they had not seen before. He picked at mosquito bites on his body incessantly, prompting Larry to put socks on his hands; still, Andrew would not stop scratching and eventually developed a staph infection on his arm. His tantrums grew longer and more extreme, and he often banged his head against the floor. Sometimes he cried inconsolably for hours.

Overwhelmed, the Overtons sought guidance in prayer. Fellow church member Anita Miotti remembers them telling her and her husband, Rich, that they were struggling. "They said Andrew was going through a very difficult time," she said. "They asked us, 'Can you pray that we have discernment and wisdom in helping him through this?'"

Andrew's preoccupation with eating intensified, and he began getting out of bed at night to forage for food in the kitchen. Hoping to show him that his behavior was self-destructive, Larry told Andrew one morning that he could have as much as he wanted for breakfast. "I knew it would probably make him sick, but I wanted him to understand why we were setting limits," Larry explained. At Andrew's request, he made a plate of sausage and more than a dozen eggs, all of which the boy eagerly devoured. Andrew continued eating until he threw up. Then he asked for more.

Perplexed, Larry installed a baby monitor equipped with a video camera in the boys' room so that he and Hannah could observe if Andrew was wandering into the kitchen at night. It was while watching the monitor that Hannah saw him trying to eat part of his foam mattress and paint off the wall. She reported Andrew's unusual eating habits to his adoption supervisor when she visited the Overton home on September 25. The supervisor suggested that Andrew might have an eating disorder called pica, which is characterized by a desire to consume things that have no nutritional value, and she recommended that he be evaluated by a specialist if his behavior continued.

That Sunday, October 1, Larry took the other kids to church while Hannah devoted some extra attention to Andrew. Before the family returned home, Andrew asked if he could have lunch, and Hannah told him that he needed to wait; Larry was bringing them something to eat, she explained, and he would be back in a few minutes. Andrew flew into a rage. He defecated on the floor of his bedroom, then smeared feces on the bed, the dresser, and the walls.

Larry attempted to restore order upon his return, putting Andrew's soiled sheets in the garbage and hosing off the boy and his foam mattress in the backyard. While Larry tried to scrub down the bedroom, Andrew pulled his sheets out of the trash several times, despite repeated warnings not to do so. Losing his patience, Larry took the sheets to the family's fire pit and burned them. "Not the brightest thing to do," Larry conceded. "But I was frustrated. The sheets were filthy, and he was getting poop everywhere. I made sure that he saw that we had an identical set of Spider-Man sheets so he would calm down."

That evening Larry laid a sleeping bag on top of Andrew's plywood bed frame, where, he told the boy, he would have to spend the night while his mattress finished drying. The three oldest Overton children had gone to their aunt's house to see their cousins, who were visiting from out of town, and Andrew grew increasingly agitated and restless, throwing a tantrum at three o'clock in the morning. "Before we ever tried to adopt, we had been warned that this was going to be difficult, that this was not going to be the *Little Orphan Annie* story," Larry told me. "We were having a hard time, but we knew it was going to pass. We were in it for the long haul."

Larry left for work the following morning, and Hannah, who was still in considerable pain from the car accident, gave Andrew and Sebastian breakfast before bringing them into bed with her to watch cartoons. Exhausted from the previous night, she briefly dozed off, then awoke to discover that Andrew had slipped out of the room. She found him standing on a stool in the pantry, near the baking ingredients, having pulled something off the shelf. She could not recall later what, exactly, he had been holding in his hand.

According to Hannah, Andrew once again asked for an early lunch, and once again, when she told him that he would have to wait, he defecated and smeared feces across the floor. Hannah managed to clean him up, but when she reiterated that he would have to wait until lunchtime to eat, he defecated on the floor again. Finally she relented, heating up what she had on hand: leftover vegetable-beef soup flavored with Zatarain's Creole Seasoning. Shortly after noon, Larry picked her and the boys up and took them to a McDonald's drive-thru, and then the chiropractor, before returning to work. (Andrew was told that he could not have any food at McDonald's, since he had already eaten.) When Andrew complained of being hungry that afternoon, Hannah gave him more of the leftover soup. When she refused to give him a second helping, he threw a tantrum and shouted, "I hate you!" Finally, Hannah resorted to sprinkling some Zatarain's into a sippy cup of water, hoping that the taste alone would appease him. After drinking a little, he threw another tantrum that continued unabated for twenty minutes.

Then, abruptly, Andrew grew quiet and stumbled to the floor. "Mommy, I'm cold," he said, and threw up. Shortly afterward, at three-thirty, Hannah called Larry and asked him to come home since Andrew was vomiting and she needed his help. The boy's symptoms that afternoon—vomiting, chills, and lethargy—initially suggested to the Overtons that he had a routine ailment, like a stomach bug. But as the afternoon wore on, his symptoms grew troubling;

his breathing became congested, and he became less and less responsive. Just after five o'clock, the Overtons put him in their car and rushed him to a nearby urgent care clinic. A block away from the clinic, as they waited at a red light, Andrew stopped breathing. Frantic, Hannah began administering CPR in the backseat. At the clinic, she continued giving him mouth-to-mouth and chest compressions until paramedics took over, but the four-year-old lay motionless. He soon lapsed into a coma.

The next morning, Corpus Christi police detective Michael Hess paid a visit to Kathi Haller, the Overtons' next-door neighbor, who knew the family well. Like Hannah, Haller homeschooled her children, and the two mothers split teaching duties; the Haller children went to the Overton home for instruction for part of the day and vice versa. The families shared an unofficial open-door policy, and when Andrew had begun acting up the previous afternoon, Hannah had called Haller for help, asking if she could look after Sebastian for a little while. Then, as always, Hannah had been composed, despite the strain she was under. "We had known each other for ten years, and I don't think I'd ever seen her mad," Haller told me.

Hess, who investigated child abuse cases for the police force's family violence unit, had a very different impression of Hannah. The detective had been alerted to Andrew's grave condition when the boy was transported to a nearby hospital the previous afternoon and, as was protocol, had begun looking into the circumstances surrounding the boy's unusual and rapid decline. Haller, who took notes documenting her conversation with Hess and later testified about it under oath, recalled the detective's certainty that Hannah had tried to kill Andrew. According to Haller, he told her, "Look, she's pregnant and she has all these kids, but it was just too much for her. So she had to find a way out." (Hess did not respond to interview requests for this article but has previously denied Haller's version of events.) Haller was stunned by the accusation. "I kept denying that Hannah could do such a thing," she told me. "Hannah would never harm a child." Even setting aside her loyalty to her friend, the detective's theory made no sense to her. "Andrew's adoption hadn't been finalized," Haller said. "If Hannah had been looking for a 'way out,' she would have called the adoption agency and told them that she and Larry couldn't go through with it." Hess was unmoved. Before he left, Haller recalled his saying, "You might want to prepare for the media."

Hess' suspicions had developed the previous evening during an interview with Hannah, who had consented to talk to him without an attorney present. The medical staff at Driscoll Children's Hospital had determined that

Andrew had nearly twice the normal level of sodium in his blood—a highly abnormal finding—as well as bleeding in the brain, and as Hess questioned her, he tried to ascertain what had happened. But Hannah, who was bewildered by Andrew's condition, had no ready answers. Impatient to return to the boy's bedside, she gave a hurried, disjointed account of the day that omitted critical details, such as how she had found Andrew in the pantry unattended, and she made only fleeting mention of his unusual eating habits. Hess became exasperated. "I don't see what caused the trauma to the brain," he said. "I don't see what caused the high salt content. That's what I'm trying to get you to tell me." With no obvious explanations to consider, he focused his attention on Hannah. "Did you at any time strike him?" Hess asked. "Push him?" Throughout the interrogation, which spanned more than two hours, Hannah insisted that she had never harmed Andrew.

Hannah did describe how she and Larry had at first tried to treat the boy's symptoms themselves, often volunteering more information than the detective had asked for. When Andrew started "breathing funny," she told Hess, she had administered asthma medication with a nebulizer, hoping to open up his airways. And when he became "less responsive," she had pulled out her old EMT books to assess what was wrong. Larry had also tried to rouse him by giving him a warm bath. "I wasn't thinking, obviously, or I would have just taken him to the hospital," Hannah told the detective. She had studied years earlier to be an EMT, she explained, and although she had never worked as a paramedic, she had felt confident in her training. "I was just trying to fix it—to do anything I could to fix my baby," she said. When Andrew's condition worsened, she and Larry had debated whether to call 911 or to go to the nearby urgent care clinic, a concern because Andrew lacked health insurance. (CPS had not yet sent them his Social Security card, which they needed to get him insured.) She and Larry were under tremendous financial strain, she admitted, but she stressed that they had rushed for help as soon as they realized how critical Andrew's condition was.

Hess remained skeptical of Hannah's account. "It should be noted that during the entire conversation, Hannah Overton showed almost no emotion," he later wrote in his police report. In the context of a criminal investigation, the calm that she had always exhibited in the midst of crisis was suddenly a liability—an indication, perhaps, that she was cold-blooded enough to have killed a child.

A pediatric critical care specialist who treated Andrew at Driscoll, Alexandre Rotta, grew equally troubled. EMS records show that the boy was admitted with no more than a bruised knee and sores on his right elbow, but during his hospitalization, other significant black-and-blue marks emerged—in particular, on his trunk and nose. EMTs and hospital staff had vigorously poked and prodded the boy as they attempted to revive him, first at the clinic, then in an ambulance, then at Christus Spohn Hospital, where he was initially taken, and finally at Driscoll, where he was transferred to the intensive care unit. CPR had also been performed for an extended period by Hannah and later by medical personnel, who had squeezed the boy's nose and administered chest compressions for thirty-five minutes. But Rotta was alarmed by his overall appearance. "This was not a child that came into the office looking well, with a story of, you know, 'He's just a tomboy, and he falls and hits himself,'" Rotta would later testify. "This is a child that came in (to the emergency room) in cardiopulmonary arrest and was dying. So it is the context and the totality of the injuries that worried me ... I was convinced that we were in the presence of a crime."

Within hours of Andrew's arrival at the hospital, the Overtons' home had been searched, and soon more facts seemed to bolster the notion of abuse. There was Andrew's bed—just a bare piece of plywood, with no mattress—and a "security camera," as the baby monitor was later called at trial, trained on it. There were the charred remnants of his Spider-Man sheets in the fire pit. And then there was the abnormally high sodium level, coupled with Hannah's account of feeding him Creole seasoning after he had misbehaved. Taken together, the disparate details formed a disturbing picture. It did not matter that Haller, who had seen Andrew in the days leading up to his hospitalization and who was frequently in the Overton home, had never observed any suspicious bruises or indications of abuse. In the eyes of law enforcement, Hannah and Larry were not grieving parents but perpetrators of an appalling crime. As Andrew's condition deteriorated, CPS barred the Overtons from visiting their son. They were not allowed to be at Andrew's bedside on the evening of October 3, when he experienced massive organ failure. He died at 9:30 p.m.

The death of a child—particularly a sudden, unexplained death in which abuse is suspected—evokes strong emotions, even among seasoned investigators, doctors, forensics experts, and prosecutors. A more thorough investigation would have uncovered ample evidence to suggest that Andrew had an undiagnosed eating disorder, raising the possibility that he had unintentionally consumed too much salt on his own. But law enforcement officials are accustomed to handling child abuse cases, not medical mysteries, and salt poisoning is rare enough that most emergency room doctors will never encounter a case during their careers. Against the backdrop of possible abuse, authorities wasted little time. Larry was charged with injury to a child for failing to get Andrew timely medical attention. The onus for the boy's death fell on Hannah, who was charged with capital murder.

The state's case would be predicated in part on the findings of Ray Fernandez, the Nueces County medical examiner, who ruled Andrew's death to be a homicide. Fernandez determined that the boy had died as a result of acute sodium toxicity, with "blunt force head trauma" as a contributing factor. That Andrew had sustained a head injury was based on the presence of a half-inch area of hemorrhaging under the scalp. There was no evidence of external bleeding or injuries to Andrew's head, however, and at a pre-trial hearing, Fernandez conceded that the hemorrhaging could have been related to elevated sodium in the blood. State district judge Jose Longoria, who would oversee Hannah's trial the following fall, would later rule Fernandez's finding of blunt force trauma to be inadmissible because it was not based on sufficient data or reliable methodology. Nevertheless, the idea that Andrew had sustained a head injury propelled the case forward, further casting Hannah as an abuser.

That perception would throw her other children into the investigation as well. During a wide-ranging interview with a social worker to determine if he had ever been abused, Isaac mentioned that he and his siblings had been given pepper, which he described as "spicy stuff," as a punishment for lying. (A former pastor of Hannah's had advocated reprimanding children when they were dishonest by putting a single red pepper flake on their tongues.) Given that Hannah was suspected of poisoning Andrew with Creole seasoning, the suggestion that the Overtons had used pepper to discipline their children raised immediate concerns. On October 3, while Andrew was still hospitalized, the agency removed Isaac, Isabel, Ally, and Sebastian from their parents' custody, placing them in two separate foster homes in Beeville, sixty miles away. The following day, family court judge Carl Lewis awarded temporary custody to Hannah's mother and stepfather. Larry and Hannah were granted supervised visits. Once reunited with their children—who were terrified by the ordeal—Larry and Hannah had to break the awful news to them about Andrew. Weeping, they told the children that their brother had gone to be with Jesus.

A funeral for Andrew followed at Seaside Memorial Park, alongside Corpus Christi Bay, at which Pastor Rod Carver officiated. He and Noreen had recently lost their own son, who had been stillborn, making his grief particularly acute. As he grasped for the right words to convey the depth of pain a parent feels over the loss of a child, he noticed a row of unfamiliar faces. "Hess and a group of CPS workers were standing in the back with dark glasses on, their arms crossed, scowls on their faces," Carver said. "That was the most uncomfortable service I have ever done. It was very tense. By that point, Hannah had completely broken down emotionally."

Corpus Christi's introduction to Hannah came the following week, when she and Larry were arrested and led past a bank of TV cameras outside the Nueces County jail. News reports that followed, prominently featuring their grim-faced mug shots, cast the Overton home as a house of horrors. ("More shocking details on abuse suffered by four-year-old before death," began one breathless report.) Veteran defense attorney John Gilmore, whom the Overtons had retained using funds raised by their church, was stunned to learn of the arrests from reporters, who called asking for comment. "Channel Three, Channel Six, Channel Ten, the *Caller-Times*—they all knew ahead of time," Gilmore said. "Hess had given me his word that he would tell me if and when warrants were going to be issued, so that Hannah and Larry could turn themselves in." Instead, law enforcement officials had apprehended the Overtons by making a felony traffic stop, a practice usually reserved for suspects believed to be armed and dangerous. With guns drawn, police officers had surrounded Hannah and Larry's car as they returned from an errand, forcing them to the ground and handcuffing them. "It was like they were arresting Bonnie and Clyde," Gilmore said.

The media coverage of the case stirred widespread outrage. The *Corpus Christi Caller-Times'* online comments section filled with the vitriol of readers, some of whom called for Hannah to receive the death penalty. ("You can just tell by looking at her how evil she is," one wrote.) Fueling the public's antipathy was an affidavit written by a CPS child abuse investigator named Jesse Garcia, who claimed that Hannah had admitted to forcing Andrew to drink two cupfuls of "chili with water" and quoted her as saying that she then "beat the shit out of him." Garcia never produced any documentation or witnesses to corroborate his claim, and internal police memos show that law enforcement officials doubted the veracity of his story. Hess disavowed Garcia's account at a court hearing regarding the Overton children, and prosecutors never entered Garcia's affidavit into evidence or called him to testify at Hannah's trial. (He was subsequently fired by CPS after having three car accidents on the job in less than six months.) But the damage was done: that Hannah had confessed to force-feeding Andrew and beating him was repeated, uncorrected, on the local news.

Even more devastating to Hannah were the actions that CPS took that January. Days after she gave birth to her daughter Emma, CPS took the newborn into protective custody. At a subsequent family court hearing, in which Hannah's civil attorney argued that she should be given access to the infant so that she could continue nursing her, Judge Lewis returned Emma to her parents, but with conditions. The Overtons had to remain at the Carvers' home, where they had been staying to avoid the camera crews that were camped out on their own doorstep, and they were never to be left alone with the baby. Hannah—who had already lost a child and was now living apart from her four older ones—was in a fragile state of mind. "There were days I had to remind her to eat, to brush her teeth, to get out of bed," Noreen told me.

The Carvers, like most members of Calvary Chapel, never doubted her innocence. "Knowing Hannah, it was inconceivable that she would ever hurt a child," said Noreen. Hannah's supporters included a young churchgoer named Dawn Werkhoven, who had lived with the Overtons the year leading up to Andrew's death. Hannah and Larry had taken her in after her marriage ended in divorce, giving her their extra bedroom while she got back on her feet. "I never saw Hannah be anything but patient and loving with all the kids," the now-married mother of two told me. Being in the Overtons' home had afforded Werkhoven an intimate view of the family. Her bedroom was just a few feet away from the children's rooms, which were always open; their doors had been removed so that the kids could easily come and go as they pleased. The children liked to hang out in her room and talk to her, particularly Andrew, who always visited her for an extra hug before bedtime. "If anything had been wrong, I would have known it," she insisted. "Would I really have stayed with a family that would abuse a child?"

The most unsettling aspect of *The State of Texas v. Hannah Ruth Overton*, which got under way in August 2007, was how effectively a woman who had spent most of her life as a do-gooder could be recast as a monster. The particulars of her crime, as sketched out by the prosecution, were vague; assistant district attorney Sandra Eastwood, a passionate child advocate, conceded in opening arguments that she was not sure how Hannah had made Andrew eat so much salt. "We don't know precisely how she got it down Andrew, but we know that he was very, very obedient," Eastwood told the jury, standing before the TV news cameras that Judge Longoria had allowed inside the courtroom. "And we do have some evidence of bruising to his nose (which could indicate) his nostrils were squeezed and he was made to drink it."

Over the course of the three-week-long trial, Eastwood sought to convince jurors that a mother with no history of violence or mental illness had force-fed her child to death—a scenario that each prosecution witness helped, incrementally, to suggest was possible. Patricia Gonzalez, a nurse at the urgent care clinic, told the jury that Hannah had not behaved like a panic-stricken parent and had "had a smile on her face" as she performed CPR on the boy. Another nurse, Dina Zapata, remembered Hannah smirking as she tried to resuscitate him. Both women's accounts were problematic; Gonzalez had never made a statement to police and was testifying from memory after nearly a year's worth of negative media coverage, while Zapata had failed to mention anything about Hannah smirking when she wrote her initial report about the incident. Yet the image they conjured—of a woman grinning at the sight of a comatose four-year-old—was devastating. Gemma Mitchell, a phlebotomist, recalled overhearing Hannah tell medical staff that Andrew had stopped breathing after he was "punished." No one could corroborate her story, and under cross-examination, she admitted that she had never told anyone this fact until taking the stand. Still, the overall impression was a damning one.

Other witnesses testified that they had detected signs of abuse. One paramedic recounted how he had seen two sores on Andrew "that looked to me like cigarette burns because they were round." Another paramedic also believed the sores were cigarette burns, though he admitted he had only looked at them "from a distance." Fernandez, the medical examiner, said he had observed "burn-like scarring" on Andrew's arm that had likely been caused by "contact with a hot surface." But neither Larry nor Hannah smoked. Not until shortly before closing arguments did jurors hear from the defense's expert witness, a Harvard-educated pathologist and assistant medical examiner in San Francisco, Judy Melinek, who offered her opinion that the sores were consistent with mosquito bites that had been scratched and picked at.

The prosecution's most persuasive testimony came from Rotta, the pediatric critical care specialist who had originally expressed concern that Andrew had been mistreated. "A comment someone made was that it appeared that this child had been in a fight with a porcupine," the physician stated. "There were so many bruises and scratches that it would be difficult to describe them all." Rotta allowed that the appearance of Andrew's body may have been due in part to the fact that he was coagulopathic, or not able to clot blood properly, a condition that occurs after a person has gone into cardiac arrest and can cause excessive bleeding and bruising. But he was adamant that the boy's death had not been accidental. Andrew had never been diagnosed with pica, Rotta reminded jurors. "We have a child that was well until that afternoon, that had behavioral issues, that was having temper tantrums, that was then given something . . . probably to punish his behavior, that then goes into cardiorespiratory arrest."

Rotta stopped short of describing the manner in which he believed Andrew had been made to eat a lethal amount of salt—a dose that, after analyzing Andrew's blood, he determined would have consisted of twenty-three teaspoons of Zatarain's Creole Seasoning or six teaspoons of salt. The physician only said that the scratch marks he had noticed on the boy's neck had been caused, he believed, by another person. The marks "could be consistent with many things, including a fight, an altercation, someone trying to hold this child's neck forcefully," he said.

Andrew's former foster mother, Sharon Hamil, who was devastated by the boy's death, testified that Andrew had not exhibited significant developmental or behavioral problems, aside from his speech delay, during the time that he lived with her—a characterization that was rebutted by numerous members of Calvary Chapel later in the trial but that cast Hannah's credibility into doubt. "He was always happy," Hamil testified. She believed that Andrew's eating habits were not the stuff of pathology but those of a growing boy. "Andrew liked to eat every day, all day, any time," she said.

By the time Hannah took the stand, jurors appeared to have made up their minds. Several crossed their arms; others looked away. By that point, they had already been shown numerous photos of Andrew's small, bruised body postmortem. They had also watched the video of Hess questioning Hannah, during which she described calling a paramedic friend in Oklahoma for guidance when the boy's condition deteriorated, and even using her camera's flash to check if his pupils were reactive, but never calling for an ambulance. Sitting in the courtroom, she tried to explain how she had failed to recognize that Andrew's condition was life-threatening. "I realized that it was something serious … a few minutes before we actually took him in," she testified. Until then, she said, Andrew "was doing nothing that my other kids hadn't done with the flu … There wasn't anything that I thought was dangerously wrong with him at that point. I didn't realize the seriousness of the situation." Eastwood questioned how Andrew had come to have scratches on his neck. "Could it be that you held his nose, held his neck, and made him drink this horrible concoction?" the prosecutor challenged her during a withering cross-examination. "Absolutely not," Hannah shot back.

Despite Eastwood's zeal, there were still basic questions that the prosecution could not explain. How had Hannah, who was six months pregnant and recovering from whiplash, managed to overpower Andrew? How had she known how much salt would kill him? And how had she forced him to choke down the lethal slurry through a sippy cup—a drinking container that is, by design, able to release its contents only when sucked on? Yet according to the unusual wording of the jury charge, jurors had to believe just one of two scenarios to find Hannah guilty: that she deliberately made Andrew ingest a lethal amount of salt or that she purposely neglected to get timely medical attention, knowing that this would kill him. In other words, if the jury could not agree conclusively that she had poisoned Andrew, it could still rule that she was guilty of capital murder "by omission," or by failure to act.

Gilmore and his defense team, which included two civil attorneys versed in the intricacies of medical testimony, tried to counter the prosecution's claims that Hannah had poisoned Andrew and purposely delayed medical treatment. (In his thirty-two years of practicing law, Gilmore told me, he has never run across the charge of "capital murder by omission" before or since.) Melinek, the defense's expert witness, testified about pica and an array of factors that could have contributed to Andrew's death, including undiagnosed diabetes. And a succession of witnesses, nearly all of them members of Calvary Chapel, recounted Andrew's unusual eating habits and Hannah's attentive parenting. During closing arguments, Gilmore emphasized that Hannah had no motive to kill Andrew and that the state had failed to prove that she had intentionally caused the boy's death.

But just as the prosecution could not show exactly how Hannah had forced Andrew to ingest a lethal dose of salt, neither could the defense give precise details for how the four-year-old had come to have so much sodium in his body. Prosecutors exploited that uncertainty in final arguments, asserting that Andrew did not have pica. Throughout the trial, Eastwood had suggested that the Overtons had withheld food as part of a larger pattern of abuse, and as she addressed the jury, she insisted that Andrew had scavenged for food because he was hungry. "The defendant has portrayed herself as a nurturing Christian woman," Eastwood proclaimed. "Does God want a child to go to bed hurting, in pain, fearful, being looked at by closed-circuit television? Any God, Christian or not, would have wanted a better mother for Andrew."

The burden on the state to prove its case beyond a reasonable doubt was, Gilmore told me, perhaps less than it should have been. "There was a dead child," he observed. "The jury was not just going to let her walk." Capital murder carries two possible punishments in Texas—the death penalty or life without parole—and the district attorney's office had already decided not to seek death. If convicted, Hannah would receive an automatic life sentence. However, Judge Longoria could allow the jury to consider a lesser charge if he felt that the evidence did not support capital murder, and after hearing the state's case, he did so, telling both the prosecution and the defense that he was willing to let the jury consider manslaughter or criminally negligent homicide. (Both carry shorter sentences and differ from capital murder on the issue of intent; a motorist who hits and kills someone while driving too fast is often deemed to be criminally negligent in that he did not set out to take a life but was aware of the danger of speeding.) Gilmore urged Hannah more than once to agree to have the jury consider a lesser charge, but she was uneasy with what she perceived as an underlying suggestion of wrongdoing. She could not consent to a lesser charge, she told her attorneys, because she felt it would mean she was admitting fault.

It was a catastrophic decision. After nearly eleven hours of deliberation—during which jurors sent out thirteen notes to the judge, primarily seeking to clarify medical testimony—the jury found her guilty of capital murder. As the verdict was read, Hannah looked horror-struck. Larry, who was sitting behind her, broke down. Before she was led away in handcuffs, the couple embraced for several minutes, overcome with emotion.

But had jurors fully understood the decision they had been asked to make? When Gilmore polled the jury afterward, all twelve members stated that they had found Hannah guilty of capital murder by omission for not acting quickly enough to save Andrew; none believed that she had poisoned him. Yet to find her guilty, they'd had to believe that she *knew he would die* if she did not get him immediate medical attention. According to juror number three, a high school English teacher named Margaret Warfield, that was not the case. "The jury found that Mrs. Overton failed to procure medical care within a reasonable time frame," she wrote in an affidavit that was later filed with Hannah's appeal. "It seemed to me, based upon the wording of the charge, that we had no choice but to find her guilty of capital murder." But, Warfield added, "I do not believe that Mrs. Overton knew that her actions (or lack thereof) would kill Andrew Byrd [sic]. Although I believe that Mrs. Overton was remiss in seeking timely medical care for Andrew Byrd, I do not believe that she intended or knew that this would result in his death." The wording of the jury charge, she added, had been "ambiguous and confusing." Ultimately, Warfield wrote, "I do not feel that justice has been served."

Two days after Hannah was sentenced to life in prison without the possibility of parole, a pediatrician named Edgar Cortes took the unusual step of contacting Gilmore. The doctor had been the on-call emergency medicine physician at Driscoll the day that Andrew arrived, and he had resuscitated the boy as he was transported to the intensive care unit. Although Cortes had been scheduled to testify for the prosecution, he was never put on the witness stand. (During the third week of the trial, moments before the case was sent to the jury, Eastwood had asked Judge Longoria if she could call Cortes as a rebuttal witness, but the judge, who had grown impatient with the length of the trial, denied her request.) As a frequent witness for the state in child abuse cases, Cortes was not in the habit of reaching out to defense attorneys, but he was so angered by the verdict that he picked up the phone. "I have mitigating testimony that I think would have been very useful to your client," he said in a voicemail he left for Gilmore. "Please call me at your earliest convenience."

Unlike the three physicians who had testified for the prosecution, Cortes was the only doctor who had seen Andrew before his hospitalization; he had evaluated the boy during a routine checkup when Andrew was three years old and still living with Hamil. "Andrew was not a normal child," Cortes explained to me. "A colleague of mine who attended the trial told me that the prosecution described Andrew again and again as a normal child, and that is a great distortion of the truth. Andrew was a sweet boy who had significant neurological and developmental disorders. He had a speech disorder called echolalia, which is one of the things we see typically in children who have autism spectrum disorders. He displayed hyperactive behavior and possibly had some cognitive delays as well." The doctor's assessment of Andrew as developmentally delayed was significant because it dovetailed with Hannah's testimony. She had told the jury of the boy's unusual habits—the inappropriate eating, the obsessive picking and scratching, the head banging—but her version of events had been tainted by the specter of abuse.

Cortes believed that Andrew's death was accidental. "The intentional poisoning of a child is usually perpetrated with sedatives, anticonvulsants, or medications like injectable insulin, not food," he told me. "The sodium content of Zatarain's is not listed on its packaging. How do you poison someone with a substance you don't know the contents of?" That Hannah had not sought immediate medical attention did not change his view. "Benign conditions and life-threatening conditions look the same in the beginning," he said. "You can ask, 'Why didn't she go to the hospital sooner?' but in hindsight, everything is obvious. If she had taken Andrew to the hospital earlier, what would she have taken him in for? Because he was vomiting? Because he felt cold?" He suspected that as the boy's condition worsened, Hannah had fallen victim to what he calls "stress blindness," a phenomenon he had witnessed many times during his forty-two years of practicing medicine. "I've seen doctors and nurses freeze up when a patient comes in convulsing or in extremis," he said. "When people are under severe stress, their judgment becomes poor."

Cortes's perspective was revelatory. "He would have been witness number one for the defense," Gilmore told me. "The key issues in this case were knowledge and intent, and his opinion went directly to those issues." Hannah's attorneys would later argue on appeal that the doctor's opinion—that Hannah had never intended for the boy to die—amounted to exculpatory evidence that the state had withheld from the defense. But at a hearing on the defense's motion for a new trial, Eastwood stated under oath that Cortes had always been a passionate advocate for the prosecution; he had even remarked to her that he thought Hannah should "fry." Cortes does not dispute that story. "When I first learned Andrew had died, I was angry," he explained to me. "But I told prosecutors five months before the trial that I believed Hannah had no intent to kill him and that this was not a capital murder case. I was assured that they would be seeking lesser charges." During the trial, he said, "I sat at the courthouse for five days, waiting to testify. I came in the morning, and I left in the evening. To never have been produced—it was very strange."

Hannah's conviction was upheld in 2009 by the Thirteenth Court of Appeals. "It is unclear," read the court's ruling, "whether the state actually knew of Dr. Cortes's opinion." The court also ruled that the wording of the jury charge was "free from error." The Texas Court of Criminal Appeals declined the opportunity to reconsider the decision.

Then, in the spring of 2010, Hannah's appellate attorney, Cynthia Orr, made a startling discovery. Orr—a formidable legal mind whose work recently helped exonerate Michael Morton, a Williamson County man who was wrongly convicted of his wife's 1986 murder—had begun preparing a writ of habeas corpus, a last-ditch effort to persuade the courts to review Hannah's case. The writ is the final opportunity a defendant has to introduce new evidence into the record. Looking for any information that might bolster the appeal, Orr requested access to the prosecution's case file. Sifting through it one afternoon, Orr came across documents she had never seen before, which showed that Andrew's stomach contents did not have an elevated amount of salt when he arrived at the urgent care clinic. Orr forwarded the paperwork to a leading expert on salt poisoning, Michael Moritz, and asked him to explain its significance.

Moritz is the clinical director of pediatric nephrology at the Children's Hospital of Pittsburgh, where he specializes in children's kidney diseases. In 2007 he published a seminal paper on salt poisoning, in which he examined, among other things, documented cases of children who had accidentally ingested excessive quantities of salt. He found that they fit a narrow profile: They were between the ages of one and six, they had been in the foster system or were from abusive homes, and they had pica. Moritz, in fact, had been asked to testify as an expert witness for Hannah's defense at her trial. After examining Andrew's medical records, he had determined that the boy's death was likely accidental. Yet the jury had never heard from him. Short on time as the trial drew to a close, the defense had asked Moritz—who needed to return to

Pittsburgh—to sit for a videotaped deposition; when the deposition ran long and could not be completed, the defense was unable to enter it as testimony.

The paperwork Orr now forwarded to him, which showed that Andrew's stomach contained a great deal of water, only confirmed the clinical director's initial conclusion. "If someone was trying to murder Andrew, they would have restrained him and prevented him from drinking water," Moritz subsequently wrote in an affidavit. "The very dilute gastric sodium contents suggest ... that he had unrestricted access to water." Given these facts, he explained, "There is not a single piece of evidence which suggests that Hannah Overton salt-poisoned Andrew." Instead, Moritz added, the most likely scenario was that Andrew "accidentally salt-poisoned himself."

In light of this information, Moritz felt certain that Andrew's prognosis would have been the same whether or not Hannah had called an ambulance. "It is unlikely that any intervention would have made a significant difference as Andrew had already taken the most critical step to save himself (by consuming) copious amounts of fluid," he wrote. The newly discovered documents, Moritz later told me, were "a monumentally important piece of evidence."

The discovery soon exposed strains among the prosecution team. Former prosecutor Anna Jimenez, who had assisted Eastwood as second chair at Hannah's trial, subsequently wrote a letter to Orr claiming that a sheaf of medical records that Eastwood had asked her to fax to an expert witness before trial had not included the documents that Orr had uncovered. "I fear she may have purposely withheld evidence that may have been favorable to Hannah Overton's defense," Jimenez wrote in her letter, which Orr would include in the writ. She also described her unease with Eastwood's "trial strategy," claiming the prosecutor had told her that they would not be calling Cortes because a record in his file indicated that Andrew had behavioral problems. Finally, Jimenez stated, "I do not believe that there was sufficient evidence to indicate that Hannah Overton intentionally killed Andrew Burd." In response, Eastwood penned an affidavit, asserting that she did not engage in any misconduct. "(I) fully disclosed the DA's office's case file to the defense," she wrote in the lengthy statement. "If I failed in my duties of disclosure before the Hannah Overton trial (which the record corroborates I did not), then so did Ms. Jimenez."

Orr filed the writ in April 2011, and soon afterward *San Antonio Express-News* reporter John MacCormack—whose reporting has raised questions about the fairness of Hannah's conviction—made a routine call to the office to gauge the reaction to the recent developments in the case. He reached Doug Norman, who was part of the prosecution team at Hannah's trial and who is now responsible for fighting her appeal. (Like Eastwood, neither Norman nor

Jimenez would comment for this article.) Norman's remarks were hardly the stuff of a cocksure prosecutor. "I may harbor doubts, but a jury heard this case and made a decision, and everyone has to respect that decision," he told the *Express-News*. "I'll put it this way. My job requires me to be an advocate for the state. As long as I can make a non-frivolous argument, I'll make it, but nothing in my job prevents me from praying for a more just outcome."

Every Saturday for the past several years, Larry has ridden his motorcycle from Corpus Christi to the Murray Unit, the maximum-security women's prison west of Waco where Hannah is incarcerated: a squat, concrete building walled off from the world with cyclone fencing and coils of razor wire. He and Hannah are allotted two hours, during which they sit together in the dayroom, flanked by other inmates and their families. Once a month, Larry loads the kids into his van and they make the trip together, although on those visits, no contact is allowed. Hannah must sit on the opposite side of a metal divider, behind Plexiglas. There are two phones that the kids can speak into, and they eagerly pass the receivers back and forth, recounting the month's events in stereo. "They get to see her for two hours, once a month—twenty-four hours in a year," Larry said. He and the kids return home the same day so that he can teach Sunday school the next morning. Round-trip, the journey is 632 miles.

That Larry is able to be with the children at all, much less raise them, is "a huge blessing," he told me. Not long after his arrest, a grand jury upgraded the charges against him to capital murder, and he feared that he too might face life in prison. But after Hannah's conviction, the DA's office offered him several plea deals, each of which required him to acknowledge that he had intentionally caused Andrew's death. Larry turned them down. Finally he agreed to plead no contest to criminally negligent homicide. "The way it was explained to me, that's how I would be charged if I accidentally ran a stoplight and hit somebody," he said. "Pleading out to that was much better than having my children grow up without a mother or a father." In exchange for his plea, Larry was given five years' probation and a $5,000 fine. (Hannah's mother and stepfather—whom the courts had named "managing conservators" of the children—were then able to return them to Larry's custody.) While he was relieved not to have to serve prison time, the discrepancy between his wife's punishment and his own left him stupefied. "How can one person get probation and another get life without parole for the same thing?" Larry said.

I visited Hannah at the Murray Unit one bright, cloudless afternoon, when the warden granted her a few hours to speak with me. She was even slighter in person than I had expected, and as she related the events of the past five years in her soft voice, she looked hopelessly out of place in her white prison jumpsuit. Yet her life behind bars, however incongruous, has taken on its own rhythm. She is awakened every morning at 2:45 a.m., rarely sleeping well; the overhead light above her bed never shuts off, and announcements blare throughout the night over the loudspeaker. At 4 a.m., she reports to the laundry, where she folds shirts and hands out clean clothes to inmates. After her shift ends in the late morning, there are letters to write home, in which she tries to stay present in her children's lives by choreographing what she can from a distance. "I plan their birthday parties from here," she told me. "I pick out the games and I make the decorations, if I can." She devotes most of her evenings to Bible studies, leading groups of inmates through careful examinations of Scripture. One of her favorite books to revisit is Ruth. "It's about trusting God and seeing how he is a god of redemption and restoration," she said.

As we sat across from each other in the dayroom, Hannah and I discussed her case and the anguish that had consumed her following Andrew's death. "I spent many nights beating myself up over 'Could I have done this or could I have done that?'" Hannah told me, staring at her hands. "I regret that I didn't push harder from the beginning to find out what was wrong with him—that I believed his problems were just due to his previous abuse and neglect, and that, when I finally decided he needed to see a doctor about his pica, we didn't get him in quicker." When I pressed her to explain why she and Larry had not called 911, she leaned forward, as if pleading with me to understand. "Because we were not thinking we were in a life-or-death situation," she insisted. "For us to go to (the clinic) was a lot faster than it would have been had we called, at that point."

As we talked about Andrew, she had to stop several times to compose herself. "I'm supposed to be done crying," she said apologetically at one point, brushing away tears. Despite all the pain, she told me that if she could do it over again, she would not change their decision to bring Andrew into their home. "It's not even a consideration," she said. "I wouldn't give up that time we had with him and that he had with us."

I asked Hannah if her faith had been shaken by Andrew's loss and the suffering that she and her family had experienced. "There was a time when I questioned how God could allow this to happen," she said. "But what I've realized is that I can trust his heart, even though I don't understand his plan." The reality that Hannah, who is thirty-four, may spend the rest of her life in prison for capital murder—a sentence usually reserved for violent criminals who pose a continuing threat to society—is one she is still struggling to understand; even harder to grasp is the possibility that she might never be reunited with her children. "I miss everything," she later wrote to me. "Good-night kisses, bedtime stories, playing in the yard, birthdays, loose teeth, Christmas plays ... movie nights, waking up to their beautiful faces." The Court of Criminal Appeals is currently reviewing her writ, which contends that the information about Andrew's gastric contents are grounds for a new trial. The court, which could rule imminently or years from now, could send the case back to Judge Longoria for a hearing or—far less likely—overturn her conviction. Because the court has not been inclined to intercede so far, members of Calvary Chapel have begun a letter-writing campaign to the Texas Board of Pardons and Paroles in hopes of securing a pardon or a commutation.

Meanwhile, those who once pursued Hannah with such certainty have undergone their own trials. Detective Hess was put on administrative leave in 2008 after it came to light that he had disclosed confidential information to the suspect in an ongoing investigation for indecency with a child. Hess was allowed to return to the force and is now a patrol sergeant. And Eastwood was fired from the DA's office in 2010. Then-district attorney Jimenez did not publicly disclose the reasons for the termination, but it occurred one week after Eastwood informed her superiors that she had been romantically involved in the past with a sex offender; she reported that she feared the information had been used by the offender's defense attorney to get him probation in a criminal case. (A subsequent investigation by the attorney general's office found that no crimes had been committed.)

As the Overtons wait on the appellate courts, Larry goes about the task of raising their five children, while also trying to rebuild his business. (After his arrest, he lost most of his clients. "One woman said she didn't want to work with a child killer," Larry told me.) In his role as single dad, he is aided by his extended family and his many friends from Calvary Chapel, who pitch in to do cleaning, grocery shopping, laundry, and babysitting. A church member who homeschools her daughters educates the Overton children, using lesson plans Hannah sends her. (Haller, their next-door neighbor, has since moved to Houston.) The kids now range in age from four to twelve, and when I visited them late one afternoon, not long after I had seen Hannah, they seemed unencumbered by the tragedy that had engulfed their family. They were no different from other children their age: exuberant, funny, guileless. As Larry stood in the kitchen and peeled potatoes, the kids—excited to have a visitor—showed me around their house, pointing out their favorite hiding places and the plaster cast of their footprints in the hallway, which includes the letter A for Andrew. The absence of their mother and their late brother was quietly acknowledged. "This is where Andrew used to sleep," Isaac told me softly as he led me into the boys' room. "There have been a few tear-filled nights because one of the kids misses Andrew," Larry told me later. "I remind them that the Lord loves him more than anyone could and he is with Him now and we will see him again someday."

The kids took me out back, where they jumped on the trampoline and played hide-and-seek in the salt grass. Emma, the youngest, trailed behind them with a doll, occasionally running inside to bang on the piano. It was Emma whom Hannah was pregnant with when Andrew died, and she is the child Hannah knows least. When Emma took her first steps, Larry brought her to the parking lot outside the county jail so that Hannah could watch from her cell above.

Larry called out that dinner was ready, and we gathered inside around a rough-hewn oak table he had made years ago. Dinner was potato soup—"It's good and filling, and it's cheap," Larry told me—which the kids dived into after saying grace. They chattered about an upcoming birthday party and discussed the merits of their favorite colors, finishing each other's sentences between slurps of soup. Had Andrew sat among them, I realized, he would have been nine years old.

After dinner the kids settled down in front of the TV to watch a movie that was Isabel's pick: a Japanese animated film that her brothers and sisters showed less enthusiasm for, fidgeting as they lay next to each other on the carpet. Before they headed to bed, Larry turned up the lights for their nightly devotions. Isaac read John 9 aloud while Larry helped him sound out the difficult words ("synagogue," "Pharisees"). A short discussion followed about the passage, in which Jesus heals a blind man, and then Larry closed his Bible and said, "Okay, guys, let's pray." One by one, the kids spoke their prayers, each of which ended with the same wish.

"Dear God, thank you for the soup," Isaac said, his head bowed, his eyes closed tightly. "And thanks for the movie, even though it was kind of weird. I pray that you will bring Mom home soon."

AUTHOR'S AFTERWORDS...

I wish that all stories fell into my lap the way that this one did. One day in early 2011, I got a call from a reporter here in Texas I revere: John MacCormack of the *San Antonio Express-News*. I didn't know John personally, but I had admired his work for a long, long time. I would dare to say that he's the best newspaper reporter in Texas, and he has held that distinction for a long time. Back when I was twenty-five, and had just been hired by *Texas Monthly*, and had absolutely no idea what I was doing, I was lucky enough to get to write about a trial in Amarillo that John was also covering. I never got up the guts to talk to him, but I watched him—cultivating sources, shaping the day's narrative—and I learned a lot from his example.

John called me out of the blue and told me about Hannah. He explained that he had written a few stories about her case, but that he had done as much as he possibly could with it in newspaper form. I had read one of his stories, so I was familiar with the broad strokes of the case. He said, "It's a really important case, and I wish you would look into it." John ended up driving to Austin and giving me a box of documents, contact information for sources, and all of his notes. He is incredibly generous like that.

So I started reading, and of course there were a lot of things about the case that were troubling on its face. The trial transcript alone took a long time to read, because the trial lasted for almost three weeks. I also learned as much about salt poisoning as I possibly could. After I did that initial research, I made some phone calls and discovered that no one—literally no one—from the prosecution side of the case was going to talk to me, even off the record. So I went into this story knowing that I would not have any input from the cops, the District Attorney's office, or prosecution witnesses. That was really disheartening, but also interesting to me. Why would no one talk? Usually when someone has already been convicted, sources aren't so wary.

I went down to Corpus Christi and spent a substantial amount of time with Larry Overton. I also spent time with Hannah's friends and extended family, her pastor, the people she attended church with, and her children. Of course, everyone was an advocate for Hannah, and I had to keep that in mind. At the same time, if you spend enough time with people, it's hard for their true nature to not come to the surface at some point. (I am not a particularly religious person, so there was a natural distance between me and the people I was interviewing that was helpful, I think. I didn't want to get too close, particularly since the prosecution had decided not to cooperate.) The picture that emerged of Hannah was so radically at odds with the picture of her that had been presented at trial that I started thinking about that as a theme of the story. She was either an angel or a monster, and nothing in between.

After spending some significant time with Larry, I asked him if he would be comfortable with me coming over to the house and being a fly on the wall one evening. I did this because I had already figured out how I wanted to end the story. Larry had mentioned to me during an interview that the kids prayed every night for Hannah to come home. The moment he said it, I knew that was the end of the story. I just had to figure out a way to actually witness that moment myself, so that I could write about it. Often the first thing I figure out about a story is how to end it, and then I try to figure out how to get to the end as efficiently as possible. Figuring out a story's first section can unhinge me, but endings are pretty intuitive. Larry agreed, and so I was able to be there one night when the kids prayed for Hannah's return.

I was hugely pregnant with my second child when I was reporting this story, and my pregnancy came in handy when I went to interview Hannah. I had been allotted one hour by the prison to interview her, which was ludicrous, because we had so much to cover. When I showed up to the warden's office, I tried to look as pathetic and physically uncomfortable as possible so that the prison officials would take pity on me. Long story short, the warden gave me four hours with Hannah. That was still barely enough time to cover everything, but I was so grateful. The fact that I was pregnant also helped break the ice with Hannah, whose dealings with the press (other than John MacCormack) had been pretty traumatic. She was a bit wary of me at first, so we started off talking about our children, and then she started asking about my pregnancy. Once we found common ground there, everything was okay.

I wrote half the story before I had my daughter, and then returned to write the second half of it after three months of maternity leave. That might sound hard, to write a story with such a large break in the middle of the writing, but it was actually wonderful. I had been able to marinate in the ideas of the story for three months, and so I found that finishing the story was relatively easy, which writing never is for me.

A month after the publication of the story, Texas's highest criminal court ruled that a lower court should examine Hannah's claims of actual innocence. An evidentiary hearing was held in the spring of 2012, and now the case is before the high court for review. There are several different possible outcomes: Hannah could be freed, she could receive a new trial, or her conviction could be upheld. I always try to figure out the ending of my stories first, but I have no idea, at this point, how this case will end.

Luke Dittrich

L uke Dittrich began working as a journalist in 1997, while living in Egypt. The first article he ever submitted for publication, an article *The Middle East Times* initially accepted and then later killed, was a personal account of finding a dead body floating down the Nile. He has since written about lost atomic bombs, teenaged hitmen, Chuck Berry, and various other topics. His stories have appeared in several anthologies, including *The Best American Crime Writing, The Best American Travel Writing,* and *The Best American Science and Nature Writing.* An article he wrote about something terrifying and beautiful that happened during a tornado won the 2012 National Magazine Award for feature writing. He's been a contributing editor at *Esquire* since 2007, and is currently working on his first book, about a memorable case of amnesia, for Random House.

Tonight on *Dateline* This Man Will Die

A cop guards the open gateway that leads from the house's driveway to the side yard, in case the man inside attempts to flee. At first the camera is static and the shot is simple: the cop, the gateway, vertical red fence planks, a right foreground portion of green bush. After a few minutes of this, the cameraman starts playing with the composition. The screen fills almost entirely with the bush, and then the view pans left from the bush to the cop, who is big and bald and has three upside-down blue V's—sergeant stripes—on the sleeve of his shirt. The cameraman zooms in past the cop to the patio area beyond, to a lattice of firewood and the blur of something green. The camera stills, focuses. The blur becomes a wheelbarrow. A green wheelbarrow leaning belly-exposed against a red wall.

While the shot of this particular wheelbarrow is superfluous to the television program being filmed here today and will be edited out along with most of the rest of this raw footage, there happens to be a story about the man inside the house in which a wheelbarrow plays a much more prominent role. The story begins more than two decades ago, at a party in another house not far from this one. The man inside was there, as were many of his friends, which meant that the attendees were a hodgepodge of the most notable lawyers and doctors and businessmen in Terrell, Texas. Anybody compiling a list of local luminaries back then might have placed the name of the man inside at or near the top. His high school class, of which he was president, had voted him most likely to succeed, and he had done so. At the time of the party, not much more than a decade out of law school and still in his thirties, he was already district attorney of his home county.

The party's host had hired a local kid named Eric Bishop to provide entertainment, and Bishop—who would eventually change his name to Jamie Foxx and move west—was playing old R&B covers, pounding them out on a borrowed piano. The man inside stood near the keyboard, watching. Watching and drinking. A couple drinks and then a few and then who knows how many until he was well and truly lit, until he was finally a staggering mess, until he was finally so far gone that the prospect of walking home, never mind driving, was an Everest summit attempt. And finally: The host and another friend poured the shambling young district attorney into, yes, a wheelbarrow. They delivered him to his home, legs and arms flopping out to the sides like the limbs of an upended turtle.

The reason people remember this story and still tell it twenty years on is that it is so remarkably uncharacteristic of the man inside. He is a man so proper, so predictable, that when he occasionally dons a blue shirt, the color jolts the eyes of his friends, who are unaccustomed to seeing him in anything other than solid white. Imagine how an episode of flagrant public drunkenness in the life of such a man might sear itself into the memories of those who witnessed it. Twenty years later and they still laugh at the thought of him being barrowed home with a brain full of booze.

The cameraman pulls back, revealing again all the ingredients at once: the bush, the cop, the wheelbarrow, the red fence. A few seconds of this and then the view drifts upward to a chaos of tree branches against an overcast November sky.

A long view from a different camera shows the same cop in the same gateway. More of the house is visible, along with the broad driveway. Three voices are audible off camera.

"We should have craft services bring it in here," the first voice says, referring to the catering truck. The other voices laugh.

"If he's not in there, [inaudible] gonna take some heavy abuse," the second voice says.

"Oh, yeah," says the third voice.

The third voice is exceptional. A deep and furred rumble. Even on the basis of just those two syllables, most would intuit that the owner of the voice is either a radio or television reporter. Get a look at him and it's obvious he's the latter, standing self-consciously erect, hands on narrow hips, a plumb line between the top of his head and his heels, posture and hair perfect.

It is past 3 p.m. and Chris Hansen, the host of "To Catch a Predator," a recurring series on NBC's *Dateline* television news program, arrived here at 8:30 this morning, having gotten hardly any sleep the night before. He never gets much sleep on these shoots. Although aspects of his show are tightly choreographed, Hansen and the rest of his production team must always remain loose limbed, ready to adapt to changing circumstances and unpredictable hours. The show's protagonists, after all, are recruited on the fly, and everything depends on them. They drive the plot, and Hansen never knows exactly where that plot is going to take him. Before the unexpected series of events that began yesterday afternoon, for example, Hansen had no intention of ever being here, outside this house, waiting for a SWAT team on an overcast Sunday afternoon.

Yesterday, at around 1 p.m., a young actor named Dan Schrack leaned back against a folding table and held a tubular, bendable microphone close to his lips. Headphones pinioned his blond Prince Valiant hairdo over his ears. A coffee cup, a can of Diet Dr. Pepper, and a packet of Pepto-Bismol sat on the table, as did a Motorola cell phone. The cell phone was plugged in to a recording device. Before placing the phone in its cradle, Schrack had punched in the number of a man he knew as Wil, and now he was listening to the ringing in the headphones. Schrack had assumed so many different identities during the last few days that he had to actually pause a few moments before in order to quiz himself on some of the vital stats of his newest alias to make sure he didn't screw anything up.

My name? Luke.

Age? Thirteen.

Family? Parents divorced, dad neglectful, stepdad no good.

Current location? In the empty home of neighbors who are paying me to walk their dogs while they're away visiting an elderly relative.

In reality, the home he was in was not empty at all. Far from it. At the moment, it contained almost two dozen people. There were cameramen and technicians and producers from *Dateline*. There were people from a group called Perverted Justice. There was Chris Hansen. There was security: a former NYPD lieutenant and an off-duty police detective from a nearby city. And these were only the people actually within the house. Just outside, hidden in a moving van, there were at least a half dozen more people—local city cops, the so-called Takedown Team— all armed and ready to spring at a moment's notice.

A couple of months ago, when Schrack showed up at an audition at the NBC studios in Burbank, California, he hadn't really known what he was getting himself into. He had been in Los Angeles a few years, a twenty-one-year-old whose naturally rosy cheeks and guileless smile make him appear much younger. The biggest gig on his résumé was a Toys "R" Us commercial, and like many struggling actors, Schrack tried to squeeze in so many auditions that he didn't have time to properly research the roles he was reading for. So though he had known that he was auditioning for *Dateline*, he thought *Dateline* was just looking to film one of those dramatic reenactments that other programs like *America's Most Wanted* sometimes used. He'd never seen *Dateline's* "To Catch a Predator" series and didn't have any idea how it worked. A producer at the audition brought him up to speed.

The typical episode works something like this: *Dateline* leases a house in a small town somewhere in America and wires it for sound and video. Members of Perverted Justice, a group to which *Dateline* pays a consulting fee, pose in online chat rooms as underage teens living in that small town. If an adult man starts hitting on one of these fake kids, the Perverted Justice decoys save the transcripts of his chats. Eventually, the man is invited over to the wired house for a liaison. When he arrives, Chris Hansen confronts him with a printout of Perverted Justice's chat transcripts and attempts to interview him. As soon as he leaves the house, local cops (the Takedown Team) arrest him and charge him with online solicitation of a minor. Each episode focuses on a decoy house in a single city and documents the catching of six or seven men.

Schrack's role in all of this would be as the real-life incarnation of the fake boys that Perverted Justice creates. (An actress would be hired to portray the fake girls.) His picture would be used in the online profiles, he would conduct any telephone or Web-cam conversations, and when the men showed up at the house, he'd be there to greet them at the door and invite them inside, usually getting a few moments of screen time before Chris Hansen makes his appearance.

A few hours after he left the Burbank audition, NBC offered him the gig: $5,000 per shoot, with each shoot lasting three or four days.

By this time, standing there with his headphones on, waiting for the man he knew as Wil to pick up his phone, Schrack had already wrapped two episodes and was one day away from finishing his third. This would be his last, since the first had just aired, effectively blowing his cover. Though he liked the money, he wasn't going to miss much about working for "To Catch a Predator." He wasn't experienced in improv, and he'd come to realize that improv was what this job amounted to. Before making this phone call, he'd had to read the alternately mundane and smutty transcripts of all the chat sessions conducted between the Perverted Justice decoy and Wil over the last two weeks. The transcripts gave him the parameters of the character he was playing and of his character's relationship to Wil: Luke was a thirteen-year-old dog walker, and Wil was a nineteen-year-old college student. Luke lived at home with his parents, who had not given him the Razr cell phone he'd asked for last Christmas, and Wil lived with a straight roommate, who had once walked in on him having sex with another man. Luke had confessed to falling in love with Wil, and Wil had confessed that he liked young boys. Within the broad parameters laid down in the chats, however, the actor was given conversational freedom. His only mandate now was to entice Wil to come visit him in the real world, at this new house about a half hour's drive north of downtown Dallas in Murphy, Texas, a house that NBC had leased and booby-trapped for television.

The actor's favorite roles had been in musicals. He preferred productions like that, where every line and verse and dance step was preordained before the curtain rose, and he knew going in whether the show was a comedy or a tragedy.

"Hello?"

"Hey, is this Wil?"

"Yeah."

"Hey, Wil, this is Luke!"

"Hey! How are you? Did you get the dogs walked?"

"Yes, I did. So what are you doing?"

"Not anything. Well, actually, I'm sort of watching a football game."

Until this last line, everything about the beginning of their conversation, both its words and its premises, was false: The name of the man inside was not Wil, he was not nineteen, he lived alone, without a roommate, and he'd stopped being a college student more than three decades ago.

But there is reason to believe that the man inside was telling the truth about watching a football game. He was probably referring to Texas Tech's noontime rout of Baylor University, which Fox Sports Net was broadcasting at the time of the phone call. He graduated from law school at Texas Tech and usually pulled for the team, though with nothing like the passion he displayed for the Longhorns of the University of Texas, his undergraduate alma mater. He'd been a Longhorns fan forever. One of the precious gifts of his childhood had been a ticket to the 1964 Cotton Bowl, when the Longhorns beat Navy and seized the national championship. His parents had swaddled the ticket in multiple layers of wrapping paper and boxes of descending sizes, a Russian doll of a present that he'd remember for the rest of his life.

Before the kickoff of Saturday's game, the man inside had gone out for a little while: He'd dropped some of his white shirts off at the cleaners, he'd shopped for groceries, he'd bought a Texas Two Step lottery ticket.

Then he had come home, where he'd probably turned on his RCA and tuned in FSN shortly before his phone rang.

As Dan Schrack leaned against a folding table and talked on the phone, a number of Perverted Jutice employees sat at nearby desks, working on computers. At some point, after Schrack hung up, some of these people ran the screen name and email address and phone number of the man known as Wil through a variety of Internet search engines. They made certain discoveries, among them Wil's real name and occupation.

A cameraman recorded a scene shortly thereafter, when one of the Perverted Justice employees informed Chris Hansen. He told Chris Hansen that the man they thought was nineteen was actually fifty-six, that his name was Bill Conradt, that he was not a college student but rather an assistant district attorney of a neighboring county, the county's chief felony prosecutor.

In the two years since the first episode of "To Catch a Predator" aired, Chris Hansen had exposed men from a variety of professions. A doctor. A handful of soldiers. A couple of cops. Teachers. A rabbi. A minister. But he'd never exposed a prosecutor before.

The Perverted Justice employee rubbed his hands together, clapped them, obviously energized by the news he was imparting.

Chris Hansen's usual on-camera listening expression—lips tight, eyes slightly narrowed, just the hint of a furrow to his brow—did not change.

Bill Conradt was a good prosecutor. All of the judges and lawyers who knew him best, even the ones who served on the opposite side of the aisle from him, the men and women who defended their clients against him, say he was very good at his job. He had a near photographic memory for the law, they say, and this made him either a formidable opponent or a valuable ally, depending on where you stood.

So Conradt no doubt knew that statute 33.021 in the Texas penal code description of the crime of "online solicitation of a minor" states that an adult offends when he "communicates in a sexually explicit manner with a minor," and defines "minor" as anyone who represents himself or herself as being under the age of seventeen. And yet here are some of the things Bill Conradt wrote during the two-week-long online relationship he had with thirteen-year-old "Luke":

"could I feel your cock"

"how thick are you"

"i want to feel your cock"

"maybe you can fuck me several times"

"has anyone sucked you"

"just talking about this has me hard"

Bill Conradt, a good prosecutor, was used to straddling mires of facts and statutes and circumstances. It is hard not to wonder what he would have made of his own case.

"Did you leave yet?"

"No."

"You didn't leave yet?"

"No."

"Are you gonna come or not?"

Dan Schrack drenched the last line with all the petulance and neediness he could muster, so the final syllable stretched like taffy and leapt at least an octave in pitch: Are you gonna come or *nahhhhhhhttt?*

The desperation sounded genuine. It was about 3 p.m. on Saturday, and this was their third conversation in as many hours. Schrack had likely concluded their first conversation with an invitation to come visit him here at the decoy house, and Bill Conradt had accepted. He'd accepted and then he never showed up. By this point, everyone in the house, including Schrack, knew Conradt's real identity, and by this point the same question was on everyone's mind: Was he gonna come or not?

"Yes, I shall," said Conradt.

"Well when are you gonna come *overrrrr?*"

"Well, a little later."

"A little *laterrrrrr?*"

"Yeah. Is that all right?"

"Yeah, I *guessssss.*"

The arrests made yesterday at the decoy house, like the arrests made the day before and the day before that, were all filmed. The footage played out in real time on monitors in one of the rooms on the first floor. Jimmy Patterson, an off-duty detective whom NBC was paying thirty-five dollars an hour to protect its employees in case one of the suspects got violent, had watched the first few arrests on these monitors. Then he had stopped watching. He knew if he kept watching, he would have to say something to somebody about all the stupid mistakes the Murphy Police Department's "Takedown Team" was making.

Detective Patterson had worked for a suburban Dallas-metro-area police department for the last twenty-two years, had spent the last twelve of those years on SWAT, knew his tactics, knew his weapons. And he knew that Murphy was just a small town, with a population of ten thousand, and so you couldn't expect all the cops in Murphy to be as well trained as he was. They didn't have the resources. But still. How hard was it to avoid a cross-fire situation? Because that's what he saw on those little gray-scale monitors every time an arrest was made: cross-fire situations. The cops on the Takedown Team would rush the suspect and surround him, guns leveled, and Detective Patterson winced when he saw it, because he knew that if those officers ever had to actually fire their weapons, well, they'd be just as likely to kill one another as the suspect. Sometimes he'd get a view right down the barrel of a Murphy cop's gun, a perspective straight out of Doom, courtesy of a *Dateline* buttonhole camera, and in the same shot he'd get a view of another cop's back.

Not to mention that the whole intensity level of these arrests, the way the Takedown Team would holler at the suspect, the way they'd throw him to the ground, the whole idea of even having their weapons drawn in the first place, all of that struck Detective Patterson as ridiculous. Just the other day, he'd been in a supermarket parking lot when he noticed someone who fit the description of a suspect in a bank robbery he'd been working. He called the sergeant, told him to send over some of the boys. And when his colleagues got there, you know how many guns were drawn, how much shouting was done? None. The officers walked up, introduced themselves, asked the guy to show some ID, and that was that. Sure, they had their holsters unsnapped, one hand near, but they didn't need to take it to the next level. You hardly ever have to, not in the real world. All that business— the guns, the tackling, the shouting—struck Detective Patterson as pure and simple TV: It might look good on camera, but if you're letting a camera influence how you do your takedowns, you've got a problem.

All of this stuff was on Detective Jimmy Patterson's mind when he heard people on the second floor start throwing around the name Bill Conradt. He asked them to spell the surname. Sure enough. With a t. He knew a Bill Conradt. Had worked with him. Bill Conradt was the chief felony prosecutor of the county that included part of Detective Patterson's city. Bill Conradt had prosecuted people that Detective Patterson had arrested. Couldn't be the same Bill Conradt.

Early Saturday evening, Detective Patterson asked to listen to the tapes of the telephone conversations. The voice was familiar, but he couldn't be sure. Does he have a son? Sons often sound like fathers. Anyway, a voice wasn't enough. Something like this, somebody like this, you've gotta be extra careful. You're talking about law enforcement taking down law enforcement. You've gotta take extra precautions. But the way things had gone these last few days, what with the overzealous made-for-TV cops outside and the real TV people here inside, Detective Patterson wasn't at all sure that the necessary precautions would be taken.

As the evening wore on, Detective Patterson learned that Bill Conradt had stopped responding to Dan Schrack's phone calls. He'd also stopped responding to the AOL instant messages that the Perverted Justice chat decoy was sending. The IMs were starting to read like semiliterate poems of longing and anxiety:

> i tried callin you alot
> an u didn't answer :(
> and i cried cuz ure so hot

At a little after 9 p.m., Detective Patterson overheard Lynn Keller, the lead producer of "To Catch a Predator," discussing Bill Conradt with another *Dateline* employee, trying to come up with different strategies they might employ to lure him to Murphy. Detective Patterson was the only law-enforcement officer inside the decoy house, and at that moment, standing there listening to a couple of civilians devising ways to lure an assistant district attorney, he was beginning to feel very uncomfortable. He felt as if he was being made party to something he was not at all sure he wanted to be involved in. Finally he approached Keller, told her that as an officer with the Rowlett Police Department, he felt obligated to call his boss, the chief of police, and give him a heads-up regarding the whole matter brewing with Bill Conradt. Lynn Keller stopped him cold.

"You're working for *Dateline* now," she said.

A day or two prior to the beginning of the sting operation, NBC technicians had installed a high-tech video-projection system in a room at Murphy Police Department headquarters. Along with the projector, NBC installed all the equipment necessary to stream multiple live video and audio feeds from the decoy house a mile or so away. The room was normally the police department's training classroom and was usually referred to as such, but after the arrival of *Dateline's* impressive array of electronics, some officers began referring to it as "NORAD" or "the War Room."

Just around midnight on Saturday, the War Room was still busy, as it had been all day long. The whole *Dateline* crew was planning to pack up and fly out tomorrow evening, yet though the operation was nearing its conclusion, new men continued to arrive at the decoy house. Many of the Murphy detectives, whose job it would be to interrogate these men once they'd been hauled to the station, stopped by to watch Chris Hansen interview them first, getting a real-time preview of the next episode of "To Catch a Predator." The chief of police, Billy Myrick, was here, too, as well as one of the chief's lieutenants, a woman named Adana Barber.

Chief Myrick had held his current job for about a year and a half. He'd never been chief anywhere else but had been in law enforcement for more or less his entire adult life. He was now forty-eight years old, a naturally burly man drifting toward middle-aged paunch. When he applied for a job here in Murphy, the department ran a pretty comprehensive background check on him. Most of the officers Myrick had previously worked with, in various departments around north Texas, all said pretty much the same thing: He was a good officer but not a great leader. When he began getting into supervisory positions, he changed, one of his former coworkers said. "A bull in a china closet" who "blusters around" is how another put it. "He probably shouldn't be in supervision but is a great officer," the background report stated. But shortly after Myrick started working as a cop in Murphy, the sitting chief and city manager departed, and the new city manager, who has hiring powers at the police department, promoted Myrick to chief.

On July 22, 2006, an officer named Kevin Carter approached Chief Myrick and told him that a group called Perverted Justice had offered the Murphy Police Department its services. Two days later, Perverted Justice demonstrated what it could do, feeding the department information regarding an east-Texas ophthalmologist who'd been chatting with a Perverted Justice decoy. The doctor, Perverted Justice informed the police, had set up a liaison at a Murphy convenience store. Chief Myrick dispatched officers to the store, and sure enough, there was the doctor, waiting patiently in the front seat of his Ford Expedition, with a brand-new teddy bear. After the cops arrested the doctor, they seized his vehicle, which became de facto city property. Chief Myrick, who would eventually use that Ford Expedition as his ride-around vehicle, was hooked. When Perverted Justice broached the subject of doing something more ambitious in Murphy, a "To Catch a Predator" sting operation with *Dateline*, he didn't hesitate. Soon after, in early fall, he called a full departmental meeting, got all his officers together, and told them that "To Catch a Predator" was coming to town.

Not everyone in the department was sold on the idea. One of the chief's detectives, a man named Sam Love, stood up during that initial meeting and told the chief that the sting operation was going to generate a lot of cases, but the department wouldn't have the means to work them. Detective Love said it was hard enough for the Murphy PD to handle all the homegrown cases here in Murphy without luring in who knows how many perverts from out of town.

And the Collin County District Attorney's office, which encompassed Murphy, wasn't on board, either. A few weeks ago, Perverted Justice had faxed Collin County, notifying officials of the upcoming sting and requesting logistical and planning support. John Roach, the district attorney, was very surprised that a civilian group, not the Murphy Police Department, was the first to inform him of the sting. Roach directed Chris Milner, the head of his special-crimes unit, to draft a response and send it back to both Perverted Justice and Chief Myrick: The DA's office, the letter read, "will take no part in the planning or execution of the sting operation ... must take pains not to implicitly authorize or direct non-law-enforcement entities to act as our agents during law enforcement operations ... the Collin County District Attorney's office is in the law enforcement business, not show business." Roach worried that the involvement of *Dateline* and Perverted Justice might badly compromise the sting operation, and he hoped that his letter might serve as a wake-up call to Chief Myrick, giving the chief an out.

But all this nay-saying aside, Chief Myrick, standing there in the War Room late on Saturday, seemed to think the operation a resounding success. As he had told several officers, he hoped *Dateline* would "put Murphy on the map." He was in a joking mood: Whenever a suspect pulled up in a particularly nice automobile, he would lean over to Lieutenant Adana Barber, a petite woman with short-cropped hair, and say something like, "That one's mine!"

At about 12:30 a.m., according to Detective Sam Love, who was also in the War Room, Lieutenant Barber's cell phone rang. The conversation, recalls Love, was brief and mostly one-sided, and afterward Barber relayed a message to the chief: Chris Hansen wants the police to get an arrest warrant and a search warrant for Bill Conradt. He and the rest of the *Dateline* crew have decided that since Conradt is no longer responding to IMs or answering his telephone, he is probably not going to come to the decoy house in Murphy. Since he won't come to them, they've decided to go to him. Conradt lives in a small town called Terrell, about an hour's drive southeast of Murphy. Hansen plans to go to Conradt's house the next day. They're hoping Conradt might have some sort of Sunday routine, might go out for coffee or something. If he does, the *Dateline* crew will follow, and Chris Hansen will attempt to interview him. In the parlance of television news, they will ambush him. Then, if the Murphy police get the warrants, Bill Conradt will be arrested and carted away on camera. Basically, the producers want the interview and arrest of Bill Conradt to follow the standard "To Catch a Predator" formula, despite Conradt's evident unwillingness to visit the decoy house. And they want the warrants ready by morning.

Approximately fifty minutes after Lieutenant Barber relayed this message, at about 1:20 a.m., in a quieter room at the police department, Chief Myrick approached Detective Walter "Gator" Weiss. He told him they were about to net a big fish. A woman from Perverted Justice accompanied the chief, and she handed Gator a sheaf of papers that contained printouts of some Internet chat logs and a freshly burned compact disc that contained recordings of some telephone conversations. The chief ordered the detective to review the material and prepare a search warrant and an arrest warrant for Bill Conradt. And he told Gator they needed the warrants by morning.

Gator stared at his computer screen, wrestling with the assignment. He'd had qualms about the sting operation from the beginning, same issues that Detective Love had with it—too many arrests, too much paperwork for a small department to handle—but he figured that in the end, if it succeeded in taking some bad guys off the streets, they would have done some good. He'd been in and out of interrogation rooms for the past twenty-six hours straight, no sleep, talking with these suspects, and some of them, well, he sure wouldn't want them anywhere near his teenage son. And the suspects had, after all, come to the decoy house. That showed intent—a willingness to take their whole mess off the Internet and into the real world.

This thing with Bill Conradt, though...it bothered Gator. When the chief told Gator about Bill Conradt, the first thing Gator thought was, we can't do this alone. This guy, he never came to the decoy house. And this guy, he was a chief felony prosecutor. He told the chief maybe they should call in the Rangers. He told the chief he'd also like to call Chris Milner, the guy in charge of special crimes at the Collin County District Attorney's office, get his advice. Don't worry about Chris Milner, the chief told Gator. Just worry about getting the arrest warrant and the search warrant together tonight.

So Gator sat down at his computer and he read the transcripts and he listened to the telephone conversations and then he started putting what he read and heard into the form of an affidavit for an arrest warrant. He wrote. He continued writing. He stared at the screen. He stared at the keyboard. He closed his eyes for a second. He woke with a start.

Goddammit. He'd fallen asleep at his computer. Just before dawn. Pages to go.

Even in the hurry he was in, trying to push everything to the back of his mind, a bad feeling was gnawing at him, creating a bigger and bigger pit in his stomach. Too much of a rush job. Why do they need to get this guy so fast, right now?

When *Dateline* airs the episode documenting this sting operation a few months later, Chris Hansen, narrating, will offer one explanation: "For some reason," Hansen will explain, "[Conradt] abruptly stopped chatting, and Perverted Justice discovered he'd deleted his MySpace page." Similarly, in a blog posting on the "To Catch a Predator" website, Hansen will write: "We'll never know why Conradt abruptly ended his conversations with the decoy and why he apparently started to delete material from a MySpace account, but in the eyes of law enforcement, he'd already committed a crime. That night, Murphy Police began the process of obtaining an arrest warrant and a search warrant for Conradt." And in interviews after the sting has ended, Xavier Von Erck, the head of Perverted Justice, will offer a similar account to both The *New York Times* and Bill O'Reilly, an account summed up on Perverted Justice's own website: "We began to notice that information was disappearing ... and when we advised the police of this they chose to act." The implication was that the police had to get Conradt as soon as possible, since he was working posthaste to cover his tracks by deleting information from his MySpace account.

When asked this summer if Perverted Justice had saved any versions of the page that was mentioned during the broadcast, Von Erck will respond: "His MySpace is still up. It was very blank then and it's still very blank." And then Von Erck will provide a Web link. The page will indeed still be up. And it will show that nobody had accessed or deleted information from it since August of 2006, three months prior to the sting operation. Von Erck will not respond to follow-up emails for eleven days, at which point he will write back that "the MySpace you were linked to is just another of the profiles of his that we found afterwards." Neither he nor NBC nor the Murphy Police Department will produce any other evidence regarding Bill Conradt's alleged vanishing MySpace page.

In any case, Gator had never been told about a MySpace page. Nor had he been given any other information that made the rush for these warrants explicable to him. He began to suspect the Murphy PD was trying to accommodate *Dateline's* schedule. If they're not gonna call in other agencies, Gator thought, at least send the evidence to a grand-jury referral. A confidential inquest. Get them to look at the facts, decide if warrants are warranted. Gator knew there was one easy way he could slow this down. He could leave. He could walk out the back door of the police department, drive home to his family, and sleep for a whole day. He could quit. He thought about it.

But that's not what he did.

At a little before 11 a.m., Gator finished writing the arrest warrant. A local municipal judge, Cathy Haden, came to headquarters and signed it. Chief Myrick told Gator to start in on the second warrant, the search warrant, immediately, and to radio him as soon as he'd gotten it signed.

When the cops arrive at Bill Conradt's door on Sunday afternoon, a dog starts barking somewhere inside the house. Short, sharp, expulsions of nervous energy. Unmistakably a small dog. Bill Conradt has shared his home with a mini schnauzer named Lukas for the last several years. Before that he shared it with another mini schnauzer, Bismarck. Bismarck's ashes sit in an urn on a mantel in the den. His sister, Patricia, used to tease him about those ashes and his reluctance to part with them, told him to just bury Bismarck already, but then she lost her own dog and she didn't tease him about the ashes anymore after that.

A sergeant from the Terrell Police Department knocks on the door. The Terrell sergeant is here because early this afternoon Lieutenant Barber called the chief of the Terrell PD, Todd Miller, and asked for his department's assistance in making this arrest. Chief Miller complied. Along with the Terrell sergeant, a Terrell patrol officer and Murphy detective Snow Robertson are also at the door. Chief Myrick and Lieutenant Barber are about thirty feet away, hiding behind trees. Another man, a cameraman, is hiding behind a different tree, much closer to the door, evidently trying hard to stay out of the footage being recorded by the other NBC cameramen, perhaps for aesthetic reasons, perhaps because it is generally illegal for news cameras to be on private property without permission.

Dateline's cast and crew outnumber the five cops here by a factor of two. One of their cameras captures the sergeant as he presses a door buzzer that has not worked in years. The Murphy detective then draws his gun and holds it in both hands, angling it down so it aims at a spot a foot or two in front of his feet. The sergeant knocks again on the door, which does not lead into the house but rather into a large open courtyard. He tries the doorknob. He presses the useless door buzzer. He waits. Eventually the cameraman stops filming.

The video picks up again a few minutes later. Chief Myrick and the Terrell sergeant are talking, facing the camera as much as each other. Sometimes the camera zooms out a little and the back of Chris Hansen's head enters the frame. About twenty minutes ago, at 2:20 p.m., Gator finally Nexteled in news of the completion of the search warrant, straight from the living room of the district judge who'd just given it his signature. Hansen and his crew got here hours before the police did, but they never got their hoped-for chance to ambush Bill Conradt. During the *Dateline* crew's long and lonely stakeout, they didn't see much of note, though they themselves were seen and noted by many: Numerous residents phoned in suspicious-persons reports during the five hours that *Dateline's* three crowded vehicles were in the area, sometimes parked in front of the neighborhood watch sign.

Actually, Hansen and his crew did notice one thing. They saw the Sunday edition of the *Dallas Morning News* sitting just outside Bill Conradt's door. And then, the next time they looked, they didn't see it. Which is what the chief is talking to the sergeant about.

"And I just clarified," Chief Myrick says. "They didn't actually see him come out. But when they got here on surveillance, the paper was there. And then they look up again, the paper was gone."

"But no one's left the residence?" the sergeant asks.

Chief Myrick repeats the question to someone off camera.

"Yeah," Chris Hansen answers. He hasn't seen anyone leave the residence. "Okay," says the sergeant. "In view of that, and the dog's barking, it's evident that if there's someone in there, they know we're out here. My chief says he's more comfortable calling the tac team out and, um . . ."

"Make an entry?" asks Chief Myrick.

"Make a forced entry," says the sergeant. "If it has to be like that, that's what he wants to do."

Many will eventually question the decision to call in SWAT. Ed Walton, at the time the sitting district attorney of Kaufman County, which encompasses Terrell, will label the Terrell Police Department "the most incompetent bunch of buffoons you've ever seen" and wonder whether the decision had something to do with an embarrassing and locally well-publicized incident that took place just weeks earlier, in which the Terrell police were forced to drop charges against the prime suspects in a murder case because of what Walton calls a "bollixed" investigation. Calling out their SWAT team for what they knew was going to be a nationally broadcast police operation was, in the opinion of Walton, "their great white hope. You know, to try to come in and show they really weren't a bunch of lummoxes." When asked about the matter later, Terrell chief Todd Miller will answer, "The Conradt case was not a Terrell Police Service case, it was a Murphy Police Department case," and refuse further comment. Mike Minor, an attorney who has worked in Kaufman county for thirty years and was a friend of Bill Conradt's, calls the decision to send in the SWAT team "the stupidest and most unnecessary thing that I have ever heard of in law enforcement. If they really wanted to do the right thing, they could have waited until Bill came out. [Or] they could have gone to the courthouse [where he worked] and arrested him. You know, he was not like John Dillinger. That was all for sensationalism."

But this afternoon, on Bill Conradt's lawn, nobody questions the decision, though one man takes pains to make clear that the decision doesn't come from him: Chief Myrick splays his fingers wide, holds a hand out sternum-high and tilted slightly upward, palm down, a universal sign for abdication of responsibility.

"This is y'all's call on that one," he says.

A few feet away from the chief, a man wearing blue jeans, an untucked olive-green button-down shirt, a brim-forward baseball cap, and a pair of big dark sunglasses says something.

Everyone here knows the man with the conspicuously incognito look as Frag, though Frag is not his real name. All the members of Perverted Justice have fake names. For example, the person who spent the last two weeks conducting an on-again, off-again chat-room relationship with Bill Conradt calls himself Jay Alternative, though his real name is Greg Brainer. Ostensibly the members of Perverted Justice adopt these fake names so that the men they trap do not seek them out in the real world, but the cartoony, superhero-like aspect of most of their aliases perhaps also says something about the way the members of Perverted Justice perceive themselves. Online, Jay Alternative is a faceless crusader patrolling the dark side of the Internet. Offline, Greg Brainer is a middle-aged man who lives in Milford, Michigan, and spends upwards of forty hours a week sitting at a computer pretending to be a sexually available boy. Sometimes the fake names become real. A few years ago, Phillip John Eide, the founder of Perverted Justice, legally changed his name to that of his alter ego, Xavier Von Erck.

Von Erck, formerly a computer tech-support worker, launched www.perverted-justice.com after witnessing how commonplace it was for adults to hit on children in the Portland, Oregon, chat rooms he frequented. The website was a sort of online equivalent of that medieval punishment, the stocks: Von Erck and other volunteers would pose as minors in chat rooms and then post and widely distribute the names, photographs, and other personal information of men that sexually solicited them. There was no law-enforcement aspect to Perverted Justice's early work, just a public shaming.

As Perverted Justice grew, it attracted increasing media attention. In 2004, Kevin Dietz, a television reporter at an NBC affiliate in Detroit, ran a piece on Perverted Justice. Dietz was a friend of Chris Hansen's, who saw the report and was inspired. *Dateline* ran its first story on Perverted Justice in September of 2004. In that first report, *Dateline* documented how Perverted Justice decoys lured men to a house, and then Chris Hansen interviewed these men once they arrived. But although that first episode drew high ratings, viewers complained that *Dateline* was not actually doing anything about the problem it was documenting and assailed local law enforcement for not arresting the men *Dateline* exposed. So starting with episode three, the arrest of the suspect became an essential and always-present ingredient in the show's formula: It serves as the climax of every vignette. The show's title, after all, is not "To Catch and Release a Predator."

Hansen and NBC News maintain that law enforcement and *Dateline* simply conduct "parallel investigations" that never influence each other, and that Perverted Justice creates an impermeable "wall" between the two entities.

But by this afternoon, in front of Bill Conradt's house, whatever wall may have once divided *Dateline* and the police has essentially collapsed.

"You know we've got the number," Frag says to the cops standing on Bill Conradt's lawn. He points at Lynn Keller, the *Dateline* producer. "If somebody wants to call in and try to talk him out."

Neither the chief nor the sergeant nor any of the other officers on the scene have previously considered contacting Bill Conradt by phone. They nod approvingly at the idea.

The sergeant flips open a cell phone. Chris Hansen shuffles through a pile of papers, finds what he's looking for, then slowly dictates ten digits. The sergeant punches them in and settles the phone to his ear. "Might make an easy way to resolve it," says the chief.

Fifty-four seconds later, the sergeant hangs up. He doesn't leave a message.

Months from now, when *Dateline* has finished editing its raw footage, SWAT's arrival will be dramatic. The image on television screens will suddenly divide in three, 24-style, and the subscreens will host a confusing but portentous jumble of squad cars and body armor.

Today, in real time, SWAT's arrival is a dull trickle. The team leader, Ken McKeown, arrives first, strolls around the house, chooses a point of entry: a glass sliding door in the rear. The Murphy detective, Snow Robertson, has posted himself at the door. Through it, the detective can see a turned-on laptop screen glowing in a dark and empty room, and he's informed Chief Myrick that he plans to bust in without waiting for SWAT if he observes Bill Conradt making a move toward his computer, so that Conradt can't destroy any evidence the computer may contain. When the SWAT leader finishes his lap of the house, he waits across the street for the rest of his men. Time passes. A *Dateline* cameraman lingers on the branches of a sun-limned tree rising above an idle sergeant.

Eventually, SWAT is finally all here and ready. A camera tracks them left to right as they march in slow formation across the front yard, toward the door in the gateway that leads to the side yard. Their heads swivel in synchrony with their pace, eyes always on the house. In the foreground of the shot, a campaign sign rises on two wire stalks from Bill Conradt's lawn. White letters on a red background: HOWARD TYGRETT, who's running in the upcoming election for district judge.

Four years ago, during the last election cycle, Conradt ran for that same position. In fact, a bunch of his old campaign signs, dusty failures, sit in a pile in the closed garage that the SWAT team is now marching past. At the time of that election, Conradt had been the district attorney of Kaufman County five times in a row, twenty-two years of service in all. Becoming district judge seemed like the next logical step. So when the sitting district judge announced his retirement, Bill Conradt announced he was quitting his district attorney's post in order to pursue the position. He campaigned hard, driving his dad's old pickup truck around the county, attending barbecues and fish fries. And then, for the first time in his political career, he lost.

Maybe he lost for macro reasons, because he was a Democrat and his opponent was a Republican, and 2002 was a year in which a Republican wave swept through Texas, scouring away not just Bill Conradt but hundreds of other Democrats. Maybe he lost for micro reasons, because the pastor at the Good Shepherd Episcopal Church, a church Bill Conradt had attended faithfully his entire life, a church he had served as a cross-bearing acolyte when he was a boy, had unexpectedly decided to support his opponent. Maybe he lost because he was an unmarried middle-aged man in a rural county in Texas, and people talk.

Whatever the reasons, the loss devastated him. He didn't work at all for about a year. Then he went into private practice and slogged efficiently but without passion through the duties of a small-town defense lawyer. His heart wasn't in it. He hardly ever even bothered to collect on his bills.

In the aftermath of what is about to happen today, some of Bill Conradt's friends, trying to reconcile the exceedingly proper man they knew with the sordid and improper content of his chat transcripts, will reexamine their own memories, looking for signs. Some of them will dwell on the period following the last election. They will make oblique, tentative attempts to formulate some sort of explanation: Perhaps he lost more than an election. Perhaps the man they knew as the epitome of restraint somehow lost, during those hard days, control of himself.

Although trying to make sense is what humans do, sometimes it is senseless. Because four years ago, Bill Conradt fell, yes. But then he got up, and moved on.

For proof, look no further than that campaign sign on his front lawn. Howard Tygrett, the man whose name resides there, is the same man who beat him in the last election.

Bill Conradt is no longer wearing the ill-fitting suit of a defense lawyer. He is again a prosecutor, and while he is now only an assistant district attorney rather than the top guy, he has told some people that he prefers it this way, prefers focusing on the cases rather than managing an office. Just two days ago, on Friday afternoon, his best friend, Mary Gayle Ramsey, a woman he has known forever, a fellow lawyer who helped him through the rough times following that lost election, ran into him in the hallway of the Rockwall County District Attorney's office and they laughed and joked and talked shop like they always did. And when they parted, he said what he always said, asked her if there was anything he could do for her, and she told him no, and he smiled, and when he walked away, she never would have guessed...

SWAT files through the gateway into the side yard. Many of Bill Conradt's neighbors, none of whom knew him well, have been gathering on their own front lawns, watching. He's always been friendly enough, but he's a hell of a private guy, even though he's got no private life at all, as far as they can tell: This is the first time most of them can remember anyone besides the postman actually setting foot on his property.

The last SWAT officer through closes the gate behind him.

Gator slumps in the front seat of the same Ford Expedition they seized from that doctor back in July. He's got the signed warrant, though his weary hands had riddled it with errors, including the wrong city, county, and date. A woman named Sandra, a Murphy animal-control officer, is at the wheel. Sandra is driving because Gator's too tired. Might fall asleep behind the wheel, something he has been known to do.

When they're just pulling into Terrell, Gator radios, lets them know he's almost on the scene. Nobody responds for a minute. Then his Nextel crackles to life.

"A tactical situation has developed," he hears someone say, and then it goes dead, and nobody responds when he asks for clarification. The pit in his stomach grows.

The nimblest of the SWAT members scale the low chain-link fence that encloses about a fourth of the two-acre backyard, then turn and help some of the bigger cops over, before a quick reformation under trees. Bill Conradt's father planted these trees: a maple, a cedar, a pear, a loblolly pine. His father, a small-town physician who eventually became the medical director of the Texas division of Blue Cross Blue Shield, built this house. Moved in with his wife, his young son, his younger daughter. His children grew up here. And eventually his wife died here. And then, in 2000, he died here. And his daughter and his son decided to keep the house, and his son, who'd never married and lived alone with his mini schnauzer, sold his own house and moved here, back home, with Bismarck, who could run outside in this half-acre plot of fenced-in old cotton field.

SWAT's slow march resumes for a few more paces, delivering them past a coiled hose, past a lawn chair, past a grill, to a glass sliding door that leads into the house. One of the officers holds a black metal battering ram the size of a parking meter and is about to swing it. The leader of the team stops him, pulls out a device called a Halligan bar, and uses it to lever the door until the lock busts under the pressure and the door slides open. The SWAT team pushes through a floor-length curtain covered with a print of ducks and geese and rifles and enters a dim room. The screen of a Sony VAIO laptop provides scant illumination. The laptop sits in a far corner of the room, on an upside-down old-fashioned leather trash can, next to an easy chair. Eyes adjust and flashlights flare.

This is a den. Four easy chairs. A couch. A wood-paneled RCA television set. Recessed bookshelves contain very old copies of *National Geographic* and *Gourmet* and dozens of medical texts that belonged to Bill Conradt's father. Two old sepia-tone portraits of Bill Conradt's parents, taken when they were children, hang in oval frames on the wall. Among the few things in this dusty-feeling room definitely belonging to Bill Conradt, and not simply left-over belongings of his parents, is a tidy stack of books sitting on an end table by the sofa. Atop the stack: a recently published, book-length account of the pivotal 1969 showdown between the University of Texas Longhorns and the University of Arkansas Razorbacks.

A green-and-white-checkered wool blanket puddles half on and half off the easy chair nearest the laptop, a note of dishevelment in the otherwise clutterless room. Somebody left this chair in a hurry.

SWAT sweeps the den, then files into the next room, a dining area adjacent to the kitchen.

"Terrell Police!"

"Search warrant!"

The kitchen is visible from here: wide open, with a cooking island in the middle where Bill Conradt's mother used to prepare the recipes she gleaned from *Gourmet*. Conradt is a good cook himself, though the cupboards aren't as well stocked as they once were. The team turns right, enters a large living room with floor-to-ceiling windows that would, if the shades were not drawn, look out onto the backyard. The living room offers two paths: Either cut through the room and to a door in the rear, or head left, down a long hallway. Sergeant Hanks from Terrell SWAT shouts an order—First four, follow me!—and heads for the door in the rear of the living room. The remaining men, with an officer named Todd Wiley fronting them, turn left and head down the hallway.

One side of the hallway is glass. Beyond the glass, a concrete walkway borders a rectangle of grass in the house's interior courtyard. On the far side of this small lawn, to the right of an American flag, the door to the front yard, the one with the busted doorbell, remains closed. On the other side of that door: all the cameras and the neighbors and the cops wondering what's going on here, inside. Large plants in earthen pots line the hallway, growing so close together that the foliage brushes at the arms and legs of Todd Wiley and the men behind him. They hold their guns square and close to their chests and march forward.

Up ahead, at the end of the hallway, an open door.

Bill Conradt steps into view.

Today he's wearing one of his colored shirts.

Black slacks, a blue shirt, the same shock of thick fright-white hair he's had since his thirties. His small mouth, his wide-set eyes. His skin still ruddy, the trace of a burn from a district-attorneys conference he attended down on South Padre Island a month ago. He'd stayed out on the beach so long that he'd come home with serious carnage on the tops of his feet.

The wall behind him bears a framed illustration from a book about Australian wildlife: a trio of striped kangaroos. Conradt loves Australia. He travels there whenever he can, as often as once a year, pure vacation time, never on business. A friend who once accompanied him on one of his trips thinks Australia appeals to Bill Conradt so much because it is about the farthest he can get away from his hometown. His love for the country has left its mark on his home, and also on his language. Australian idioms creep into his speech and writing sometimes. During his chat-room dialogues with "Luke," for example, he sometimes typed both "good on you" and "no worries," unusual terminology for a native Texan.

The few other decorative touches that Bill Conradt added to this house consist of framed historical memorabilia. If he looks slightly to his right, at the wall beside the doorway that leads into the plant-lined hallway, he will see a poster-sized collection of Abraham Lincoln relics: a sliver of wood from his house, another from his law office, and a penny-sized scrap of fabric that once decorated the president's coffin.

But Conradt is looking straight ahead. All he sees is Officer Todd Wiley and his men behind him.

From the account Todd Wiley will write approximately two and a half hours from now: "He stepped back into dark room. His hands came up. I could see something shining."

All of the officers will eventually write down their best recollection of what Bill Conradt says now, and their memories are pretty consistent. If the testimony of at least one of the officers is perfectly accurate, then Bill Conradt says one of the following things:

"I am not gonna hurt anybody."

"I'm not going to hurt anyone."

"Guys, I'm not going to hurt anyone!"

"I'm not going to hurt nobody, guys."

And, of course, that means his last words, whatever their exact phrasing, are a lie.

Although the microphones outside of Bill Conradt's house have no trouble picking up a mini schnauzer's barks, none record Bill Conradt's Browning .380 handgun, which he places muzzle-first against his own temple and discharges.

The cops inside radio to the cops outside.

Lieutenant Barber enters and sees Bill Conradt lying faceup with part of the side of his head missing. A SWAT officer is trying to put Conradt's legs up on a large pot, to keep the blood flowing toward his vital organs. After noting that "the scene is secure," Lieutenant Barber goes back to the front yard to tell Chris Hansen what she's seen.

"He shot himself," she tells him, then explains she's not sure exactly when he pulled the trigger, whether it was the moment he heard SWAT making entry, or later.

Chris Hansen outlines the scenario he prefers to a crew member.

"Well, I mean, there's gonna be some controversy," Hansen says. "So it's better that he did it as they were coming in, as opposed to . . ."

The noise of approaching emergency vehicles swallows the rest of his words.

The camera settles on one of the SWAT-team members standing outside the closed door of the ambulance after they load the body inside. A middle-aged man in slacks and a sport jacket walks haltingly into the frame. He approaches a cop, one of the Terrell officers who now swarm the lawn wrapping trees with yellow tape. He's asking questions, though you can't hear what they are.

The guy in the sport jacket is named Greg Shumpert. He's the assistant city attorney for Terrell, has known Bill Conrad for decades. A friend. The first friend on the scene. And soon he'll call other friends, mostly other lawyers, and the news will spread. And the questions that Greg Shumpert is asking, the initial questions of what the hell is going on here, will lead to other questions. Friends will question their memories of their friend. Could he have done what the police say he did? Those transcripts. The ghastly sordidness of it all. It's so hard to imagine a man who never tells a dirty joke having a such dirty mind. Some will conclude that no, he couldn't have done it. Word will pass from friend to friend about a possible explanation. An excuse. Did you know that in the room where he worked on his laptop, on an ottoman not two feet from his own, he had a work-book from a conference he'd attended back in June? Did you hear what the conference was about? The title of the workbook? *Investigation and Prosecution of Child Sexual Abuse*. Doesn't that mean something? Doesn't that mean that he was probably working when he was typing those repulsive things? He was probably working on a little homegrown sting operation of his own, and then he got swept up in a larger sting operation himself. A tragedy, this whole thing, but at least Bill Conradt was innocent.

Of course the excuse doesn't really make any sense—if he was trying to catch predators, he would pose as a child, not an adult teen—but people, even smart people, invest themselves in explanations that provide them with the least painful world to live in. A world where their friends, their friend, the one who wears pressed white shirts and lives alone with his dog and always asks if there's anything he can do for you, doesn't, didn't, harbor unpleasant sexual fantasies.

Most of his friends won't even bother with this sort of speculation, will just leave the gray areas gray. They'll try to dwell on the good things, recount his many kindnesses: This was a guy who, when the Longhorns played for the championship, in 2006, had rustled up four tickets to one of the biggest Rose Bowls in history for his niece and her husband, his nephew, and his sister, even though he couldn't go, since he was in Australia. But they won't be able to stop wondering about his last hours. How long did he know what was coming? Did he see *Dateline's* vans early in the morning, like so many of his neighbors did? Did he realize then? Or did he not realize until the police arrived? Or even until SWAT busted in? When did he know for sure? And when did he decide what he was going to do?

Five hundred friends of Bill Conradt will attend his memorial service a few days from now, and for a little while they'll stop asking questions and just sit in receptive silence.

What happens after a police officer arrests a suspect in Murphy, Texas, and charges him with a felony (say, online solicitation of a minor) is that the suspect is detained and a magistrate sets bail and then, eventually, the police send their evidence to the Collin County District Attorney's office. It is up to the DA's office to decide whether to present the evidence to a grand jury for indictment or, if there is insufficient or problematic evidence, to drop the case. The woman responsible for making the initial review of evidence is Doris Berry, one of the most experienced felony prosecutors in the 108-person office.

In the months following today, Doris Berry will review the cases the Murphy Police Department submits to her against the twenty-three men they arrested outside *Dateline's* decoy house, and she will find a variety of problems.

Some of the problems will be technical. For example, in most of the cases, she will find so-called venue problems. In order to pursue a case on an online-solicitation-of-a-minor charge, you've got to prove that either the suspect or victim in the case was physically present in Collin County at the time the crime was committed. The location of the decoy house is irrelevant: What's important is where the chat suspect and the chat decoy were when they were actually doing their chatting. But in sixteen of the cases that the Murphy Police Department will submit to her, Doris Berry will find it impossible to prove that either the Perverted Justice decoy or the suspect was inside Collin County when the crime was allegedly committed.

Some of the problems will be more fundamental: She will find that all of the arrests may have been illegal. Under Texas law, there are only certain circumstances under which a police officer can make an arrest without a prior warrant. But in all of these "To Catch a Predator" decoy-house arrests, it will come to light that not only was there no warrant but the police had done literally no prior investigation. Instead, they simply camped outside the decoy house and arrested the men who emerged after receiving a prior signal from the *Dateline* crew inside. The only thing Doris Berry won't quite be able to figure out is whether this means that *Dateline* had become an agent of the Murphy Police Department or whether the relationship was the other way around. She'll discuss this question with her boss, John Roach, the district attorney, and Roach will eventually form the opinion that "the Murphy Police Department was merely a player in the show and had no real law-enforcement position. Other people are doing the work, and the police are just there like potted plants, to make the scenery."

The thing is, Doris Berry is a prosecutor. She wants to see bad guys punished. She's read the transcripts, which means she knows most of these men are bad and a lot of them are probably dangerous. And if she rejects the cases, she knows what will happen: Instead of receiving the incarceration and supervision that might prevent them from someday soliciting real kids, not fake ones, they'll receive only *Dateline's* nationally televised shaming.

But the law is the law, and you can't just wish a batch of mangled cases good.

On June 1, 2007, seven months after the end of the sting operation, three months after *Dateline* airs the relevant episode of "To Catch a Predator," the Collin County District Attorney's office will announce that it has decided not to pursue indictments for any of the suspects Murphy police arrested outside the decoy house.

Gator arrives at the house soon after the SWAT team secures it. He enters and hastily executes the search warrant, seizing Conradt's Sony VAIO and a mainstream pornographic DVD called *DreamBoy*, as well as a bunch of other things that his sleep-deprived and shocked mind falsely thinks might have some relevance to this case, including an inflight magazine called Red Hot and packets of imported Australian Vegemite.

Months later, Gator will learn that a forensic analysis of the laptop has verified that Bill Conradt was the person who chatted online with "Luke," but that the computer hard drive was otherwise devoid of anything illegal or indicative of sexual predation. Soon afterward, Gator will resign from the Murphy Police and consider never returning to law enforcement. He will make ends meet working at a private security firm. He will meet with a reporter in the reporter's hotel room, recount what he did and what he didn't do, and he will start to cry and then apologize for making a fool of himself.

Of the people directly involved in the events leading up to the death of Bill Conradt, only a couple of others besides Gator will express anything close to regret.

Dan Schrack, the actor, will feel terrible, as if he is somehow responsible. He will be at the decoy house when Frag phones in with the news. A few minutes later, *Dateline* will announce that it's shutting down the operation right away. Schrack will be hustled to the airport early. After he boards his flight, he will mull over his feelings that the pursuit of ratings was behind what happened today, and he will decide that he won't recommend auditioning for "To Catch a Predator" to his actor buddies. It's too real.

District judge Mark Rusch, who signed the search warrant, won't necessarily feel guilt, but he'll feel anger when he learns that *Dateline* was present during the arrest attempt, a possibility the affidavit had not warned him of. He'll call the Murphy police, rip into an officer there: Did it ever occur to them that maybe, just maybe, an assistant DA who sees a camera crew out front and knows what he has been up to on his own damn computer can put two and two together, and had that camera crew not been out there, maybe he'd still be alive?

But most of the people involved won't express any second thoughts at all. (Chief Billy Myrick and Lieutenant Adana Barber will decline repeated interview requests.)

Xavier Von Erck, the founder of Perverted Justice, will say his only regret is that Bill Conradt died before he could face justice.

And Chris Hansen, during a phone interview eight months later, will say that though Conradt's suicide was very sad, something "nobody can feel good about," he doesn't have any regrets about how things were handled in Murphy or Terrell. He will say that the "To Catch a Predator" concept of "parallel investigations" works "pretty darn well" and that the police and *Dateline* are completely independent of each other: "Just like the police don't tell me how to do the interviews, we don't tell them how to do their business. Aside from saying hello in the beginning, I really don't have contact with law enforcement." He will deny that *Dateline's* presence constituted "surveillance," as Chief Myrick had characterized it on site, and deny that its cameramen were ever on Conradt's property. When asked about Frag's actions in Terrell, he will insist that "Frag was not out there," and then angrily suggest that the question stems from some "notion that Perverted Justice was calling the shots. Nobody from Perverted Justice was out there. I was there." It is only when it is described to Hansen what Frag was wearing that day, in detail, that he will put the phone on hold to consult with his producer, Lynn Keller (who declined to be interviewed), and then come back on the line and concede he was wrong. Similarly, he will heatedly deny that Perverted Justice or NBC personnel ever encouraged the Murphy Police Department to get warrants for Bill Conradt.

A spokeswoman for *Dateline*, Jenny Tartikoff, will decline to comment on the future of "To Catch a Predator" or on the show's relationship with Perverted Justice, other than to say, "We always evaluate our news-gathering procedures before and after each broadcast."

Among the final footage *Dateline* shoots today is a view of a CareFlite chopper that squats thundering in Bill Conradt's backyard, ready to take him to Parkland Memorial Hospital in Dallas, where the pronouncement will be made. The shot pans from the chopper to Lieutenant Adana Barber. She's on her cell phone. Although you can't hear what she's saying because of the helicopter, it's possible that she is on the phone with Jimmy Patterson, the off-duty detective NBC had hired to work security. Detective Patterson will later recall that it was at about this time that he called Lieutenant Barber. He knew Lieutenant Barber because she used to work at his department, in Rowlett. Detective Patterson had left the decoy house, was on his way out of the neighborhood, and had just noticed two Murphy Police Department squad cars pulling in behind him, lights flashing. He was in his black Ford F-150 pickup truck. *Dateline* had earlier advised the Murphy Police Department Takedown Team that one of the suspects scheduled to come to the house that day owned a black Ford F-150 pickup.

Detective Patterson tells Lieutenant Barber that the Murphy Police are pulling him over for some reason.

"Jimmy, you look like a pervert!" she says, laughing.

He tells Lieutenant Barber that several Murphy police officers have surrounded his truck. "Your guys are pointing guns at me," he tells her.

"You can take them!" Lieutenant Barber responds, still laughing.

The cops have yanked the F-150's door open and are now trying to physically haul Detective Patterson out of his vehicle.

"Tell your people to get their fucking guns out of my face," he says to Lieutenant Barber, and then drops his cell phone.

Eventually, a few minutes after the cops push Detective Patterson against his truck and handcuff him, the misunderstanding is resolved.

But the larger questions provoked by the last few days remain.

Is it possible that Bill Conradt, an adult pretending to be a teenager, might have suspected, correctly, that "Luke" was also an adult pretending? Yes: Everybody knows that the Internet is a swamp of false identities. And is there any evidence that Conradt had ever acted on the longings that his chats illuminated? On the contrary, he chose not to when presented with the opportunity. Was it morally wrong for Bill Conradt to engage in online sex chats with an apparent child? Of course. But did his actions merit the response to them? Before answering this question, a man should take stock of the history of the desires he has never acted on, and consider whether he would ever like to defend that history in court, or see it detailed on television.

After ending her cell-phone call, Lieutenant Barber looks at the camera. She asks the cameraman a question, speaking loudly enough to be heard above the rumble and whine of the rotors. Although the events of the last few days provoke a lot of questions, perhaps the one Lieutenant Barber now asks is the most pertinent. When law enforcement and television entertainment have commingled so completely and so lethally, perhaps there is really only one question left that matters at all.

"We having fun?"

She asks the question, she smiles wide, and then she relays an update Frag gave her a little while ago, something about a three-hundred-pounder nabbed back at the decoy house.

A few minutes later, the tape ends and the screen goes blank.

AUTHOR'S AFTERWORDS…

In February of 2007 I was in Chile, on my way down to Antarctica to run a marathon, when I got an email from an editor at *Esquire* named Dave Katz. He wanted to pitch a story idea. "I'm sure you've heard about these *Dateline* stings," he wrote. Actually, I hadn't. I'd been living in Whitehorse, in Canada's Yukon Territory, and didn't have cable. Dave explained that *Dateline* NBC's "To Catch a Predator" was a hit series about online sting operations, and that it involved television producers teaming up with civilian vigilantes and local law enforcement agencies to lure would-be sexual predators into trysts with fake underage boys and girls. He mentioned that one of the sting operations had gone wrong, and that one of the so-called predators, Bill Conradt, an assistant district attorney in rural Texas, had killed himself while a SWAT team stormed his home and a production crew loitered outside.

Was I interested?

As soon as I got back from Antarctica, I flew to Texas and began reporting.

From my first interview to the final edits on the final proof, I spent about three months working on this story. Like most long projects, this one involved lots of tedium punctuated by occasional breakthroughs. The breakthroughs, of course, are the memories that stand out.

I remember sitting in a shabby hotel room with my laptop and a stack of unlabeled DVDs, watching, for the first time, the raw footage that NBC's cameramen had shot before, during, and after the fatal raid on Bill Conradt's home. I'd worked hard to convince a source to turn the DVDs over to me, and the relief of finally having them in my possession turned into something else as it dawned on me how different NBC's official account of the day was from the actual events that the network's own raw footage revealed.

I remember sitting in another hotel room on a different day, with Detective Walter "Gator" Weiss. In particular, I remember when Gator started to cry. He had played a pivotal role in the investigation that led to Conradt's death, and in the months since, he'd been wracked by feelings of guilt. His bravery—speaking to me on the record was nothing if not brave—gave the story a whole new dimension.

I remember walking through Bill Conradt's house. The blood had been scrubbed away, but everything else was almost exactly as it had been the day of the raid. I remember retracing the steps that the SWAT team had taken, snapping pictures from various angles with a little digital point-and-shoot, trying to imagine what the scene had looked and felt like to the cops. I remember Bill Conradt's potted plants brushing against my arms and legs as I walked down the long hallway that led to the spot where the shot was fired.

I remember finally getting Chris Hansen, the host of "To Catch a Predator," on the phone. I had printed out several pages of single-spaced, small-font questions in preparation for the interview, but pretty soon I stopped looking at the questions and just started digging in. Hansen's voice, that confident baritone, had inhabited my days and nights for months prior to our interview, and I remember how strange it felt to finally engage that voice in a dialogue. I remember his voice changing, losing some of its poise, as the interview progressed. Toward the end of our phone call, after I'd honed in on a discrepancy in Hansen's story and he'd started flailing out at me with a lame interrogation about who I'd spoken with and what my agenda was, I remember having to stifle the impulse to borrow one of his own catchphrases: "I'm asking the questions here."

I remember sitting in a coffee shop and cuing up that first snatch of ideo, the scene I open with, over and over. And then I remember starting to write. I remember turning in my longest-ever first draft—nine thousand words or so—and I remember when Dave told me that he liked it, but that he thought the second draft should be a lot longer.

The final version is still, at about thirteen thousand words, my longest article ever. Rereading it now, I worry that maybe it's too long, that maybe it has too many characters, that it might get confusing and clumsy in certain sections. But I'm not sure what I'd cut.

I like to think that my story, when it came out, made some sort of difference. You can make a strong argument that, at the very least, it killed "To Catch a Predator." While occasional reruns still air, NBC produced only one new episode after the article hit the stands, and then, after settling a mammoth lawsuit brought against it by Bill Conradt's sister, the series was quietly cancelled.

I regret I haven't kept in touch with Gator and some of the other people I got to know down in Texas. That's one of the bittersweet parts of my job: I develop these short, intense relationships, and then those relationships tend to dissolve. In a perfect world, I'd throw an amazing Christmas party every year and bring together all the people I've ever written about, even the ones who probably don't like me very much.

Todd C. Frankel

Todd C. Frankel is an enterprise reporter with the *St. Louis Post-Dispatch*. His stories have received national recognition with National Headliners Awards for feature writing and beat reporting, an American Society of Newspaper Editors award for deadline writing and a Society of Professional Journalists award for feature writing. He was published in *2008-2009 Best Newspaper Writing* and was part of the newsroom team that was a finalist for the 2009 Pulitzer Prize for breaking news. He teaches at Washington University in St. Louis; previously he has written for newspapers in Washington, West Virginia and Kentucky. Born in Washington D.C., he is a graduate of the University of Delaware. Frankel lives in St. Louis with his wife, Stephanie, and two young sons, Eli and Asher.

The $1 Million Bill

The shades were drawn against the morning sun, as if Rodney Dukes was trying to block out his doubt about the $1 million bill. The room was dark. It was hard to see the dishes in the sink, the unpaid bills on the table, the gray in his black hair. The TV was muted. The only sound was the slow beep of a smoke alarm battery dying.

Rodney often thought about the bill while sitting in the darkness of his daughter's place in the Villa Griffin public housing project. A million dollar note. A life-changing sum in a scrap of paper. A bill he had discovered five months earlier on the street—his ticket out, away from all this.

At first, he was certain the bill was fake. Or stolen. Just another false promise in "this dead-ass, beat-down town." He hadn't held a steady job since working as a parking lot attendant six years ago. He and his wife recently lost their house. Now they were staying with his daughter. Rodney, a father of three, was a man close to bottom, a place where even dreaming of escape can feel like too much weight to bear. Better to let it go.

But now he believed. He believed in the possibility of the $1 million bill. He allowed himself to think that luck might be smiling on him at long last, finally, after fifty-one years, tapping him on his worry-worn shoulders.

He had set out to discover the truth of his find. Months trickled by. He kept searching. The answer seemed just out of reach. But he felt he was closing in. You could laugh it off as a quixotic quest—except for the way he went about it. No short cuts. No scams. He moved with deliberation, like a man aware of the stakes.

And along the way, as he pressed and pressed, nearing despair, he found something else rare and unexpected.

But first he needed to learn about the $1 million bill.

"I want to see if it's real. I really do," Rodney said in the dark room. "I've just got to hope that sonabitch is real."

He found it. Just ... found it. Like someone uncovering a Picasso in the basement. It was late May. He needed to call his wife. He didn't own a cell phone. He stopped at a pay phone and spotted what looked like money lying on the phone's metal table. A $20 bill? He looked around as he stood outside a Shell gas station in University City. Traffic did not stop. People pumping gas did not glance his way.

He returned to the bill. He turned it over and over in his callused hands. He pulled a $10 bill from his wallet and compared.

The $1 million note looked real. Crisp, like it never had been outside a bank. The greens and blacks and grays were just right. Rodney didn't recognize the stern, bearded man in the center portrait as nineteenth president, Rutherford B. Hayes. He figured there were enough obscure old men to go around. The "1,000,000" was printed in the top corners. He noted what appeared to be the stamps of the U.S. Federal Reserve and Department of Treasury. Some words on the back were too small to make out.

The bill was too perfect, its location too obvious. But for Rodney, that made perfect sense.

"Somebody wanted to give it to somebody. Who is going to sit a $1 million bill in a phone booth? Somebody put it there," Rodney recalled. "Unless it's not real. But you might find a twenty. A fifty. But a million dollars?"

He put the bill in his pocket and headed home, forgetting all about the phone call.

He didn't tell his wife. First, he needed to know more.

The idea of a search suited Rodney, a high school dropout who retains a restless curiosity about the world. He is the type of person who tries piecing together how a new neighborhood gas station makes its money; who wants to know how the Internet is changing people's lives, yet rarely has sat at a computer; who slips several coins into a charity donation box at a fast-food place, then wonders aloud if his money really goes to a good cause.

He wanted to know more about the bill.

Still, his mind couldn't help but wander, to conjure up what it would feel like to be secure. More than secure. Rich. He would buy a place in Hazelwood. Nothing fancy. A fixer-upper in a nice subdivision. Someplace safe. He wanted to get his family out of the projects. No more struggle. No more worrying about ever being flat broke again.

But Rodney's old man knew better. He knew that money could be a curse, too. Maybe that's why Rodney went to him first with the $1 million bill. Rodney looked up to Willie Dukes, father of eight. Now seventy-three and retired from airport maintenance work, Willie Dukes spent his days helping his children and hanging out with other retired men in his North St. Louis neighborhood.

Willie Dukes had money once, but it disappeared like the old North Side houses replaced by empty lots. When he was a teen, he had been good enough at poker to amass a small fortune. He remembers he had a duffle bag so stuffed with $20 bills he could sit on it like a chair. He drove a pink Cadillac. The money flowed until he joined the Army at the urging of his mother. She wanted better for her son.

Willie Dukes never saw that kind of money again. But he learned a lesson: Manage what you have. Handle your money with care. "If you don't have a budget, it will go away."

The old man worried over Rodney and the potential windfall. Rodney had struggled for so long. And the old man had other plans for his son. Willie Dukes recently had been eyeing an old pickup he wanted to buy for Rodney so they could go junking—collecting and reselling scrap metal.

Yet Willie Dukes thought the bill looked real. He recalled a TV show about $1 million bills and how they were no longer in circulation. Maybe this was one that slipped out. It had happened before: A few 1933 double-eagle gold coins ended up with collectors despite never being released by the government. One sold for $7.6 million.

He showed the bill to some of the other retirees, men whom Rodney trusted because they had been around. They agreed. It looked real. Willie Dukes told his son to see someone who knows money.

"Like with diamonds," Willie Dukes said, "you've got to go to the folks who know them."

So Rodney went to a bank—a U.S. Bank branch in downtown St. Louis. He wasn't trying to deposit the bill. He didn't even have an account there. He remembers the teller was stunned. She had never seen a $1 million bill before. "They were telling me there was nothing they could do with it," Rodney said.

The teller suggested he try the Federal Reserve Bank, a few blocks away.

Rodney walked into the stone fortress that is one of twelve banks controlling the nation's money supply. He passed through the automatic revolving door and into a wide lobby of soaring marble walls. The Reserve Bank's massive brass emblem sat on a wall above him. It looked like the one printed on U.S. currency. And on Rodney's $1 million bill.

He was met by blue-uniformed security guards. He explained his mission. The guards told him the Federal Reserve dealt only with other banks. Then one guard pulled out a tattered manila folder and handed Rodney two pieces of paper.

It was a printout from the U.S. Bureau of Engraving and Printing, detailing how it verifies and refunds damaged money. It was an opening he could try.

Rodney decided first to put the bill through one more test. He stopped at a corner store the next day and asked the clerk if he could borrow a counterfeit money pen. The felt-tip marker, filled with an iodine solution, leaves behind a brown mark on the wood-based paper of most fakes. Real U.S. currency is printed on fiber.

The clerk handed Rodney the pen. He swiped it down one end of the bill. A dark line trailed behind. Then he watched as it faded, along with his doubt.

Rodney decided it was safe to tell his wife.

She laughed. No way that bill was real. No way.

But Rodney, he was starting to believe.

And so a week later, in early June, he was at a post office in St. Louis. He was nervous. He was about to mail the $1 million bill to the bureau of engraving. He had studied the instructions for sending currency to its examiners in Washington. The bureau "will issue a written confirmation of receipt," his handout explained, for cases expected to take longer than four weeks to process.

He took a deep breath. He mailed it off.

Rodney left the post office with a registered mail receipt and tracking number, which would show the letter arrived in Washington at 1:55 p.m. on June 7.

That was the last tangible proof of his dream.

Four weeks passed. Five. And six. No word from Washington. Seven weeks.

Rodney thought about calling the bureau, but his long-distance bill was already out of sight. Eight weeks. Nine. Then Rodney got an idea. He would ask a judge to demand a response from the bureau of engraving.

In late August he walked into the federal courthouse in St. Louis and with the help of a clerk, Rodney filed a lawsuit by hand, writing that he wanted to "... request bill return or replace the currency, 1 million dollar bill..."

"Please!" he wrote.

Three weeks passed. A district court judge dismissed Rodney's plea. The judge didn't see how the court could help. "The complaint is incoherent."

Rodney figured the judge misunderstood. He filed again six days later. "Maybe with help from Honorable Judge may I ask for help. Unemploy(ed) and cannot afford long distance call."

The judge waved him off. Rodney filed a third time. And was rejected.

Now Rodney sat in the dark living room, the shades drawn tight.

He stewed about the delay. He imagined the judge was afraid to demand that federal officials answer for his missing money. He suspected the bureau didn't believe a guy from East St. Louis could have found something so valuable. And he thought of one more possibility.

"Maybe there's something to it—it being a million dollars and all," he said. "They're making me think something good because it's taking so long."

Now he planned to call the bureau. He dialed the number on a borrowed cell phone. He got a recording. The message warned it could take twelve to fourteen weeks for a response. Rodney already had waited seventeen. A beep. Rodney spoke slowly.

"My name is Rodney. I'd like to receive a call back from you people." He recited the bill's serial number and his phone number. "Please return my call as soon as possible. Please. Thank you."

By the middle of October, Rodney worried that he would never see his bill again. But maybe he could find out if even the possibility of such a bill existed.

He headed to the library. It was a dreary, cold Wednesday. He slipped on a black leather jacket and matching hat. After the library he was going to work for a guy. Wouldn't say doing what. "I need to earn some money, man," was all Rodney said.

He walked out, past fresh plywood sheets covering windows and doors of neighboring apartments. Loose dogs roamed a grass lot across the street.

"I've got to get a house, get out of the projects, change things," Rodney said, walking to his car, a blue Volvo that a friend swung him a deal on.

"Nothing good happens around here."

He drove to the main library building in downtown St. Louis. He bounded up the library's wide stone steps in a hurried stride, the $1 million bill on his mind.

"Do you think it exists?" he asked suddenly, walking in the door.

Inside, Rodney was pointed to the online library catalog. He stood above the keyboard. He fumbled with the mouse. He pecked at the keys with one hand. "I don't know how to use this," he said.

Frustrated, Rodney walked over to a library worker.

"I'm trying to find something out about a million-dollar bill," he said.

"You're looking for what now?"

"A million-dollar bill. To see if it's ever been made."

He was passed off to another researcher, who walked to another computer. Rodney stood over his shoulder. The librarian typed "million dollar bills" into Google. He clicked on a story link, "Georgia Man Tries to Deposit One Million Dollar Bill." The librarian silently scanned the article. Rodney noticed a photo of the suspect note, President Grover Cleveland on the front.

"Mine didn't look like that," Rodney said, relieved.

The librarian surfed through several other pages before announcing he couldn't find any evidence that a $1 million bill had ever been produced. A

$10,000 bill, briefly. Even a rare $100,000 bill. Then the librarian searched for "million dollar bill" on the bureau of engraving's website.

"Hmmm," the librarian said. "It's not matching anything."

"But you can't say for sure, can you?" Rodney countered.

No, the librarian allowed. He pulled out a World Book reference volume. He walked back to the computer and called up Google. "Has a million dollar bill ever been issued," he typed.

The search results were the same: No mention of a $1 million bill.

"So it never really answered your question either, though," Rodney said.

"Yes, no," the librarian said, flustered. "It never directly said no."

Rodney started to persist, but he sensed the librarian was done. He thanked him, slipped back on his leather hat and walked into the hallway.

"I don't know, man. I don't know. I'm not going to doubt the man," Rodney said outside. "But he's not going to undoubt me, either."

It was cold. He needed to head to work.

"I'm not no fool," he said now, raising his voice. "I'm not no fool."

One morning a week later at Villa Griffin, Rodney pulled a small chicken pot pie from the oven. He wrapped it in tin foil and prepared to head out. On the kitchen table was a phone bill with a red slip of paper and the stark words "Disconnection notice" peeking through the cellophane window.

Next to it was a letter from the bureau of engraving.

The letter had arrived two days earlier. Registered mail. A manager in the Mutilated Currency Division announced case No. 9-11579 was closed: "Your note(s) were thoroughly examined and determined to be play money, not genuine United States currency. Therefore, it has no monetary value and cannot be redeemed."

The letter ended with a condolence: "I apologize that my reply is not favorable."

No explanation for why it had taken so long. And the letter was addressed to "Rooney Dukes." At that, Rodney shook his head. Suffocating, that's what he had been doing. Suffocating while this played out. And they didn't even care to know his name.

But Rodney had his answer. He had that much.

His wife laughed. She knew, just knew all along. "I told you that wasn't real," she said, no longer laughing.

He figured she didn't understand. He had to try. At least, he wasn't so far down that he couldn't imagine his way out. The bill was fake, yes. But his faith in that bill was real. He wasn't ready to surrender his dream. The search had awakened something inside him. It was like believing in something false allowed him to feel something real.

"I'll make something happen," he said now.

He felt his luck was out there. He just had to find it. His life's path was not set. Recently, he had been thinking about going back to driving trucks. He knew a guy who was getting 75 cents, even a $1 a mile. He had driven short-haul routes before. He had his commercial drivers license. Maybe he could do that. And his old man's offer of a pickup and a chance to go junking—that was out there, too.

First, though, he had some unfinished business. Because tucked inside that letter from D.C. was his $1 million bill.

The bureau of engraving shed no light on the bill's origins for Rodney. Turns out that for years a California-based evangelical ministry—Way of the Master, perhaps best known for its late-night TV ads with "Growing Pains" sitcom actor Kirk Cameron—has been distributing fake $1 million bills with religious tracts on the reverse. A tract was on Rodney's bill asking, "Will you go to heaven when you die?" Except the type was so small, it was nearly unreadable.

Some people see the fake bills as a good bait-and-switch for spreading religion. Online, people brag about leaving the bills in public places. You can buy a hundred of them for $5.

But the bills are a sore spot for the Treasury. Several years ago the Secret Service seized thousands of the bills claiming they too closely resembled real money. A judge overruled the agency because a true $1 million bill had never been produced. It wasn't counterfeit. Still, people across the country sometimes try to deposit the bills at banks or use them in liquor stores, trying to make a quick score, pull one over.

But Rodney knew none of this.

Now, he was going to try one last place. He wanted to see if even a fake bill had a price.

With his car in the shop needing $400 in repairs, he got a ride into St. Louis. Along the way, he talked about a guy who gave him five can't-miss numbers for the lottery. "He's been working with the numbers for two, three months. He's an old hand," Rodney said. "Said they were his best five. I could use some money right now—get out of this hole I'm in."

Thirty minutes later he was at Midwest Money, a coin shop in South St. Louis. His old man had recommended he come here months back. Now Rodney was there, a $1 million bill in his pocket.

The store bustled behind a buzz-in security door. Silver coins clinked through an automatic counter. Workers examined bracelets and necklaces for customers looking to cash in on the soaring price of gold. Glass cases filled with paper bills stood just inside the door.

Rodney bent down to look. A 1914 series $5 bill, selling for $70. Lincoln looked shrunken.

"This can't be real. Heck, no," he said quietly.

He noticed a $1 Elvis Presley novelty note going for $5. He walked round and round the displays, fascinated. Mostly $1 notes, different designs. He pulled the $1 million bill from his leather jacket's inside pocket. It looked just as it did five months earlier, except for three deep creases from Rodney's repeatedly unfolding the bill to look at it. He laid the bill on the display glass. "Whoever printed it printed a helluva bill," he said.

A worker broke free from another customer and asked Rodney if she could help. He showed her the $1 million bill, his eyes cast down.

"Okay, I'll have to ask about this," she said, taking the bill and walking to another worker. She returned seconds later.

"Yeah, this isn't real," she said.

Rodney managed a slight smile and slipped the bill in his pocket.

"It's not real," he said. "Okay, thank you."

He walked outside. The late morning sun glared down. The promise of driving trucks or collecting scrap metal could wait one more day. Right now, he needed a ride to the gas station. He carried $10 in his pocket and the lucky numbers on his mind, still struggling to imagine a world without $1 million bills.

AUTHOR'S AFTERWORDS…

I liked Rodney Dukes. You don't have to like the people you write about. But I really liked Rodney. So when he would ask me, as he did on occasion, what I thought about the $1 million bill, if I thought it was real, it was hard to know what to say.

Yes? No? The answer wasn't that simple. For most of our time together he didn't have the bill in front of him. It was off in Washington, D.C. I didn't know for sure the bill even existed. Maybe it was a hand-drawn joke. Or Monopoly money. Who knew what he'd found. And if he didn't get the bill back, if he never got a definite answer, the story probably wouldn't run. Or it would be very different. That made a lot of my time with Rodney feel like a theoretical venture in reporting. So I usually answered Rodney by reminding him of what I said when we first met: I was there to follow him, not to offer doubts or encouragements.

Some readers (thankfully, very few) were upset that I didn't take Rodney by the lapels and urge him to abandon his quest early on. They pointed out it took only a quick online search to learn the bill wasn't real. (Everything online is true, of course.) And preemptive worries about these readers led to the inclusion of an editor's note that said I "avoided interfering with the course of events, so that the story could unfold as naturally as possible." That only drew attention to me. For these doubting readers, the article read even more like I did nothing to break Rodney's inevitable fall.

But that's not how it went down. It's not how it felt chasing this. Rodney's biggest concern was looking like a fool. It was mine, too. But that worry faded the longer I spent with him. The earnest way he went about it, trying to sort it all out, fighting to understand, daring to take a chance, it felt closer to heroic. Stories shouldn't celebrate only the people who succeed in their efforts, but also the ones who tried and failed, odds be damned. Those might be the better stories.

The story never hinged on Rodney being right. It hinged on his belief and determination.

And it wouldn't have mattered how I answered Rodney's question. He was told the bill was likely fake by just about everyone. His wife said it. The bank said it. The librarian said it. The U.S. Treasury finally said it. I would've just been adding my voice to a chorus of people Rodney wasn't hearing.

One day, standing outside the library where he'd tried to research his $1 million bill, Rodney explained why he believed the bill was real. His world was largely circumscribed by two towns on either side of the Mississippi River. There were many things he'd never seen, yet believed in. He'd never had need of a $1 million bill. But, he said, what about the world's super-rich? If they had so many millions, didn't they need $1 million bills? Wouldn't that make sense? It was like off-shore tax shelters or some painted canvas worth more than he'd earn in a lifetime. Those were real. Why not $1 million bills? Outside the library, Rodney's world came into view. It made sense.

Most readers loved the story. They got it. It was great to see. About a week after the story ran, I caught back up with Rodney. A reader had mailed me a $100 cashier's check to give to him, along with a letter saying it wasn't a $1 million, but, hey, it was something. Rodney was happy to have the money. He was happy about how the people he knew reacted to the story.

He didn't feel like a fool. He also didn't have a banking account.

So we drove to a check-cashing store in East St. Louis. The store's giant yellow sign offering "Check cashing / Food stamps" poked out from a dense, rundown block of downtown storefronts—a wig shop, pawn shop, discount store, boarded-up night club—set among beautiful old buildings that had been falling apart for so long that thick trees now grew from their crumbling rooftops. From here, believing in much of anything felt like a stretch.

Vanessa Grigoriadis

V anessa Grigoriadis is a contributing editor at *New York, Rolling Stone,* and *Vanity Fair.* She's been with *New York* on and off since she graduated from Wesleyan University, beginning as an editorial assistant. She was promoted to contributing editor a couple years later, when she was twenty-five years old. She lives in Los Angeles with her husband and daughter, but she grew up on the Upper West Side of New York City, where she played classical violin and danced with Alvin Ailey in her teens

Grigoriadis also worked as a writer on the Style desk at the *New York Times* in 2003. Prior to that, she spent a year studying the sociology of religion at Harvard University. In 2007, Grigoriadis won an American Society of Magazine Editors award for profile writing for a story about of Chanel designer Karl Lagerfeld.

"Long-form magazine writing is a bit anachronistic these days, but that's what I do. I'm also generally classified as a "generalist," which means that I don't cover one beat. I write lengthy cover stories and feature articles on a number of topics—some weighty, some not at all. Some of my articles can be controversial, but I pride myself on dealing with my subjects and sources honestly at all times," she says.

The Tragedy of Britney Spears

A pop star at the mall is an eternal cause for happiness, especially on a Sunday afternoon in the Valley. One moment, shoppers in the Westfield Fashion Square Mall, in Sherman Oaks, CA, are living in the real world, monotonously selecting a new shade of eye shadow or rubbing perfume on wrists, but upon the rapture of Britney Spears, they are giggling, laughing, orgasmic, already sharing their secret on cell phones. "Her legs are actually really skinny," an adolescent whispers into her Sidekick, as Britney beelines for the Betsey Johnson boutique, pseudo-punk designer of evening dresses and splashy heels worn to suburban high school proms. In person, Britney is shockingly beautiful—clear skin, ruby lips, a perfectly proportioned twenty-six-year-old porcelain doll with a nasty weave. She cuts through the crowd swiftly, the way she used to when 20,000 adoring fans mobbed her outside a concert, with her paparazzi boyfriend, Adnan Ghalib, trailing behind.

Only a few kids are in the store, a young girl with her brother and two blondes checking out fake-gold charm bracelets. Britney rifles the racks as the Cure's "Pictures of You" blasts into the airless pink boutique, grabbing a pink lace dress, a few tight black numbers and a frilly red crop top, the kind of shirt that Britney used to wear all the time at seventeen but isn't really appropriate for anyone over that age. Then she ducks into the dressing room with Ghalib. He emerges with her black Am Ex.

The card won't go through, but they keep trying it.

"Please," begs Ghalib, "get this done quickly."

One of the girls runs to Britney's dressing room, explaining the situation through a pink gauze curtain.

A wail emerges from the cubby—guttural, vile, the kind of base animalistic shriek only heard at a family member's deathbed. "Fuck these bitches," screams Britney, each word ringing out between sobs. "These idiots can't do anything right!"

Ghalib dashes over to console her, but she's already spitting, growling, throwing a big bottle of soda on the floor so that it begins to spill underneath the curtain, and then she's got a box of tissues and is throwing them on top of the wet floor along with piles of discarded merchandise. A new card finally goes through, but by then Britney is out the door, leaving her shirt on the ground and replacing it with the red top. "Fuck you, fuck people, fuck, fuck, fuck," she keeps screaming, her face splotchy and red as she crosses the interminable mall floor, the crowd behind her growing larger and larger. "Leave us alone!" yells Ghalib.

The siblings run after Britney to get a video to put up on YouTube, and some of the shopgirls run after her to hand off the merchandise she left behind, and there's an entire bridal party wearing yellow T-shirts who have pulled out camera phones too. A crush of managers in black shirts and gold name tags try to keep the peace, but the crowd running after Britney gets larger, and now the shopgirls have started to catch up to her, one of them slipping spectacularly in her platform shoes, grazing her elbow. She pulls herself up, mustering the strength to tap Britney's shoulder. "Um, I'm from the South too," she mumbles, "and I was wondering if I could get a picture with you for my little sister."

Britney turns to Ghalib and grabs his arm. "I don't want her talking to me!" she screams. She whirls around and stares the girl deep in the eyes, her lips almost vibrating with anger. "I don't know who you think I am, bitch," she snarls, "but I'm not that person."

If there is one thing that has become clear in the past year of Britney's collapse—the most public downfall of any star in history—it's that she doesn't want anything to do with the person the world thought she was. She is not a good girl. She is not America's sweetheart. She is an inbred swamp thing who chain-smokes, doesn't do her nails, tells reporters to "eat it, snort it, lick it, fuck it" and screams at people who want pictures for their little sisters. She is not someone who can live by the most basic social rules—she is someone who, when she has had her one- and two-year-old sons taken completely out of her care, with zero visitation rights, appeared at Los Angeles' Superior Court to convince the judge to give her kids back, but then decided not to go inside, and she's someone who did this twice. She's the perfect celebrity for America in decline: Like President Bush, she just doesn't give a fuck, but at least we won't have to clean up after her mess for the rest of our lives.

If Britney was really who we believed her to be—a puppet, a grinning blonde without a cool thought in her head, a teasing coquette clueless to her own sexual power—none of this would have happened. She is not book-smart, granted. But she is intelligent enough to understand what the world wanted of her: that she was created as a virgin to be deflowered before us, for our amusement and titillation. She is not ashamed of her new persona—she wants us to know what we did to her. While it may be true that Britney suffers from the adult onset of a genetic mental disease (or a disease created by fame, yet to be named); or that she is a "habitual, frequent and continuous" drug user, as the judge declared; or that she is a cipher with boundless depths, make no mistake—she is enjoying the chaos she is creating. The look on her face when she's goofing around with paparazzi—one of whom, don't forget, she is dating—is often one of pure excitement. "For years, everyone manipulated Britney," says a close friend. "There was always a little game. If she didn't want to come out of the trailer, the label would come to me, saying, 'Please talk to Britney, make sure she performs, and we'll take you on a shopping spree.' Now this is her time to play."

More than any other star today, Britney epitomizes the crucible of fame for the famous: loving it, hating it and never quite being able to stop it from destroying you. Over the past year, it's looked several times like she was going to get it together, but then girlfriend messes up again. She started off with a bang—the head-shaving, plus attacking a paparazzi car with an umbrella—followed by rehab, a magazine shoot where she let her dog poop on a $6,700 gown, a hit-and-run (the charge was dropped), an investigation by the Department of Children and Family Services, the sad performance at the VMAs and her hospitalizations on January 3 and January 31. Even Michael Jackson never deteriorated to the point where he was strapped to a gurney, his madness chronicled by news choppers' spotlights. Before her first hospitalization, Britney shut herself in the bathroom with her youngest son for three hours, wearing only panties, arguing with cops who tried to give her a sweater. "Don't cover me up," she said. "I'm fucking hot"—meaning warm, although the other interpretation of the word is funnier. Britney's assistant told police she demanded her "vitamins" (Britney's code for pills), though it's not known what kind she is taking.

Today, Britney is alone: Arrogant, anxiety-ridden and paranoid, she has lost faith in everyone. "She goes through people like she goes through dogs," says a close friend. "There's one instant with everyone where she freaks out and suddenly says, 'I don't trust you, and I don't know what's going on.'" She does not have a manager, agent or publicist (Jive Records no longer speaks to her directly, and the publicist at the label assigned to Britney refused to participate in this article). She has no stylist, image consultant, crisis-control manager or driver. She has pushed away her family: her brother and father ("It is sad that all the men in my life do not know how to accept a real woman's love," she explained); her sister Jamie Lynn, whom she speaks to on the phone and sees rarely; and, most important, her preening, difficult mother, Lynne, whom Britney considers poisonous. Famous for two saccharine books about her fabulous relationship with Britney, Lynne is now desperately trying to help her family, but her attempts have fallen flat: She was the force behind selling Jamie Lynn's pregnancy photos to *OK!* magazine for $1 million and encouraged Dr. Phil's visit with Britney in the psychiatric ward of Cedars-Sinai Medical Center. Ironically, it may be Britney's family who succeeds in retaining control of her now, in collaboration with doctors who are advising that she remain in a hospital setting as long as legally possible.

Britney wasn't allowed to see her kids in January, and it is unclear when she will get them back. Under the terms of their prenup, Kevin Federline was due only $1 million of Britney's estimated $30 million fortune, and his sole route to future riches is custodial support, although his intentions are widely considered to be more honorable. Federline currently receives $20,000 a month, and his hope is to keep at least part-time custody—a goal his lawyer, diminutive powerhouse Mark Vincent Kaplan, is well on his way to achieving in the court of Commissioner Scott Gordon. In her legal case, as otherwise in her life, Britney has alienated those trying to help her—her divorce attorney, Laura Wasser, dropped her a few months ago, and her current legal team of Trope & Trope requested removal at one point. "You can tell Britney all day that she has to follow court orders to get her kids back, and she will lucidly and rationally listen to what you have to say," says an attorney. "But there's a disconnect, and she'll be right back to asking, 'Why does this fucking flea need to take my deposition for me to mother my children?'"

There is one group of people who love Britney unconditionally, and whose love she accepts: Every day in L.A., at least a hundred paparazzi, reporters and celebrity-magazine editors dash after her, this braless chick padding around town on hilariously mundane errands—the gas station, the pet store, Starbucks, Rite Aid. The multibillion-dollar new-media economy rests on her slumped shoulders, with paparazzi agencies estimating that she has comprised up to twenty percent of their coverage for the past year. It's not only bottom feeders running after Britney—a recent memo leaked from the Associated Press, which plans to add twenty-two entertainment reporters to its staff, announces that everything that happens to Britney is news (they have already begun preparing her obit). The paparazzi feed the celebrity magazines, which feed the mainstream press, while sources sell their dirtiest material to British tabloids, and then it trickles back to America. "She is by far the top person I have written about on my Web site, ever," says Perez Hilton. Harvey Levin, founder of TMZ: "We serialize Britney Spears. She's our President Bush."

This mob lurches around town after Britney, descending on her with its notepads and cameras, and passing wild speculation from outlet to outlet. New players enter the gold rush by the minute, with people from around the world getting into the game: The flashiest new player is Sheeraz Hasan, a Pakistani-British immigrant who recently founded Hollywood.tv with backing from investors for His Highness of Dubai. A devout Muslim who can be found at the mosque on Fridays for prayers—and also drives a yellow Lamborghini—he was on the hajj to Mecca when he stopped in a small town on the side of a mountain for a bottle of water, and there he saw a newspaper, and on the cover was Britney. "It seemed to me she was the number-one star in the world, not Tom Cruise, not Will Smith," says Hasan. "Everything Britney does is news—Britney pumps gas, Britney forgets to put milk in her coffee—and there's a war going on, man!" Hasan realized it was his calling to build a paparazzi agency and brand with Britney's soap opera as the centerpiece: "By the blessing of God, my logo is on AP, *Entertainment Tonight* and CNN," he says, looking prayerful. He leans in and confides, "I'm going to take Paris to Dubai—the sheiks said any amount of money she wants is fine—and next I'm going to take Britney," he whispers. "She can have her own island!"

Trying to get an interview with Britney is a whole other level of craziness: A friend of a friend sets me up with a guy she says will introduce me to Britney, but it has to happen right away. The man insists that I have a signed contract from *Rolling Stone*, and he's also going to want money. I tell her to make the meeting. An hour later, a good-looking Danish guy, Claus, pulls up to a Beverly Hills street corner—he was the host of Britney's twenty-sixth birthday party, at his swag event, the Scandinavian Style Mansion (Paris Hilton and Sharon Stone attended). He's the kind of guy who gets the celebrity boutique Kitson to open its doors for Britney at 2 a.m., like he did in January (in yet another shocking image of Britney, she arrived in fishnet tights and without a skirt, her white panties visibly stained with menstrual blood). He gets out of a blue Porsche in a T-shirt that reads fuck rehab! It seems to be an unironic shirt. I grab my laptop case.

"Is that the contract?" he asks, pointing at my case. He leans in, "For the interview, are you offering $2 million?"

Of course, I have zero dollars to offer him, but I decide to play along. He tells me to get into his car.

"Britney and I are really, really good friends," says Claus. "That's my contract for her, for a million-dollar deal. But it's all friends. We're going on vacation together soon, on the jet to a supersecret location." He zooms down winding streets. "I'm so sick of everyone in this town thinking that they can get celebrities to come to their events for a free tube of lip gloss. My celebrities get free furs and diamonds. Britney is a queen." He sighs. "You know, the media probably made $12 million off the pictures they took of Britney at my party, and what do I get?" he says. "At least someone could reimburse me for the birthday cake."

These days, Britney may not care much what we think of her, but when she was younger it was all that mattered. Britney was a sort of JonBenét baby, encouraged to enter the pageant circuit early by Lynne, the daughter of a strict Baptist dairyman and a British war bride with dreams of escaping the small-town life of Kentwood, Louisiana. Lynne was raised in the town of 2,200 with Britney's dad, Jamie, a young rogue who popped wheelies on his motorcycle in front of the VFW and divorced his first wife two weeks before he married Lynne. His own mother committed suicide when he was fourteen. An hour inland of New Orleans and the dairy capital of the South until the seventies, Kentwood was in the death spasms of a faltering economy during Britney's childhood, with few new businesses opening other than a mineral-water bottling plant. Lynne worked as a second-grade teacher, and Jamie as a contractor, with projects in Memphis, a few hours' drive away. He generally came home on weekends and drank too much. "Jamie is clean now, but when Britney was growing up he was a horrible addict," says a former manager. "She is the product of some very, very bad genetics."

Lynne became transfixed on her talented daughter, partially as a way of relieving some of the marriage's pressure. By age three, Britney was enrolled in choir, dance and gymnastic lessons, and by six she'd won Miss Talent Central States. At eight, daughter drove with mom eight hours to an audition for *The Mickey Mouse Club* in Atlanta. She was too young for the show, though Lynne tried to pass her off as nine, but Britney caught the casting director's eye, and he recommended a New York talent agent. The family began to fall into debt as Jamie's construction business took a downturn, but they decided to wager their fortunes by sending Britney to Manhattan. Over the next few years, she and Lynne would split their time between New York and Kentwood as Britney booked commercials, played the lead in a Broadway play, *Ruthless*, and performed on *Star Search*. The family declared bankruptcy before Britney attained her dream: At twelve, she landed a role on *The Mickey Mouse Club*, alongside Christina Aguilera and Justin Timberlake.

After thriving in Disney's world of chaste adolescence, Britney applied her skills to a nearly identical demographic with a rapidly changing sense of what modern teenhood meant. Thanks to the Gen Y boom, teen music began to explode with the Backstreet Boys and the Spice Girls, the perfect music for America's pre-9/11 optimism. Britney was picked up by Larry Rudolph, an entertainment lawyer turned manager who was in the process of packaging 'NSync with Johnny Wright, manager of New Kids on the Block and the Backstreet Boys. They sent Britney to Sweden to record with Swedish pop maestro Max Martin, who had already written her future smash, "...Baby One More Time." Then Britney headed back to her Christian day school in Mississippi. She loved it: She had basketball practice and a handsome boyfriend, Reg Jones. She reportedly lost her virginity to him at fourteen. (Britney denies this.)

If true, this was a secret she couldn't share, particularly because Rudolph's plans included marketing her as the teenage Lolita of middle-aged men's dreams. In January 1999, Britney emerged on the national stage with the video for ". . . Baby One More Time," as a Catholic schoolgirl in pink pompom hair barrettes. The genius stroke of her creation was that her next single was a ballad, with a video featuring her dancing in a white outfit on a pier: By emerging as a vixen and then reverting to a child, she allowed the world to breathe a sigh of relief that her temptress act was make-believe. She played along. "All I did was tie up my shirt!" she said to *Rolling Stone.* "I'm wearing a sports bra under it. Sure, I'm wearing thigh-highs, but kids wear those—it's the style. Have you seen MTV—all those girls in thongs?"

On the road, Britney was humble—washing her dishes, doing her laundry, calling older female assistants "ma'am." "We would wake up Britney at 6 a.m., and she'd work on a video for three or four days straight for twenty hours a day," says Abe Sarkisyan, her driver for five years. "She was a kind, generous sweetheart with a big heart and no poor habits." An unedited goofball and girlie girl who wrote flowery notes to friends, burped a lot and liked practical jokes, Britney was almost comically naive—she covered "Satisfaction," but when she found herself in an elevator with Mick Jagger, she had no idea who he was. Lynne retained a minor management role over the years, but she disappeared from Britney's side, enjoying her newfound wealth and laying the star-machine groundwork for Jamie Lynn, a tomboy more interested in her scooter than becoming a star. Jamie was not in the picture. "It was upsetting for Britney to be around her dad," says a friend. "He came backstage one night, and he was wasted. She was devastated." Britney would tell friends that her father was emotionally abusive, and in 2006 she wrote a poem about "sins of the father": "The guilt you fed me/Made me weak/The voodoo you did/I couldn't speak."

The first big blow to Britney's golden-girl image was her breast implants. According to a source, she and Lynne had made the decision for her to get them, on the assumption that the culture demanded it, but the press leapt on her scornfully. (Britney has denied having implants.) "When Britney saw the papers, she was crying in the bathtub uncontrollably, asking, 'Why is everyone being so mean to me?'" says a friend. "It was very hurtful for her to go through something so private so publicly." Britney regretted the implants, particularly because her chest was still growing, and when her natural breasts became larger, she had the implants removed. "When other girls did their boobs, they were like, 'Yeah, I did my boobs, move on,' but Britney was brought up to lie about herself," says Darrin Henson, the choreographer of several videos from Britney's first album and Christina Aguilera's "Genie in a Bottle." Gradually, she began to lose her confidence. "Britney would come offstage after performing in front of 15 to 16,000 people and start crying because she thought she was terrible," says Henson. "The girl doesn't know who she is."

Britney's first two albums sold more than 39 million records, making her part of a teen-pop trifecta, with the Backstreet Boys and 'NSync, that comprised the best-selling acts in Jive's history. Some in her camp argued that Britney was too young to be pushed so hard, and wanted her to return to Kentwood to reconnect with girlfriends. "There were meetings where people would fight about giving Britney a break, but in the end the machine always won," says a friend. "Britney wanted it too, but she wasn't aware of the price tag." Those who advocated too much were shoved aside. Even though she had a squeaky-clean image, things changed backstage. "There were all these slick businessmen for Britney who let seedy people come around, offering her drinks and drugs, and she thought it was fun," she says. "If Britney wanted to party to blow off stress, that's what her team wanted her to do."

Britney's savior was Justin Timberlake, whom she started dating around 1999. "Justin had his head screwed on so straight, and he rescued her from that world," says a friend. "He became the great force in her life, but it started a pattern—she began to look for guys to help her get away from the people who control her." Even though Britney was one of the biggest stars in the world and Timberlake was still just another guy in 'NSync, the power balance in their relationship was solid. "She wasn't competitive about attention," says a close friend. "She just wanted to be in love with him." Once again, her manager gave her instructions: The partnership was to be kept under wraps, and they had to tell everyone they planned to stay abstinent until marriage. "They were always running in between each other's buses, and one night Justin came back to the bus and said to me, 'Dude, smell my fingers,'" says Henson. "Justin slept with her that night." It was another year before they admitted publicly that they were a couple.

Although the world thought Britney was an innocent sexed-up for the cameras, she was always lobbying to appear sluttier, which she thought would make her appear more mature. From the time she was young, Lynne and Jamie let her walk around the house naked. "Every girl in America was wearing crop tops and booty shorts, and Britney felt like she was being held back," says a friend. "She would joke about wanting to do videos topless." Her managers didn't want to scare off her fan base. "These middle-aged guys were so intense about her not being sexual that they pushed her the other way," says the friend. "They'd tell her to put on a bra or that her lip gloss was too dark. They were literally picking out her panties for her."

With her third album, Britney was told that she could change—a little. It was time to enter the "Not a Girl, Not Yet a Woman" phase, but she was ready to leave it behind. All the gay dancers and stylists were always having dirty conversations around her backstage, and one day Britney piped up: "God, I want to have hot sex too! I want to have throw-down, hot sex!" Her primary creative collaborator on her tour, choreographer Wade Robson, agreed that it was her time to blossom, and she owned her new image by draping the proverbial snake around her neck while performing "I'm a Slave 4 U" at the 2001 VMAs. Her sexual curiosity got the better of her, and she reportedly began sleeping with Robson, a friend of Timberlake's who co-wrote 'NSync's "Pop" with him. (Both Britney and Robson have denied the affair.) In February 2002, Timberlake discovered a mash note from Robson in Britney's room. Britney and Timberlake were performing on *Saturday Night Live* that night, and they sat backstage, miserable—he refused to accept her apologies. The breakup was a terrible shock, particularly as it was followed by Britney's parents' divorce two months later. "No one took the time to say to Britney, 'Let's take some time off here, let's get you some counseling,'" says an ex-assistant manager. "They expected her to have the drive, to dust it off."

Britney realized that the machine wasn't going to bring her satisfaction anymore—she needed a man. She began desperately seeking love in nightclubs with inappropriate guys like Colin Farrell and in the studio, most notably with Fred Durst, who violated her trust by boasting about their exploits on *The Howard Stern Show*. Without a strong sense of self, she'd take on the characteristics of whomever was around at the moment, and after her kiss with Madonna at the 2003 VMAs, she decided they were soul mates. "Britney and Madonna became friends after the performance, and she started to think she was Madonna," says an ex-manager. "She said, 'Madonna calls her own shots, I can do that.' But Madonna doesn't need to be told what to do. Britney does." (Britney on Madonna: "Maybe she was my husband in another life.")

Britney returned to Kentwood for Christmas in 2003, staying in a small house on her parents' property with old friends, including childhood crush

Jason Alexander, a junior at Southeastern Louisiana University. After fighting with Lynne one morning, she packed her pals on a plane for three days of partying in Las Vegas—cocaine during the evening, Ecstasy in the early morning and Xanax to sleep, according to Alexander. At 3:30 a.m. on January 3, 2004, after watching the *Texas Chainsaw Massacre*, she and Alexander took a lime-green limo to the Little White Wedding Chapel, where she strapped a white garter over her ripped jeans and held a small bouquet of roses in cardboard for their forty-dollar wedding. Eleven hours later, they called their parents to give them the big news. Lynne flew to Vegas, the couple were separated, and lawyers worked to annul the marriage. Shipped home with a false promise that Britney wanted to stay together, Alexander cracked under the national spotlight and dropped out of school.

This was to have been the new Britney, and she was genuinely disappointed, wearing a wedding ring in defiance. Lynne tried to circle the wagons around her furious daughter, keeping her in Kentwood on the day of the Grammys and taking her to a church service instead, but within a few months, the road called—Britney went back on tour with *In the Zone*, a much more mature album with songs about early-morning sex and masturbation. By the time she filmed the video for the ballad "Everytime," she was down the rabbit hole: Her concept was to die in an overflowing bathtub with pills and booze strewn around, and get reincarnated as a baby. There were demons that she was battling, and she wanted everyone to know. Jive insisted on a different method of death, so she ran away from the paparazzi before drowning in the tub. Britney was compliant on the first day of the shoot, but on the second, she refused to leave her hotel room. "Finally, Britney agreed to do it, but first she said, 'I need three Red Bulls, and call my doctor,'" says a friend.

She found her soul mate a few weeks later, on the dance floor: Kevin Federline, a twenty-five-year-old cornrowed white boy who had been a dancer for Timberlake, a high school dropout and son of a Fresno, California, auto mechanic with one baby by his girlfriend, Shar Jackson, and another on the way. Nicknamed "Meat Pole," he was a fixture on the L.A. club scene, and one broke-ass dude: Before he met Britney, Federline's Chevy had been repossessed. Britney got stuck on him—"part of it was that she wanted to pimp Justin's dude, get his spot and throw it in Justin's face," says a friend—and invited him on her tour, where they got matching tattoos of dice on their wrists and filmed each other obsessively with video cameras, movies that would become the basis for their reality show, *Chaotic*. With little else on her mind, Britney was relieved when her knee gave out in the middle of the tour, and Jive announced that doctors had prescribed four months of rest. But the next week, she asked Federline to marry her (he refused, mock-horrified, and proposed a few minutes later), and they got hitched immediately, with Juicy tracksuits for the bridesmaids (in pink) and groomsmen (in white) embroidered with MAIDS and PIMPS.

Two weeks after the wedding, Britney fired her manager, Rudolph and Lynne. "Kevin convinced Britney that he was going to get the users out of her life, and they were going to run her business together," says a friend. Their life became the main business: They sold their wedding photos to *People* for $1 million, and Britney began to blog on her fan site, charging a $25 club-membership fee. She popped out two kids quickly—Sean Preston, a year after she and Federline were married (the baby pictures were also sold for $1 million to *People*), and Jayden, one year later (she kept him under wraps for months, in hopes of a big payday, but a paparazzi caught her carrying him on a beach in Maui, Hawaii). Her interest in her recording career was minimal. She recorded three songs in three years.

Federline gave Britney license to fully embrace her white-trash side—walking into gas-station restrooms barefoot, dumping ashtrays out hotel windows, wearing novelty tees like I'M A VIRGIN, BUT THIS IS AN OLD SHIRT and, most notably, not strapping the kids into car seats. But he liked the high life, buying a $250,000 silver Ferrari with monogrammed rims and getting stoned in their home recording studio while cutting his rap album. "Kevin didn't step up to the plate and be a man to Britney in their relationship," says a close friend. "He was a boy to her, turning his back on her for his bros and that fame." He made her feel a lot of her old insecurities—loneliness, fear of abandonment—and she started partying and spiraling downward again, attributing her crying jags to postpartum depression. "When Britney had children, that should've been the end of her wild ways, and it wasn't," says a friend of Federline. "She turned into someone who only wanted to hear 'yes,' and if you're not going to say it, get the hell out of her way."

Meat Pole wasn't the one for Britney, and she asked him for a divorce by text message in November 2006. (His response: scrawling on the wall of the nightclub bathroom, "Today I'm a free man—Fuck a wife, give me my kids, bitch!") She rehired Rudolph immediately, and he took her ice-skating at Rockefeller Center in Manhattan for a photo op. But she wasn't ready to be a little girl again. Night after night, she hit the L.A. scene lost, vomiting in public, exchanging clothes with a strip-club cocktail waitress, and, perhaps most dangerously, hanging out with Paris Hilton—the two of them even splitting a pair of fishnet stockings, each wearing one leg, and she copied Paris' cootchie-flashing stunts three times before Rudolph quashed their friendship (Paris' nickname for Britney: "The Animal," because she doesn't think before she acts).

The Animal had to go to rehab: Eric Clapton's Crossroads, in Antigua, but she stormed out one day later, flying to Miami and then coach-class to Los Angeles to see her family. She arrived at Federline's house for her babies, but he had joined forces with Lynne and Rudolph, and wouldn't talk to her until she registered at the Malibu rehab center Promises. She circled his house three times, furious at having to concede to their demands, before pulling into a random hair salon in the Valley and taking her hair off in big clumps, less as a penance than a liberation. Then she stayed up for forty-eight hours straight, driving around, sucking down dozens of Red Bulls, afraid that she was being followed by demons, or that a cell-phone charger was taping her thoughts, and obsessively listening to the radio for news about Anna Nicole Smith's death earlier that month. That was her fate, she declared—she was next.

After rehab, Britney was deeply angry and cut out every person in her life who had argued for it—her parents, Federline, Rudolph, even old best friends. She claimed not to have a drug problem, and stopped returning calls to her disloyal subjects, changing her phone numbers. "She was queen of the ghost moves," says singer Keri Hilson, who did backup vocals and co-wrote "Gimme More." "She'd be in the booth one second and then security would come get her, and we wouldn't know she was gone." Britney's former bodyguard claimed in an interview with a British tabloid that she suffered a near-overdose with singer-songwriter Howie Day, whom she met at Promises, in a Los Angeles hotel room—the room was trashed, a glass pipe alongside a white substance that the bodyguard claimed was cocaine or meth.

Jive was cautious about booking Britney on the 2007 MTV Video Music Awards, but it was too good a promotional opportunity to pass up. Britney signed a new management contract with the firm and started working out a few times a week. The day of the show, she arrived early to the arena. Timberlake was rehearsing. Suddenly, her face fell, and she started getting panicked, nervous, afraid—what was he going to think of her performance? What about the rest of her peers? She headed backstage and was pacing in her dressing room when Timberlake knocked on the door. She refused to come out. She didn't want to see him yet.

Soon, she was going to put on her hair, and maybe she would feel better. There was a wig waiting for her by master coiffeur Ken Pavés, who created Jessica Simpson's cascading fake tresses—it had been seven months since Britney shaved her head, and her real hair was less than six inches long. All she had to do was sit for the afternoon so the wig could be glued to her head, piece by piece, then remain very still for an hour so it could set, and she would be the old Britney again.

Suddenly, Britney declared that she didn't want Pavés to touch her. She asked for his assistant, but the assistant didn't want to betray Pavés. The hair divas turned on their heels, leaving the firm to try coaxing them back while insisting to Britney that she must change her mind. When she finally granted Pavés entree an hour before the show began, it was too late to apply the wig, so someone grabbed Nelly Furtado's stylist, who glued on some straight blond hairpieces. Britney sat for those in her glittery black bikini and then stepped into the rest of her outfit, a Posh Spice-style corset-dress. Then she took it off, refusing to wear it. She wanted to go onstage without artifice, as naked as possible, and for us to love her just the way she was.

The edge of Mulholland Drive is the lip of a pit, a vertiginous fall into destruction. Britney's house sits at the top, jutting over the glittering city. It's a rainy weekday a couple of months after the VMAs. She knows she messed up her performance—"Afterward, she kept asking, 'Was I terrible? Was it terrible?'" says a friend. "This is just the way it is with her: It's circular, manic thinking"—and because she's not doing any promotion for *Blackout*, other than a seven-minute radio interview with KISS-FM, there's not much else going on. The firm stepped down from managing her, without making a cent, because they were no longer able to speak with her directly: Her phone is now answered by Osamah Lutfi, also known as Sam, a jovial thirty-three-year-old who a friend of Britney's describes as her "life coach." They met at a party in 2007, and he called her then-assistant, Kalie Machado, to meet at a Santa Monica Starbucks. According to Machado, Lutfi told her that he worked for Federline as a private eye, and he knew that there was a tap on Britney's phone and a warrant to search her Malibu home for drugs. (Federline's rep has denied any connection.) Lutfi has had two temporary restraining orders issued against him for harassment.

It's Lutfi who has kept Britney together through the months, filling in as her assistant and trying to be a manager, talking to her record label, and driving her around town. There are constant breakdowns about all the people who have sold Britney out to celebrity magazines—the assistant she forgot to pay, the bodyguard who claims he's seen her do cocaine and regularly walk around the house nude, the twenty-one-year-old college kid she made out with topless in a hot tub on the roof of a hotel in downtown L.A. A new rumor crops up every day: She feeds soda in baby bottles to her toddlers (whose teeth she also asked a dentist to whiten), her choice of poison is the Southern rap scene's "Purple Monster" (vodka, Red Bull and NyQuil) and she has a sex dungeon in her Beverly Hills villa with spanking paddles displayed in a glass jar (and a large covered candy dish of lotions and toys she calls her "pleasure chest"). In this embattled state, Britney has become a recluse, in a way—she's never out to dinner or at a nightclub, spending most of her nights at the Four Seasons in Beverly Hills.

For weeks, she slept there almost every night, and Lutfi is often downstairs at the hotel, like everyone else who is working this story—the red-carpeted lobby bar has become the de facto center of Britney operations, with reporters, paparazzi and lawyers from the child-custody case holding meetings with hope that the object of everyone's desire might come wandering by. It's like the United Nations in this bar, with folks from myriad ethnicities, and everyone acting deadly serious. I have coffee on separate occasions with two men from Federline's attorney's team: Aaron Cohen, a former Israeli operative, who served the subpoenas to some of Britney's friends, including Lutfi—along with his regular job, which is training SWAT teams in Israeli anti-terrorism techniques. "With Britney, I penetrated the inner circles of Hollywood," he tells me. "It was not unlike counterterrorism, in that I worked with both enemies and friends." I also meet with Michael Sands, the media liaison for Kaplan, who gives me a key-chain light stamped with a picture of the Pentagon, an FBI lapel pin and another from the CIA, and a commemorative Navy coin—one might think he works for one or all of the agencies. The rumor flies around the lobby that the government is looking into Lutfi, curious about his connection to the Saudis.

Britney's Danish pal Claus makes an appearance at the Four Seasons as well, with two business associates. They'd like to talk about the $2 million, which now, for some reason, everyone is talking about as $1 million. This is how it will go, they explain: I will give them the money, and the cash will be held in escrow. Britney will know that she won't get any money until she completes the interview and photo shoot (they will take a ten percent finder's fee, payable whether or not she shows up). They will be at the shoot, making sure Britney is happy—I will have to bring five photographers, five stylists and five makeup artists in case she is not. They do this all the time: They just took Paris to Moscow, and did the deal for Britney's New Year's Eve 2007 appearance at the Vegas nightclub Pure, the one where she passed out. "My guy was behind her, holding her up that night," boasts one guy.

Ryan Seacrest stops by the table. "Hey, guys, what's up?" he asks.

"We made Ryan $3 million last year," they say after Seacrest leaves. "It's all friends, so friendly."

The next night, Claus, again in his FUCK REHAB! shirt, has a new plan: He will tell Britney that he's going to give her $1 million. I'll give him the $1 million, and then he'll give it to her. "This way, no one will ever know that *Rolling*

Stone bent over to pay Queen Britney," he says. He is very pleased. He calls Lutfi to tell him. "Sam says that *OK!* magazine was going to pay $2 million for an interview with Britney," he says.

Claus takes off for Citizen Smith, a rock bar in Hollywood, to meet Lutfi and Britney's twenty-six-year-old cousin, Alli Sims—a naive climber with hopes of releasing her own album. It's a birthday party for Jason Kennedy, an E! reporter who may or may not be dating Sims.

"We really just want someone to tell the truth," says Sims. "Britney's such a good girl." She screws up her face, thinking about nice things to say. "Britney never talks bad about anyone behind their backs, ever, seriously," she says.

"That is one of her best characteristics," agrees Lutfi. He turns to me. "Just to let you understand something as far as her psyche goes, she really doesn't need to do another thing in her life. Her big thing with me is that she doesn't want me defending her against anything fake in the magazines. But she understands that's the way they make their money, because it's the way she made hers too. She really doesn't care anymore."

"We're going to need pre-approval over the article," says Claus.

"Also, Britney has a friend who is a photographer whom we would want to shoot the photos," says Lutfi. He thinks for a moment. "You know, this is so much more than a magazine article—we've been doing dictation, she's been telling me her story, and I've been writing it all down. It would make a great book!"

It's 1:30 a.m., and the bar is closing. The lights flick on, and we hug goodbye.

After explaining to Claus that there is no money, I write to Lutfi many times, explaining that we are still very interested in interviewing Britney and telling her side of the story.

No response.

As 2007 comes to a close, Britney starts to really enjoy her paparazzi chases. She races around the city for two or three hours a day, aimlessly leading paps to various locations where she could interact with them just a little bit and then jump back into her car. A Britney chase is more fun than a roller coaster, but with the chance that the experience could cause lasting harm. "Britney is the most dangerous detail in Hollywood," says Levin of TMZ.

There are twenty paps in the core Britney detail, a bunch of hilarious, slightly scary thugs who use expert drag-racing skills to block off new guys who try to get in the mix. It's like a game of Frogger, with everyone jostling to be the first car behind Britney, the better to shoot all over her when she stops (and then watch their feet, because several have found themselves on crutches after she speeds away). "She's nuts," says Craig Williams, a photographer for

Hollywood.tv. Williams, a former beatmaker for Death Row Records with a long braid slithering down his back and multiple silver rings on his fingers, gets in front most of the time, riding her Mercedes SL65 hard. Almost all the paps drive rental SUVs, most with dents and scrapes on the sides, because no one wants to get their real cars messed up. A plastic bag swings from the door to the trunk of the SUV in front of us—the pap had been using it for trash all day and forgot to dump it.

Britney pulls into her driveway, and Williams waits down the street. He puts Blackout on his CD player. "Let's summon Britney," he says. "She's gonna come back out after she does her drugs or changes her clothes, whichever comes first," he jokes, lighting a cigarette. "She didn't get enough chase today."

An hour later, the white Mercedes whizzes by, and it's on: up and down Coldwater Canyon and across Mulholland Drive for one hour, with paps jostling behind. Then she flips a bitch and heads right back where she came from. The other cars get lost as she circles a Ralphs supermarket twice, dumps her assistant at the Starbucks and zooms down the street to a red light. Williams pulls out his video camera.

She waves hi. "Hey, Brit, I listened to that new album," says Williams. "It's awesome! Good album. Good job. Vocals were tight, girl."

"I know," Britney yells. "I'm the shit."

Williams laughs. "You the shit!"

"I know it, baby," she yells, with a coy smile. "It's hard to be this hot."

"Tell me about it," says Williams, laughing. "It's Britney, bitch!"

This kind of flirtation is a daily occurrence, and she starts to prowl the pool for a dude—of all the guys, Adnan Ghalib is the hottest one, and she knows it. He's a British Afghani who has claimed he fought for the Mujahdeen and has the shrapnel scars to prove it, a smoldering thirty-five-year-old in Gucci sunglasses (far more appealing in person than he is on the news). Once Britney asked him into the bathroom of a Quiznos; his wife has filed for legal separation, and he has said that he plans to marry Britney and get her pregnant. The unimaginable happens one night right before Christmas, when Britney decides that she's had enough of being lonely—she pulls over on the Pacific Coast Highway, jumps into Ghalib's car, pops on her pink wig and takes him to the Peninsula hotel for a late "lunch," as he called it.

For the past few years, Britney has begged friends to help her run away, to leave everything behind and become a stylist or schoolteacher, or move to an island where she can work as a bartender. Ghalib helps her achieve her goal, evading the paparazzi for weeks on violent, terrifying chases. The relationship is just starting to build when Britney is taken to the hospital for the first time, and as soon as she comes out, Ghalib absconds with her to crisscross the West Coast, listening to their favorite music in the car (her: Dixie Chicks and Janet Jackson; him: System of a Down), making stops in Palm Springs and Mexico with his buddy, a paparazzi who would shoot the two of them for exclusive sale by Ghalib's then-agency. The other agencies are having nervous breakdowns. Ghalib gets on the phone with *Rolling Stone* because he's a fan of the magazine. "You must understand something about Britney," he says, in arguing her side of the story. "People turned on her. They were only there when the getting was good. She has become very Columbo-esque—she acts a certain way so that people don't think she's intelligent, and then people volunteer information, and she is able to put together what is going on. It's not the blogs or magazines or the people on the street she cares about. She knows that the people who had a responsibility to support her bailed out and is very hurt by their actions."

A tug of war begins between Ghalib and Lutfi for control of Britney, and on January 20, when Ghalib goes to a funeral in Northern California, Lutfi invites a few paparazzi from a friendly agency, X17, over to Britney's house, and shows them what he claimed was a restraining order against Ghalib. "He folded it over so they couldn't see what he was showing," says Ghalib, chuckling. "I'll give it to you, he's good, he's very good at what he does." Lutfi has spread rumors that Ghalib sleeps on the couch when he's at Britney's house. A pap catches a text message: Lutfi writes, "You're a manic trigger. If you continue to have any contact with her, you'll kill her. It's your decision."

Britney finds herself right where she used to be: Again, there's control, pressure, fighting. She argues with Lutfi, and Ghalib rushes in to save her, but Lutfi calls security to keep him off her property. Lynne arrives, dragging her daughter around town, and Britney begins to spin out, staying up for sixty hours straight. On January 30, she arrives back home after a day at the Beverly Hills Hotel, and meets with a psychiatrist, according to X17. They put out the news at 11 p.m.: She's attempted suicide.

Seventy-five paps gather around the entrances to Britney's gated community, stamping their feet in the chilly winter night, as a police helicopter circles overhead. "You don't want an ambulance to roll out with a body bag and miss that," says a French photographer, checking his battery. These guys are jaded after all that's happened. "Man, Britney can't die, because then I don't get my money!" says a guy in a Famous Stars and Straps baseball hat. Someone starts running down the block, and everyone runs after him; they hide in a driveway and laugh when everyone catches up. Although she doesn't seem to have tried to commit suicide, the doctors are on their way again: Police and paramedics descend as the LAPD blocks off all exit paths from her house, stations twenty cops in her driveway and takes her out (her code name: "The Package") without a single picture. The next day, her parents file a restraining order against Lutfi.

A world without Britney, where she is set aside in rehab or a psychiatric center, is hard to contemplate: She's the canary in the coal mine of our culture, the most vivid representation of the excess of the past decade. She didn't think there was a tomorrow worth saving for, and neither did we. After blaming everyone else for her problems, Britney's finally starting to realize the degree to which she's messed up, but her sense of entitlement keeps her from admitting it to herself, or to anyone who is trying to help her. We want her to survive and thrive, to evolve into someone who can make us proud again. Or maybe, we just don't want the show to end. "Look at George Foreman: He's the oldest heavyweight champion ever," says Ghalib. "That's what Britney's going to be. She said it best to me: She refuses to live her life anymore reflected in the eyes of others." Then he gets very quiet. "Be gentle to her," he says. "That's a personal request."

AUTHOR'S AFTERWORDS...

When my editors at *Rolling Stone* approached me about doing this Britney Spears story, I resisted on the grounds that the subject matter was too horrific. But they pushed me, and I'm glad they did. The assignment was to follow around Britney Spears—or those in her orbit—for a couple days. It was 2008 and she had either gone loco because she was on drugs, or gone loco because she wasn't on drugs. She'd shaved her head. You knew that. What you might not have known is that she had also fired her bodyguard, manager, and publicist, plus she wasn't returning calls from her parents, both of whom had helped keep her in line over the years. The first thing I did when I started my reporting was call her record label, but they didn't call me back. Let's say that again: a *Rolling Stone* writer called a record label to tell them that their artist was going on the cover, and the label didn't return the call. That's how far off the reservation Britney was at that point. I heard later that they couldn't get in touch with her either.

So she was alone up on the top of Mulholland Drive in her big fancy house. I figured it wouldn't be too hard to knock on her door, so I printed out her address and hopped in the car, but I forgot about the guard stationed outside her housing development. Needed a new strategy. I went out a couple nights in West Hollywood to parties that I would usually have blown off because they were filled with coke heads, talent agents, and airheads (female and male varieties of the preceding). I made a point of asking everyone I talked to whether they knew anyone who knew anyone who knew Britney. At a director's house in the hills, I struck up a conversation with a young brunette publicist for a big agency. She said she was friends with a guy named Claus. He ran something called the "Scandinavian House of Style," and he'd just hosted some sort of weird event sponsored by a furrier—Britney had showed up, probably lured by the promise of a free white mink wrap, but now Claus was telling everyone that they were best friends. The publicist wanted a hookup with *Rolling Stone*, I wanted to meet Claus.

A meeting was arranged for a couple days later. I hopped in the car again, and was about fifteen minutes from the location when the publicist called. She said Claus was now demanding that I pay him for his "information." I asked how much he wanted. She said $2 million, or at least he needed a contract saying that I was going to pay $2 million. We went back and forth for a while, and I told her I wouldn't pay anyone, but he said I needed money or there wasn't going to be a meeting. I called my editor at *Rolling Stone*, and we decided to see where this went. There are some people who might feel like we made some sort of trespass here, but we were never going to pay a cent, so that was our justification for continuing to pursue the story in this way.

Anyway, when I pulled up to the corner of Sunset and Doheny to meet Claus, he wasn't hard to miss. He was standing in front of a beat-to-shit navy-blue Porsche, about five-foot-three, with bugged out light blue eyes and a T-shirt that said FUCK REHAB. I was like, *Shit, I guess I've got to play this one out.* I had my laptop in a black briefcase, so I grabbed it as I got out of the car, and gave it an ostentatious swing as I walked toward him. He stared at me as I walked over. "Is that the contract?" he asked.

That's just one of the weird things that happened while I was reporting this story. After it came out, an editor at Gawker emailed me because he had received a nasty letter about how I had copied a lot of my reporting from videos I had watched on YouTube, particularly the opening scene where I trailed Britney through a mall—a scene that I only got from hopping in the car again after convincing a paparazzi to call me with the name of the mall she'd gone to, then running through two stories of the building asking everyone I saw if they had seen Britney. I slapped the Gawker inquiry down immediately. I worked incredibly hard and even put myself in harm's way during shockingly dangerous car chases to get this story. And yeah, I know it's just a dumb story about Britney Spears, but I'm proud of it.

Justin Heckert

J ustin Heckert is a native of Cape Girardeau, MO, and now lives in Indianapolis, IN. His first journalism job was at *Atlanta*, writing long-form stories about the people and issues of Georgia, including the transgender community, a spelling bee, the science of neuromarketing at Emory University and the making of an *Adult Swim* show on Cartoon Network. Heckert was named writer of the year by the City and Regional Magazine Association in 2005 and 2012. For five years he wrote for *ESPN The Magazine*, where he chronicled (among other stories) the start-up football team at Georgia State University for a twelve-part series, tracked down a Pittsburgh Steelers imposter, lifted 1,000 pounds with a Russian weight trainer, and went to the Egg Bowl with a poet named Chico in Oxford, MS.

A 2002 graduate of the University of Missouri School of Journalism, Heckert has written for *Esquire, Men's Journal*, the *Oxford American*, and the *Washington Post*. He's been anthologized in *The Best American Crime Reporting* and *The Best American Essays*.

Lost in the Waves

The ocean at night is a terrible dream. There is nothing beyond the water except the profound discouragement of the sky, every black wave another singular misfortune. Walt Marino has been floating on his back for hours, the ocean on his skin, his mouth, soaking the curls of his graying hair. The water has cracked his lips, has formed a slippery glaze on his shoulders and arms. The salt has stuck to his contact lenses, burning the edges of his eyes. A small silver pendant of the Virgin Mary sticks to his collarbone on a link chain. He can no longer see the car key floating below his stomach, tied to the string of his floral swim trunks. The water licks against his ears. Every familiar sound is gone.

He arches his neck, contemplates again how far of swim it might be to shore. He can't know how many miles. He tries to convince himself he might be able to make it back to the beach, to the rock jetty from which he was swept out to sea. He starts dog-paddling, but after about thirty minutes his arms give out, his back tires, and he decides that he'll die if he tries.

In the dark, he can make out only the outline of his hands. He can see a faint glow in the distance, orange and premonitory, like a small fire, what he guesses to be the hotels and condos of Florida's northern coast. He wonders if someone in a living room watching TV could look out far past the shore and see him floating here.

No, he decides. That's crazy. Even if they were looking through binoculars, they could probably see only the water, and maybe the ripples beneath the stars. Even the rescue helicopter hadn't been able to spot his head sticking above the surface, as it traced a search grid just beyond where the tide of Ponce de Leon Inlet empties into the Atlantic. Below the helicopter, patrol boats and Jet Skis had gone back and forth like sharks in the distance. He had waved his arms and screamed until his throat cracked, until the blue search signal and the light of the beam had thinned and disappeared. He now wonders if he'll ever need his voice again.

That was hours ago. When Christopher was floating beside him. Christopher, his little boy. When the two of them, father and son, were still together in the waves.

The ocean was always one of Christopher's favorite places. The shallow water near the jetty rocks of Ponce Inlet, pale and green at the curve of the beach—Walt took him there as much as he could. Like a lot of autistic children, Christopher was drawn to water. By the sensation of it, by its sounds, its placidity—Walt could only guess. Christopher could never explain the ocean's hold on him, could only put on his swim trunks and stand barefoot on the wooden floor of the house, or find the car keys from the table and try to place them in Walt's hand, or just wait impatiently at the door of his convertible. As his son grew up, his main communication turned out to be the sounds of his laughter, his hands slapping at the tide foam, his giddy squeal as he climbed onto his father's back, swimming for hours until it was time for them to go home.

On September 6, 2008, a Saturday, Walt took him to Ponce Inlet late in the afternoon. It was his weekend with the kids. As he did every two weeks, he picked up Christopher from the group home where he lived, then picked up Angela, his fourteen-year-old daughter, at her mom's house in Oviedo. Christopher sat next to Dad in the front seat of Walt's red Celica, the top folded back, wind running through Christopher's short dark-brown hair. Angela sat squished along with two of her friends in the back. It was a perfect day to go to the beach. They stopped at McDonald's, Christopher's favorite, on the way.

Christopher ate his double cheeseburgers slowly, maddeningly, the exact same way he did every time. He took off the top bun, held it in his hand, and ate the pickles. Then he ate the lettuce. Then the top bun. Then he ate the meat. Then the bottom bun, then each french fry, one at a time. He chewed vigorously, with his mouth open, loud enough for Walt to ask him to stop. Occasionally, when he became anxious or upset, he might stand beneath the spout of the soda fountain and press the button, and try to catch the spill in his mouth.

As Walt watched Christopher eat, he tried not to think about the meeting he'd had earlier in the day with his ex-wife Robyn and her husband Ed. Walt had lost his accounting job a few months before and asked if he could cut back on child-support payments. He'd split with Robyn eight years earlier, and whenever they spoke anymore it was briefly, tensely, and only in regard to the kids. During this meeting, in which Robyn and Ed agreed to reduce but not eliminate payments, they asked Walt what he planned to do with the kids that day. "I don't know," Walt replied, though he did know.

They arrived at New Smyrna Beach around 6:30 pm. The five of them walked the long wooden boardwalk, Christopher plodding behind, sometimes staring down. Walt followed him. The Ponce Inlet Lighthouse was the one thing, long and orange, that rose above the sparse landscape in the distance. The boardwalk ended at stairs that went down to the sand; by the time Walt and Christopher caught up to them, the girls had ignored the signs posted and were sliding down the backs of the white dunes as if on a playground. Walt and Christopher watched them for a while, then put their bags and towels down on the hard sand close to the water.

Christopher, in floral trunks like his dad, took off ahead of Walt, toward the south jetty, and splashed in, wading along the rocks. The tide on the protected side of the jetty looked serene. A group of people, their dark fishing poles like long weeds sticking up between the jetty rocks, watched them. Walt waded in to get Christopher, unaware that the tide had begun to go out, or of how strong it was, or that he was actually disobeying a county ordinance; no one was supposed to swim within 300 feet of a pier or jetty. Robyn and Ed had repeatedly asked Walt not to put Christopher in any situation that could be dangerous, and they asked him in particular not to take Christopher to the beach. But Walt didn't listen to them. He was certain that it made Christopher happy to be here.

The current grabbed father and son almost immediately. They floated past the glistening rocks, and then it pulled them faster, the sand disappearing beneath their toes. Within a minute, Walt and Christopher were fifty feet out, the ocean in their faces and ears.

"Do you need help?" one of the fishermen yelled at Walt as he watched him being pulled away.

"We're okay!" Walt shouted back, giving a thumbs-up. He still thought he had things under control, that they could make it back. They had waded into this water a thousand times, he and Christopher.

But this time the current was much stronger. Another two minutes, 200 yards farther out to sea. Walt knew they were in trouble now. His heart thumped in his ears. "Don't come in!" he screamed to Angela, who was now staring out at them in fright from the jetty. "Call 911! 9-1-1! 9-1-1!" He repeated this instruction, hands cupping his mouth, over and over, trying to keep his head above water as the waves grew, but Angela was now out of earshot.

One second Walt could see the beach, and the next he was below the horizon. He tried to focus on Christopher's head, the dark-brown hair wet and matted, the only part of him above water. Christopher was about 20 feet ahead of Walt now, bobbing and laughing hysterically. Walt yelled at Christopher to swim back to the jetty with him—"Come on, let's go, let's swim!"—but they had been raked into the middle of the inlet, where the current's pull was even stronger.

After twenty minutes, they were about a mile out, at the mouth of the open sea. A green navigational buoy bobbed there, tall and round, with a rusted bell clanging back and forth. Walt reached out to try and grab onto the buoy but struggled against the current. Christopher just kept laughing, unaware of the danger, of the situation, of the fading shore and the strength of the current, of the ocean ahead. As they floated past the buoy, there was nothing else to stop them from drifting into the sea.

Walt studied Christopher as the sun went down. It was a game to his son, he decided—floating there without a care in the world. Farther out from shore, the light dwindling, the land itself was less visible. The current seemed to relax, and it was hard to tell how fast they were moving anymore.

Staying afloat was all there really was to do. Walt told himself to keep his eye on Christopher, to make sure his head stayed above the four-foot waves. But his mind wandered to his own mom and dad waiting for them back at the house, to the girls left on the beach, to nothing at all. He forced himself not to consider what could be swimming below them. The only sounds to keep them company were the lap of the waves and the slap of the fins of the small fish that jumped onto the surface. Walt could see the white point revolving at the top of the lighthouse, counted the seconds of its revolution. He decided the coast guard would probably be coming for them soon. They had been in the water for two hours, he guessed. They were beginning to tire.

Christopher was no longer laughing, so Walt decided it was time to give him a break. He dog-paddled to his son, grabbed his arm, and let Christopher climb on his back. Walt, who'd become a certified lifeguard because Angela's Girl Scout troop needed him to get his license, took a deep breath. Then he arched his back and dipped his head forward below the surface, arms slightly extended from his sides—the dead man's float.

He lay facedown in thirty-second increments, coming back up for air, wiping the water from his cheeks, spitting the ocean out of his mouth. Each time he would clutch Christopher's hands, then lift him up on his back. Christopher would lay his stomach on top of Walt and wrap his arms around his father's neck. Each time Walt rose to take a breath he ached more; after only a few minutes he came up again and clutched his stomach. Then he vomited. He puked everything he had eaten at lunch, big chunks of his cheeseburgers, floating in a pool of bile on the surface, barely digested. He dry heaved until his throat burned; he was screaming gibberish, nonsense, "Jesus, God, help us...."

Small fish surfaced in packs to feast on the vomited meal, and Christopher reacted with panic. He began to scream. He grabbed at Walt's hair and tried to rip it out of his head. He was thrashing on Walt's back, his weight pushing Walt beneath the surface. Christopher weighed about 120 pounds, and he was tearing at his father, digging his fingernails into him, crying at the top of his lungs. Walt pulled him off of his back, wiped his eyes, and croaked, "Please, Christopher, calm down. Please be a good boy." Christopher looked at Walt, pleading with a pair of helpless eyes, as if to ask: What are we going to do, Dad? Walt had no answer. He couldn't breathe.

Christopher grabbed for him again, jumping out of the water to get away from the fish, splashing salt water into Walt's eyes. Walt went under, gulping a throatful of ocean that made him vomit again. Crying, desperate to breathe, he yelled at Christopher, at the situation. Christopher was screaming again, too. What could Walt do? There was really only one thing he could do, for the both of them. He was forced to make a horrible decision: If they stayed together, if Christopher kept clutching his father, they would both drown. Their only chance was for Walt to separate himself from Christopher, to hope that his son could stay afloat on his own. It was the only choice that made any sense. He looked at his son again, then pushed him away into the ocean.

When he was fifteen months old, they knew something was wrong. He didn't pay attention, didn't make eye contact, didn't cry. He would just scream and grunt. He didn't say a real word until he was four. After Christopher was diagnosed with autism as a toddler, Walt spent twenty grand on a couple of miracle cures, including an injection of pig hormones into Christopher's leg. He also looked into another form of treatment called "patterning," an exercise designed to improve neurologic organization that required several people to help lift and move the patient's legs and arms and head for several hours a day. But it cost $10,000, and Walt thought it looked like torture.

He knew where the bathroom was because Walt and Robyn showed him, but he didn't know how to ask for it when he needed it. Sometimes he would pee or shit in his pants and laugh, or smear his feces on the walls. He would make high-pitched noises when Robyn handed him the telephone and told him his dad was on the other end. He could say "goodbye," "hello," "thanks," "water," "hungry," "candy." He could repeat the phrases "I love you" and "Hi, Dad" and "Wow." A cadre of therapists had worked with him over the years, tried to teach him skills like brushing his teeth and buttoning a shirt, how to chew quietly. Some of them had quit because he bit them.

He ignored other children, mostly. He'd pick up an object—say, a string of thread—and let it drop, over and over, to see how it behaved on its way to the floor. Sometimes he would spin madly in a circle.

He had so much energy it was exhausting, and he required constant supervision. As he got older, he would sit in the backseat on his way to school with Angela and would bite her on the arm or pull her hair as she screamed. He was fearless and reckless because he didn't have a concept of danger. There was just a connection missing somewhere. That was the easiest way to describe it.

He couldn't carry on a conversation, but he could listen and understand. He could follow directions: Pick this up, please, Christopher. Take it over there and come back. He responded to sign language, because it was visual. He could point to a flash card to indicate what he wanted to eat. He was in an eighth-grade class with ten other autistic kids, some who didn't speak or even act like they knew the teacher was there. The teacher once had a student who spoke only by reciting an infomercial: "If you didn't buy it here, you paid too much!"

In the callous terms of the DSM-IV—the *Diagnostic and Statistical Manual of Mental Disorders*—Christopher displayed "markedly abnormal nonverbal communication." To his father he was shy and curious, and sometimes so quiet and so temperate that Walt could imagine his son was perfectly normal.

The first rescue helicopter appeared just before nightfall, then the boats in the distance, engines breathing on the water. Walt called over to Christopher, who had drifted maybe ten feet away. He told him that he was a good boy and a great swimmer. He pointed his finger to the blinking helicopter high in the sky near shore, and said, "Blue lights. Blue lights. Blue lights coming to get us." Walt felt like he understood.

Christopher certainly understood what it meant to be in the water. Walt pictured him floating on his back at the YMCA in Oviedo, where he'd learned to swim. Walt had spent hours there teaching him to float, Christopher with his green goggles strapped across his face, laughing, looking up at the ceiling painted to look like a sky.

At the Y, Christopher was a regular boy. The lifeguards knew him by name, let him go into the utility closet and pick out a foam ring to play with in the water, the same green one every time. He always walked the tiled stoop around the pool, feeling the water on the tops of his feet. Then he'd jump in. Walt would show him how to fill his stomach with air so he could float, then pull him along by his shoulders, walking him around the left lane of the pool.

Out at sea, in the fading light, Christopher rose and dipped from Walt's line of sight. Walt tried to talk to his son to keep him calm, reciting his favorite lines from his favorite movies. Christopher loved to sit right in front of the small television in his room and watch Disney videos all day. Sometimes he would put his eyeball as close to the screen as he could get it without touching. His all-time favorite scene was Buzz Lightyear in *Toy Story*, flying into space, saying his trademark phrase: "To infinity ... and beyond!"

"To infinity!" Walt yelled to Christopher over the waves. He waited for Christopher to respond.

"To infinity, Christopher!"

"... and beyond!" lightly from atop the wave, as Christopher was lifted back into view. It didn't sound like that when Christopher said it, though. It always sounded like "infin' a beyon'..." And he'd always send his fist into the air. That little fist pump—Walt did it in the water then, too, even though he was trying to conserve energy.

After a while the first helicopter left and another took its place, its blue light flickering over the open water. Looking out toward the black sky, Walt began to wave his arms, certain now that no one could hear him. Christopher pounded his fist against the waves. A group of jellyfish interrupted them, swimming into Walt's and Christopher's legs, clutching onto them and burning like strands of electric hair. Christopher shrieked. Then Walt was lifted up at the same time Christopher was lowered. When the tide evened, Christopher was even farther away, thirty or forty feet. Walt tried to swim toward him, flapping his arms as hard as he could. Then a wave lifted Christopher, and Walt was caught on the other side. When the wave broke, Christopher was no longer there.

Only his breath in the darkness, a silence as everything settled in. For half an hour, Walt had yelled, begging for Christopher to answer. He had given up conserving energy, had been swimming as hard as he could to try and find his son. "Who's my best boy?" Nothing. "Christopher, who's my buddy?" Only the fish beneath him, brushing against his back and legs.

"Christopher?!"

Walt spun in every direction, trying to spot the small white face and the dark-brown hair.

But he was gone.

Walt wiped his eyes, took a breath. He's gone. It was a thought as dark and fathomless as the ocean itself. At that moment, he couldn't see it any other way—Christopher was dead. So Walt stopped yelling and shivered as a trail of bright green phosphorescence floated past him. He stared at it, amazed by its arrival, the only color on the sea, passing behind him like lights beneath the water. He told himself it was probably peaceful, told himself that Christopher just got tired and finally let go. Just slipped away under the sea.

But Walt's mind wouldn't fully accept that. Christopher was a terrific swimmer. He had nine lives, Walt liked to say. Maybe he was merely playing a game. Maybe he was floating, just beyond where Walt could see. Maybe he just wanted to be alone for a while, like he sometimes did.

Christopher had wandered off so many times, Walt learned to expect he would always be okay. "Eloped" is the word used to describe the way an autistic person sometimes wanders off—is there one second, then vanishes.

Christopher had eloped at the mall, at the hardware store, from Walt's parents' house, and after a search they would often find him playing in water. At first it was the lake in their old neighborhood, then the retention pond at the bottom of the street—the police had sent a helicopter to search for him. Then it was the neighbors' pool: floating on his back, naked. The neighbors called the cops, who came and pulled Christopher out and saw the silver chain bracelet on his left wrist with his identification and phone number.

Once when Christopher wandered off, the police searched for him again, and half an hour later, he turned up in the fountain at the Oviedo mall. Christopher had walked across a busy intersection, crossed through six lanes of traffic, had navigated the winding road back to the parking lot at night. He had taken his clothes off and was splashing beneath the falling water in his underwear, his feet brushing the pennies people had tossed in to make a wish.

After each of these episodes, Robyn would fume at Walt. She no longer trusted him. She and Ed held their breath whenever Christopher was with Walt. When Christopher was with Robyn and Ed, they never let him outside without maintaining physical contact. But Walt wanted Christopher to experience the world like a regular boy, wanted him to walk the stadium stands without holding his hand and feel the beach sand and breathe the air, wanted him to make choices.

Walt couldn't even bear to call him autistic, to label him that way, and his voice always cracked when he talked about his "little buddy." He took the good days, swimming together at the Y, sitting together in the front pew of church, eating at McDonald's without incident, and weighed all of that against the tantrums, the outbursts, the moments in which his son would lunge at him, out of the blue, and sink his teeth into his arm. That's when Walt would sob. He'd lament having to shout at Christopher, asking him why he'd attack his own father. For every good day there was always some kind of reminder of the bad.

But now he was gone. They shouldn't have come out to the beach, he told himself. He should've rented a movie and spent the day at home. He could never face his own family. He wouldn't know what to say to his mother and father, to his daughter, to the coast guard, to Robyn and Ed. The guilt, too, the realization that he had been responsible for his son's death.

He decided that he should take his own life. It would be easier. Bawling, his tears mixing with the salt water on his face, he took a deep breath, exhaled, and slipped like he imagined Christopher did beneath the surface.

But there was Angela. He had almost forgotten about her. He kicked his legs and came up for air, expelling a mouthful of water. She needed a father too.

The ocean at dawn is a wonderful dream. He thought the night might last forever and now considers the morning itself a sign, too. The birds dive to the surface, stretching out their patternless wings as if to yawn. A seagull, white and with crystal eyes, lands right next to Walt. It looks directly at him, opens its orange beak like it's trying to get him to talk. Walt can suddenly see the life of everything, the fish swimming on the surface, the actual blue of the water. His neck aches like hell. His hands and wrists are swollen stiff. His lips are chapped and bleeding. He's numb and warm. His tongue is swollen, his eyes dry.

He thinks he's floated much farther out, but he really has no point of reference. No one even knows the exact direction in which he and Christopher floated. He has survived the night, he realizes, for nothing. He stares forward, shielding his face from the sun with his arm, and then looks back down to the water, thinking of Christopher.

At 7:15 a.m., on the deck of a recreational fishing boat called the Open Range, Shawn McMichael looks out and sees a reflection in the water. Just turns his head, while the five other men on the deck are staring forward toward the horizon. A glitter, something sparkling, something that maybe on a thousand other days would never catch his eye. It could be anything, maybe one of the cruise-ship balloons that frequently float off the deck and then settle and shimmer on the surface. Shawn looks again and sees movement. Stanley Scott, the boat's owner, realizes it's a man. Floating. By himself, waving his arms. The boat slows, turns hard, comes within fifty feet of him.

"How did you get here?" Stanley shouts. "Where's your boat?"

The man is delirious, won't stop yelling—they can't get a word in. He asks about someone named Christopher. The men ease up to him, extend a boat pole out on the left side so he can grab onto it, and walk him around to the platform on the back end, by the engines. It takes two guys to haul him in. Dripping water, swollen, pale, shivering, jellyfish stings like long red scars on his legs. The silver pendant dangling below his chin—that's what Shawn had seen reflecting.

"I lost him!" They sit him on a beanbag in the back of the boat. "I lost him!" He repeats that phrase until they can get him to stop shouting and ask what he's talking about. "Christopher, Christopher...have you seen him? Oh, my God, have you seen him?" The men drape a windbreaker over his shoulders, hand him a bottle of water. He drinks six, one after the other. "He's a great swimmer. He's a great swimmer.... Oh, God, he's gone."

He has an amazing, preposterous story, all right. He's floated nine miles northeast into the ocean from Ponce Inlet. The men don't say a word. They're in awe. They get the coast guard on the radio and tell them they've found a man named Walter Marino, and his autistic son is still missing.

Walt shivers and sniffles in the boat. He calls his younger sister, Linda, and tells her that he's alive. The night before, Linda had not been able to sleep, knowing her brother and nephew were missing. She stayed up with her elderly mother and father, calling the pastor at the church and asking him what to do. "We're going to pray for a miracle," he had told her. Robyn and Ed stayed up too, in fear for Christopher's life, Robyn convulsing, so sick that Ed almost called 911. Angela had gone to sleep thinking about how her dad had once told her he wanted his ashes scattered, and that she couldn't remember where.

Walt tells Linda now that Christopher is still missing, that he's been in the water thirteen hours.

"My God, that's a long time," she says.

He calls Robyn, too, gritting his teeth. "Tell Angela I'm alive," he says.

His voice is weak, raspy. She can barely tell it's him. "Walt?" she shouts.

"We've lost Christopher," he says.

"What? *What?* How? *Where is he?*" She's hysterical, asking about her son. She's talking so fast, asking so many questions that he doesn't want to answer, so he hangs up.

An orange-and-white coast guard boat pulls up next to the Open Range at 9 a.m. For an hour and a half, Walt has been sitting on the beanbag, moaning. A door opens on the side of the boat, and two men pull Walt inside. He waves goodbye to the guys on the Open Range, who stand in stupefaction.

The ship's captain asks Walt if he wants to be taken to the hospital or stay on the boat as they go search for Christopher. "Let's go," Walt says. But he chooses to sit below in the cabin, because he doesn't want to be there when someone spots Christopher floating on his stomach, bloated, dead—he doesn't want to be the one.

So he's escorted down a flight of stairs to a room filled with life jackets and flare guns. An officer in charge of keeping an eye on Walt sits opposite on a bench and says only, "You look like you regret something. Do you regret something?" Walt just shakes his head in his hands—he doesn't want to talk.

All the way from Clearwater, out of the skies above northeastern Florida, the Jayhawk helicopter rides a hundred feet above the water. It's got a bright orange tail and white-striped body, like the fish from *Finding Nemo*. At three hundred feet the trained men aboard can see gulls hitting the surface, but they're flying even lower this morning, as low as they can go, because they're looking for a twelve-year-old boy.

The helicopter goes into a right-hand orbit, circling once, then again, initially lowering to fifty feet. The flight mechanic had seen the dark-brown hair and white face in the tide line, had seen a body floating there, bobbing. Tom Emerick, a rescue swimmer, is already wearing a shorty wetsuit and puts on a black mask with a snorkel.

Lowered twenty feet down by a thick hoist cable, Emerick hits the water feet first. He swims toward Christopher, the boy's small pale eyes staring at him, unblinking. Emerick signals for the helicopter to send the basket down. It's 9:15 a.m., three miles from where his father had been discovered two hours earlier.

"Hi, how you doing, my name is Tom," Emerick says.

Christopher says nothing, barely makes a move—just watches as Emerick pulls him into the stainless-steel basket. "Don't climb out of it, okay, buddy?" he shouts. It's deafening beneath the whir. The rotor wash is coming down so hard that it stings them, nearly suffocates them.

Christopher rides up in the basket silently, looking down at Emerick still in the water, studying him like a piece of string.

In the stomach of the helicopter, Emerick wraps a wool blanket over Christopher's shoulders, checks his breathing, his pulse, has him track his index finger with his eyes. He asks him if he wants something to drink, and when Christopher doesn't answer, he makes a motion with his hands to emulate taking a sip from a cup, and Christopher nods. Sitting on a bench in the helicopter, he shivers, freckles beneath the dark hair. His skin is warm; he's slightly hypothermic. But other than the jellyfish stings, there doesn't appear to be anything the matter with him.

Robyn and Ed take Christopher home on September 8, after he stays one night at Halifax hospital in Daytona. He can barely walk, so they carry him back and forth from his bed to the bathroom. He can't put any weight on his legs because of the jellyfish stings. He's dehydrated. He eats carrot sticks, bananas, pieces of chicken. They let him watch Disney movies, tuck him under his Tigger and Pooh bed sheets. Robyn goes in and sits beside him, asks him softly what he saw out there in the ocean, what it was like. Two days, and she asks him this several times, and finally he tells her: "It was dark." A whole sentence.

Robyn and Ed have a beautiful home on a quiet street with a pool out back that Christopher can play in. The property is bolted down so tight, Christopher can never elope. The front and back doors have key locks on the inside as well as the outside. The garage is locked. There are locks on all the sliding doors. The house has an alarm system, with a chime function.

When Robyn was living alone with Angela and Christopher, he was nearly impossible to care for, and as a single mother she felt she had no other choice but to put him in a place where other people could take care of him twenty-four hours a day. He got kicked out of day care because he bit other children. They had to put a harness on the bus for him, a five-point seat belt, because without it he'd run up and down the aisles, hitting students and even the driver. Christopher split his weekends between Robyn and Walt and stayed at the group home on weekdays.

When Robyn and Ed first saw Walt after the incident, it was on the dock, as he stepped off the coast guard boat; he was sunburned and babbling like a child. They didn't have the energy to confront him, to yell at him, to tell him they had been right. They were just happy that Christopher was alive.

Three weeks after he comes home from the hospital, Christopher is named grand marshal of the parade at Disney World. Robyn and Ed make sure to keep a sharp eye on him the whole time and to hold his hand. He gets a Florida Safety Hero award. He gets to stand on the bridge of a coast guard cutter and pretend to drive.

In January, Walt moves to Vancouver, Washington, just across the bridge from Portland. He takes a job contracting with the FDIC, closing a bank, for good money, and thus has to live so far away. He flies back to Florida on Friday evenings every two weeks just so he can spend a day and a half with Christopher and Angela before getting up at 4 a.m. on Mondays and flying back. When he drops Angela off at Robyn and Ed's house, they do not wave at him as he leaves.

He lives in a hotel room, a suite with comfortable furniture and a nice bed, big wooden cabinets where he can store his things. He goes to the bank in the morning, watches cable in the hotel after work, and lounges around in his sweatpants and gray Columbia fleece pullover. He shares a white Pontiac Vibe hatchback with one of his co-workers. He's a tall guy, forty-six years old, a little pudgy, with high blood pressure.

In March, Walt goes to Florida and takes Christopher back out to the beach at Ponce Inlet. They sit up in the front seat of the Celica listening to an audiotape of *The Aristocats.* Christopher eats a bag of Doritos Cool Ranch chips and, later, two McDonald's double cheeseburgers, layer by layer. "Aaah, eeehh, uhhhhh!" he shouts, off and on. They drive by the mall where he was found in the fountain with the pennies. "Wow, dude!" Walt says, looking into the empty bag. He leans in and puts his face right up to Christopher's, almost touching his nose, and says, "You're my best buddy." Christopher giggles and then stares at the passing cars.

Christopher walks on the beach and looks around, then goes into a bathroom to put on his swim trunks. He dips his feet into the water, recoils upon discovering how cold it is. The waves press into the rocks, the jetty long and uneven out to the ocean. Christopher lies on his stomach in the sand, laughing.

But when Walt takes him back to the group home at around 9:30 that night, Christopher, who had been silent and mostly calm the entire day, looks at his father, then throws his cup of McDonald's water at the car window. When Walt gets out of the car in front of the group home, Christopher runs into the empty street and sits on the concrete of the cul-de-sac, beneath the streetlight. He looks lost and frightened in the glow. He starts hitting his head with his fists and shouting at the top of his lungs.

"Please, buddy, please," Walt begs.

Walt puts his hands under Christopher's arms and tries to stand him up. Christopher won't budge. Walt's voice quivers, "I know you don't want me to leave, man, but I have to."

He manages to stand Christopher upright and drag him about twenty feet toward the door of the home, and then Christopher jumps at him, sinks his teeth into Walt's arm, so Walt lets go and falls halfway to the ground. It had been so easy to forget all day.

Walt cries out in pain.

"Why, Christopher, why?"

Tears are running down his face, with nothing but the back of his bitten arm to wipe them away.

Christopher just stands there.

Walt has tried to imagine what that night was like for Christopher. He has imagined it repeatedly, in his sleep, at his work, in his rented hotel suite with the curtains drawn, the empty plastic soup containers on the counter. He has imagined Christopher giggling and splashing, the fish touching his back and arms; Christopher staring in awe at the dolphin snouts and falling stars, soothed by the foam tops of the waves; has imagined the whole night was like this one big adventure, the biggest adventure Christopher will ever have in his life, floating on his back as the water warmed his ears, in wonder as the sounds changed beneath the surface; has imagined that those sounds captivated his son's imagination, and that since Christopher loves to float and swim more than anything, perhaps he even had fun. And the phosphorescence, the most colorful thing, he hopes it passed his son in a trail on the top of the water, long and thin, sparkling there like something hopeful; prays that Christopher got to see it. He has to believe he did. He can just picture Christopher sticking his hand in the filmy substance, holding it up to the moonlight, slick and shiny and Disney green. In fact, he cannot bring himself to imagine anything else. Walt aches for the day, a day that will probably never come, when he'll be able to actually talk to Christopher, and ask him about what he saw and what he felt and what he was thinking, how he survived.

But really, all he can do is wonder.

AUTHOR'S AFTERWORDS...

I spent forever trying to come up with the first sentence of Lost in the Waves. Or at least it felt like forever—the better part of two days, at least. In a Word document on my computer, I had written an entire page of sentences, two spaces between them. And all those sentences, each one a possibility, eventually gave way to the final sentence, the one that worked, the one that sang: "The ocean at night is a terrible dream." If memory serves I woke up one morning and those words spoke to me in a half-sleep haze. This sentence is often a talking point when people ask me about the story. Of course, it's a long story, with a first act, a denouement, and a second act, a story filled with what I would describe as the elements of short fiction: foreshadowing, metaphor, and tension throughout. And the story is way more important, as a whole, than any one damn sentence. But I worked hard for that sentence. It didn't exactly just happen—though there's admittedly some magic involved.

Critiquing my process, I can often spend a lot of time on a single sentence or a paragraph, or any one part of the story. So this wasn't unusual. I have been known to obsess. I'm not promoting my way as the right way to do this, nor am I always convinced that the very first sentence is by far the most important part of the story. Though, for any story I'm writing, I have to get the first sentence before I can write anything else that follows. No matter if I have two days or a week to write the entire story (for Lost in the Waves it was the latter), I have to be able to see the sentence, and have the realization that it's right. Then, I have to re-read that sentence several times in order to be able to write the second sentence. And then I have to read the first, and the second, together, and only then can I write the third. Repeating this process the whole way through is tedious. I end up reading and re-reading and re-reading. But that's just the way I write.

I wanted the first section of this story to be about the ocean. I wanted to put the reader in the water immediately, with Walt, in the wake of one of the story's most dramatic moments, after he pushed Christopher away. Wanted the reader to be able to taste the ocean, feel it and smell it, as if they, too, had been treading for hours. I wanted to establish that it was going to be difficult for anyone to stop reading the story. In that way, the beginning really is the most important part, though I am fond of this piece's ending, and other parts throughout.

The ocean is something, I think, that nearly every great writer has tried to wrap his arms around. It was certainly one of the reasons I was drawn to this story in the first place. In Lost in the Waves, the ocean is not only vast, not only impossible to fathom, it is equal parts sinister and hopeful, and turned out to be an actual character.

Before I began, I re-read Stephen Crane's short story "The Open Boat," which takes place in a small boat, in the middle of the ocean, in the midst of a desperate predicament; I think it's the most captivating thing ever written about the sea, and the first sentence of that story, the mood it sets and the way it shapes what's to come, had a huge influence on me: "None of them knew the color of the sky." Amazing first sentence. And his story just roars along from there.

I read some other stuff, too. I re-skimmed *Moby Dick* and read *The Story of a Shipwrecked Sailor*. My goal was to write something completely new about the ocean. One of the reasons I love to write is I take pride in the labor of creating something, trying to write something that's never been written before, experimenting with words. Even though I'm writing on a computer, this can feel like scraping into a piece of stone.

As a reader, I was weaned on fiction; I have an expectation—a kind of appetite—to read the beginning of a story and expect it to be creative, have it immediately compel me to continue. This is also how I want to present my own work. I write for me. Every time out. As a writer, my goal is to be in complete control of where I'm taking you (the phrase "Let the story tell itself" has always seemed like bullshit to me).

I won't technically quit reading after the first sentence of anyone's story. I can appreciate different kinds of writing, different styles, and style can depend on the publication, of course. But, honestly, a writer has about two or three paragraphs to hook me. My favorite stories have first sentences and first paragraphs that I can remember almost verbatim, that I can recite.

I wanted readers, and other writers, to remember this first sentence.

Wil S. Hylton

Wil S. Hylton is a contributing writer at the *New York Times Magazine*. Over the years, his work has appeared in *Harper's, Esquire, GQ* and *Rolling Stone*, and has been collected in *Best Political Writing, Best Music Writing*, and *Best Business Stories*. He teaches creative nonfiction in the graduate writing program at Johns Hopkins University, and is a recipient of the John Bartlow Martin Award for public interest reporting, granted by the Medill School of Journalism. In the line of duty, Hylton has scaled the world's tallest active volcano, crawled inside a nuclear reactor, cycled a thousand miles across rural Cuba, and plumbed the depths of the U.S. prison system to examine the state of inmate healthcare. He is completing a book about the lasting legacy of grief among families of the disappeared.

The Unspeakable Choice

She had to lie. She stood in the window of the little white house and looked outside at her boys on the lawn.

It was warm for September, and they seemed happy, throwing a baseball in the afternoon light under a huge Nebraska sky. The hill behind them sloped away to the Missouri River, and beyond it the plains of Iowa stretched toward the eastern horizon, with rocky bluffs at the far edge like sentinels against the dawn. Her own dawn was coming. All she had to do was lie.

Lavennia Coover took a breath and stepped outside. The sun streamed over her shoulders as she walked toward the boys, casting shadows in their direction. "Guys," she called out. It had to sound casual. "Let's go for a ride." For a moment, the words seemed to hang in the air, and she wondered if they already knew, but then they were ambling toward the pickup, oblivious to what was coming.

Yes, she thought. *It's happening.*

She closed them into the backseat and steered down the long driveway through acres of corn, the boys babbling mindlessly about sports and whatever—Lavennia paid no attention. She felt numb and jittery all at once, every fiber in her body strained in anticipation of what might come, some lapse in the environment, some change in the atmosphere, some hint that the trick was up. At the base of the driveway, she turned onto the river road, heading toward town. Time was everything, and she played for more.

"You guys hungry?" she asked, pulling into a McDonald's drive-thru. They called out their orders, and she smiled. *Today*, she thought, *they can have anything they want—just keep them distracted.* She ordered a Big Mac and nuggets, Cokes and fries, passing the cups and bags into the backseat, and in the crinkling of wrappers and happy chatter, she slipped onto the highway, heading south toward Omaha. *Sixty miles to go.*

"Where are we going?" Colby asked suddenly.

"Just driving," she said. She braced herself, but they let it pass, rummaging through their bags of food, and she exhaled, watching the miles tick past:

five, then ten; fifteen, now twenty. Silently, she began to pray: *Please, God. Just let us get there.*

It would all depend on Skyler, of course. Everything did. He was the youngest of her three, only eleven, but he missed nothing and trusted less. Eventually, he would finish his nuggets and his fries and his Coke, and he would look up and out the window, and in that instant he would know. And then... Lavennia winced at the thought. Then, it was impossible to predict. He might leap from the truck onto the open road. He'd done worse. Or lunge into the front seat, pummeling her with his fists and feet, sinking his teeth into her arms. He'd done that before, too.

When she finally saw the exit in the distance, she angled the truck toward the ramp, glancing over her shoulder at Skyler...and there it was: the storm of recognition gathering on his face. His eyes narrowed, his fists clenched. The air seemed to withdraw around her. "You're taking me to that place!" he shouted.

"No," she said. "We're just driving."

"Yes, you are!" he screamed. "YOU LIAR!"

She looked back in the mirror again, searching his face for the little boy within, but he was gone, consumed with fear and fury. For the first time, she felt a flash of alarm. The violence was coming. She reached for her cell phone and dialed quickly. "Hello," she said, tears beginning to stream down her face. "I'm bringing my son. I need security to meet us."

In the back, Skyler slumped into his seat. He began to cry, then plead. "Mommy," he sobbed, "I'll be good. I promise, I'll be nice. I'll do whatever you want..."

She felt lost. She felt like turning around. She felt like holding him close, and crying together, and going home. She felt like dying. But she said nothing, and the truck fell silent. Up ahead she could see the hospital.

She was almost there. He was almost gone.

It has never been easier to abandon a child. Over the past ten years, every American state has been working to make the process simpler. Simpler, that is, to haul a newborn baby into a police station, a hospital, or even a firehouse, and just walk away—without signing anything, or telling anyone your name, without providing any medical records or proof of custody, or even a reason why. For the first 200 years of U.S. history, to do such a thing was regarded as an abomination and a crime, punishable under a host of charges, from reckless endangerment to child abuse. Today, in all fifty states, it is every parent's right, enshrined in law.

In theory these new laws, commonly known as safe havens are written to *protect* newborns, and to prevent so-called Dumpster babies—by giving desperate parents a way out. The first safe haven was passed in Texas in 1999, after thirteen abandoned infants were discovered in a ten-month period, and as other states have followed suit, this Dumpster-baby scenario has become a rallying cry for the safe-haven movement: Faced with the specter of babies left in alleys, gullies, and backyards, few state legislators are willing to drag their heels while they demand proof that such laws actually work. Yet after ten years, it is increasingly clear that "safe havens" are anything but.

For one thing, the promise of anonymity is a double-edged sword. While it may draw some parents from the brink of disaster, it can also create disasters of its own. Under the shield of a safe haven, for example, a frustrated young father, overwhelmed by his new responsibilities, can easily deliver his infant to a remote police station and be rid of the burden in a stroke—knowing that nobody can stop him or ask him any questions, that there is no way of tracking him down, and that the child's mother, who may not even be aware of his decision, will almost certainly never find her baby. For that matter, a jealous boyfriend might do the same thing with a child not his own; under the protective banner of safe havens, there is no way to verify that an adult who leaves a child is related in any way.

Just as troubling is the question of who actually uses the laws. Many experts are concerned that the parents most in need of the safe haven laws are the least likely to use them. As Michelle Oberman, an expert on infanticide at Santa Clara law school, points out, parents who kill newborn children tend to fit a very narrow demographic. "They are, for the most part, young girls under the age of eighteen," she says. "They are terrified by the thought of having a baby. They conceal the pregnancy from friends and family. They have little to no prenatal care. And in the vast majority of cases, the baby is delivered in the bathroom, into a toilet. So their state of mind speaks for itself: the panic, the confusion, the exhaustion, the pain."

According to Margaret Spinelli, a psychiatrist at Columbia University and author of *Infanticide*, that state of mind has a clinical name: psychosis. "The idea of pregnancy is so overwhelming to these women that they mount a kind of dissociative defense," she says. "When they deliver the baby, there is a break with reality. Many of them become psychotic."

Given this grim reality, the basic premise of safe havens—that these traumatized young women, after hiding their pregnancies for nine months, rejecting all medical attention, and birthing in shame, will, in the midst of a psychotic episode, spontaneously achieve a moment of clarity and march into a police station to expose their darkest secret to a complete stranger, and surrender the child they have worked so hard to conceal—begs credulity.

Exactly who does use the safe-haven laws is more difficult to discern. Most states make no effort to study the cases or compile any data, and the anonymous nature of the process makes outside research nearly impossible. But certain evidence does lend insight. Over the past decade, for example, many of the parents who have used safe havens, and spoken publicly about it, defend the laws not as a way to protect infants from harm, but as an alternative to the adoption process, which can be slow and bureaucratic. For these parents, then, the real value of safe havens is not to save children's lives but parents' time.

Despite these concerns, the drumbeat for states to pass a safe-haven law has only grown louder with time, and last summer, after years of wrestling with the issue, Nebraska became the final state to enact one. Yet as that bill made its way through the legislature, something odd happened: When senators couldn't agree on an age limit for the law (in other states, it applies to children from three days to one year old), the Nebraska legislators decided on...no age limit at all.

In a stroke, the law was transformed: from the last passenger on the safe-haven bandwagon, to a pioneer into uncharted territory. For the first time in American history, it was not only legal to relinquish a baby; in Nebraska it was now okay to abandon any child of any age, and for any reason at any time—with the full protection of the law.

Child abandonment was no longer a crime.

"Another safe haven!" the registration nurse shouted, and Lavennia wanted to disappear. She stood at the counter, with Skyler and Colby sulking beside her and security guards lingering nearby. In the back, nurses and medical staff scurried around, gathering paperwork. "Safe haven," they muttered to one another, shooting disapproving glances in her direction.

She had never felt so alone.

For years she struggled to avoid this day. The sickness struck when Skyler was only seven—epic tantrums, earth-shattering fits. At the slightest provocation, the gentlest rebuff, he would break into a rage, hysterical, red-faced and feverish, thrashing around the room and destroying things. Most of his fury was directed at her. He would launch himself in her direction, biting her arms and legs and face, scratching and kicking and punching all at once, a torrent of violent motion. At first, she wondered if it was all an act, a cry for attention. She would search his eyes for some hint of recognition, but all she found was anger. "It's like his soul is gone," she told her mom. In the midst of the fits, she would try to calm him, pulling him close and whispering to him beneath incessant shrieks of curdling rage. Eventually, he would crash into sleep; hours later, when he awoke, he would blink his eyes and ask what had happened. She studied his eyes again for some clue that he might be feigning innocence, but all she saw was confusion and fatigue.

It was like lightning had struck her twice. Her oldest, Natosha, had struggled with mental illness for years. Now, at eighteen, she was out of the house, but the years of turmoil consumed her childhood, turning their home into a hellish battlefield. Her father left when she was eight. By nine, Natosha was throwing fits like Skyler's. By twelve, she was refusing to attend school. By fourteen, she was staying out late, doing drugs with boys, and viciously beating her brothers. One morning she kicked Lavennia in the face. Lavennia took her to special schools; she tried therapy, group homes, anything she could find, paying thousands of dollars, but one by one, the programs sent Natosha back. There was nothing they could do. She was too far gone. By the the end of that year, she'd slipped away entirely—after one too many encounters with police, she was remanded to state custody. Over the next three years, she would pass through fourteen placements—a new home every eleven weeks, running away or being expelled each time.

Through it all, Lavennia struggled to make a normal life for Skyler and Colby. She finished college when Natosha was young, with a major in elementary education and a teaching certificate for early childhood. She had always wanted to work with disadvantaged kids, so she took a job on the Omaha reservation, teaching second grade, then kindergarten. She attended graduate school one weekend a month, earning a master's degree in 2006. And last year, she made a down payment on a new home, moving into the little white house on the hill. But just as the family was settling in, just as Natosha was graduating from state services and moving into an apartment with her friends, Skyler's illness began to peak.

The degeneration was slow but relentless. It began in second grade, the outbursts spilling from home to school—two or three days a week his teacher would call, interrupting her at work. Skyler was having a fit again. He was beyond control. No one could stop him. He was throwing chairs against the walls, hurling scissors and pencils, shrieking and knocking over desks. Lavennia would leave her class, drive twenty-five miles to Skyler's school, talk to him and calm him, wait for the episode to pass, and then drive the twenty-five miles back.

One day she found him pinned beneath a teacher on the floor behind a secretary's office. She registered a complaint and transferred him to the school where she worked; they made the drive together each morning, and his classroom was right next to hers, but nothing changed. Within a week, he was having fits again, throwing desks and books and chairs. She could hear the clamoring through the walls of her classroom. Eventually, his teacher would evacuate the other students, then come next door to get Lavennia. She would go in alone, try to calm him, and pray it wouldn't happen again. It always did.

After one of Skyler's rages, when he was asleep, Lavennia carried him to her truck and took him to a hospital emergency room. He was admitted for a psychological evaluation, then transferred into a psychiatric unit. In the structure of the hospital, with therapy and care, he seemed to improve. But her insurance covered only three days, and on the fourth Skyler was sent home. He brought a medley of new medicines—Depakote and Seroquel for bipolar disorder, Adderall for hyperactivity. He was eight years old. It was enough medication to tranquilize a horse.

Now Skyler merely slept. He slept in class, through the evenings, through the night. When he wasn't sleeping, he still raged—demolishing the house or the classroom or the car, wherever he happened to be. Lavennia waited ten days for the medicine to work, then she brought Skyler back to the hospital. This time, her insurance covered five days.

After that she enrolled him in an outpatient program for behavior modification and took three weeks off work to drive him—ninety miles each way. She spent each day in the waiting room, doing homework for her master's program or just staring into space, listening to the second hand of a wall clock and wondering how it had come to this. Each evening they drove the ninety miles home.

When the program was over, he returned to school, but there was still no change. If anything, he was more violent. She placed him in a special class for difficult kids, but he fought with the other kids and flew into rages, crashing to sleep on the classroom floor. He was, she realized, not a child but a zombie—between the drugs and the episodes, he was never just a boy. She tried alternative treatments—a Reiki master, biofeedback—but after a few sessions he refused to cooperate.

A year drained by and Skyler was nine; then another and he was ten. In the special class, his language became coarse—in the midst of a fit, he would curse at her and spit. Evenings, he took it out on Colby, who was a year older but quiet and subdued. Lavennia felt imprisoned in her own house. Her options were vanishing by the day. Her insurance had dried up. With her teaching job, she didn't qualify for Medicaid. She had no money for private care. And she was more than $10,000 in debt from the programs she had tried already. Worst of all, she had lost the upper hand with Skyler. He was just eleven, but he was five feet tall and 120 pounds. In the thrall of a rage, he could easily overpower her. When school began, he refused to go. She tried dragging him to the truck, but he fought her off—kicking, punching, spitting, biting, cursing, tearing at her face. Finally, she gave up. For three weeks, she left him at home alone. When she returned each day, she found the house demolished—food smeared on the walls and strewn on the floors, toys smashed in pieces everywhere. He would go into her bedroom and pillage her jewelry box, scattering her personal things through the house. He emptied cupboards onto the floor. He began taking the deck apart, ripping off the wooden arm rails. She came home one day and found the family cat nearly dead, limping and wheezing, covered with cuts and gashes, hair ripped out. There was a broken piece of wood beside the house, with nails hammered halfway through like a primitive club. She brought it to Skyler, but he denied that it was his. She pushed him for answers, but he answered with rage.

At night Lavennia huddled in her bedroom, whispering into the phone with her parents. One day her mother mentioned a new law she had read about in the paper: If Lavennia took Skyler back to the emergency room, now they had to take him, and keep him, and help him, and treat him. They had no choice. And the state would pay.

Lavennia found that hard to believe. She called the hospital in Omaha to see if it was true. Would they really take him? Yes, a nurse told her. And would he really get help? "Oh, definitely," the nurse said.

After that, Lavennia began to wonder: Not whether, but how. How would she get Skyler into the truck? How could she convince him to go? For weeks, he had refused to leave the house.

She would have to trick him. She would have to lie.

Now she stood at the registration desk, watching nurses scramble for admission papers. She could feel their scorn wash over her like heat—or was she only imagining that? She felt broken. Sickened. Terrified. In a few hours, she would leave the hospital and drive home with Colby through the night, leaving Skyler behind forever. Her own son, no longer hers. She wondered how she would find the strength to walk away. She wondered if he would ever forgive her. She wondered if she would forgive herself. This was what it had come to: To save her son, she had to give him up.

Within weeks of the safe haven's passage, children like Skyler began pouring into Nebraska hospitals. During the first month, fourteen kids were dropped off. In the second, the number rose to twenty-four. And in the third, November of last year, it reached thirty-six.

But not a single infant was among them.

Whatever else one thought of safe-haven laws, this was clearly something else: The kids in Nebraska were not unwanted; they were sick—mostly teens and preteens, in various stages of distress. There was the eleven-year-old boy who had violently attacked his grandfather. The twelve-year-old who sexually assaulted girls. The seventeen-year-old, in and out of psychiatric wards since the age of six. The thirteen-year-old driven to the hospital by his mother, aunt and grandmother—a family decision, endured together. They came from all over Nebraska but also beyond. They came from Michigan, Indiana, Georgia, Florida, Arizona, California. And the one thing they had in common was a history of mental illness. According to a report by the state's Department of Health and Human Services, out of the first thirty children relinquished in Nebraska, all but three had a history of psychiatric problems. Some, like Skyler, were so far gone that they were transferred into lockdown units immediately, remaining there for weeks, even months to come.

They appeared at the hospitals like ghosts emerging from some hidden world, a place that most of us never see, where hope has died and parents give up, where children disappear into themselves. Some struggled and fought on the way in. Others cried and begged in desperation. Still others showed no reaction at all, too tired, too confused, too sick to understand. In the cold abstraction of political debate, one could argue the role of government endlessly, the balance between the individual and state, between parental responsibility and social assistance, but here was something that seemed to rise above all that: Here were children. Sick children. Sad and lost and damaged children, whose parents—rightly or wrongly, it made no difference to a nine-year-old girl—had lost hope and given up. If there was ever a cause to help anyone, if there was ever a moment for public intervention, if there was ever a time to help anyone, if there was any social contract at all, weren't these children, tormented by demons, forsaken by parents, weren't these eight-year-olds and eleven-year-olds, six-year-olds and twelve-year-olds, the founding imperative of society itself?

In Nebraska the question was long begging for an answer. A year earlier, the legislature had convened a task force to assess mental healthcare for kids, and the report came back blistering: In eighty-six of the state's ninety-three counties, facilities were either understaffed or nonexistent. Children spent months on "long waiting lists" for care. Communication between agencies that was "uncoordinated," and the road to treatment that was so convoluted that it was nearly impossible for parents "to understand myriad eligibility requirements, assessment processes, service models, funding requirements, service coordination structures, and data collection mandates." Worst of all, there was nobody keeping track—no oversight agency or internal accountability. "It is impossible," the report concluded, "to determine systematically whether the expenditures of public funds have resulted in a benefit to the state and its citizens."

Not that Nebraska was unique. The influx of kids from so far away—from the north and south, from both coasts—was a reminder that children's mental health is deteriorating everywhere. In a society where 46 million people have no health insurance at all, and where even the best policies offer little psychiatric care, the emotional well-being of low-income children has virtually dropped off the radar. According to the most recent report from the Surgeon General, there are as many as 9 million children in America today who suffer from "serious emotional disturbances," but 70 percent won't receive any care at all. That's more than 6 million children with nowhere to turn—no therapy, no medication, no recovery, no future. For their parents, it didn't matter if the law in Nebraska was called a "safe haven" or a "broken piano." It made no difference whether this safe haven was different from other safe havens, or whether other safe-haven laws actually worked. What mattered to them, all that mattered, was that, like Lavennia Coover, they could finally bring their children to a hospital.

And this time, nobody could turn them away.

It was a frigid November morning, clear and bright, when Lavennia's bus pulled up to the state capitol in Lincoln. She stepped outside and cinched her coat, staring up at the wide limestone steps rising toward the white megalith of the capitol. She had never wanted to come to this place; she had to come.

It was eight weeks since she dropped Skyler at the hospital, and for eight weeks, he'd been getting help. For eight weeks, he'd lived in a psychiatric ward, with group sessions and personal therapy, with twenty-four-hour care and a surplus of staff. For eight weeks, she watched him stabilize and improve; for eight weeks, she called and visited, sent him clothes and cards and snacks. And for eight weeks, she listened to the director of the state's Division of Children and Family Services, a man named Todd Landry, attack everything she was doing.

The Nebraska safe haven was national news now, and the *New York Times* had come to town, and *Time*, and ABC News, and Landry found time for all of them, answering their questions and preening for their cameras, seething with hostility toward the parents who used the new law.

It was all a matter of laziness, he explained. The parents just didn't care.

Almost every day, there seemed to be a new quote from him. The morning after Lavennia dropped Skyler, he was in the Lincoln paper, discussing her case. "It's the job of the parent to be a parent," he said. "I am very concerned that people are deciding they no longer want to be a parent and are taking advantage of the law." A few days later, he was in *the New York Times*: "The appropriate response is to reach out to family. What is not appropriate is just to say, 'I'm tired of dealing with this,' and drop the child off." Soon after, he assured the Omaha paper that the only problem in Nebraska was the safe-haven law itself. "You fix that situation," he explained, "and I think all these other questions disappear."

Disappear? Lavennia thought as she read it. *You take away the help and our problems will disappear?*

As the days went by, with each new quote and condemnation from Landry, Lavennia became more upset, then angry, then determined. This was the director of Family Services? This was the man whose $130,000 salary she paid with her taxes? She wrote a letter to the newspapers explaining her decision, and when a state senator, Amanda McGill, called to offer support, Lavennia agreed to visit the capitol and tell her story to McGill's committee. If Landry was going to be on the offensive, she figured, someone had to fight back.

But now, as she found a seat in the hearing room, Lavennia began to have second thoughts. All around her, senators and reporters swarmed, setting up laptop computers and cameras and lights, shaking hands and slapping backs. She felt removed from it all, an outsider, just a girl from the plains with a sick kid and a sad story.

One of the senators made her especially nervous. Nobody in Nebraska opposed the new law more than Ernie Chambers. He had blocked its passage for nearly a decade, squelching versions in 2002, 2004, 2006, and 2007. He finally relented in 2008, allowing the safe haven to pass, but now that it was getting national attention, with children flooding state hospitals, Chambers felt more than a little vindicated. "I never supported this," he reminded everyone. "I'm the one who tried to stop it."

At seventy-one, Chambers was both an icon and a legend in Nebraska. He'd been in the legislature more than half his life, but he retained the attitude and appearance of an outsider: Where other senators wore suits and ties to work, Chambers arrived each day in faded jeans and a T-shirt; while others accepted the $12,000 salary as symbolic, Chambers subsisted on it for thirty-eight years, saying with a shrug, "My needs are meager." With his casual clothes and informal manner, he could appear docile at first glance, and the illusion was only reinforced by his office, which looked less like a five-room senatorial suite than the ruins of a ransacked law library: Sheaves of paper were strewn in every direction and nearly all the floor space was crammed with detritus—stacks of cardboard boxes six feet high, typewriters buried under piles of clothing, paper plates and coffee mugs, and a white miniature poodle, Nicole, meandering among it all, disappearing through tunnels in the cardboard jungle. Yet beneath the surface, Chambers was lit with a ferocious energy. He had first come to prominence during the civil rights movement, rousing customers at an Omaha barbershop with polemics against the white oppressor, and condemning any talk of nonviolent resistance. In the 1967 film *A Time for Burning*, he can be seen excoriating a white preacher with characteristic zeal: "We've studied your history. You did not take over this country by singing 'We Shall Overcome.' You're treaty breakers, you're liars, you're thieves. You've raped entire continents and races of people. Your religion means nothing. And here's what I'll say: I wish you would follow Jesus like we have followed him, because if you did, then we'd be in charge tomorrow." In the forty years since, Chambers had not mellowed much, suing to remove the state legislature's chaplain in 1980, and in 2007 going even farther, suing God himself in state court for all the calamities of the world. As a senator, he was known for fiery speeches and merciless inquisitions—interrupting witnesses, challenging their answers, demanding the truth, and threatening charges of contempt. Today, his witness would be Lavennia Coover—defending a law that Chambers despised.

As Lavennia waited for her turn to speak, Chambers reiterated his case against the safe haven. "What difference does it make if the law is three hours, three days, or like now, no age limit at all?" he asked. "I don't believe a person on this panel can know what it means to feel abandoned. My parents never abandoned me, but I was certainly abandoned when I went to school. When I was in that white teacher's classroom, she read *Little Black Sambo*, and I was the only black child there. *Little Black Sambo* made me. That white teacher made me. I felt abandoned. I didn't even tell my parents. I couldn't fight back. So when I read about these children—these children get treated like Ping-Pong balls! Then they get old enough and they get a gun, and suddenly everybody's saying, 'Why? Why? Why?' "

As Chambers spoke, Lavennia felt her face grow hot. The rest of the room seemed to blur, then disappear; it was like Chambers was speaking directly to her, reprimanding her, accusing her. In the midst of it, a page knelt beside her in the aisle and whispered, "You'll be next," but the voice sounded far away to Lavennia; she heard her name crackle through a loudspeaker and she found herself standing, dazed, floating toward the witness stand and sinking into a cushioned seat, blinded by the haze of television lights and the laser beam of Ernie Chambers' glare.

She put her hands in her lap, then on the table, then back in her lap, fumbling through her purse for the statement she had prepared, unfolding it and leaning into the microphone. "My name is Lavennia Coover," she began, as flashes erupted around her. "My son Skyler was admitted to Immanuel hospital on September 24 through the safe-haven law." As she spoke, she felt numb, as though she were listening from another room, listening to herself and to her own story, the most intimate and humiliating details of her own life ricocheting off the stone walls. "While I was at the hospital," she said, "I tried to let all the staff know why I was bringing my son. I told them I was unable to give him the help that he needed. I stayed with my son, even though the hospital staff kept telling me that I could leave." She was crying now, but she kept on. "Around 11:45 that night, I gave Skyler a kiss and a hug, and I told him that I loved him, and I went home." Her voice cracked and she stopped for a moment, then she straightened herself in her chair. "Many families and myself have received harsh criticism from Todd Landry. Landry states that we are taking advantage of the law. According to the court documents I received, I am being charged with neglect, due to the fact that I dropped off my child at Immanuel hospital. I am being prosecuted for invoking the law."

When she finished, she looked up again and found Ernie Chambers' eyes. There was a long silence as he studied her face. "I have a question," he said finally. "Has anybody from the state told you what the plan of treatment for your son will be?"

"Right now, he's still in the hospital," she said. "They are having a difficult time finding the proper level of treatment."

"Do they tell you that you're going to be removed from your child's life?"

"Yes," she said. "And I have a daughter who went through the proper process to get help, and all I got was criticism, as I'm getting now. I had a judge tell me I was a worthless parent."

Chambers' eyes darkened.

"Did the judge say that in court?" he asked.

"He did."

"How long ago?"

"Probably four years."

"If you can get a copy of that transcript, I wish you would share it with me."

Lavennia nodded. "I will," she said.

Chambers fell silent again. He looked like he wanted to say more but wasn't sure what. Before he could find the words, the chairman of the committee dismissed Lavennia. She stood and stepped from the witness stand and walking down the aisle and out, into the hallway, with a battery of cameras flashing around her as she hurried toward the front exit.

"Ms. Coover?" a voice called from behind. She turned and saw Chambers jogging to catch up. When he did, he smiled. "I hope you will send that transcript to me," he said. There was a helpless look in his eyes, like he wanted to help but was unsure how. It didn't make sense—of all the senators in that room, this was the man most opposed to the safe-haven law, most opposed to her decision, a man who, just minutes ago, had accused her of abandoning her son and treating him like a Ping-Pong ball, yet here he was...

"You said you're being prosecuted?" he asked.

"Yes," she said. "I was just served papers."

Chambers shook his head. "The county attorney told us that nobody is being prosecuted. Can you send me those papers as well?"

"Sure," she said.

He paused, then nodded. "Thank you, Ms. Coover." Chambers turned back toward the hearing room, and Lavennia watched him disappear, then she walked slowly toward the front door, stepping outside into the midday light. She felt an unfamiliar sensation in her chest, and she realized it was hope. If Ernie Chambers had listened, if Ernie Chambers understood, if the most resolute opponent of safe havens had finally grasped that it wasn't about safe havens, not anymore; that it wasn't about newborns, or Dumpsters, or neglect, or abandonment; that it was about desperate families turning to the worst and only option they had left, their broken surrender manifest in this last unspeakable choice; if Ernie Chambers could see that now, and turn toward her, and want to help, then maybe there was a shard of hope that the rest of the senate would understand, too.

Privately, many of Nebraska's senators were considering the law for the first time. They had passed it quickly and carelessly in the spring, but now, it seemed urgent to reconsider what it meant. Now the stakes were impossible to deny: Without meaning to, or knowing they would, they had opened the floodgates to families in crisis, families with nowhere else to turn. Whatever changes they made going forward, their first priority was to make sure those families continued getting help.

"We obviously need to deal with this problem," Senator Arnie Stuthman, the author of the safe-haven law, said in early November as the children poured in. "This isn't what I intended, but these people are crying out." The chairman of the state's Health and Human Services Committee, Senator Joel Johnson, agreed. "You hear a lot of comments saying how bad a decision it was to leave the age open, but this is filling a real need." And the chairman of the state Judiciary Committee, Brad Ashford, went a step further. "It's not the law's fault," he explained. "Nebraska is in the bottom nine states for health care eligibility for kids; we're the bottom state for child-care subsidy, bottom 10 percent for school breakfast, highest rate of youth in custody. So if anything is a fiasco, that is."

Yet when the governor of Nebraska, Dave Heineman, convened an emergency session of the legislature that month, he instructed senators not to consider any of those issues. In a written proclamation, Heineman gave the legislature a narrow focus: They would convene for one week, insert an age limit, confine the law to infants only, and then close the session and head home for the winter break. Any effort to address the larger problems, or to help the families who actually used the law—any effort to acknowledge the plight of mentally ill children or provide assistance to their desperate parents—was entirely off-limits. If the experiment in Nebraska had lifted a curtain on the suffering of families with sick kids, the governor's solution—the only one he would consider—was to pull that curtain down again.

By the end of the week, the legislature had complied, caving to the governor's demand and limiting the law to infants only. Two months later, the senate reconvened for its 2009 session but moved on from safe havens to the most pressing issue in Nebraska: setting up new laptop computers—seventy sleek MacBook Airs, purchased at a cost of more than $100,000. A few of the members who had supported the safe-haven law proposed new legislation to help mentally ill children. But so far, not one of those bills has come up for a vote.

Help was not on the way.

If the short-lived safe-haven law seemed to promise one thing, it was that parents who used it could not be prosecuted for abandonment. But Lavennia Coover was prosecuted anyway. Two days after she dropped Skyler, she was indicted in Juvenile Court for neglect. How this can happen is murky at best; there is no particular nuance or clever rationale to explain how it is possible to convict someone for what is not a crime. But there it is. So it goes. This is the world Lavennia Coover inhabits.

Each morning she and Colby wake up early. Colby feeds the cats while Lavennia prepares breakfast; then they drive together to the reservation for school. She doesn't know what Skyler is doing, or even how he's doing. After nine weeks in the hospital, he moved into a foster home, last fall, but he's hard to reach and rarely calls. By early this year, she had only seen him twice: once on Thanksgiving, for a few hours at the mall, and once on Christmas, at the foster agency. In February, after four months without him, Lavennia made another impossible choice: Against every instinct in her body, every principle and conviction, she stood in court and admitted to the charges against her, admitting to something she did not think was wrong, admitted to put the issue behind her. She hopes that now she can see Skyler more often. Life is quieter without him, and maybe a little better, too. But on weekends and evenings, the emptiness sets in. She has trouble sleeping; for months, she cried herself through the night. Even now, she lies in bed, wondering what she might have done differently. What she should have done. Maybe she was too stern, or not stern enough. Maybe there was some other way, and she didn't see it. There must have been. There has to be. These are the questions she asks herself, sleepless in the little white house on the hill, overlooking the winter landscape of her life. A good mother. A loving mother. A hardworking, committed mother, fighting to build a life and a home, to raise three kids, work a full-time job. One bad break, and it crashes down. For Lavennia Coover, it was never about abandoning Skyler. It was never about wanting to walk away. Never about taking the easy way out. It was always about one thing: Getting help for her child. It's about the little spare room in the back of her house, with an old computer and a modem screeching, with pages fluttering from the printer, and Lavennia hunched over the keyboard, pounding out letters—to senators, to the governor, and to her son, a son she could find no other way to help.

She was never able to save Natosha. Fourteen placements in three years, and today they rarely speak. To save Skyler, she tried something new. To save him, she gave up more than custody; she gave up the most fundamental thing of all: her pride. Her pride as a mother, as a provider; her joy in those precious moments, however scarce, when the family was one, and it worked. Gone now, gone forever. And the irony is, if you wanted one signal of a parent's intentions, one clue of a mother whose commitment was total, it would be her willingness to sacrifice everything for her child—not only the child, but the essence of herself. It would be the mother willing to die for her children, to die inside. And Lavennia Coover is dying.

AUTHOR'S AFTERWORDS...

When the news broke, in 2008, that a new law in Nebraska allowed parents to abandon their children without any explanation or paperwork, and that a stream of parents were doing just that, dropping off their toddlers and teens into the hands of bewildered firemen and nurses, without so much as a signed release, the potential for a human-interest story seemed obvious. Less clear was what the story meant. I am a firm believer that narrative nonfiction offers both the opportunity and responsibility to do more than gawk. That is, the form should not merely provide a window on the world, but something more like a lens, helping focus the reader's attention on the details that give rise to a larger resonance. But what was the resonance of child neglect and cruelty, of parents ditching their kids in a hurry? This is what troubled me on the flight to Nebraska, as I left behind my own young family. Beyond the sordid tale of negligence and trauma, did the episode reveal anything larger?

It took perhaps a week in Nebraska before I began to see the larger contours of the story. I tried to remain open, and not pollute my impressions with those I had formed from afar. I think staying open is the reporter's truest goal. It is impossible, of course, to be truly objective; but it is necessary to be receptive and fair. As I spoke with state health officials, legislators, charity workers, and doctors associated with the new law, I began to see common threads in the cases I was permitted to review. Two things in particular challenged my own assumptions. In many of the cases, parents had traveled overwhelming distances to drop off their kids—not just across the state, but all the way from Michigan, Indiana, Georgia, Florida, Arizona and California. This seemed like an awful lot of trouble for parents who couldn't be bothered with their children. Then too, looking through the records, it was impossible to avoid the conclusion that most of the children in question were seriously ill. Of the first thirty who had been surrendered, all but three had a history of psychiatric institutionalization, and some were in such rough shape that they'd been transferred immediately into lockdown facilities.

Reaching the parents was tricky at first. The very nature of the law allowed them to remain anonymous, and many chose to stay that way. In some cases, even the state was unsure who the parents were. But others stayed in contact with their children, and it was possible to begin reaching out to them, tentatively, though contacts I was making among public health officials. As I finally began to locate the parents, it became clear to me that the story was not really about the new law, or even about child abandonment. It was a story about mentally ill children, and the struggle their parents endure, and the dearth of public services to help them. It was about families in search of any way possible, however painful or humiliating, to deliver their children to psychiatric help. By relinquishing custody, they were in fact making the ultimate sacrifice: Giving up their pride and dignity, and foregoing the right to share their child's life, all to keep their children safe.

In time, I chose to focus the story on one mother and one child. Partly this was a matter of access. I could not reach all the parents, or even enough to draw complete statistical conclusions. But the decision to focus on Lavennia and Skyler also reflected my belief about long-form as a lens. The role of the lens is to narrow and clarify; to look intimately within spaces and pull the details into focus. By keeping my view on a single mother and child, I hoped to give readers a more visceral sense of how this crisis feels from within, and what the statistics really mean.

Writing the story broke my heart. Reading it does still. In some ways, things have improved for Lavennia Coover and her son, Skyler. But what I realized through this story was that the problems they faced went farther and deeper than I'd ever known. The parents who availed themselves of the Nebraska law had been living in a shadow world, without any other recourse, where countless other families remain. Despite so much discussion about national healthcare in recent years, we continue to offer little aid to struggling families with mentally ill children. Even the best insurance policies tend to limit mental healthcare drastically, yet public services are woefully underfunded. The result is a constellation of families like the Coovers, for whom the only option is the unimaginable.

Chris Jones

C hris Jones is a writer at large for *Esquire* and the back-page columnist for *ESPN The Magazine*. He has won two National Magazine Awards for Feature Writing. He lives in Port Hope, Ontario, Canada with his wife and two boys.

Roger Ebert: The Essential Man

For the 281st time in the last ten months Roger Ebert is sitting down to watch a movie in the Lake Street Screening Room, on the sixteenth floor of what used to pass for a skyscraper in the Loop. Ebert's been coming to it for nearly thirty years, along with the rest of Chicago's increasingly venerable collection of movie critics. More than a dozen of them are here this afternoon, sitting together in the dark. Some of them look as though they plan on camping out, with their coats, blankets, lunches, and laptops spread out on the seats around them.

The critics might watch three or four movies in a single day, and they have rules and rituals along with their lunches to make it through. The small, fabric-walled room has forty-nine purple seats in it; Ebert always occupies the aisle seat in the last row, closest to the door. His wife, Chaz, in her capacity as vice-president of the Ebert Company, sits two seats over, closer to the middle, next to a little table. She's sitting there now, drinking from a tall paper cup. Michael Phillips, Ebert's bearded, bespectacled replacement on *At the Movies*, is on the other side of the room, one row down. Steve Prokopy, the guy who writes under the name Capone for *Ain't It Cool News*, leans against the far wall. Jonathan Rosenbaum and Peter Sobczynski, dressed in black, are down front.

"Too close for me," Ebert writes in his small spiral notebook.

Today, Ebert's decided he has the time and energy to watch only one film, Pedro Almodóvar's new Spanish-language movie, *Broken Embraces*. It stars Penélope Cruz. Steve Kraus, the house projectionist, is busy pulling seven reels out of a cardboard box and threading them through twin Simplex projectors.

Unlike the others, Ebert, sixty-seven, hasn't brought much survival gear with him: a small bottle of Evian moisturizing spray with a pink cap; some Kleenex; his spiral notebook and a blue fine-tip pen. He's wearing jeans that are falling off him at the waist, a pair of New Balance sneakers, and a blue cardigan zipped up over the bandages around his neck. His seat is worn soft and reclines a little, which he likes. He likes, too, for the seat in front of him to remain empty, so that he can prop his left foot onto its armrest; otherwise his back and shoulders can't take the strain of a feature-length sitting anymore.

The lights go down. Kraus starts the movie. Subtitles run along the bottom of the screen. The movie is about a film director, Harry Caine, who has lost his sight. Caine reads and makes love by touch, and he writes and edits his films by sound. "Films have to be finished, even if you do it blindly," someone in the movie says. It's a quirky, complex, beautiful little film, and Ebert loves it. He radiates kid joy. Throughout the screening, he takes excited notes—references to other movies, snatches of dialogue, meditations on Almodóvar's symbolism and his use of the color red. Ebert scribbles constantly, his pen digging into page after page, and then he tears the pages out of his notebook and drops them to the floor around him. Maybe twenty or thirty times, the sound of paper being torn from a spiral rises from the aisle seat in the last row.

The lights come back on. Ebert stays in his chair, savoring, surrounded by his notes. It looks as though he's sitting on top of a cloud of paper. He watches the credits, lifts himself up, and kicks his notes into a small pile with his feet. He slowly bends down to pick them up and walks with Chaz back out to the elevators. They hold hands, but they don't say anything to each other. They spend a lot of time like that.

Roger Ebert can't remember the last thing he ate. He can't remember the last thing he drank, either, or the last thing he said. Of course, those things existed; those lasts happened. They just didn't happen with enough warning for him to have bothered committing them to memory—it wasn't as though he sat down, knowingly, to his last supper or last cup of coffee or to whisper a last word into Chaz's ear. The doctors told him they were going to give him back his ability to eat, drink, and talk. But the doctors were wrong, weren't they? On some morning or afternoon or evening, sometime in 2006, Ebert took his last bite and sip, and he spoke his last word.

Ebert's lasts almost certainly took place in a hospital. That much he can guess. His last food was probably nothing special, except that it was: hot soup in a brown plastic bowl; maybe some oatmeal; perhaps a saltine or some canned peaches. His last drink? Water, most likely, but maybe juice, again slurped out of plastic with the tinfoil lid peeled back. The last thing he said? Ebert thinks about it for a few moments, and then his eyes go wide behind his glasses, and he looks out into space in case the answer is floating in the air somewhere. It isn't. He looks surprised that he can't remember. He knows the last words Studs Terkel's wife, Ida, muttered when she was wheeled into the operating room ("Louis, what have you gotten me into now?"), but Ebert doesn't know what his own last words were. He thinks he probably said goodbye to Chaz before one of his own trips into the operating room, perhaps when he had parts of his salivary glands taken out—but that can't be right. He was back on TV after that operation. Whenever it was, the moment wasn't cinematic. His last words weren't recorded. There was just his voice, and then there wasn't.

Now his hands do the talking. They are delicate, long-fingered, wrapped in skin as thin and translucent as silk. He wears his wedding ring on the middle finger of his left hand; he's lost so much weight since he and Chaz were married in 1992 that it won't stay where it belongs, especially now that his hands are so busy. There is almost always a pen in one and a spiral notebook or a pad of Post-it notes in the other—unless he's at home, in which case his fingers are feverishly banging the keys of his MacBook Pro.

He's also developed a kind of rudimentary sign language. If he passes a written note to someone and then opens and closes his fingers like a bird's beak, that means he would like them to read the note aloud for the other people in the room. If he touches his hand to his blue cardigan over his heart, that means he's either talking about something of great importance to him or he wants to make it clear that he's telling the truth. If he needs to get someone's attention and they're looking away from him or sitting with him in the dark, he'll clack on a hard surface with his nails, like he's tapping out Morse code. Sometimes—when he's outside wearing gloves, for instance—he'll be forced to draw letters with his finger on his palm. That's his last resort.

C-O-M-C-A-S-T, he writes on his palm to Chaz after they've stopped on the way back from the movie to go for a walk.

"Comcast?" she says, before she realizes—he's just reminded her that people from Comcast are coming over to their Lincoln Park brownstone not long from now, because their Internet has been down for three days, and for Ebert, that's the equivalent of being buried alive: C-O-M-C-A-S-T. But Chaz still wants to go for a walk, and, more important, she wants her husband to go for a walk, so she calls their assistant, Carol, and tells her they will be late for their appointment. There isn't any debate in her voice. Chaz Ebert is a former lawyer, and she doesn't leave openings. She takes hold of her husband's hand, and they set off in silence across the park toward the water.

They pass together through an iron gate with a sign that reads ALFRED CALDWELL LILY POOL. Ebert has walked hundreds of miles around this little duck pond, on the uneven stone path under the trees, most of them after one operation or another. The Eberts have lost track of the surgeries he has undergone since the first one, for thyroid cancer, in 2002, followed by the one on his salivary glands in 2003. After that, they disagree about the numbers and dates. "The truth is, we don't let our minds dwell on these things," Chaz says. She kept a journal of their shared stays in hospitals in Chicago and Seattle and Houston, but neither of them has had the desire to look at it. On those rare occasions when they agree to try to remember the story, they both lose the plot for the scenes. When Chaz remembers what she calls "the surgery that changed everything," she remembers its soundtrack best of all. Ebert always had music playing in his hospital room, an esoteric digital collection that drew doctors and nurses to his bedside more than they might have been otherwise inclined to visit. There was one song in particular he played over and over: "I'm Your Man," by Leonard Cohen. That song saved his life.

Seven years ago, he recovered quickly from the surgery to cut out his cancerous thyroid and was soon back writing reviews for the *Chicago Sun-Times* and appearing with Richard Roeper on *At the Movies*. A year later, in 2003, he returned to work after his salivary glands were partially removed, too, although that and a series of aggressive radiation treatments opened the first cracks in his voice. In 2006, the cancer surfaced yet again, this time in his jaw. A section of his lower jaw was removed; Ebert listened to Leonard Cohen. Two weeks later, he was in his hospital room packing his bags, the doctors and nurses paying one last visit, listening to a few last songs. That's when his carotid artery, invisibly damaged by the earlier radiation and the most recent jaw surgery, burst. Blood began pouring out of Ebert's mouth and formed a great pool on the polished floor. The doctors and nurses leapt up to stop the bleeding and barely saved his life. Had he made it out of his hospital room and been on his way home—had his artery waited just a few more songs to burst—Ebert would have bled to death on Lake Shore Drive. Instead, following more surgery to stop a relentless bloodletting, he was left without much of his mandible, his chin hanging loosely like a drawn curtain, and behind his chin there was a hole the size of a plum. He also underwent a tracheostomy, because there was still a risk that he could drown in his own blood. When Ebert woke up and looked in the mirror in his hospital room, he could see through his open mouth and the hole clear to the bandages that had been wrapped around his neck to protect his exposed windpipe and his new breathing tube. He could no longer eat or drink, and he had lost his voice entirely. That was more than three years ago.

Ebert spent more than half of a thirty-month stretch in hospitals. His breathing tube has been removed, but the hole in his throat remains open. He eats through a G-tube—he's fed with a liquid paste, suspended in a bag from an IV pole, through a tube in his stomach. He usually eats in what used to be the library, on the brownstone's second floor. (It has five stories, including a gym on the top floor and a theater—with a neon marquee—in the basement.) A single bed with white sheets has been set up among the books, down a hallway filled with Ebert's collection of Edward Lear watercolors. He shuffles across the wooden floor between the library and his living room, where he spends most of his time in a big black leather recliner, tipped back with his feet up and his laptop on a wooden tray. There is a record player within reach. The walls are white, to show off the art, which includes massive abstracts, movie posters (*Casablanca*, *The Stranger*), and aboriginal burial poles. Directly in front of his chair is a black-and-white photograph of the Steak 'n Shake in Champaign-Urbana, Illinois, one of his hometown hangouts.

He believes he's had three more surgeries since the removal of his lower jaw; Chaz remembers four. Each time, however many times, surgeons carved bone and tissue and skin from his back, arm, and legs and transplanted them in an attempt to reconstruct his jaw and throat. Each time, he had one or two weeks of hope and relief when he could eat a little and drink a little and talk a little. Once, the surgery looked nearly perfect. ("Like a movie star," Chaz remembers.) But each time, the reconstructive work fell apart and had to be stripped out, the hole opened up again. It was as though the cancer were continuing to eat away at him, even those parts of him that had been spared. His right shoulder is visibly smaller than his left shoulder; his legs have been weakened and riddled with scars. After each attempt at reconstruction, he went to rehabilitation and physical therapy to fix the increasing damage done. (During one of those rehabilitation sessions, he fell and broke his hip.) He still can't sit upright for long or climb stairs. He's still figuring out how to use his legs.

At the start of their walk around the pond, Ebert worries about falling on a small gravel incline. Chaz lets go of his hand. "You can do it," she says, and she claps when Ebert makes it to the top on his own. Later, she climbs on top of a big circular stone. "I'm going to give my prayer to the universe," she says, and then she gives a sun salutation north, south, east, and west. Ebert raises his arms into the sky behind her.

They head home and meet with the people from Comcast, who talk mostly to Chaz. Their Internet will be back soon, but probably not until tomorrow. Disaster. Ebert then takes the elevator upstairs and drops into his chair. As he reclines it slowly, the entire chair jumps somehow, one of its back legs thumping against the floor. It had been sitting on the charger for his iPhone, and now the charger is crushed. Ebert grabs his tray and laptop and taps out a few words before he presses a button and speakers come to life.

"What else can go wrong?" the voice says.

The voice is called Alex, a voice with a generic American accent and a generic tone and no emotion. At first Ebert spoke with a voice called Lawrence, which had an English accent. Ebert liked sounding English, because he is an Anglophile, and his English voice reminded him of those beautiful early summers when he would stop in London with Chaz on their way home after the annual chaos of Cannes. But the voice can be hard to decipher even without an English accent layered on top of it—it is given to eccentric pronunciations, especially of names and places—and so for the time being, Ebert has settled for generic instead.

Ebert is waiting for a Scottish company called CereProc to give him some of his former voice back. He found it on the Internet, where he spends a lot of his time. CereProc tailors text-to-speech software for voiceless customers so that they don't all have to sound like Stephen Hawking. They have catalog voices—Heather, Katherine, Sarah, and Sue—with regional Scottish accents, but they will also custom-build software for clients who had the foresight to record their voices at length before they lost them. Ebert spent all those years on TV, and he also recorded four or five DVD commentaries in crystal-clear digital audio. The average English-speaking person will use about two thousand different words over the course of a given day. CereProc is mining Ebert's TV tapes and DVD commentaries for those words, and the words it cannot find, it will piece together syllable by syllable. When CereProc finishes its work, Roger Ebert won't sound exactly like Roger Ebert again, but he will sound more like him than Alex does. There might be moments, when he calls for Chaz from another room or tells her that he loves her and says goodnight—he's a night owl; she prefers mornings when they both might be able to close their eyes and pretend that everything is as it was.

There are places where Ebert exists as the Ebert he remembers. In 2008, when he was in the middle of his worst battles and wouldn't be able to make the trip to Champaign-Urbana for Ebertfest—really, his annual spring festival of films he just plain likes—he began writing an online journal. Reading it from its beginning is like watching an Aztec pyramid being built. At first, it's just a vessel for him to apologize to his fans for not being downstate. The original entries are short updates about his life and health and a few of his heart's wishes. Postcards and pebbles. They're followed by a smattering of Welcomes to Cyberspace. But slowly the journal picks up steam, as Ebert's strength and confidence and audience grow. *You are the readers I have dreamed of,* he writes. He is emboldened. He begins to write about more than movies; in fact, it sometimes seems as though he'd rather write about anything other than movies. The existence of an afterlife, the beauty of a full bookshelf, his liberalism and atheism and alcoholism, the health-care debate, Darwin, memories of departed friends and fights won and lost—more than five hundred thousand words of inner monologue have poured out of him, five hundred thousand words that probably wouldn't exist had he kept his other voice. Now some of his entries have thousands of comments, each of which he vets personally and to which he will often respond. It has become his life's work, building and maintaining this massive monument to written debate—argument is encouraged, so long as it's civil—and he spends several hours each night reclined in his chair, tending to his online oasis by lamplight. Out there, his voice is still his voice—not a reasonable facsimile of it, but his.

"It is saving me," he says through his speakers.

He calls up a journal entry to elaborate, because it's more efficient and time is precious: *When I am writing my problems become invisible and I am the same person I always was. All is well. I am as I should be.*

He is a wonderful writer, and today he is producing the best work of his life. In 1975 he became the first film critic to win the Pulitzer Prize, but his TV fame saw most of his fans, at least those outside Chicago, forget that he was a writer if they ever did know. (His Pulitzer still hangs in a frame in his book-lined office down the hall, behind a glass door that has THE EBERT COMPANY, LTD.: FINE FILM CRITICISM SINCE 1967 written on it in gold leaf.) Even for Ebert, a prolific author—he wrote long features on Paul Newman, Groucho Marx, and Hugh Hefner's daughter, among others, for this magazine in the late 1960s and early '70s and published dozens of books in addition to his reviews for the *Sun-Times*—the written word was eclipsed by the spoken word. He spent an entire day each week arguing with Gene Siskel and then Richard Roeper, and he became a regular on talk shows, and he shouted to crowds from red carpets. He lived his life through microphones.

But now everything he says must be written, either first on his laptop and funneled through speakers or, as he usually prefers, on some kind of paper. His new life is lived through Times New Roman and chicken scratch. So many words, so much writing—it's like a kind of explosion is taking place on the second floor of his brownstone. It's not the food or the drink he worries about anymore—*I went thru a period when I obsessed about root beer + Steak + Shake malts*, he writes on a blue Post-it note—but how many more words he can get out in the time he has left. In this living room, lined with thousands more books, words are the single most valuable thing in the world. They are gold bricks. Here idle chatter doesn't exist; that would be like lighting cigars with hundred-dollar bills. Here there are only sentences and paragraphs divided by section breaks. Every word has meaning.

Even the simplest expressions take on higher power here. Now his thumbs have become more than a trademark; they're an essential means for Ebert to communicate. He falls into a coughing fit, but he gives his thumbs-up, meaning he's okay. Thumbs-down would have meant he needed someone to call his full-time nurse, Millie, a spectral presence in the house.

Millie has premonitions. She sees ghosts. Sometimes she wakes in the night screaming—so vivid are her dreams.

Ebert's dreams are happier. *Never yet a dream where I can't talk*, he writes on another Post-it note, peeling it off the top of the blue stack. *Sometimes I discover—oh, I see! I CAN talk! I just forget to do it.*

In his dreams, his voice has never left. In his dreams, he can get out everything he didn't get out during his waking hours: the thoughts that get trapped in paperless corners, the jokes he wanted to tell, the nuanced stories he can't quite relate. In his dreams, he yells and chatters and whispers and exclaims. In his dreams, he's never had cancer. In his dreams, he is whole.

These things come to us, they don't come from us, he writes about his cancer, about sickness, on another Post-it note. *Dreams come from us.*

We have a habit of turning sentimental about celebrities who are struck down—Muhammad Ali, Christopher Reeve—transforming them into mystics; still, it's almost impossible to sit beside Roger Ebert, lifting blue Post-it notes from his silk fingertips, and not feel as though he's become something more than he was. He has those hands. And his wide and expressive eyes, despite everything, are almost always smiling.

There is no need to pity me, he writes on a scrap of paper one afternoon after someone parting looks at him a little sadly. *Look how happy I am.*

In fact, because he's missing sections of his jaw, and because he's lost some of the engineering behind his face, Ebert can't really do anything but smile. It really does take more muscles to frown, and he doesn't have those muscles anymore. His eyes will water and his face will go red—but if he opens his mouth, his bottom lip will sink most deeply in the middle, pulled down by the weight of his empty chin, and the corners of his upper lip will stay raised, frozen in place. Even when he's really angry, his open smile mutes it: The top half of his face won't match the bottom half, but his smile is what most people will see first, and by instinct they will smile back. The only way Ebert can show someone he's mad is by writing in all caps on a Post-it note or turning up the volume on his speakers. Anger isn't as easy for him as it used to be. Now his anger rarely lasts long enough for him to write it down.

There's a reception to celebrate the arrival of a new ownership group at the *Sun-Times*, which Ebert feared was doomed to close otherwise. Ebert doesn't have an office in the new newsroom (the old one was torn down to make way for one of Donald Trump's glass towers), but so long as the newspaper exists, it's another one of those outlets through which he can pretend nothing has changed. His column mug is an old one, taken after his first couple of surgeries but before he lost his jaw, and his work still dominates the arts section. (A single copy of the paper might contain six of his reviews.) He's excited about seeing everybody. Millie helps him get dressed, in a blue blazer with a red pocket square and black slippers. Most of his old clothes don't fit him anymore: "For meaningful weight loss," the voice says, "I recommend surgery and a liquid diet." He buys his new clothes by mail order from L. L. Bean.

He and Chaz head south into the city; she drives, and he provides direction by pointing and knocking on the window. The reception is at a place that was called Riccardo's, around the corner from the Billy Goat. Reporters and editors used to stagger into the rival joints after filing rival stories from rival newsrooms. Riccardo's holds good memories for Ebert. But now it's something else—something called Phil Stefani's 437 Rush, and after he and Chaz ease up to the curb and he shuffles inside, his shoulders slump a little with the loss of another vestige of old Chicago.

He won't last long at the reception, maybe thirty or forty minutes. The only chairs are wooden and straight-backed, and he tires quickly in a crowd. When he walks into the room of journalistic luminaries—Roeper, Lynn Sweet, Rick Telander—they turn toward him and burst into spontaneous applause. They know he's earned it, and they don't know even half of what it's taken him just to get into the room, just to be here tonight, but there's something sad about the wet-eyed recognition, too. He's confronted by elegies everywhere he goes. People take longer to say goodbye to him than they used to. They fuss over him, and they linger around him, and they talk slowly to him. One woman at the party even writes him a note in his notepad, and Ebert has to point to his ears and roll his eyes. He would love nothing more than to be holding court in a corner of the room, telling stories about Lee Marvin and Robert Mitchum and Russ Meyer (who came to the Eberts' wedding accompanied by Melissa Mounds). Instead he's propped on a chair in the middle of the room like a swami, smiling and nodding and trying not to flinch when people pat him on the shoulder.

He took his hardest hit not long ago. After Roeper announced his departure from *At the Movies* in 2008—Disney wanted to revamp the show in a way that Roeper felt would damage it—Ebert disassociated himself from it, too, and he took his trademarked thumbs with him. The end was not pretty, and the break was not clean. But because Disney was going to change the original balcony set as part of its makeover, it was agreed, Ebert thought, that the upholstered chairs and rails and undersized screen would be given to the Smithsonian and put on display. Ebert was excited by the idea. Then he went up to visit the old set one last time and found it broken up and stacked in a dumpster in an alley.

After saying their goodbyes to his colleagues (and to Riccardo's), Ebert and Chaz go out for dinner, to one of their favorite places, the University Club of Chicago. Hidden inside another skyscraper, there's a great Gothic room, all stone arches and stained glass. The room is filled mostly with people with white hair—there has been a big push to find younger members to fill in the growing spaces in the membership ranks—and they nod and wave at him and Chaz. They're given a table in the middle of the room.

Ebert silently declines all entreaties from the fussy waiters. Food arrives only for Chaz and a friend who joins them. Ebert writes them notes, tearing pages from his spiral notepad, tapping his fingers together for his words to be read aloud. Everyone smiles and laughs about old stories. More and more, that's how Ebert lives these days, through memories, of what things used to feel like and sound like and taste like. When his friend suddenly apologizes for eating in front of him, for talking about the buttered scallops and how the cream and the fish and the wine combine to make a kind of delicate smoke, Ebert shakes his head. He begins to write and tears a note from the spiral.

No, no, it reads. *You're eating for me.*

Gene Siskel died eleven years ago, in February 1999, from a brain tumor. He was fifty-three years old. He had suffered terrible headaches in those last several months, but he was private about his pain. He didn't talk about being sick or how he felt or what he expected or hoped for. He was stoic and solitary and quiet in his death. Siskel and Ebert were both defined, for most of their adult lives, by comparative measures: the fat one, the bald one, the loud one, the skinny one. Siskel was also the careful one. He joked that Ebert's middle name was "Full Disclosure." Ebert's world has never had many secrets in it. Even at the end, when Siskel knew what was coming, he kept his secrets. He and Ebert never once spoke about his looming death.

There are pictures of Siskel all over the brownstone—on the grand piano, in the kitchen, on bookshelves. The biggest one is in the living room; Ebert can see it from his recliner. In almost all the pictures, Siskel and Ebert—never Ebert and Siskel—are standing together, shoulder to shoulder, smiling, two big thumbs-up. In the picture in the living room, they're also wearing tuxedos.

"Oh, Gene," Chaz says, and that's all she says.

All these years later, the top half of Ebert's face still registers sadness when Siskel's name comes up. His eyes well up behind his glasses, and for the first time, they overwhelm his smile. He begins to type into his computer, slowly, deliberately. He presses the button and the speakers light up. "I've never said this before," the voice says, "but we were born to be Siskel and Ebert." He thinks for a moment before he begins typing again. There's a long pause before he hits the button. "I just miss the guy so much," the voice says. Ebert presses the button again. "I just miss the guy so much."

Last February, to mark the tenth anniversary of Siskel's death, Ebert wrote an entry in his online journal called "Remembering Gene." He calls it up on his screen. It is beautifully written, filled with stories about arguments, even pitched battles, but nearly every memory is tinged with love and humor. Ebert scrolls through each paragraph, his eyes brimming, the smile winning again. The first lousy balcony set had painted pop bottles for rail supports. Siskel had courtside tickets for the Bulls and thought Phil Jackson was a sage. His beautiful daughters, Cate and Callie, were the flower girls for the Eberts' wedding.

And then comes the turn. Gene's first headache struck in the back of a limo on their way to be on Leno, which was broadcasting from Chicago. In front of the audience, Siskel could manage only to agree with everything Ebert said; they made it a gag. That night Siskel went to the Bulls game because they were in the playoffs, but the next day he underwent some tests. Not long after that, he had surgery, but he never told anyone where he was going to have it. He came back and for a time he continued taping the show with Ebert. Siskel's nephew would help him to his seat on the set, but only after the set was cleared.

Our eyes would meet, the voice reads from Ebert's journal, *unspoken words were between us, but we never spoke openly about his problems or his prognosis. That's how he wanted it, and that was his right.*

Gene Siskel taped his last show, and within a week or two he was dead. Ebert had lost half his identity.

He scrolls down to the entry's final paragraph.

We once spoke with Disney and CBS about a sitcom to be titled Best Enemies. It would be about two movie critics joined in a love/hate relationship. It never went anywhere, but we both believed it was a good idea. Maybe the problem was that no one else could possibly understand how meaningless was the hate, how deep was the love.

Ebert keeps scrolling down. Below his journal he had embedded video of his first show alone, the balcony seat empty across the aisle. It was a tribute, in three parts. He wants to watch them now, because he wants to remember, but at the bottom of the page there are only three big black squares. In the middle of the squares, white type reads: "Content deleted. This video is no longer available because it has been deleted." Ebert leans into the screen, trying to figure out what's happened. He looks across at Chaz. The top half of his face turns red, and his eyes well up again, but this time, it's not sadness surfacing. He's shaking. It's anger.

Chaz looks over his shoulder at the screen. "Those fu—" she says, catching herself.

They think it's Disney again—that they've taken down the videos. Terms-of-use violation.

This time, the anger lasts long enough for Ebert to write it down. He opens a new page in his text-to-speech program, a blank white sheet. He types in capital letters, stabbing at the keys with his delicate, trembling hands: *MY TRIBUTE*, appears behind the cursor in the top left corner. *ON THE FIRST SHOW AFTER HIS DEATH.* But Ebert doesn't press the button that fires up the speakers. He presses a different button, a button that makes the words bigger. He presses the button again and again and again, the words growing bigger and bigger and bigger until they become too big to fit the screen, now they're just letters, but he keeps hitting the button, bigger and bigger still, now just shapes and angles, just geometry filling the white screen with black like the three squares. Roger Ebert is shaking, his entire body is shaking, and he's still hitting the button, bang, bang, bang, and he's shouting now. He's standing outside on the street corner and he's arching his back and he's shouting at the top of his lungs.

His doctors would like to try one more operation, would like one more chance to reclaim what cancer took from him, to restore his voice. Chaz would like him to try once more, too. But Ebert has refused. Even if the cancer comes back, he will probably decline significant intervention. The last surgery was his worst, and it did him more harm than good. Asked about the possibility of more surgery, he shakes his head and types before pressing the button.

"Over and out," the voice says.

Ebert is dying in increments, and he is aware of it.

I know it is coming, and I do not fear it, because I believe there is nothing on the other side of death to fear, he writes in a journal entry titled "Go Gently into That Good Night." *I hope to be spared as much pain as possible on the approach path. I was perfectly content before I was born, and I think of death as the same state. What I am grateful for is the gift of intelligence, and for life, love, wonder, and laughter. You can't say it wasn't interesting. My lifetime's memories are what I have brought home from the trip. I will require them for eternity no more than that little souvenir of the Eiffel Tower I brought home from Paris.*

There has been no death-row conversion. He has not found God. He has been beaten in some ways. But his other senses have picked up since he lost his sense of taste. He has tuned better into life. Some things aren't as important as they once were; some things are more important than ever. He has built for himself a new kind of universe. Roger Ebert is no mystic, but he knows things we don't know.

I believe that if, at the end of it all, according to our abilities, we have done something to make others a little happier, and something to make ourselves a little happier, that is about the best we can do. To make others less happy is a crime. To make ourselves unhappy is where all crime starts. We must try to contribute joy to the world. That is true no matter what our problems, our health, our circumstances. We must try. I didn't always know this, and am happy I lived long enough to find it out.

Ebert takes joy from the world in nearly all the ways he once did. He has had to find a new way to laugh—by closing his eyes and slapping both hands on his knees—but he still laughs. He and Chaz continue to travel. (They spent Thanksgiving in Barbados.) And he still finds joy in books, and in art, and in movies—a greater joy than he ever has. He gives more movies more stars.

But now it's getting late, which means he has his own work to do. Chaz heads off to bed. Millie, for the moment, hasn't been seized by night terrors, and the brownstone is quiet and nearly dark. Just the lamp is lit beside his chair. He leans back. He streams Radio Caroline—the formerly pirate radio station—and he begins to write. Everything fades out but the words. They appear quickly. Perfect sentences, artful sentences, illuminating sentences come out of him at a ridiculous, enviable pace, his fingers sometimes struggling to keep up.

Earlier today, his publisher sent him two copies of his newest book, the silver-jacketed *Great Movies III*, wrapped in plastic. Ebert turned them over in his hands, smiling with satisfaction—he wrote most of it in hospital beds—before he put them on a shelf in his office, by the desk he can no longer sit behind. They filled the last hole on the third shelf of his own published work; later this year, another book—*The Pot and How to Use It*, a collection of Ebert's rice-cooker recipes—will occupy the first space on a fourth shelf. Ebert's readers have asked him to write his autobiography next, but he looks up from his laptop and shrugs at the thought. He's already written a lot about himself on his journal, about his little childhood home in Champaign-Urbana and the days he spent on TV and in hospitals, and he would rather not say the same thing twice.

Besides, he has a review to finish. He returns his attention to his laptop, its glow making white squares in his glasses. Music plays. Words come.

Pedro Almodóvar loves the movies with lust and abandon and the skill of an experienced lover. Broken Embraces *is a voluptuary of a film, drunk on primary colors, caressing Penélope Cruz, using the devices of a Hitchcock to distract us with surfaces while the sinister uncoils beneath. As it ravished me, I longed for a freeze-frame to allow me to savor a shot.*

Ebert gives it four stars.

AUTHOR'S AFTERWORDS…

It's funny how stories sometimes change in your mind with time. I've felt probably a dozen different ways about this story—a full gamut of emotion, especially if I go back far enough in the process. When I first started emailing with Roger Ebert, and he finally agreed to talk to me, I was excited. When I walked up his front steps and knocked on his door, I was nervous. When I first met Roger that afternoon, when I first shook his hand next to his shining grand piano, I was some weird combination of happy and sad. Over the next few days and weeks, I was elated, stunned, embarrassed; I was many, many things. But one emotion I never felt was doubt. Through every last minute of it, through all those rises and falls, through the reporting, writing, and editing of this story, I had an overriding feeling of peace about everything. I felt as though everything was as it should be.

That doesn't happen very often for me. I have colleagues who sit down and I'm sure they feel the words pour out of them like liquid. Charlie Pierce seems capable of spinning out a few thousand words, perfectly constructed, every thirty minutes. I'm not like that. I love writing, but it's hard work for me. (I've taken a lot of shit over the years for daring to call writing "hard work." Someone once told me I should try social work or something like that so I could really know what hard work was. Well, that someone can bite me. I've had many dirty, physical jobs in my life, from working at a drycleaners to castrating hogs on a farm, from ferreting raccoons out of lumber piles to bussing tables at Red Lobster. And none of those jobs, as hard as they were, taxed me the way writing does. To hell with anybody who thinks writing is easy.) In this very particular case, however, I will confess that everything just kind of happened. I'm not sure writing about Roger ever felt like work.

In the more than ten years I've been at *Esquire*, I've felt something like that level of bliss maybe—maybe—a half-dozen times. Perhaps not coincidentally, those five or six stories are probably my favorites. I think it's a bit like the way athletes talk about slipping into "the zone," those too-brief stretches of time when your movements become almost automatic, as though you're more machine than human. Then something bad inevitably happens (you start thinking about how well everything's going, for instance), and your touch just as suddenly leaves you. There's a scratch, and the record stops playing.

If there were a conscious way to put ourselves into that zone, of course, we'd all do it all the time. Unfortunately, it just happens, and I've never been able to figure out why it does when it does. All I know is the feeling. For me, usually, it comes late at night, when the house is quiet, and I'm listening to music I love, and I'm writing essentially from memory—I'm not looking at notes, I'm not listening to tapes—and the hours just disappear and full pages take their place. It's as though I can't work fast enough, because I have this fully formed story in my head and I need to get it out before it vanishes. I'll look at the clock or out the window and the sun is coming up, and on my computer screen are however many words, and when I finally go to bed and wake up and read them again, they're still right. All the words are sitting in some magical order and they feel as though they belong exactly where they are.

A half-dozen times in more than ten years. That's not a very high joy-to-work ratio, or at least it might not seem like it on paper. But maybe it's the elusiveness of that feeling, of those stories, that's the great lure of them. If they were easy, if we could just snap our fingers and make them happen, we'd probably get bored and lazy. (That happens to plenty of writers enough already.) For me, that feeling is so good, and so rare, I'm happy to chase it. I'll grind through the stories that don't quite feel that way—one significant measure of a professional writer is his ability to deliver a solid story even when nothing's going his way—in that mostly vain hope that the next story will be the one that I'll remember forever.

I'll remember that time I spent with Roger forever. I'll remember all those feelings I had; I can still feel them in my stomach. But if someone asks me about this story now, a few years removed, I'll tell you what first flashes in my head: the single most perfect night of my writing life. It might never be that good again, but if this all ends tomorrow, at least I had that night.

We were living in Missoula, Montana, at the time, and the house we were renting had a little desk built into a cubby in the basement. My wife and kids were sleeping upstairs; I was down there, boxed in. It was dark except for the white of my screen. I was listening to "Little Motel" by Modest Mouse on a loop—literally, that was the only song I listened to, again and again. I felt almost high, fuzzy and sharp at the same time. I was writing without thinking. And I can remember very specifically the moment when I wrote the part of the story when Roger finds out that his tributes to Gene Siskel have been taken down. That whole scene just came out of me in one long torrent, and I can remember reading it back and feeling as doubtless as I have ever felt. So many times, I've looked at what I've written and been unhappy or disappointed. That night, I felt perfect.

Then I sent the story to my editor, and he read that scene, and he cut out the last line. Because even those half-dozen times when I've felt perfect, I wasn't actually perfect. No writer is. I was just closer to perfect than I've ever been.

Michael Kruse

M ichael Kruse is a staff writer on the enterprise team at the *Tampa Bay Times* (formerly the *St. Petersburg Times)* and a contributing writer for ESPN's *Grantland.* In 2012, he won the Paul Hansell Award for Distinguished Achievement in Florida Journalism; in 2011, he won the American Society of News Editors' award for distinguished non-deadline writing; in 2010, he won the award for best short story of the year from the Society for Features Journalism. Before the *Times,* he worked at the *Times Herald-Record* in New York's Hudson Valley, where he covered two towns and Major League Baseball and was the paper's writer at large. He's the author of *Taking the Shot: The Davidson Basketball Moment,* and has written for *Yahoo! Sports, Charlotte* and *Parade.*

Kruse was born outside Los Angeles, raised outside Boston and educated at Davidson College in North Carolina. He lives with his family in St. Petersburg, FL.

A Brevard Woman Disappeared

Last year, a week before Thanksgiving, a man in Cape Canaveral bought in a foreclosure auction a two-story stucco run-down townhouse on a short, straight street called Cherie Down Lane. He went to see his purchase he hoped to fix up and sell.

He found in the kitchen dishes stacked so high on the counter they almost touched the bottoms of the cabinets. In the living room on the carpet was a towel with two plates of mold-covered cat food. Empty orange pill bottles were everywhere. In front of the couch, open on a single TV tray, was a *Brevard County Hometown News*, dated July 24, 2009.

Both bedrooms were the same: stuff strewn all over, clothes and fake flowers and plants and a dusty treadmill pushed into a far corner, a mattress propped against tightly shut drapes, and stacks and stacks of books, about religion, about weight loss, about wiping out debts and making fresh starts.

Next to the door to the garage was a bulletin board with a thirteen-year-old receipt from Home Depot and an inspirational quote: "I may not be totally perfect, but parts of me are excellent."

He opened the door to the garage.

Inside was an old silver sedan. The doors were locked. He looked inside and saw a white blanket on the back seat. There was a pillow on the floor. Hanging from the rearview mirror was an air freshener shaped like a pine tree. Wedged against the console was a thin white candle. He stopped on what he saw in the passenger seat: the mummified body of what looked like a woman.

The call to the Sheriff's Office came on Nov. 18, 2010, just before noon. The townhouse, deputies learned, had belonged to a woman named Kathryn Norris, and the 1987 silver Chevy Nova was registered to her, too. She had used a normal amount of electricity in July 2009 and much less in August and none after that. She had paid her mortgage in August and then stopped. Her head was on the floor and her feet were on the seat. The corpse, deputies wrote in their report, was wearing a dress.

Television trucks showed up. Local reporters talked to her neighbors.

The neighbors said that they seldom saw her but that for more than a year they hadn't seen her at all. One called her "a little strange." Another said she "just disappeared."

How could a woman die a block from the beach, surrounded by her neighbors, and not be found for almost sixteen months?

How could a woman go missing inside her own home?

Kathryn Norris moved to Florida in 1990. She was intelligent and driven, say those who knew her back in Ohio, but she could be difficult. She held grudges. She had been laid off from her civil service job, and her marriage of fourteen years was over, and so she came looking for sunshine. She knew nobody. Using money from her small pension, she bought the Cherie Down townhouse, $84,900 new. It was a short walk to the sounds of the surf and just up A1A from souvenir stores selling trinkets with messages of PARADISE FOUND.

She started a job making $32,000 a year as a buyer of space shuttle parts for a subcontractor for NASA. She went out on occasion with coworkers for cookouts or cocktails. She talked a lot about her ex-husband. She started having some trouble keeping up at the office and was diagnosed in December of 1990 as manic depressive.

After the diagnosis, she made daily notes on index cards. She ate at Arby's, Wendy's, McDonald's. Sometimes she did sit-ups and rode an exercise bike. She read the paper. She got the mail. She went to sleep at 8 p.m., 1:30 a.m., 6:30 a.m. Her heart raced.

"Dropped fork at lunch," she wrote.

"Felt depressed in evening and cried."

"Noise outside at 4 a.m. sounded like a dog."

She found it difficult to focus when she went back to work. She told people all the pills to settle her moods made her feel like she was taking whole bottles of Nyquil. There were times when she just sat at her desk. She was demoted. In the summer of 1993, she spent a week in a psychiatric hospital, where she was under suicide watch. She visited her sister in Ohio to try to get well. She went back to work in the fall. It wasn't long, though, before she was let go.

Stronger pills made her sluggish. She slept constantly. She gained weight on her five-foot-one frame, 150 pounds, 160 pounds. "I'll be fine here," she wrote to her sister, "until April 1994 when the unemployment runs out."

She met a man at the post office that May. They were married in October.

Bill Kunzweiler was fifteen years older. Their marriage was more utilitarian than romantic. They lived in the Cherie Down townhouse, and he was to pay the mortgage, and she would provide "wife-type services and support," is how she put it. He had his activities, softball, garage sales, Sundays at the Baptist church, and she had done some of those things during their brief courtship. Not anymore. They didn't sleep well together. She snored. He wiggled. He had told her he'd been married three times, but the number, she discovered, was actually eleven. She was the second Kathryn. She moved into the other bedroom and locked the door.

They separated in June of 1995. He called her a money grubber. She called him a fraud and a predator of lonely women like herself.

When she was alone, she explained during a divorce hearing in 1996, she grew unreliable and reclusive.

"I have learned I attach myself to one person," she said, "and they become my safety person."

And if there's no safety person?

"I stay within my home."

She did go outside and leave the townhouse, occasionally, to go to the doctor, to go pick up pills, to go get takeout from Olive Garden or Outback, to go to Walmart to buy things she didn't need, like eight of the same dresses, mostly so she could take them back later. She worked some in her garden during the day, planting trees of lemons, limes and tangelos. She once walked across the street and gave a neighbor a banana tree. Late at night, she dragged her garbage can to the end of her driveway, wearing her housecoat, and neighbors heard her call for her cats. She set up cinder blocks in front of her yard that said NO PARKING. She put boards on her windows for hurricanes and left them there for months.

Inside, as a year became five and as five became ten, she saved coupons and recipes, birthday cards and Christmas cards. She lived on dwindling savings and her small pension and $526 a month of Social Security disability pay. She had credit card bills and owed doctors money and had trouble paying them back. She made contributions to the Christian Broadcasting Network. She joined AARP. She started sleeping on the couch.

She sued a man who years before had bumped her in the parking lot of a Cocoa Beach Publix. A judge dismissed it because the man was now dead. She continued to haggle over money with her second ex-husband. She accused a man she had worked with of sexual harassment. She sued her former company for back pay.

"And your ability of clear judgment is impaired?" an attorney for her old company asked her in a deposition.

"Still," she said, "yes."

She hired attorneys and then stopped responding to them. She stopped paying them. She filed motion after motion in courts, on her own, which judges dismissed as nonsense. She stopped showing up for court hearings. She didn't go to scheduled depositions. "Avoiding service," process servers wrote in their notes. "Defendant is barricaded in her condo."

Her brother-in-law called to tell her that her mother was ill and near death. She didn't answer the phone. This was in 2002. He called the Sheriff's Office to get a deputy to go to the townhouse to let her know. She didn't answer the door. He called the Sheriff's Office again two days later to tell her that her mother had died. She didn't answer the door.

Finally, in 2003, a judge issued a warrant for her arrest for contempt of court because of the missed depositions and hearings, and deputies managed to coax her out of the townhouse, taking her away in the back of a cruiser. The arrest report said her hair was brown and her build was "stout." She now weighed 220 pounds. She was sentenced to a week in county jail.

Neighbors talked. They decided she had been arrested for using the Internet to steal people's identities. It wasn't true, but she was on the Internet, leaving wee-hours posts on genealogy forums like Cousin Connect and Ancestry.com.

At the time, she was around fifty years old, and totally disabled. Her mental illness and now also a thyroid condition and a circulatory disease left her aching and fatigued, with dry skin, a dull mind and a slow heart. She was not who she was. The Internet didn't have to know.

"I am the grandchild of Joseph Mulford and Elizabeth Downey," she wrote on Ancestry.com.

"I am the granddaughter of Zelma's oldest sister."

"I have copies of many of the Yenger family records."

"I am very eager to talk with you."

"Contact me."

She ripped out a page from the local section of *Florida Today*, on Aug. 18, 2006, and underlined information about free adult games of Scrabble, checkers and cards. "Come out and enjoy a game with friends," it said, "or just socialize and meet new people."

She started making long phone calls back to Ohio, eighty-five minutes, 134 minutes, 200 minutes. She called her friend from high school and for hours she stayed on the phone as her friend recovered from knee surgery. She called her first husband, Jim Norris, to try to make amends, she told him, and he kept answering her calls because it sounded like she needed someone to talk to. She called her nephew, Brent Henninger, more than anybody else, he said, and he tried unsuccessfully to make her stop crying. He told her he was going to come down from Ohio to visit, but she told him no, please.

"I won't let you in."

Toward the end, in the last few years, she called the Sheriff's Office to say a white truck was parked in front of her townhouse. She called to say now it was a black car. She called to say her water line was broken and she couldn't shut it off. She called to say there was somebody outside in the dark, pounding on her windows, and she was home alone and scared, and now there were two voices, and the pounding was getting louder. A deputy was sent to Cherie Down Lane. Nothing. She didn't answer the door.

She put up a camera by her front door and a camera on her back porch. She watched a monitor inside. She drilled holes in her garage door so she could look out without others looking in.

On July 23, 2009, she called the Sheriff's Office again to say she believed her ex-husband and some of her neighbors had conspired to make her car stop running. A deputy went to check and concluded there were no signs of vandalism or mischief and the car was just old and broken down.

She started writing a letter to a friend. The last couple months, she said in her shaky-handed writing, had been confusing. She no longer knew what was real. She never sent the letter. She called her nephew and left a message. *"It's Aunt Kathy. Everything between you and me is fine. I love you."*

She left her car keys in her dark blue purse on the cluttered kitchen table. She went out to the garage. She shut off the electricity. She got in her car. Maybe she felt safe inside her locked townhouse, inside her locked garage, inside her locked car. The thin white candle was the only light. At some point, the flame flickered, then went out.

In Brevard County, in Cape Canaveral, and on Cherie Down Lane, where the affordable, same-shaped, sun-strained units are filled with retirees and winter-only residents and year-round tenants who struggle to pay the rent, here is some of what happened around Kathryn Norris over the next almost sixteen months:

An elementary school started a new year, ended the year, started another. A space shuttle took off and came back five times. A neighbor saw her cats. A neighbor crossed the street and picked her limes. A neighbor noticed her garbage can hadn't moved. A neighbor saw some fluid leaking out from under the door to her garage and wondered if it was motor oil or something else. A neighbor had a Christmas party. A neighbor on New Year's Eve sat down on his couch and put a .22-caliber pistol to the side of his head behind his right ear. Pulled the trigger. People walked by to the beach.

Her nephew from Ohio called the Sheriff's Office in March 2010 and said he hadn't been able to get in touch with her, which wasn't so unusual, because once he and his family hadn't heard from her for two years, but now he was worried. A deputy went to the townhouse to check on her. No signs of forced entry. No insect activity on the windows. Nothing suspicious. She didn't answer the door.

A neighbor called the Sheriff's Office to say her gates were broken and the townhouse seemed vacant.

The bank foreclosed. People hired by the bank went inside and took pictures of her stuff. They took pictures of her car. That happened twice. "Diligent search and inquiry," they wrote. "Confirmed residence is unoccupied."

And Kathryn Norris had her fifty-sixth birthday. And her fifty-seventh. The summer heat made decomposition quick. Eager flies found ways inside, through tiny slits and vents, seeking their sustenance from the moisture of death. Her neighbors who shared a wall were still in Cincinnati for the summer. Winter months brought cooler weather. The air dried out, and so did she, as her skin turned brown and thick. The flies moved on. She could have stayed that way for years.

The man who found Kathryn Norris fixed up the Cherie Down townhouse and sold it in April to a woman from Orlando. She uses it as a weekend getaway for her family and friends. The neighbors hear their music and laughter. The woman says her neighbors seem friendly. The neighbors say so does she. They say hello.

The remains of Kathryn Norris had to be kept as evidence until the county finished the investigation of her death. That was just last month. The medical examiner identified her using DNA from her hair that matched DNA from her sister. She had no drugs in her system, but that was expected, given the extent of the decomposition.

The autopsy used words that were clinical and factual but also incomplete. Her remains were labeled unremarkable. The cause and manner of her death were listed undetermined.

The manner is a mystery. The cause is not.

She disappeared long before she died.

She was buried in Ohio. There was a short service. Her brief obituary said she would be missed.

AUTHOR'S AFTERWORDS...

In November 2010, a man in Brevard County, FL, bought in a foreclosure auction a townhouse in Cape Canaveral a block from the beach. He got the keys and opened the front door and walked around downstairs and then upstairs and then walked back down through the kitchen and into the garage, where he found an old Chevy hatchback, inside of which he saw what looked like the mummified remains of a human being. He called the sheriff. Deputies came quickly. The home and the car belonged to the same woman. Her name was Kathryn Norris.

I sat at my desk in the main office of the Tampa Bay Times, on the other side of the state in St. Petersburg, and read a brief about this. I clicked around some of the other early coverage from local papers and TV. Neighbors saying she kept to herself. Neighbors saying they hadn't seen her for probably a year and maybe more than that.

Who was she? How had she become a corpse in a dress in her car? How had she died so alone? I sent her name to one of the news researchers in the Times' library. What came back was a standard background, things I look at no matter the subject, no matter the piece. Every one of us makes paper tracks that are public records, some more than others, and Kathryn Norris had left behind more than I was expecting. I could see on my computer screen in St. Pete that she had been married and divorced, twice, and I could see that she had sued people and that people had sued her—fat, rich files, no doubt, in the courthouses near where she had lived. Public records are like the bottom rungs of rope ladders. They're something to grab onto. Names lead to names. Information leads to information. Material leads to material. What I saw were lots of rope ladders.

It was more than enough to justify a trip over there. I scheduled three days and two nights and left St. Pete early one morning and drove east, past Orlando's fantasy lands and on over to Cape Canaveral on the opposite coast, where the ground used to shake when the space shuttle launched.

Then I got lucky.

Most stories in newspapers aren't actually stories. They're parts of stories. They're usually beginnings or endings. Someone's opened a shop. Someone's died in a crash. There's an election today. Here was an ending. My task now was to try to report back to the beginning.

I pulled up in front of 232 Cherie Down Lane. There was a big red dumpster on the front lawn. The man who had bought the townhouse was inside, cleaning it out, and I introduced myself and told him what I was doing. We talked about the day he found her. He showed me around. Lots of the place was the way she had left it. There was a bunch to get rid of. She'd clearly been a hoarder. I let the man get back to work but asked if I could stick around and make some notes. He said sure. I did that and then asked if I could take some of her stuff, and he said sure to that, too, because sheriff's investigators already had been through, and her sister and her nephew already had been down from Ohio and taken what they wanted. It was trash to him and information to me. So I picked up a laundry basket and started putting things in it. Receipts. Scraps of paper. Envelopes with return addresses. Books and magazines. Coffee mugs. Fridge magnets. Pill bottles with prescriptions stuck to the sides. At some point, the man noticed the kinds of things I seemed to be looking for, and he said to me: You know, a lot of that stuff, it's already out in the dumpster.

The rest of my trip over there was valuable. I knocked on doors up and down Cherie Down Lane. Some people told me to get lost. Some people told me not much. And some people told me about the banana tree and the housecoat and the garbage can and the boards on her windows for hurricanes she then kept up for months and the strange fluid that seeped for a while out from under the door to her garage. And I walked around the neighborhood and down to the beach. I saw there was an elementary school nearby, close enough, probably, for her to have heard the squeals and chatter of children's play. And I spent time speed-reading in courthouses. There were depositions and transcripts of hearings from her divorce. She had sued her former company for back pay and so they demanded proof of illness and need. Details about her finances. Details about her health. Notes from her doctors. She had sued an elderly man in a flimsy case involving an alleged mishap in a grocery store parking lot. More testimony in front of a judge. It was almost like she just wanted to talk.

But the most important thing I did in Cape Canaveral was take the laundry basket and go get in that dumpster. I didn't really know what I had until I started looking at it back at the hotel. I had phone bills and letters and notes on index cards about daily routines. There were dates. I could touch what she had touched. I could see her shaky hand. I organized the material as best I could in chronological order, laying it out on the desk, the dresser and the bed, standing in the quiet and staring at these intimate, little glimpses into her isolated descent.

When I got back to St. Pete, I requested more documents—all the calls for service to the sheriff from Cherie Down Lane in the sixteen months she had decomposed, some more documents from her court cases that were actually up in Atlanta, and the autopsy and crime photos that would turn public once the investigation was complete. And I made more calls. To one of her few good friends up in Ohio. To her two ex-husbands. To her nephew. To real estate agents who knew the neighborhood. To decomposition experts.

And then I waited. I feel like waiting is an under-discussed part of reporting. It's not always a possibility. It can feel like a luxury. In this case, though, it was a necessity. It took the sheriff's office and the medical examiner six months to finish. I worked on other stuff during that time. But finally the rest of the records arrived in the mail, and her remains were released to her family in Ohio, and they had a service up there and put a short obit in one of the papers. I wrote pretty fast after that.

I liked this story. Still do. I like it because I didn't want to dishonor her and I don't think I did. What I owed Kathryn Norris was what I think we owe everybody we write about—authenticity in approach and sincerity in reporting. This story is reported. It's reported more than it's written. Every sentence is earned. And I also like it because it's the closest I've come, I think, to using everything I've learned so far about how to try to do this work right. Knock on doors. Dial those numbers. Always go to the courthouse. Climb every rope ladder. And when you're wearing a shirt and a tie and there's probably some good stuff down in a dumpster? Get in.

Thomas Lake

T homas Lake is the third of Robert and Elizabeth Lake's six home-schooled children. He spent seven years working for newspapers in Georgia, Massachusetts, and Florida before he caught his big break, in 2008, when *Sports Illustrated* writer Gary Smith helped him get a freelance assignment for *SI*. That story, "2 on 5," won the Henry Luce Award for story of the year among all the magazines of Time Incorporated, the nation's largest magazine publisher.

Lake has written about a softball player who carried her injured opponent around the bases, a buzzer-beating three-pointer that actually saved people from a tornado, and the man falsely accused of cutting Michael Jordan from his high school basketball team.

Lake graduated from Herkimer County Community College in upstate New York and Gordon College in Wenham, MA. His work has been anthologized in three editions of the annual *Best American Sports Writing* collection. As of 2012, he was the youngest senior writer for *Sports Illustrated*. He lives in Atlanta with his wife, Sara, and their two children.

The Boy Who Died of Football

On the day Max Gilpin ran himself to death before nearly 140 witnesses, he did almost nothing but what he was told. He began complying an hour before dawn, when he stumbled out of bed at his father's command, and he continued through the morning and afternoon behind the brick walls of his school as the August sun parched the valleys of Kentuckiana. After school he surrendered to the will of his football coach, a man he loved as he loved his father, and he hoped this surrender would be enough to please them both.

This is a story about obedience, the kind that gives football and religion their magnetic power. Max Gilpin was an obedient boy. He was, to borrow a word from his adoring mother, a *pleaser*, and if he misbehaved, he had four parents to set him straight. They had family meetings, four against one, mother and stepfather and father and stepmother. Max's mother told him to obey his stepmother, and his father told him to obey his stepfather. So he did. And although he hated the Adderall pills—although they flattened his personality, made him smile less, made him want to hurl them off the deck into the back-yard—he took them, usually, because they also made him stare at the teacher instead of the ceiling fan.

Max had a girlfriend named Chelsea Scott, a cheerleader with green eyes and shining auburn hair. They were sophomores at Pleasure Ridge Park High in Louisville, and they'd been a couple barely forty-eight hours. It should have been much longer, but Max couldn't muster the courage to ask her out. Fortunately Chelsea was a modern woman. Since the end of their freshman year she had kept a picture of Max on her phone, with the caption "MY BABY," and over the summer, on MySpace, she had asked for and received his cell number. Still he needed encouragement. Finally Chelsea wrote Max a love note, delivered by her best friend, and he understood. That was Monday. Today was Wednesday. He had never taken Chelsea on a date. Instead they commiserated in the halls between periods, and Max complained about football.

In middle school Max's mother, Michele, struggled with Max to put his pads on. He was on the verge of quitting until Michele (head cheerleader,

Western High) called his father, Jeff, and put Max on the line, and when the conversation was over, Max was no longer quitting. He did manage to sit out for a couple of years, but at the start of high school Max told his father he was going to play football. And his father (offensive lineman, Butler High) taught him power cleans and leg presses and rhythmic breathing. He bought Max protein shakes, and his mother bought him the muscle-building substance creatine. Max tried to quit again that year, but his parents talked him out of it, and gradually he came to embrace football. By August 2008, just after his fifteenth birthday, he stood six foot two and weighed 216 pounds. He had gained about twenty-six pounds in six months and had begun wearing sleeveless shirts to show off his muscles.

One thing stood in the way of Max Gilpin and football greatness. Football demands a certain brutality, a hunger to smash the other guy's face, and Max had no such hunger. He liked to fix things—decks, porch swings, BMX bikes— and he talked about opening a mechanic's shop on Miami Beach. He didn't want to smash anything, even though he was an offensive tackle and his job was knocking people down. The coaches told him to get angry, get mean, use that helmet, quit being so nice. Max tried very hard, and his father saw him improving by the day, but he had a long way to go. In practice, as the linemen took turns facing off to improve their skills, Max stepped aside and let others go in front of him. His girlfriend from freshman year said Max was a true Christian, and this sounds about right. If Jesus had played football, He might have played like Max Gilpin.

Max's football coach also believed in Jesus and lived his life in relentless pursuit of heaven. His name was Jason Stinson, and he sat in the balcony on Sunday mornings at Valley View Church in southwest Louisville with a bible called *God's Game Plan* on a lap whose wide expanse would barely fit between the door and the center console of his Toyota Camry. Coach Stinson was six foot four and 300 pounds, and he had been such a fearsome offensive lineman at Louisville that he got an NFL tryout with the Giants before being cut in the preseason of 1996. Now he was thirty-five years old, with a wife and two children, and he saw the 104 boys on the Panthers' football team as sons of a different kind. They came to him for money when they couldn't afford lunch, counsel when their girlfriends turned up pregnant, new shoes when their old ones wore out. And although his coaching job paid only $20 a day on top of his salary as a Web design teacher, he never turned them away, because he knew God was watching. The coach liked to say he wasn't making football players; he was making good daddies, good citizens, good taxpayers. So he was more surprised than anyone when his conduct at football practice on Aug. 20, 2008, became the subject of one of the largest investigations in the history of the Louisville Metro Police Department.

It was a miserable practice. The temperature hit ninety-four degrees that day, and the boys, after staying up late all summer, came in exhausted from a new routine that had them out of bed long before sunrise. Around 5:30 that afternoon, after team stretching and individual drills, Coach Stinson called the twenty-two varsity starters to join him near the center of the field. This is how he remembers it:

"Offense, huddle up!" he said. "Defense, put your skivvies on!" (Skivvies in this case were jerseys of an alternate color.) The boys either ignored him or didn't hear.

"OFFENSE, HUDDLE UP! DEFENSE, PUT YOUR SKIVVIES ON!"

Still they did not come. Perhaps they were distracted by the girls' soccer game beginning on the next field.

"OFFENSE, HUDDLE UP! DEFENSE, PUT YOUR SKIVVIES ON!"

Only four or five boys obeyed. Later, several witnesses would use the words *mad* and *angry* to describe Stinson's reaction. But Stinson insisted he was not angry. He was just disappointed, and now he needed a new plan.

"ON THE LINE!" he bellowed. "IF WE'RE NOT GONNA PRACTICE, WE'RE GONNA RUN."

The command applied to everyone, not just the starters, and the boys got on the line. They knew what was coming. In helmets and pads they would run across the field and back and across the field and back again, a total of about 220 yards, or one eighth of a mile. Each of these runs counted as a single gasser, and today the boys were starting the gassers earlier and running them longer than usual. Yes, it was good preparation for the hard running they would do in games. But this early running was also widely seen as a punishment. Max Gilpin was not a varsity starter and therefore not one of those who had misbehaved. He was, however, a poor runner. And so he quietly accepted a punishment he had not earned, which fell harder on him than it did upon those who deserved it.

The events of the next fifty minutes are a case study in the limits of eyewitness testimony. No video footage surfaced in the police investigation, and the roughly 140 spectators told stories that ranged from the plausible to the mathematically impossible. They couldn't even agree on whether Stinson was wearing a whistle that day. Nevertheless, a parade of witnesses said they heard the coach say one thing that set the tone for the gassers. It seems strange that Stinson still denies saying it to the runners, because it wasn't just soccer parents who said they heard it. It wasn't just assistant coaches and disgruntled players. In the opening statement at Stinson's trial for the reckless homicide of Max Gilpin, the coach's own defense attorney acknowledged, "Jason said it."

And what Jason Stinson said to his players, according to many people, was this: "WE'RE GONNA RUN TILL SOMEBODY QUITS."

Football coaches have a long and rich tradition of daring their players to quit. It probably didn't start with Bear Bryant, the most revered college coach of all time, but he did it as well as anyone. Bryant believed any boy who quit on him in practice would quit on him in the fourth quarter, and he did horrible things to make sure no quitter ever got the chance. In 1954, his first year with Texas A&M, he led 111 young men to a thorn-infested wilderness camp in Junction, Texas, and proceeded to nearly kill them. Bryant didn't believe in injuries, because he'd once played a whole game on a broken leg, and he didn't believe in water breaks, because he thought his boys would be tougher without them. His radical expectations are described in the following passage from Jim Dent's 1999 book, *The Junction Boys.*

"All of these boys need some time off," [trainer Smokey Harper] said. "Some got bad injuries in there, Coach. Joe Boring can barely walk with that bum knee, and another boy looks like he's got a fractured ankle."

Bryant nodded and said nothing. Then he swung open the screen door and marched into the trainers' room. He jabbed at the air with his index finger and shouted, "You, you, you, you, you, you, and you! Get your butts dressed for practice. Be on the field in ten minutes. I want no more excuses out of you candy asses!"

So the boys limped out for more punishment. Players who collapsed from heat exhaustion had to crawl to the sideline or be dragged off by student assistants. When a boy fell face-first to the ground from heatstroke, Bryant kicked his fallen body. Sure enough, he ran off all the quitters. Seventy-six boys quit during those ten days, and another ten were too badly hurt to play in the opener. The Aggies lost nine of their ten games that season, but two years later they went undefeated and finished fifth in the national rankings. The survivors of Bryant's hell camp discovered that nothing in life could stop them. They became doctors, lawyers, engineers, chief executives. By the time of their team reunion twenty-five years later, many were millionaires.

In the genealogy of football coaches, you can draw a line from Bear Bryant straight down to Jason Stinson. Bryant begat Howard Schnellenberger (he played tight end for the Bear at Kentucky in the 1950s and served as his assistant coach at Alabama from '61 to '65), and Schnellenberger coached Stinson at Louisville in the early 1990s. In '89 Schnellenberger recruited a lineman named Thomas Sedam. According to Sedam, water was never available at practices. Schnellenberger, who declined to comment for this story, made his boys run gassers, just as Bryant had and Stinson would, and when thirsty players took mouthfuls of the ice that was kept to cool down injuries, coaches forced them to spit it out. One day Sedam collapsed from heatstroke after running too much. He spent almost a month in the hospital and later sued Schnellenberger for negligence. They settled out of court.

After Louisville, Schnellenberger went to Oklahoma. He resigned at the end of a mediocre season during which two players quit because of heat illness. One of them, defensive tackle Brian Ailey, nearly died of heatstroke. He filed his own lawsuit, but Schnellenberger said water was not restricted at his practices, and a federal judge threw the case out for lack of evidence. According to a 1996 *Tulsa World* story, "Schnellenberger dismissed Ailey's incident as unfortunate but insisted his coaching techniques were not out of line. He points out that he had been doing business like that for years." Schnellenberger, who coached Miami to a national championship in 1983, is still doing business, at seventy-six, as coach at Florida Atlantic.

Sedam played for Schnellenberger before Jason Stinson did; Ailey played after. You might expect Stinson to tell stories similar to theirs. He will not. He says the coach was demanding but never abusive and always provided sufficient water at practice. He says he would play for Schnellenberger again. And if this is hard to understand, remember that the Junction Boys—that is, the ones who survived Junction—would almost certainly play for Bear Bryant again. They wore those ten days like a badge of honor for the rest of their lives. Jason Stinson says his father made him a man. But when Stinson left the care of Howard Schnellenberger, he considered himself even more of a man.

In the '60s at Southern High in Louisville there was another football coach who didn't believe in injuries. When a player broke his thumb and said, "Coach, I broke my thumb," and it was all swollen and purple, the coach told him to spit on it and get back in the game. Around that time a boy named David Stengel decided to tend his horses instead of attending the coach's unofficial spring practice, and when the coach punished him that fall by giving him old equipment and shoes that didn't fit, David quit.

Nearly fifty years later, after David Stengel became Louisville's chief prosecutor, after he had Jason Stinson indicted for the death of Max Gilpin, he would say Stinson reminded him of his old football coach. And when Stengel got emails from around the world telling him what a "sissy" he was, going after a football coach for doing nothing but coaching football, well, Stengel begged to differ. In his younger days he could bench-press 370 pounds, and he kept a picture of the Mohawk OV-1A in which he flew 127 combat missions over the

Ho Chi Minh Trail, including one in which he was shot down. Football is a pale imitation of war. Sissy? David Stengel would like to see you walk through this door and say that.

About a month after the fatal practice, under questioning by the police, Coach Stinson made a casual remark that explains quite a lot about Max Gilpin's collapse. "Now, but Max is the kind of kid," he said, "if you don't see him, you wouldn't notice him." Even though he was six foot two and 216 pounds, Max was not a commanding presence. He could be almost invisible. And visibility made a crucial difference on that sweltering afternoon.

The boys were allowed to run at their own pace, but they had an incentive to run as hard as they could. It went beyond merely impressing the coaches. If Stinson noticed a boy giving extraordinary effort, he might dismiss him from the running and let him cool off in the shade. One of the team's best runners was Antonio Calloway, a safety who also sprinted for the track team, and Antonio ran angry that day. First he was angry at the other boys for goofing off, and then he was angry at Stinson for not rewarding him with a license to quit. At some point the soccer spectators heard a horrible sound, something deep and strange and very loud, which turned out to be Antonio Calloway gasping for breath. His reward for blind obedience was a precautionary trip to the hospital.

The boys ran on. They took turns. The smaller players ran while the big boys (including Max) rested, and then they switched. Most players agree that Max ran hard, but there is a wide range of stories about how the running affected him. Some say he had no trouble breathing. Others say he vomited, fell to his knees, struggled for breath. There were many reports of players vomiting, and one boy said he heard others crying. None of this was enough to make Stinson call off the drill. "If we stop the drill every time somebody got hurt," he said later in a deposition for the wrongful-death suit filed by Max's parents, "we wouldn't have any drills left to do."

MICHAEL COOPER, PLAINTIFF'S ATTORNEY: Well, let's say that we have players, one or more, that are vomiting—

STINSON: No, sir.

COOPER: —would you stop a drill?

STINSON: No, sir.

COOPER: One or more players that are vomiting, another player had to quit the drill because he had passed out.

STINSON: No, sir.

COOPER: Players vomiting, passing out, they want water, do you quit the drill?

STINSON: No, sir. I mean, you can keep building on this all day long and keep adding up, and eventually, yes, you quit the drill, but it's not to the point of if a child is vomiting do we stop the drill, no, sir.

COOPER: I'm just trying to figure out, is there something you as head coach can tell me if I saw these events occur with my players I would stop the drill because I think they're getting overheated. Can you give me any scenario where that would occur?

STINSON: Not that I can think of.

In any case, Stinson had other things to worry about. Some boys were running and some were not. Understand: This was not an elite squad. If you wanted to play football at Pleasure Ridge Park High, you just showed up and took the physical. You might not get playing time, but at least you'd get a jersey, and some boys just wanted that jersey. They were called the jersey-wearers, and they had no intention of overworking themselves. As one of them later told the police, "We wasn't really runnin' for real, we was walkin' and laughin' and stuff, 'cause we wasn't about to run for no hour in the sun." (Not that it was even an hour; the best estimates put the running at thirty-five to forty minutes.)

Those boys demanded attention, and Stinson gave it to them. He called them away from the group and supervised them in a drill called up-downs, which involved running in place and then dropping to the ground and then running in place some more. Even at this they performed badly, which, according to the court transcript, led the coach to say something like, "We're gonna do 'em right or we're gonna do 'em until somebody quits." Today the coach says that this statement might have been misconstrued as applying to all the players, including the ones still running gassers. He claims to have said at the beginning of gassers, "If you don't want to do what we're asking you to do, please feel free to quit. We'll still be friends, we'll still high-five you in the hallway, but you can't play football." All this may be true, but there is a loose consensus that the boys running the gassers believed Stinson was telling them to keep running until someone quit the team.

Which someone did.

Now, a word about quitting. Stinson believed that if you quit in practice, you wouldn't just quit in the fourth quarter. You would quit in life. Bear Bryant actually wanted the boys to quit—that is, he wanted the quitters to quit—but Stinson, despite appearances, actually wanted to keep them. If they stayed on the football team, he kept his leverage. He could make sure they made good grades and behaved in class. He could keep trying to mold them into good daddies, good citizens, good taxpayers. And if they really did quit—if they called his bluff—he lost that leverage. Which is why he tried to bring them back. A player named David Englert had quit three times, and Stinson always talked him into returning. Sure enough, he was in the up-down group, the incorrigible group, and sure enough, he quit again. And sure enough, a few days later he was back on the team. (Not long after that, he quit for the last time.) Later he wrote Stinson a letter that read, in part, "You have always been there for me in everything I do. I haven't been able to sleep for the past couple of days, I walk around with a lump in my throat...I love you...Please pray for me as I pray for you."

Jason Stinson didn't believe in quitting on anyone. After all, Jesus never quit on the dying thief.

But there is another way to see David Englert, and in this light he needs neither mercy nor forgiveness. What he deserves is a round of applause. "I congratulated the child for quitting the team," a soccer spectator named Timothy Moreschi testified at Stinson's trial. "I said, 'You're the only man out on that field.'"

Take a moment now to go with Max Gilpin as he runs the last mile of his life.

Early in the running, before the damage is irreversible, he can look to the right through the face mask of his steaming helmet and see his father watching him. And this sight must give him the courage to run harder. Max is a pleaser, remember, and he wants to make his father proud. His father played lineman too, for Butler High, class of '80, and Butler won the Kentucky Class 4A championship his senior year. But his father quit football before that season and missed his chance at immortality.

Max has a shot at starting for the jayvee, and what he lacks in meanness he can try to make up in determination. At a scrimmage just last Friday, his father saw him take on a powerful defensive end from another school and play better than he'd ever played: "Max shut this kid down. He knocked him down two or three times. He turned him. He got under him. This kid never made another tackle or another play that I saw. In fact, Max played so well that they put him on defense. He's never played defense on a high school level. He didn't even know the plays. They just told him to go for the ball."

Later, when presented with Jeff Gilpin's account of that scrimmage, Stinson will refuse to confirm it. ("Didn't see it happen, didn't hear about it and didn't have any film to review.") Which will leave two ways to interpret the story. Either Jeff Gilpin is imagining things or Coach Stinson is oblivious. And both possibilities leave Max with the same mandate. Either he must close the gap between his actual performance and his father's vision of his performance, which means he must work even harder; or he must play so surpassingly well that Coach Stinson finally takes notice—which means he must work even harder.

Like most sons, Max regards his father with a blend of love and fear. Jeff will later say Max was his best friend. He will talk about driving Max to guitar lessons, about missing the way Max laughed so deeply that his eyes nearly shut. And while both Jeff and Michele want Max to go to college, Max would rather be an auto mechanic just like his father. But in other ways Max is nothing like Jeff. There is some indication that Jeff is capable of violence and coercion. In 1999, when Max was five and his parents had separated, Jeff was arrested and charged with aggravated assault after allegedly punching and bruising his live-in girlfriend. (Records of the case's outcome are no longer on file at the courthouse.) Max's stepmother, Lois Gilpin, will later say Jeff used to slap Max on the back of the head and drag him around by the ear. Jeff will deny all this, but Lois will not be the only one to say Max saw Jeff as a bully. She and Katlin Reichle, who dated Max during freshman year, will say Jeff monitored Max's performance at football practice and, if Max didn't play well enough, left him there and made someone else pick him up. Lois will say Jeff sent Max text messages to express shame in Max's performance. Katlin will say Max told her, "I'm trying my best, but I don't know what more I can do."

All around him now on this August afternoon, Max's teammates find ways to get out of running. Fast ones are dismissed for good effort. Freshmen are dismissed because they're freshmen. Some of the fat kids are barely running. The goof-offs are pulled out to do up-downs. Max is a slow runner, of course, so running hard doesn't make him stand out more. It makes him stand out less. It puts him closer to the middle of the pack. It ensures that he will run the maximum distance at maximum effort. And if he shows signs that something is wrong—if he vomits or falls to his knees or stands up only with the help of his teammates, as witnesses will later testify at the trial—Stinson doesn't notice. He's distracted by the jersey-wearing goof-offs who can't even do the up-downs right.

Max's temperature is rising to catastrophic levels, to 105 degrees, 107 degrees, perhaps 109 degrees. The cells in his body are melting. And so, when his father sees him cross the finish line on the last sprint, fall on all fours, stand again, stagger and fall for the last time, there's no telling whether Max hears Stinson say the mystifying line that marks the end of practice. The Panthers have run until someone quit, and the quitter is not Max Gilpin. "DING, DING, DING!" the coach yells as David Englert quits once again. "WE HAVE A WINNER!"

Looking back on the practice two years later, the coach noticed a major coincidence. David Englert quit at nearly the precise moment that Max's group finished what was always going to be the last sprint. Neither event caused the other, Stinson said. He insisted that practice would have ended regardless, because everyone knew that the activity bus was on a fixed schedule and many of the boys had to ride it home.

Then, more coincidences. The coach wasn't looking when Max collapsed. Nor did he notice anything was wrong when Max's father ran onto the field, or when at least three assistant coaches hustled to Max's side, or when the athletic director drove toward Max on a John Deere utility cart. A lot was happening right then, with nearly a hundred players leaving the field and a soccer game proceeding a few feet away. The coach was busy. He had a team meeting to conduct, but first he had several goof-offs to yell at once again. They'd gone straight to the water, which was forbidden until after the meeting, and he had to round them up. And then he had to yell at everyone for the terrible practice and tell them they didn't deserve to be Panthers, which half of them probably didn't. All this time Max's cells were melting. Numerous soccer parents turned around to witness the practice, because Stinson was loud and the soccer game was boring. Some saw fit to inform the local newspaper, *The Courier-Journal*, whose reporting led to the criminal investigation.

There followed a series of natural disasters that coincided with milestones in the investigation. On September 14, the day Stinson gave his statement to the police, rare winds battered Louisville with hurricane force and caused four deaths from falling timber. The following January, just after Stinson was indicted for reckless homicide, an ice storm came upon Kentucky and deprived nearly half a million homes and businesses of electricity; at least fifty-five people were killed. And on Aug. 4, 2009, the day Stinson was indicted for wanton endangerment in the same case, many residents of Louisville fled to their rooftops to escape a rising flood. Stinson worked with his church to ease the suffering of the victims. Nevertheless he saw these events as acts of a God who cared enough to keep him off the front page.

In general the people of Pleasure Ridge Park took Stinson's side. They knew him to be a good Christian man and trusted him with their boys because their boys loved Coach Stinson. They held a silent auction to help pay for his legal defense, and Howard Schnellenberger donated an autographed football. A barbecue joint called Mark's Feed Store promised to donate a portion of its profits over several nights to Stinson's cause, and so many people showed up that one night the place had to shut down because the food was all gone. Stinson's friend Rodney Daugherty wrote a well-researched book—*Factors Unknown: The Commonwealth of Kentucky vs. David Jason Stinson & Football*—that redirected blame from Stinson to the prosecutors who brought the case. Pleasure Ridge Park High principal David Johnson (free safety, Louisville) summed up the feeling of many others when he said he knew Stinson did nothing wrong because "I know what kind of person he is."

It wasn't just that Stinson did nothing wrong. Stinson *could do nothing* wrong. Max's mother said that Stinson's wife told her around the time of Max's funeral that the coach was on "suicide watch." Not possible, according to Stinson, because he didn't blame himself for Max's death, and he would never consider suicide—that would be quitting. A soccer mom swore at the trial that Stinson said something to the boys during the running that no one else seemed to remember: "Come on, who's going to be the sacrificial lamb?" No way, Stinson says. He would never say that, because he knows of only one sacrificial lamb. And that lamb's name is Jesus.

But football is America's game, and more than 600 boys and men have been killed since 1931 as a direct result of playing football. No other team sport comes close. The National Center for Catastrophic Injury Research measured catastrophic injuries in all high school fall sports from 1982 to 2009 and found that 97.1 percent of them occurred in football. And it must be no coincidence that in an '08 Gallup poll, more Americans chose football as their favorite sport to watch than chose baseball, basketball, hockey, soccer, auto racing, golf and tennis combined. We can say we watch for the precision of the quarterbacks, the grace of the receivers, the speed of the running backs, but this is only part of the truth. We watch because football players are warriors, because they are brave, because all that throwing and catching and running is done under threat of lethal violence. There is such a thing as touch football, and such a thing as flag football. Both are safe. No one pays to watch them.

"You've got a man looking at prison time for being a football coach," defense attorney Alex Dathorne (cornerback, Miami Palmetto Senior High) said in his closing argument on Sept. 17, 2009. "Jason Stinson on August the 20 of 2008 did absolutely nothing different than every coach in this county, in this Commonwealth, in this country, was doing on that day."

This was part of the reason Dathorne and his law partner, Brian Butler (rabid fan, Notre Dame), two of the best defense attorneys in Louisville, took Stinson's case at a discounted rate. They believed the game of football was on criminal trial and a loss would be disastrous. Coaches would quit by the hundreds for fear of prosecution. The media coverage already had them terrified. During jury selection, one potential juror (a coach, apparently of another sport) said, "Literally every practice, if we're running, I make a point of telling the kids up front so people can hear me, 'You can stop, you can go on or you can do whatever you want on your own.'"

Before the trial Stengel put his chance of winning a conviction at less than 10 percent, based on how the people of Louisville felt about football. "Football coaches," he said, "are right up there with the Father, Son and Holy Ghost." This is why, during jury selection, his assistants did their best to identify football bias. They asked all fantasy football players to raise their hands. They tried to weed out college football season-ticket holders. They tried—and failed miserably—to stock the jury with women. And women might not have helped them anyway. Max's girlfriend's mother, Misty Scott, had marinated so long in football culture that she could stand in her driveway one afternoon and casually toss off this remark about Louisville coach Bobby Petrino's departure: "Louisville football went down the drain so fast that we're still washing the red out of the sink."

More to the point, the commonwealth had a fragile case. Stinson would later look back at the thirteen days of the trial and decide his attorneys had racked up twelve wins, no losses and one tie. So why did Stengel prosecute a case he knew he would lose? There are two prevalent theories, and Stengel denies them both. One says he got the indictment before he understood the science of what happened to Max, and by that time it was too late to back out because the national media had descended. The other theory says the prosecution was a kind of public-service announcement intended to make coaches be more careful. Which it did. Some coaches reconsidered their use of negative motivation, and the state passed regulations that required more first-aid training and better education on heat illness.

The prosecutors tried to prove that Stinson withheld water that day, but one player after another said they'd taken several water breaks, including one right before the sprints. Besides, dehydration wasn't a factor in Max's death. Three doctors said so: Bill Smock, who usually testifies for the prosecution in Louisville; George Nichols, who founded the state medical examiner's office in Kentucky; and Dan Danzl, a co-author of the hallowed textbook Rosen's Emergency Medicine. The best the prosecution's kidney expert could do was to conclude from the records that Max was just dehydrated enough to be thirsty.

When the commonwealth attacked Stinson for his failure to help Max, the defense was ready. Stinson's attorneys showed that several other people quickly came to Max's aid and did the same things—applying ice packs, dousing him with water, removing his socks, calling 911 after a few minutes—that Stinson would have done if he'd been there. Both sides agreed that the presence of a certified athletic trainer might have improved Max's chances, but trainers are expensive, and the school was not required to have one at the practice.

The doctors agreed that Max died of complications from exertional heatstroke. This, of course, raised a crucial question: Why was Max the only player to die? The defense proposed an answer.

Tests from the hospital showed amphetamines in Max's system. They were most likely from the Adderall, the drug Max reluctantly took for better focus in school. And while it's impossible for Adderall alone to have caused Max's collapse—he'd been taking it for a year, and other boys at the practice also took Adderall—it could have slightly raised his body temperature.

There was also the creatine. It's not a banned substance, but the NCAA forbids colleges to distribute it to athletes. Max's mother said she hadn't bought it for him since March or April, but a friend testified that he saw Max taking creatine a week or two before his collapse. While scientists disagree on the possibility of side effects, a 2002 article in the journal *Neurosurgery* said there is credible evidence that creatine might contribute to heatstroke in some people.

But Max had probably been on both Adderall and creatine at other practices, some of them hotter than 94 degrees. Something had to be different on August 20.

The prosecutors had a theory. The difference was Coach Stinson. He lost his temper and forced the boys to run much harder than usual.

Except they weren't running for that long. Many football teams practice twice a day in the summer. There was just one practice that day, and it was a short one. The boys ran sprints for no more than forty minutes; actually it was much less, because they were in two alternating groups. Each group ran for about twenty minutes. Some boys gave implausibly high estimates for the number of 220-yard sprints they ran in that time period—as many as thirty-two. It probably seemed like thirty-two, but Coach Stinson always said it was twelve, and the math works in his favor. No one was allowed to start running until everyone in the other group had finished, including the players who were barely running; that would mean Max ran about a mile and a half, the majority of it in helmet and pads.

What was extraordinary, then, about August 20? The defense had another answer: By the time he got to practice, Max was already sick.

Here the medical experts fought to a draw. They argued over his white blood cells, his elevated lymphocytes, but it all came down to guesswork. The numbers neither proved nor disproved that he had a viral infection. They could be made to support either belief.

That left eyewitnesses, who were also problematic because of their vested interests in the outcome. Max's parents, who said he wasn't sick that day, were seeking more than $19 million in a wrongful-death suit. Some of

Stinson's players, who said Max was dragging along and complaining that he didn't feel well, felt a powerful loyalty to their coach. Two girls who knew Max contradicted each other, even though they were best friends: One, who was friends with Max's mother at the time of the trial, said he had seemed all right at lunch; the other, whose parents openly supported Stinson, said Max was obviously sick after school.

The truth was in there somewhere.

The defense called Lois Gilpin.

You should know a few things about Lois, the stepmother who saw Max before school on the day of his collapse. She and Jeff Gilpin had gone through an unpleasant separation. A judge granted her a restraining order against him after she said Jeff had threatened to drag her out of the house by her hair. She was also attending Stinson's church, Valley View, and she had accepted $700 from its benevolence fund to help pay her mortgage.

But when a prosecutor suggested that Lois had pulled a new story out of thin air to help Stinson, there was evidence to suggest otherwise. Two days after Max was hospitalized, a doctor wrote in the record, "New history, that patient may not have been feeling well on day of collapse." Lois swore that her story had remained the same all along, and the doctor's note seemed to corroborate it.

This is the story Lois Gilpin told under oath about Max's last morning at home: "I asked him if he wanted juice. He was to take his medicine, his Adderall that morning. And he was cranky. And I leaned over and I kissed his head, and he told me he had a headache and he was sick and he was hot. Jeff walked in and told him, 'We're going to be late, you need to get up; you need to get your butt in gear and you need to get to school.'

"He just said he didn't feel good, he had a headache. He didn't talk back to his dad. You know, when I kissed him, I told him he was hot. You know, I imagine he would have liked to have stayed home. I wish he would have stayed home. But he did what his dad said."

Later, when he looked back at his son's last practice, Jeff Gilpin was filled with pride and wonder. "I underestimated this kid, big-time," he said. "His heart. Can you imagine the fortitude it took to keep running out there?"

It is almost unimaginable. Never mind how long Max actually ran. What matters is that he ran far longer than he should have, despite what must have been terrible pain, even though quitting would have saved his life. And in dying he probably saved the lives of several boys who might otherwise suffer the same fate.

Cold blue twilight, Salvation Army parking lot. A very large man stands by a folding table, digging for clean underwear in a cardboard box. When he finds the white briefs, he holds them up, like a merchant or an auctioneer, until a poor man steps out of the crowd to claim them.

"Got a large sweater! Anybody? Anybody?" The large man's voice carries across the parking lot. "Long-sleeve, flannel! Nah, we're outta socks right now. Still lookin'. All right, brother. You have a good one."

All right, brother. This is how the men of Valley View Church talk. They come downtown every Monday night to feed and clothe the needy, and Jason Stinson comes with them because he is a free man. To him this is an act of godly obedience, not atonement, because Stinson is not guilty of anything. The jury said so. It took less than ninety minutes to decide.

When the giving is done, Stinson walks into the Texas Roadhouse off Dixie Highway, less than a mile from Max Gilpin's grave, and orders an eight-ounce sirloin, medium, and a baked potato with butter and sour cream. Every few minutes a high school girl comes over to smile and say hello. While he was under indictment, Stinson was placed in an administrative position away from children. But he is back in the classroom now, coaching basketball this fall. He plans to coach football again. Another man might have moved to another school or even another town, but that would be quitting. Anyway, there was no need. Stinson's stature in Pleasure Ridge Park is probably greater now than it was before. His supporters rose up with him for victory.

"We busted 'em in the teeth," Stinson says, referring to the criminal trial, by way of saying he and his lawyers would have done the same thing in the civil trial if it had gone that far. It was the school's insurance companies that insisted on the $1.75 million settlement in September with Max Gilpin's parents, he says. Purely a business decision. No one admitted anything.

During a bench conference at the criminal trial, Stinson's own attorney, Dathorne, said to the judge, "I think you can almost take judicial notice that Jason Stinson was being a jerk that day. Everybody said that." Now, at the roadhouse, when Stinson is asked to acknowledge the truth of this statement, he refuses. "I don't know what Alex meant by that," he says. "You'd have to ask him."

After interviews with more than 125 witnesses, the Jefferson County Public Schools delivered their own report on the Max Gilpin incident. It was so favorable to Stinson that Stengel called it "the biggest cover-up since Watergate." Nevertheless, school superintendent Sheldon Berman had a few things to say about Stinson's conduct:

"While the evidence did not reveal any violation of ... JCPS rules, I am extremely troubled—actually I am outraged—by the statement made that day by head coach Jason Stinson—that the running would end when someone quit the team. While this kind of negative motivation may be used in some amateur and even professional sports, that kind of culture has absolutely no place in JCPS' athletic programs."

The superintendent established an annual seminar that trains coaches not to motivate their players the way Stinson did that day. Stinson has attended it twice. Now, at the roadhouse, when asked to acknowledge that the seminar is a result of what he did on Aug. 20, 2008, he seems genuinely unaware of the connection. And if this is hard to believe, consider the story he gave in his civil deposition about a brief encounter with Max Gilpin after Max had finished the running that killed him.

At the trial, one of Stinson's own witnesses said Max leaned over and breathed heavily after the running. Another defense witness said Max fell and beat the ground in anger. Other players said Max couldn't even finish the running and had to be propped up. One of them said he returned from the final sprint to find Max on his hands and knees. Soon after that, he said, Max appeared to be foaming at the mouth, and his face was pale blue. But in the civil deposition, Stinson gave this account:

STINSON: Yes, sir. He had finished conditioning and was headed where he was needed to go.

PLAINTIFF'S ATTORNEY: He really wasn't in any distress as far as you could see?

STINSON: As far as I could tell.

For a few minutes on that Wednesday, after school and before football practice, no one told Max Gilpin what to do. And what he did was a total surprise. He was walking to the bus with Chelsea Scott, the green-eyed cheerleader who became his girlfriend through sheer will and persistence, and he was wearing one of his favorite outfits: a pair of yellow plaid shorts and a butter-yellow Aeropostale T-shirt that nicely set off the tan of his arms. He may have done what he did because he knew she wanted it, but perhaps this one time he decided to do what *he* wanted, just because. Anyway, he bent down and hugged her, close enough to smell the vanilla in her Victoria's Secret perfume, and then he kissed her mouth, for at least two seconds, as if he knew exactly what he was doing. It was their first kiss, and of course their last: a glimmer of the man Max Gilpin was becoming.

Then he walked toward the locker room and returned to obedience. He never stopped obeying, not even at the hospital. He hung on for three days, never fully conscious, as his body fell apart from the inside. His best friend,

Zach Deacon, told him, "Hang in there. Keep fighting. I love you." And Max kept fighting. His heart rate seemed to rise when people prayed. A nurse asked him to squeeze her hand, which he did, and said, "Max, if you can hear me, wiggle your toes." And he did.

Toward the end he had blood in his mouth and tears on his cheeks, and he finally got permission to quit. His mother whispered into his ear, "It's OK, Max. You can let go." A minute later he was gone.

AUTHOR'S AFTERWORDS...

Before I wrote the first word of my first magazine story, I spent seven years working for newspapers. Four papers in three states, starting in 2001 at a twice-weekly in rural Georgia where I covered six beats and wore an old-fashioned camera on a strap around my neck. That first job was the hardest. I had to show up by 8:30 a.m., preferably 8, and sometimes I didn't get home until 9 or 10 at night. My career should have ended about two months in, when I interrupted a contentious Jesup City Commission meeting to ask everyone to please wrap it up because by then we'd heard all their arguments at least two times each. Fortunately my publisher thought the whole thing was funny and let me off with a reprimand. He might not have been so kind if he'd known the reason for my impertinence: My long-distance girlfriend was flying in for a visit that night, and she made it hard to keep my mind on zoning variances.

I had just turned twenty-one, and I had no idea of the hard truth, which was this: at that age, at that point in my career, I could have no more written a good story than I could have grown feathery wings and flown to Saturn. Could some theoretical, super-twenty-one-year-old write a great story? Sure, I guess. In fact, I know. Gene Weingarten did it at age twenty, for *New York* magazine. Nick McDonell was seventeen when he wrote his novel *Twelve*. So it's not impossible. All I'm saying is that I couldn't, because at that stage of my development, I didn't have the habits of mind to pull it off. I got tired of reporting. I'd make a couple of phone calls and hope they were enough. I'd watch something strange happen and then write about how strange it was without bothering to ask the right people to explain it so it all made sense. I had not become a story detective.

Now, that might strike you as an odd term. Story detective. Pretentious, even. Okay, fine. It is. But it's the best way I know to describe what I'm talking about. And what I'm talking about is a set of instincts and skills and habits that very few people, if any, are born with. They come day by day, hour by hour, bad story by mediocre story, to the few people determined to keep building them. These attributes revolve around a single crucial assumption: If I want badly enough to discover something, I probably can.

So, I was thirty years old by the time I started on "The Boy Who Died of Football." I had been developing these skills for nine years. If I wasn't a full-fledged story detective by then, I had at least worn through the soles of several pair of sixty-dollar shoes. I knew what I wanted and where to look. Most of all I knew that when I set out to find something I would not stop until I'd found it, or until I ran out of time.

Being a story detective is both easier and harder than being a real detective. Easier in that you probably aren't risking your life, although, in rare cases, you might be. Easier in that you can usually follow the trail blazed by the real detectives and use their discoveries to your own ends, which may or may not resemble theirs. Harder in that you're looking for more than the plain bare facts that could send someone to prison. You're looking for character, emotion, drama. A beginning, a middle, an end.

Here the questions were simple enough. What really happened on the day Max Gilpin ran himself to death? Why did he do it? Who, if anyone, was to blame? In seeking the answers, I had a tremendous built-in advantage. Others had already spent years seeking them. There had been massive investigations by both a police department and a school district, not to mention a civil lawsuit that had resulted in numerous sworn statements and a criminal trial—every word had been written down. The records from these proceedings can be difficult to obtain, or at least expensive, but in this case I had help from a friend of the coach who wanted to convince me that the whole investigation had been a travesty. He made most of the documents available to me online, free of charge, and I double-checked with public officials to make sure the documents were authentic. I read more than 5,000 pages and took notes on all of them. It was astonishing how many different ways 140 people could remember the same event. What you develop over the years is an internal system of weights and measures, a sense of how to sift through conflicting information and figure out what rings true and what rings false and what falls somewhere in the middle. Without that sense, I could not have written this story.

But the documents are never enough by themselves. I must have interviewed thirty people. Two of them stand out in memory. One was Chelsea Scott, the cheerleader. She was very hard to find. But the story needed her. It needed a moment for Max to be himself, to stop taking orders and instead take charge. And I knew from Chelsea's police statement that she'd seen him that day. What I didn't know were the juicy details, the little things that would illuminate that moment. Real detectives don't trifle with things like that.

Well, she had an address listed on the police statement. I punched it into the GPS and drove out there. No luck. Her family had moved away. I must have gone there three times, knocking on neighbors' doors, looking for clues. Nothing. Most adults can be found through a paid Internet service called Nexis Public Records if you know a full name and preferably a date of birth, but Chelsea was a minor. She wasn't listed. I didn't know what to do. But I kept looking. If you want badly enough to discover something, you probably can.

At the courthouse I dug through the file for the civil lawsuit. Bingo: She'd given a civil deposition too, more recent than her police statement, and that deposition contained a different address. I high-tailed it out there and knocked on the door. A friendly woman answered. I explained who I was, why I was there, how I wanted to write something nice about Max from the perspective of someone who really knew him. The woman was Chelsea's mom. She seemed to get it. She said Chelsea had cheerleading practice now but I could meet her later at the fish-fry restaurant where the mom tended bar.

That first anecdote from the City Commission meeting may have made me seem utterly shameless. I am not. At least I wasn't, before I got into this game. I was a shy kid who was afraid to ask personal questions. I minded my own business and let other people mind theirs. I'm sure that was part of my problem at first. Story detectives do not mind their own business.

So I sit down in the booth at the restaurant and there's the cheerleader with her backpack and her three-ring binder. I'm a thirty-year-old married guy with a baby at home. And I forge ahead.

So, Chelsea, tell me about your boyfriend.

Oh? He kissed you that day?

It was your first kiss with Max?

Could you please describe this kiss? About how long, in seconds?

Did he seem to know what he was doing?

The story, the story, the story. It exists whether you find it or not. Find it. Get it. Get the cheerleader's cell phone number before you leave the restaurant. Don't be ashamed to call her after you've written the scene and you decide it needs more juice. Ask her:

Were you wearing perfume that day?

What brand was it?

Oh, Victoria's Secret?

What kind of Victoria's Secret perfume?

Thank you, Chelsea. Thank you for your understanding. I'm sorry if that was weird. But this is the big scene, the big moment for Max, the glory of his first kiss with his cheerleader girlfriend. And if Max were writing the movie of his own life you can bet he'd want you to get all the details right.

The other source I remember most is Max's mother, who told me that Max wouldn't even die until he had permission. A chill passed over me when I heard that. Immediately I knew it had to be the ending. For weeks thereafter, as I finished the reporting, I couldn't wait to write that scene. It made me cry every time I thought about it. But that's the feeling you're after when you do this work. When you get up every morning to go looking for tragic beauty, for human triumph, for some silver thread of the inexpressible thing that makes us all alive. And it runs, and you chase it, and you find it, and now it is yours, found and captured, waiting for you in the back of your notebook.

D a n P. L e e

D an P. Lee is a contributing editor at *New York* magazine. He has also written for *GQ* and *Philadelphia*, among others. He asked that his picture not be included.

Travis the Menace

Throughout her life, Sandy Herold had long, straight hair so black it almost looked wet. She wore it down below her shoulders, her bangs cut straight across. She applied bright-pink lipstick and copious amounts of bronzer. She wore skintight size-seven jeans. She spoke with a strange accent, a New York–New England hybrid, and spent her entire life in Stamford, Connecticut.

She was born in 1938 to a Jewish mother and Italian father who operated a popular bakery downtown and eventually built an unassuming shingled house on a windy road called Rock Rimmon, to the north of the city. As an only child, Sandy spent much of her time playing with her German shepherd Gretchen and tending to the horses on the property. At birthdays, her parents outfitted her in silk dresses and cardigans and had her pose for photographs, smiling, near multitiered cakes, Gretchen standing at her side.

She married shortly after high school, then again in 1960. Her second marriage was romantic, intense, and desperate—she adored her new husband, with whom she had a daughter named Suzan, in 1961, but they fought violently over his frequent affairs and divorced after four years. At thirty, Sandy married her third husband, Jerry Herold, who was kind, intelligent and devoted. Her life stabilized; she, Jerry, and Sue, whom Jerry raised as his own, ultimately settled in the house on Rock Rimmon Road with Sandy's parents. Sandy and Jerry opened several businesses in Stamford, including a tow operation and an auto-body shop, that would soon make them unlikely millionaires.

For a time in the seventies, Sandy, Sue and Jerry towed their horses from state to state so that Sandy (and later Sue) could barrel-race semiprofessionally in rodeos. It was during a stint with the country singer Loretta Lynn's traveling rodeo that Sandy struck up a lifelong friendship with an eighteen-year-old runaway named Charla Nash, who was rodeoing her way around the country. One day, Sandy and Charla spotted a chimpanzee dressed in Westernwear who rode a horse around the ring. Sandy sought him out backstage. She was carrying gummy bears. He took them from her with his fingers. Later, back atop his horse and wearing a cowboy hat, the chimp spotted Sandy in the audience. He jumped down, ran on two legs, and leaped into her arms.

Between the expanding businesses, the horses in the yard, and their many dogs, the Herolds lived a happily frenetic life. Sue grew into a platinum-blonde version of her mother. The two raced side by side, country-line-danced, worked together at the businesses. Mother and daughter were engaged in one endless conversation. And so when Sue married an employee from her parents' shop and moved away, Sandy was bitter and heartbroken. Then each of her parents became sick and died. Her world narrowed further. Seemingly all of a sudden, she saw herself and Jerry drifting beyond the outer periphery of middle age.

Jerry was home tending to the businesses as Sandy landed at the Lambert-St. Louis International Airport one day in 1995. A few days earlier, she had received a call from Connie Casey, a breeder in Festus, Missouri, a rural town thirty-five miles south of St. Louis. "Sandy," she said, "your baby has arrived. It's a boy."

Sandy stood in the Caseys' living room. In her arms, swaddled and in a diaper, lay tiny Travis, named after her favorite singer, Travis Tritt. Travis was the son of Coco, who'd been snatched from the jungles of equatorial Africa in the early seventies and purchased for $12,000, and an eleven-year-old retired zoo chimp named Suzy. A day earlier, the Caseys had shot a tranquilizer in Suzy and removed Travis from her cage. Travis peered up at Sandy. Black hair covered all but the interior of his face, which was pink, and the two tiny Dumbo ears that jutted from the top of his head. Sandy cried as his hands and feet grasped at her. She paid the Caseys $50,000 in cash, and a few days later, with Travis wrapped in baby blankets, the two of them boarded a flight home.

Back in Stamford, Sandy and Jerry played with Travis, who absorbed their smells and cues and began learning their language. Sandy bottle-fed him formula, burped him, put him down for naps in a crib in their bedroom. At three months, he turned over. Soon he was scooting, then walking on his arms and legs, his knuckles absorbing much of his weight. They taught him to use the toilet. They joined him in the bathtub. They brushed his teeth, and later taught him to brush his own teeth. Sandy bought him an extensive wardrobe and dressed him every morning.

The Herolds retrofitted their house to accommodate Travis. They caged in a large room in the rear, which had a set of sliders that led to an outdoor enclosure. They installed a heavy, lockable metal door on their bedroom, creating a suite of rooms, including the caged room, where Travis could roam freely when he was left alone. When Sandy and Jerry were home, Travis had the entire house at his disposal, knuckle-running from the couch in the living room to the kitchen, swinging from the tires and ropes in his room, jumping on his bed. The Herolds also laid a mattress on the floor of their bedroom, though most nights Travis slept in bed with them.

Sandy and Jerry took Travis to work with them every day. They installed tire swings, ropes, and trampolines in a giant room above the tow shop. He was inquisitive and friendly. Even the tow drivers and mechanics melted when they saw him.

These were some of the happiest days of Sandy's life. By then, Sue had divorced her first husband, and she and her young son had returned to Stamford, moving into a spacious loft-style apartment her parents constructed next to the auto-body shop. Sandy and Sue worked together every day, in the room above the tow shop, with Travis. They joked, gossiped, talked about men. Sue's son, Tyler, and Travis were close in age, and they played well together; as Travis matured more rapidly than Tyler, his fondness for the boy grew, so that he often held him in his lap, kissing him.

Travis grew quickly. Jerry played catch with him and taught him to ride a tricycle (which was awkward at first, what with his long arms), then a bike, then a ride-on lawn mower. Sandy put on a blue bikini and big gold-hoop earrings and took him to the beach, carrying him into the water with her.

Sandy and Jerry invited Travis to join them at the table for meals. He ate oatmeal with a spoon every morning. At their favorite Italian restaurant, Pellicci's, she read him the menu, offering him choices. His favorite food was filet mignon. He also enjoyed lobster tail. He preferred Lindt's chocolates. He liked Nerds candy and taffy, and he loved ice cream, hooting and pulling at Sandy when the ice-cream man came down the street. When he was thirsty, he swung his body up onto the counter and took out a glass, opened the refrigerator, and poured himself juice or soda.

Travis had a distinct sense of humor. He'd become particularly impish when Sandy was on the phone talking. He'd change the channels of the remote furiously. He'd blast the volume on the TV. "Cut it out, you little son of a bitch!" Sandy would yell, and then laugh. "I'm gonna kill you, you little bastard!"

"I'll tell you," she'd say into the phone, "you should see how smart Travis is. Just today he …" Sandy was ceaselessly dumbfounded by Travis's humanness. Though she did not know their name, she seemed to intuit the so-called spindle cells in his brain, cells shared by humans and chimps that are believed to help us to process complex thoughts and empathize.

Sandy's old friend Charla Nash came to visit, bringing with her her young daughter, Briana. They sat outside, Charla playing with Travis, the chimp climbing all over her, messing with her long blonde hair, the two of them posing for pictures. He climbed the tall oak trees around their property, racing up them, jumping from one to the next.

Travis quickly became Stamford's most famous resident. The Herolds plastered his image on the side of their tow trucks and flatbeds. He sat shotgun on tow calls, waving as the truck pulled up. He came to love police officers especially, and virtually everyone on the force had his photo taken with him. Strangers approached in stores, on the street. Sometimes they handed him their babies to hold.

One fall day, a neighbor was out raking leaves. Across the street, he noticed a Corvette coming down the Herolds' driveway. It was Travis's favorite car—he perceived it as his own, Sandy said—and in fact there were rumors that Travis had once taken the keys and gotten behind the wheel, turned the ignition, and, half-standing in the driver's seat, his opposable-thumbed feet grabbing the pedals, steered the car down the driveway and out onto Rock Rimmon Road. The man raking leaves watched as the car drew closer. Dressed in animal prints and decked to the nines, Sandy was driving, with Travis, in a ball cap and T-shirt, sitting beside her; the windows were down, and each had an arm hanging out. Reflexively, the man raised his hand. Sandy and Travis both waved back.

When Travis was around five years old, Sue fell in love and married again. She had two more children. She and her husband eventually decided to relocate near the Outer Banks, where he was opening a mechanic's shop. Sandy did not take kindly to the news. Again, she felt abandoned; again she disapproved of Sue's husband. Within a few months, however, Sandy was calling to tell Sue she couldn't stand not talking every day. She sent money and gifts down to North Carolina. Every note Sue mailed to her mother, no matter how banal, Sandy read repeatedly, showed repeatedly to Jerry, and bound in plastic for safe keeping.

Sue was making repeated trips to Connecticut to retrieve their remaining belongings. On her way home one night in September 2000, Sue, who'd complained of back pain and taken a Percocet, was driving on a mostly empty highway. Somewhere in Virginia, her car left the roadway and collided with a tree. Her infant daughter, strapped in her car seat, was unscathed. Sue was ejected from the car. The phone rang inside Rock Rimmon Road, waking Sandy, Jerry and Travis, all asleep in bed.

At an open-casket viewing in Stamford, Sue's body lay in a floral-print dress her mother had bought her. Beside her stood an enlarged photo of her in the same dress, holding her newborn daughter. Sandy was anything but stoic in her mourning. She stalked the room, gasping, and blocked certain visitors from coming inside. "That's that bastard!" she shouted at Sue's husband. "If it wasn't for him my daughter would be alive!"

In the years after Sue's death, Sandy vacillated between combustible anger and unrelenting depression. She struggled to maintain relationships with Sue's children. She distanced herself from her friends and at one point considered suicide. Her life was now built almost entirely around Jerry and Travis, and when she finally began venturing out of the house again, it was with the two of them. One bright winter day, they all drove down to the sea. They walked out onto the beach holding hands, in a line straight across; it was Travis who held their dog Apollo's leash. Sandy now considered Travis her only child.

Travis quickly moved beyond the gangly phases of early adolescence, through puberty, and into early adulthood. One night after work, Jerry was sipping a glass of wine when Travis climbed up into the seat next to him. Travis was interested in what he was drinking. Jerry offered him a sip. Thus began their nightly ritual: a glass of wine, one for Travis, one for Jerry, served in stemware, which they clinked together as Jerry said cheers.

Travis was also growing more willful. Three years had passed since the death of Sue. It was a warm night in October 2003. Jerry, Sandy, and Travis had eaten a dinner of sausage and peppers and were sitting on the couch watching the World Series. Travis was an avid TV watcher, and he particularly liked sports. All three were cheering for the Yankees. Sandy and Jerry decided they needed to make a trip to the tow shop. They asked Travis whether he had any interest in a ride. It was a rhetorical question.

They were in the 4Runner, stopped downtown at the intersection of Tresser and Washington Boulevards, when someone, for reasons unknown, threw an empty soda bottle into Travis's partially open window. Travis looked, grunted, unbuckled his seat belt, unlocked and opened the door, and began knuckle-running across the road.

He stood, surveying the area in his extra-large adult diaper (though he was potty-trained, he often wore diapers when he was out). At one point, he lunged at a passerby. And then, all of a sudden, he lay down in the street and began rolling on his back. People in their cars honked and pointed. Traffic at the intersection came to a standstill. Neighbors came out to watch.

Travis was clearly enjoying himself, climbing over cars, hooting, smiling. He chased the dozen police officers who responded to the call for a "loose chimpanzee downtown." The spectators cheered for him as he evaded capture, smacking several officers on their behinds. Cookies and ice cream could not coax him back. Each time they lured him into the 4Runner, Travis opened the door and got out again before they could lock it. This continued for two hours.

Finally, when he began to tire, Travis climbed into the SUV and buckled his seat belt. No charges were pressed; several of the police officers who knew Travis personally wrote in their reports that his attitude was only playful. They escorted the Herolds home. Travis spent the next day in his room, grounded.

Virtually everyone made light of the escapade downtown. The state Department of Environmental Protection was aware of what happened, and also that the Herolds were in violation of a new statute that required a permit to keep a primate over fifty pounds. But they determined that pressing any action would amount to a most likely unwinnable battle to "take custody of a local celebrity" and opted not to pursue the matter.

Stamford's animal-control officer was more concerned. After contacting primatologists, she spoke with Sandy, arguing that Travis was by now a fully sexualized adult (chimpanzees in the wild have sex, nonmonogamously, as often as fifty times a day); that he had the strength of at least five men; that adult chimpanzees are known to be unpredictable and potentially violent (which is why all chimp actors are prepubescent); and that maintaining Travis for the duration of his five- or six-decade lifetime was not viable. Sandy seemed to pay an open mind to the officer's warning but ultimately concluded that Travis had never exhibited even the slightest capacity for violence.

There was one piece of information, however, that Sandy chose not to share with the officer. Two years earlier, the Herolds had received a phone call from Connie Casey, the breeder in Festus. She explained how Travis's parents, Suzy and Coco, had escaped their cages and, with a third chimp, run across the ranch to a nearby housing development, where a seventeen-year-old named Jason Coats and some friends were pulling into Coats's driveway on their way home from the Dairy Queen. Coats claimed the chimps approached his Chevy Cavalier and trapped the teenagers inside, baring their teeth and rocking the car. Coats eventually got out, ran into his house, and grabbed a shotgun. Casey had by then arrived at the driveway and tranquilized Suzy, who was now, according to Casey and several eyewitnesses, sitting at the edge of the road, stoned, fingering the grass and flowers. Casey begged Coats not to shoot. He fired three rounds at Suzy; she died two hours later.

Following several neighbors' testimony that the chimps were behaving playfully and had posed no threat, a jury found Coats guilty of property damage and animal abuse, and he served a month in jail. Coats nevertheless remained steadfast in his belief that the chimps were dangerous.

The Herolds stopped taking Travis out in public after the incident in downtown Stamford, and they spent most of their time away from work at home with him. One night, over takeout spaghetti dinners at the kitchen table, Travis was sulking. He was sitting next to Jerry, facing away from him. Jerry was eating heartily, after some dental work he'd had earlier in the day. Jerry and Sandy were trying to engage Travis.

"Daddy got his tooth fixed today," Jerry said. "Look."

Travis wouldn't.

"Come on, Trav," Sandy said. "Look at Daddy's new tooth."

Travis turned, glanced begrudgingly.

"Come on, Trav," Jerry said. "Which tooth had a boo-boo? Which one?"

Travis looked finally. Jerry opened his mouth.

"Which one?"

Travis looked for a second before extending his long index finger. He placed the tip of it directly on Jerry's left molar. Sandy and Jerry cheered: "That's the one, Travis! That's the one!" Travis's lips curled open around his gleaming white teeth. He bounced in his chair and buried his face in Jerry's chest.

"Show Daddy your teeth now," Sandy told him. Travis looked at her, looked at Jerry, puckered his lips again, exposed his teeth, and tilted his head up toward Jerry. Jerry cheered.

"Show Daddy your big tongue now!" Sandy said. Travis opened his mouth and unfurled his giant pink tongue. Once again, they cheered. By now Travis could not contain himself: He smiled broadly and grunted, his shoulders shaking in silent laughter. He patted Jerry on the back. Finally he wrapped his long arm around him.

Occasionally, Jerry complained that he wasn't feeling well. After playing with Travis one morning in March 2005, he went off to work, where his discomfort sharpened. He asked one of his employees to take him to the hospital.

Over the course of Jerry's weeks-long stay, during which his doctors tried to arrest his rapidly spreading stomach cancer, Sandy spent virtually every minute at the hospital. One night he said he wanted to talk to her about Travis. He asked her what she would do if he were to die—if it were to become just her, alone with Travis. As much as he said it pained him, he urged her to send Travis to a sanctuary. He told her Travis was too much for her to manage alone. He said it was best for both of them.

When Sandy arrived home from the hospital, Travis smelled her clothing frantically, inhaling Jerry's scent. He was at first disoriented by Jerry's sudden absence, then despondent. Several times Sandy put Travis on the phone to talk to Jerry; each time Travis became so upset that she had to take the phone away.

Travis sat rocking back and forth for hours. He lifted pictures of Jerry off the wall, put his lips to the glass, held them to his chest. Sandy took them all down and put them in a box. On April 12, Jerry died.

After Jerry's death, Sandy ignored condolences and stopped speaking to many of her friends. Travis continued his rocking. When she sat on the sofa crying, Travis gently brushed her hair. He bit her nails and used an emery board to file them.

When almost a year had passed, Sandy sat down to write a letter. She drafted it in longhand, and addressed it to a woman in Florida who runs a respected chimpanzee sanctuary. These were the last two paragraphs.

"Needless to say, after forty-five years with the most wonderful man in the world we are both lost without him and miss him dearly. Travis still waits for him especially at supper time, because at that time they both had a glass of wine with their supper and if my husband ever cooked anything you can bet it has garlic in it. Try having two guys breathing on your sleep time with (garlic breath). Travis would go to the bedroom window many nights sit on the bench seat look out, get very vocal and happy then come back to sleep, this was always very late at night. Finally I went to a psychic and she told me Jerry would visit at night and talk to Travis and my husband would always kiss me good night. P.S. (him and Travis kiss alike) that's good too.

"I have no family, my only child, Suzan had gotten killed in an auto accident four years before Jerry died and who Travis also loved. My grand kids live in North Carolina and I don't see them very often. I live alone with Travis, we eat and sleep together but I am worried that if something happens to me as suddenly as my husband what would happen to Travis, therefore I have to try to do something before that happens. I set up a trust fund for him but that's not enough, he needs someone to play with of his own kind and have the best most possible life if I'm not here to care for him. I would love to see and talk to you if that's possible. I am flying down to see your member event enclosed is our donation. I am looking forward to meeting you."

She signed the letter, "Sandy (Jerry) and Travis," and enclosed photos of Travis and the family. She wrote out a check for $250, signing it from both her and Travis. She put everything in a stamped envelope. She never mailed the letter and never made the trip.

Charla Nash and Sandy reunited around the time of Jerry's death. Charla and her then-twelve-year-old daughter had lived itinerantly, at one point staying for more than a year in a homeless shelter. Charla had taken odd jobs, picked up occasional yard work, cleaned horse stalls. The reunion was mutually beneficial: Sandy invited Charla and her daughter to move rent-free into the loft apartment that had once been Sue's. She gave Charla a job, handling towing dispatch and bookkeeping. Over time the terms of Charla's employment blurred. Charla tended to Sandy's lawn and would look in on Travis if Sandy was away.

She rarely was. For four years, Travis never left home, and Sandy only sporadically did, aside from compulsive shopping trips: She spent hundreds of thousands of dollars at stores like T.J. Maxx and Marshalls, stuffing bags of clothes in dozens of plastic bins that filled almost every room of the house. She and Travis relegated themselves to the kitchen and the suite in the rear of the house. In early 2008, construction was under way on a gigantic new addition that Jerry had designed for Travis years earlier. Travis, by this point, no longer bore much physical resemblance to his former self. He was fourteen years old, five feet tall, 240 pounds, and morbidly obese. His hairline had receded dramatically, and his center torso had gone gray. His face was black and wrinkled. His chest sagged. He spent the majority of his days snacking, watching TV, playing on the computer, and roaming the house.

It was February 16, and Sandy and Charla had just returned from a weekend at the Mohegan Sun casino; before leaving, Sandy had taken Charla to get her hair colored and curled, in case, Sandy had joked, two eligible bachelors crossed their paths. Sandy had offered Charla some gambling money. At dinner one night, Sandy had opened her purse and showed the waiter several pictures of Travis. "Do you think he looks more like his mom," she had asked, "or his aunt?"

Now it was after 3 p.m., and Sandy was in a bit of a panic. She was meeting a friend, and as she'd been cleaning Travis's room, he'd walked into the kitchen, picked up the keys from the counter, unlocked the door, and ventured out into the yard. He'd seemed agitated for a good part of the day; after eating a lunch of fish and chips and Carvel ice-cream cake, he'd not been particularly interested in watching any of the three TVs that were playing in the house. He did not want to draw or color. He did not want to pet his cat, Misty. Even the smorgasbord of food—the Popsicles in the freezer she'd labeled for him with R for red and F for Fudgsicle, the steam-in-a-bag vegetables he liked to toss in the microwave himself—was unappealing. Sandy, slightly concerned, had dropped a Xanax in his mug of afternoon tea.

She was on the phone with Charla. She told her about Travis. He was outside, she said, running from car to car, apparently wanting to go for a ride; he'd ignored her entreaties to come back inside. Later, Sandy would say that

Charla volunteered to come over and help; Charla would maintain she was asked. In any case, Charla arrived at about 3:40, opened the iron gate at the end of the driveway, and drove to the front of the house. She stepped out onto the frozen dirt and grass and held over her face a red Elmo doll she'd thought to bring with her. Travis was in the front yard, about thirty-five feet away. He knuckle-ran toward her, then came up on his two legs.

"Travis!" Sandy shouted. "Travis! What are you doing? Travis! Stop! Travis! It's Charla, Travis!"

Travis knocked her into the side of her car. Then to the ground. Almost immediately, Charla turned red with blood. Sandy screamed and grabbed a nearby snow shovel. She ran to Travis and began beating him over the head. He was screaming, too, a terrible high-pitched screech. He continued at Charla, unyielding.

Hysterical, Sandy ran back to the house. She grabbed a butcher knife. She ran back, screaming all the while. As Travis stood over Charla, chewing, ripping, pulling, Sandy plunged the knife into his back. He did not stop. She pulled the knife out and stabbed him twice more, to little effect. Travis stood up finally, turned to look Sandy in the face—directly in the face—then continued.

Sandy ran to her Volkswagen Passat, parked about fifteen feet away. She got in and locked the door. She dialed 911, still holding the butcher knife.

"Stamford 911, where's your emergency?"

"Two-forty-one Rock Rimmon Road, send the police!"

"What's the problem?"

"Send the police!"

"What's the problem there?"

"The—that—the chimp killed my—my friend!"

"What's wrong with your friend?"

Sandy gasped, pressed her feet into the floor of the car to turn around and look, her face pushing the buttons of her cell phone. She sobbed.

"Oh, please! Send the police with a gun—with a gun—hurry up!"

"Who has the gun?"

"Please, hurry up! Please hurry up! He's killin' my girlfriend!"

"I need you to talk to me, I need you to calm down. Why do you need somebody there?"

"What? Please, God!"

"What is the problem?"

"He's killing my friend!"

"Who's killing your friend?"

"Chimp—my chimpanzee!"

"Oh, your chimpanzee is killing your friend?"

"Yes! He ripped her apart! Hurry up! Hurry up! Please!"

"What is going on? What is the monkey doing? Tell me what the monkey is doing."

"He—he ripped her face off!"

"He ripped her face off?"

"Gun! They got to shoot him! Please! Please! Hurry! Hurry! Please!"

"Ma'am, ma'am, I need you to calm down. They're already on their way."

"I can't. I can't … He's eating her! He's eating her!"

"He's eating her?"

"Please! God! Please! Where are they? Where are they?"

It went on for twelve minutes.

When the authorities finally arrived, they saw a body lying mostly naked on the ground, lifeless and covered in nearly half its blood supply. Travis was roaming the property. He made his way to the police car. He swatted off its driver's-side mirror. He went to the passenger's side and tried to open the locked door. He walked back around to the driver's side. He tried the door. It opened.

The officer lurched. He struggled to remove his gun from its holster. His body became wedged against the center-console computer. Travis stared into the car, baring his blood-streaked teeth. In one swift motion the officer at last released his gun and fired four rounds. Travis staggered backward, screeched, defecated, and ran off.

The officer got out of his car. Huge chunks of scalp and fingers lay scattered around the yard. He walked slowly to the body. With the stump of what remained of her arm, Charla Nash reached for his leg.

As another group of officers set out into the woods to look for him, Travis scampered unnoticed into the house. Leaving a trail of blood, he knuckle-walked through the kitchen, the bedroom, and into his room. Then he grasped his bedpost, heaved forward, and died.

Charla Nash's injuries were overwhelming. Travis had bitten or torn away her eyelids, nose, jaw, lips, and most of her scalp. He'd broken nearly all the bones of her facial structure. He'd fully removed one of her hands and virtually all of the other. He'd rendered her blind.

And yet she did not die. Three days after the attack, in critical condition, Charla was flown by specialized jet from Stamford to the Cleveland Clinic. Fifteen months of intervention followed.

One month after the attack, her family filed a $50 million lawsuit against Sandy.

Sandy was alone.

After weeks of blistering coverage, journalists from around the world—who, hoping to coax Sandy out of the house, had left her flowers, coffee, and sympathy notes—had finally moved on. The reporting had included many inaccuracies, such as the unsubstantiated assertion (which Sandy never disputed) that Travis was the same chimpanzee who had appeared in the iconic Old Navy ads of the nineties and on *The Maury Povich Show*. *The New York Post* had accused Sandy of "weird jungle love" and all but said that she and Travis had sexual relations. Even after the press mob had lost interest in her chimp, the allegation that hurt her most was that she'd cared more about Travis than Charla. "I stabbed my own son," she cried to friends on the phone. For a long time, inside her house, she refused to clean up his blood. She sat a gigantic stuffed chimpanzee in the leather chair in his room.

"I just—you just—you can't imagine," she sobbed into the phone late at night. "They cut off his head!" She was referring to the last time she'd seen Travis, when she'd gone to the crematorium to drop off his favorite tie-dyed T-shirt and discovered he'd been decapitated for rabies testing.

She tried to reconstitute her life. She visited occasionally with friends, and made trips to the casino. She continued shopping—much of it for clothes for her three grandchildren that she would end up never sending—until her house became impassable. She sat at her kitchen table and leafed through stacks of mail, old letters, old pictures, doodling Sue's name on the back of envelopes. She tuned in nightly to Bill O'Reilly. She talked—and cried—on the phone incessantly; the subject was almost exclusively Travis. One of her daughter's friends helped her set up a profile on Match.com; she went on a date with an elderly Stamford man who appalled her by requesting oral sex as they were having dinner.

In the end, all that was really left for Sandy were animals. She put bowls outside for the raccoons. She fed deer in the yard from her hands. And she found another chimpanzee. His name was Chance. She knew she could never bring him back to Connecticut, so she contributed money to a friend out of state, and the two women were to assume a kind of joint custody. One spring day, she sat on a couch in the woman's mobile home. Chance, about a year old, stretched his young, long body out across her lap. Sandy tickled his belly. He climbed all over her. The two of them snuggled and played. They opened their mouths wide and put them up against each other's. Sandy's makeup ran with her tears.

Back in Connecticut one day last summer, shortly before sunset, Sandy was alone, outside, feeding the animals. She looked up. A cloud formation resembling a fish's backbone was unspooling against the sky. She found her camera, held it up, and clicked.

Sometime later, her chest began hurting. The pain came on quickly and intensified. Frightened, she called a friend, who drove over to her house to sit with her. A hot bath provided no relief. The friend called 911. She put Sandy in her car, in her pink bathrobe and slippers, and drove her down Rock Rimmon Road, to meet the ambulance on its way.

At the ER, tests determined Sandy's aorta was bulging. She was prepared for emergency surgery. In the operating room, two hours in, Sandy's lungs filled with blood.

And then they were all gone. All the Herolds were dead.

Last May, Charla Nash was transferred to a long-term assisted-living facility outside Boston. The innumerable cosmetic surgeries she has undergone have accomplished little cosmetically. On her fifty-sixth birthday, nine months after the attack, in what will undoubtedly go down as one of the most extraordinary moments in television history, she revealed her face—a bulbous surface of transmogrified skin—to Oprah Winfrey; she told Winfrey she remembers nothing from the attack and is disinclined to worry about how others see her. "I just look different," she said. "Things happen in life that you can't change. It's a tragedy." She is financially insolvent; her brothers and a team of representatives are apparently shopping two book ideas and weighing several movie deals on her behalf. Her daughter is in her freshman year of college. Through Brigham and Women's Hospital, she is hoping to become the world's first face- and double-hand-transplant recipient.

When her brother informed her of Sandy's death, Charla was shocked. She said: "Sandra was a troubled woman, and maybe she has some peace now."

Two-forty-one Rock Rimmon Road remains almost exactly as it was the day Sandy left, held in limbo by order of the court. Rumors abounded after Sandy's death that along with jewelry, antiques, and other valuables, somewhere in the ramshackle house she had secreted $80,000 in cash, and burglars broke in five times in the first two months. The gigantic addition is frozen in mid-construction, exactly as it had been that February day, its windows still glassless, so that leaves and small drifts of snow blot its unfinished floor. The life-size stuffed chimpanzee still sits in the oversize chair in Travis's room, gazing out the window to the backyard and the woods beyond it.

A few miles away is a cemetery that has no tombstones. A plot there belongs to the Herolds. Beside Jerry, inside a sealed vault inside a sealed coffin, Sandy Herold wears an animal-print shirt and tight jeans distressed from ankle to hip. Her fingernails are painted pink, and her hands rest atop her abdomen. Against her one side stands an urn containing the ashen remains of her daughter Suzan. On the other, in the same urn she'd slept with every night since that day in February, are Travis's.

AUTHOR'S AFTERWORDS...

In terms of a process essay, I don't really have that much to say. Like most people, I was shocked and awed by the Travis story from the moment it broke. However, I purposefully avoided following almost anything about it out of jealousy. I'm a former newspaper reporter—and a fairly competitive person in general—and I have this odd instinct to do that, to avoid following stories I wish I was covering as they're breaking. In any case, it was probably a year later that I was actually hanging out with my grandmother, and she was watching Oprah Winfrey's show, and I was half-paying attention, and then Charla Nash appeared. Suffice it to say I could ignore it no longer; it was one of the most extraordinary things I'd ever seen on TV.

It got me to thinking. I'd resigned from *Philadelphia* magazine at that time and was sort of aimless and scared to jump into the freelancing storm. Nevertheless, I drafted a pitch and sent it through a friend to an editor at New York, who, to my shock, assigned it. Of course the concern then was twofold: scorched earth from the mainstream but especially tabloid media that had descended on Stamford like vultures for months, and access, since every single major player had by then died. But—for lack of a better explanation—I was still sort of inexperienced, I felt I had a lot to prove, and I worked really hard. With a ton of luck, I stumbled onto so much the media had missed (now, I know the media's initial narrative is almost always wrong, or at least grossly simplified and distorted), including a source incredibly close to Sandy who'd never been identified or spoken to. I spent huge amounts of time interviewing this source, and wandering around Stamford, and realized soon that the real story had gone all but untold. I'd begun my reporting thinking the story was about Charla Nash, about her recovery—that seemed like the obvious and only piece with forward momentum. By the time I sat down to write, though, I knew I had to begin at the beginning. I knew that the story was, really, "the story," a gothic fairytale about this odd woman and her beloved chimpanzee.

A r i e l   L e v y

A riel Levy is a staff writer at the *New Yorker*, and previously wrote for New York magazine for twelve years. She is the author of *Female Chauvinist Pigs*, and her work has been anthologized in *The Best American Essays*, *The Best American Travel Writing*, *New York Stories*, and *Sugar In My Bowl: Real Women Write About Real Sex*. She teaches at the Fine Arts Work Center in Provincetown, MA.

Either/Or

When people in South Africa say "Limpopo," they mean the middle of nowhere. They are referring to the northernmost province of the country, along the border with Botswana, Zimbabwe, and Mozambique, where few people have cars or running water or opportunities for greatness. The members of the Moletjie Athletics Club, who live throughout the area in villages of small brick houses and mud-and-dung huts, have high hopes nonetheless.

One day in late September, twenty teen-age athletes gathered for practice on a dirt road in front of Rametlwana Lower Primary School, after walking half an hour through yellow cornfields from their homes, to meet their coach, Jeremiah Mokaba. The school's track is not graded, and donkeys and goats kept walking across it to graze on the new grass that was sprouting as the South African winter gave way to spring. "During the rainy season, we can't train," said Mokaba, a short man wearing a brown corduroy jacket with a golden Zion Christian Church pin on the lapel. "We have nowhere to go inside."

For cross-country, Mokaba and his co-coach, Phineas Sako, train their runners in the miles of bush that spread out behind the track, toward the mountains in the distance. The land is webbed with brambles, and the thorns are a serious problem for the athletes, who train barefoot. "They run on loose stones, scraping them, making a wound, making a scar," Sako, a tall, bald man with rheumy eyes and a big gap between his two front teeth, said. "We can't stop and say we don't have running shoes, because we don't have money. The parents don't have money. So what must we do? We just go on."

The athletes and their coaches apologized for not having a clubhouse in which to serve tea. They didn't like talking out in the wind and the dust. There was music playing down the road at a brick-front bar, and chickens squawking in people's front yards, where they are kept in enclosures made out of tree branches. "The most disadvantaged rural area," Sako said, laughing a little and stretching his arms out wide. "That is where you are."

The fastest runner in the club now is a seventeen-year-old named Andrew who recently became the district champion in the fifteen-hundred-metre event. The average monthly income for black Africans in Limpopo—more than ninety-seven per cent of the local population—is less than a thousand rand per month, roughly $135. (For white residents, who make up two per cent of the population, it is more than four times that amount.) "I think I will go to the Olympics," Andrew said, with conviction.

Joyce, a tiny girl in a pink sweater who is eighteen but looked much younger, was similarly optimistic. "I want to be the world champion," she said, her voice so soft it was almost a whisper. "I *will* be the world champion. I want to participate in athletics and have a scholarship. Caster is making me proud. She won. She put our club on the map."

Caster Semenya, the current world champion in the eight hundred metres, was a member of the Moletjie Athletics Club until a year ago. She was born in Ga-Masehlong, a village about fifteen miles from the track, and she was, Coach Sako said, "a natural." Even before Semenya left Limpopo for college, in Pretoria, she had won a gold medal in her event at the 2008 Commonwealth Youth Games, in Pune, India, with a time of 2:04, eleven seconds behind the senior world record set by the Czech runner Jarmila Kratochvílová in 1983. "I used to tell Caster that she must try her level best," Sako said. "By performing the best, maybe good guys with big stomachs full of money will see her and then help her with schooling and the likes. That is the motivation." He added, "And she *always* tried her level best." Semenya won another gold medal in July, in Mauritius, at the African Junior Athletics Championships, lowering her time by a remarkable seven and a half seconds, to come in at 1:56.72. This beat the South African record for that event, held by Zola Budd, and qualified Semenya for her first senior competition, the 2009 World Championships, in Berlin.

Semenya won the eight-hundred-metre title by nearly two and a half seconds, finishing in 1:55.45. After the first lap of the race, she cruised past her competitors like a machine. She has a powerful stride and remarkable efficiency of movement: in footage of the World Championships, you can see the other runners thrashing behind her, but her trunk stays still, even as she is pumping her muscle-bound arms up and down. Her win looks effortless, inevitable. "Even when we were training, I used to pair her with the males," Sako told me. "I feel like she was too powerful for ladies." It was a stunning victory for Semenya, for the Moletjie Athletics Club, and for South Africa.

After the race, Semenya told reporters, "Oh, man, I don't know what to say. It's pretty good to win a gold medal and bring it home." (Her voice is surprising. As Semenya's father, Jacob, has put it, "If you speak to her on the telephone, you might mistake her for a man.") She continued, "I didn't know I could win that race, but for the first time in my life the experience, the World Championships ..." She broke into a grin. "I couldn't believe it, man."

Since the day Semenya broke Zola Budd's record, people in South Africa had been talking about her. Semenya does not look like most female athletes. People questioned whether she was really a woman. Some even emailed the International Association of Athletics Federations, the worldwide governing body for track and field, with their doubts. Before Semenya was awarded her gold medal in Berlin, on August 20, a reporter asked about a story that had been circulating at the Championships, that Semenya's sex was unclear and that she had been required to undergo gender-verification testing before the race. The IAAF confirmed the rumor, arguably in violation of its confidentiality policies. ("The choice is that you lie, which we don't like to do," Nick Davies, the communications director, told the *New York Times*.) The story ripped around the world. Several of Semenya's competitors in the race were incensed that she had been allowed to participate. "These kind of people should not run with us," Elisa Cusma, of Italy, who came in sixth, said. "For me, she is not a woman. She is a man."

"Just look at her," Mariya Savinova, of Russia, who finished fifth, said.

Semenya is breathtakingly butch. Her torso is like the chest plate on a suit of armor. She has a strong jawline, and a build that slides straight from her ribs to her hips. "What I knew is that wherever we go, whenever she made her first appearance, people were somehow gossiping, saying, 'No, no, she is not a girl,' " Phineas Sako said, rubbing the gray stubble on his chin. " 'It looks like a boy'—that's the right words—they used to say, 'It looks like a boy.' Some even asked me as a coach, and I would confirm: It's a girl. At times, she'd get upset. But, eventually, she was just used to such things." Semenya became accustomed to visiting the bathroom with a member of a competing team so that they could look at her private parts and then get on with the race. "They are doubting me," she would explain to her coaches, as she headed off the field toward the lavatory.

South Africa has eleven official languages. The majority of people in Limpopo speak the Pedi language, and many also speak English and Afrikaans, which schoolchildren were required to learn under apartheid. Sako's English was fluent but rough, and he frequently referred to Semenya as "he." "Caster was very free when he is in the male company," Sako said. "I remember one day I asked her, 'Why are you always in the company of men?' He said, 'No, man, I don't have something to say to girls, they talks nonsense. They are always out of order.' "

On September 11, Australia's *Daily Telegraph*, a tabloid owned by Rupert Murdoch, reported that Semenya's test results had been leaked, and that they showed that Semenya, though she was brought up as a girl and had external female genitalia, did not have ovaries or a uterus. Semenya was born with undescended testes, the report said, which provided her with three times the amount of testosterone present in an average female—and so a potential advantage over competitors.

"I know what Caster has got," her aunt Johanna Lamola told the *Times*. "I've changed her nappies." Semenya's father said, "I don't even know how they do this gender testing. I don't know what a chromosome is. This is all very painful for us—we live by simple rules." Semenya did not cheat. She has not been evasive. It is very common for élite female athletes, who exert themselves to their physical limits as a matter of course, not to menstruate. There's no reason that Semenya or her coaches would have been alarmed if she were amenorrheic. "Maybe it's because we come from a disadvantaged area," Jeremiah Mokaba said. "They couldn't believe in us."

The IAAF has yet to inform Semenya whether she can continue running in international female competitions. I asked Sako what he thought would happen. "Caster," he said firmly, "will remain Caster."

Sports have played an important role in modern South African history. A crucial part of the African National Congress's strategy to end apartheid during "the struggle," as everyone calls it, was to secure international condemnation of South Africa's government through boycotts and the banning of South African athletes from all international competitions. Conversely, during the 1995 rugby World Cup Nelson Mandela managed to unite the entire country behind the Springboks, the South African team, which had been a hated symbol of Afrikaner white supremacism. It was pivotal to his success in avoiding civil war and in establishing a new sense of national solidarity. Sports are "more powerful than governments in breaking down racial barriers," Mandela said. "Sport has the power to change the world. It has the power to inspire, the power to unite people that little else has." Sometimes it can unite people against other people. The South African Minister of Sport and Recreation, Makhenkesi Stofile, has warned, "If the IAAF expels or excludes Semenya from competition or withdraws the medal, I think it would be the Third World War."

In August, when Semenya returned from Germany, thousands of cheering supporters waited to welcome her at O. R. Tambo Airport, outside Johannesburg. President Jacob Zuma met with her to offer his congratulations, as did Nelson Mandela.

Phat Joe, one of the most famous radio DJs in the country, was fired by Kaya FM for suggesting on his show that Semenya might have testicles. Lolly Jackson, the owner of a chain of strip clubs called Teazers, put up an enormous billboard in a suburb of Johannesburg picturing a naked woman lying flat on her back above the words "No Need for Gender Testing!" Jackson subsequently claimed that the billboard had nothing to do with Semenya, but he sent her lawyers, at the firm of Dewey & LeBoeuf, a check for twenty thousand rand.

"I think it is the responsibility of South Africa to rally behind this child and tell the rest of the world she remains the hero she is and no one will take that away from her," Winnie Madikizela-Mandela, an ex-wife of Mandela's and a recently elected Member of Parliament, was quoted as saying in the *London Telegraph.* "There is nothing wrong with being a hermaphrodite. It is God's creation. She is God's child." By contrast, the African National Congress Youth League, a division of the African National Congress, issued a statement saying that it "will never accept the categorization of Caster Semenya as a hermaphrodite, because in South Africa and the entire world of sanity, such does not exist."

The African National Congress is part of the Tripartite Alliance, with the South African Communist Party and the Congress of South African Trade Unions. This year's meeting of the Congress happened to coincide with Heritage Day, and many of the hundreds of delegates who assembled at a conference center outside Johannesburg were in traditional tribal dress. Winnie Madikizela-Mandela wore a Xhosa turban and cape. A representative from the police and prison workers' union, wearing nothing but a loincloth made from springbok pelts and a Swazi necklace of red pompoms, mingled with fellow union members at the back of an enormous auditorium, where delegates were debating the items of the day: whether to support the legalization of prostitution in time for the soccer World Cup, which South Africa will host in 2010, and whether to pass a resolution in support of Caster Semenya.

The sessions are meant to evoke the African tradition of villagers gathering to share opinions on local matters. Everyone gets to speak, though men speak much more than women. The prostitution question was examined from every angle: Some were concerned about "the downgrading of our women by capitalism"; others felt that every source of income was desperately needed and that sex workers, like everybody else, deserved the protection of a union. After several hours, the delegates decided that what was needed was more discussion.

The South African Minister of Women, Children, and Persons with Disabilities, Noluthando Mayende-Sibiya, went to the lectern dressed in red Xhosa regalia to speak about "the issue of our young star, Caster Semenya." Everyone applauded. "She is our own," Mayende-Sibiya said. "She comes from the working class." The crowd blew horns in support, and some people ululated. "You cannot be silent! The human rights of Caster have been violated," she concluded. The resolution passed with unusual alacrity.

South Africans have been appalled by the idea of a person who thinks she is one thing suddenly being told that she is something else. The classification and reclassification of human beings has a haunted history in this country. Starting with the Population Registration Act of 1950, teams of white people were engaged as census-takers. They usually had no training, but they had the power to decide a person's race, and race determined where and with whom you could live, whether you could get a decent education, whether you had political representation, whether you were even free to walk in certain areas at certain hours. The categories were fickle. In 1985, according to the census, more than a thousand people somehow changed race: nineteen whites turned Colored (as South Africans call people of mixed heritage); seven hundred and two Coloreds turned white, fifty Indians turned Colored, eleven Colored turned Chinese, and so on. (No blacks turned white, or vice versa.)

Taxonomy is an acutely sensitive subject, and its history is probably one of the reasons that South Africans—particularly black South Africans—have rallied behind their runner with such fervor. The government has decreed that Semenya can continue running with women in her own country, regardless of what the IAAF decides.

South Africans have compared the worldwide fascination with Semenya's gender to the dubious fame of another South African woman whose body captivated Europeans: Saartjie Baartman, the Hottentot Venus. Baartman, an orphan born on the rural Eastern Cape, was the servant of Dutch farmers near Cape Town. In 1810, they sent her to Europe to be exhibited in front of painters, naturalists, and oglers, who were fascinated by her unusually large buttocks and had heard rumors of her long labia. She supposedly became a prostitute and an alcoholic, and she died in France in her mid-twenties. Until 1974, her skeleton and preserved genitals were displayed at the Musée de l'Homme, in Paris. Many South Africans feel that white foreigners are yet again scrutinizing a black female body as though it did not contain a human being.

Mayende-Sibiya has asked that the United Nations get involved in Semenya's case, and I asked her what she thought it could do. "I would like to see it getting more information from the IAAF," she said over lunch at the Congress. "We wrote to the IAAF to ask a number of questions, including what precedents informed the action that it took on Caster. Why pick up on her? What were the reasons? The IAAF has not responded, and that to me raises questions on how it conducts business." Mayende-Sibiya is a big, warm woman, a grandmother and a former nurse, who hugs everyone she meets. She sighed. "There is a lot that has gone wrong in this process."

The IAAF has behaved erratically on the issue. On November 19, the South African Ministry of Sport and Recreation announced that the IAAF had said that Semenya could keep her medal, but the IAAF refused to confirm this. Its president, Lamine Diack, was scheduled to visit South Africa several weeks ago to talk to Semenya and to representatives of the government, but he cancelled his trip at the last minute. In late October, I got in touch with the IAAF, with questions about Semenya, and received a form-letter reply (dated September 11) that it would not comment on the case until after its council meeting, at the end of November. Then, a few hours later, Nick Davies, the director of communications, wrote back by email:

Two things triggered the investigation. Firstly, the incredible improvement in this athlete's performance ... and more bluntly, the fact that SOUTH AFRICAN sport websites were alleging that she was a hermaphrodite athlete. One such blog (from sport24.co.za) stated, "Caster Semenya is an interesting revelation because the eighteen-year-old was born a hermaphrodite and, through a series of tests, has been classified as female." With this blatant allegation, and bearing in mind the almost supernatural improvement, the IAAF believed that it was sensible to make sure, with help of ASA, that the athlete was negative in terms of doping test results, and also that there was no gender ambiguity which may have allowed her to have the benefits of male hormone levels, whilst competing against other women.

ASA is the abbreviation for Athletics South Africa, the national governing body in charge of track and field. The group's president, Leonard Chuene, who was also on the board of the IAAF, and had been in Berlin for the Championships, told reporters when he returned, "We are not going to allow Europeans to define and describe our children." South Africa would have no part in tests conducted by "some stupid university somewhere," Chuene, who also happens to be from Limpopo, said. "The only scientists I believe in are the parents of this child." He claimed to be shocked by the way that the IAAF had treated Semenya, and he resigned from the board in protest before he left Berlin. (A week later, Chuene wrote the IAAF a letter saying that his resignation had been hasty, and asked to be reinstated.)

In fact, Chuene was not only aware of the Berlin tests; he had authorized them, and, at the urging of the IAAF, he had also had Semenya tested before she left Pretoria. On August 3, the IAAF's anti-doping administrator, Dr. Gabriel Dollé, had sent an email to Harold Adams, ASA's team doctor, citing the website posting that Nick Davies mentioned to me, which alleged that Semenya is a "hermaphrodite ... classified as female." Dollé asked Adams if sex verification had been conducted—or ought to be. (Debora Patta, the host of a South African investigative program called "3rd Degree," obtained the email exchange and forwarded it to me.) Adams then sent the following email to Leonard Chuene and ASA's general manager, Molatelo Malehopo:

After thinking about the current confidential matter I would suggest we make the following decisions.

1. We get a gynae opinion and take it to Berlin.

2. We do nothing and I will handle these issues if they come up in Berlin. Please think and get back to me ASAP.

Malehopo replied the same day, agreeing to the exam. Semenya was taken to the Medforum Medi-Clinic, in Pretoria, for tests by a gynecologist.

"They did not even consult us as parents," Semenya's mother, Dorcus, told the *Star*, a South African daily. "They acted like thieves. They did whatever they wanted to do with our child without informing us."

On August 8, Adams and Semenya flew to Germany to join the rest of the South African team and the A.S.A. staff at the training camp. Adams, who is also one of President Zuma's personal physicians, told Chuene that the Pretoria test results were "not good." He recommended that they withdraw Semenya from the competition, rather than subject her to further testing.

"The reason for my advice was that the tests might prove too traumatic for Ms. Semenya to handle, especially without the necessary support of family and friends around her," Harold Adams wrote in a subsequent report to Parliament. "The other reason was that being tested at the World Championships would not give her enough time to consult extensively and perhaps arrive at a decision to refuse the testing."

Leonard Chuene did not take Adams's advice. Instead, Semenya ran in a qualifying heat on August 16 and then in the semifinals, the next day. After her success in the semifinals, a television reporter outside the stadium blurted out, "With that comes rumors. I heard one that you were born a man?" The video is very hard to watch. As the reporter speaks, Semenya's breathing quickens, and she appears to be on the verge of panic. Then she looks at the ground and says, "I have no idea about that thing...I don't give a damn about it," and walks away from the cameras. August 18 was supposed to be a rest day before the finals. Semenya spent it undergoing a second round of tests. The next day, after two weeks of confusion and scrutiny, Semenya won the gold medal.

In September, the Johannesburg weekly *Mail & Guardian* exposed Chuene's dishonesty about authorizing the tests in Pretoria and Berlin.

Chuene contends that he was simply following IAAF procedure, and that his deceit was a well-intentioned attempt to maintain confidentiality. After the story broke, he held a press conference to apologize for lying to the nation, but the apology was not unconditional. "Tell me someone," he said, "who has not lied to protect a child."

Semenya is back at the University of Pretoria now, training with her coach, Michael Seme. I asked Seme how he thought she was doing. "Sometimes you can look at somebody thinking he is OK," Seme said. "But you find out in his heart, maybe it is complaining. I can't see what's happening in her heart."

At a meeting of the British Gynaecological Society on April 25, 1888, Dr. Fancourt Barnes declared that he had "in the next room a living specimen of a hermaphrodite." The person was nineteen years old, and had always believed that she was female. Barnes thought otherwise. He cited "1) the appearance of the head, 2) the *timbre* of the voice, 3) the non-development of the breasts," and "the utter absence of anything like a uterus or ovaries," as evidence of the subject's insufficient femininity.

Other members of the society who examined the patient disagreed. Dr. James Aveling asserted that "the face was feminine, the throat was decidedly that of a woman." Dr. Charles Henry Felix Routh argued that Barnes's diagnosis was "guess work," and claimed that "the mere fact" that this patient might not have a uterus was "no argument against its being a woman." (Routh was not entirely convinced that the patient lacked a uterus and suggested that unless Barnes tried to "pass his entire hand into her rectum" they could not be sure.) Dr. Heywood Smith finally "suggested that the Society should divide on the question of sex," and so it did. Before the doctors sent their patient home with her mother, they took a photograph. In the foreground, a "medical man" holds the "living specimen's" genitals with his thumb and forefinger for the camera, between her spread legs. In the background is the blurred image of the subject's head, not quite obscured by the blanket that covers her torso. The subject's face is grainy, but it is set in an unmistakable expression of powerless panic.

The society's inability to reach consensus was due, in part, to its failure to locate either testicles or ovaries in the patient. Until 1915, that was the generally accepted determining factor for sex. In "Hermaphrodites and the Medical Invention of Sex," Alice Domurat Dreger calls the period from 1870 to 1915 "the Age of Gonads."

The way doctors, scientists, and sports officials have determined sex has changed radically over the years. Before 1968, the International Olympic Committee verified the sex of female athletes by looking between their legs.

Athletes complained about these humiliating inspections—which weren't always conclusive—and, for the 1968 Olympics, in Mexico City, the IOC decided to implement chromosomal testing. (There were rumors that some men from Eastern Bloc nations had plans to masquerade as women.) These assessments proved problematic, too.

In normal human development, when a zygote has XY, or male, chromosomes, the SRY—sex-determining region Y—gene on the Y chromosome "instructs" the zygote's protogonads to develop as testes, rather than as ovaries. The testes then produce testosterone, which issues a second set of developmental instructions: for a scrotal sac to develop and for the testes to descend into it, for a penis to grow, and so on. But the process can get derailed. A person can be born with one ovary and one testicle. The SRY gene can end up on an X chromosome. A person with a penis who thinks he is male can one day find out that he has a uterus and ovaries. "Then, there is chromosomal variability that is invisible," Anne Fausto-Sterling, the author of *Sexing the Body*, told me. "You could go your whole life and never know."

All sorts of things can happen, and do. An embryo that is chromosomally male but suffers from an enzyme deficiency that partially prevents it from "reading" testosterone can develop into a baby who appears female. Then, at puberty, the person's testes will produce a rush of hormones and this time the body won't need the enzyme (called 5-alpha-reductase) to successfully read the testosterone. The little girl will start to become hairier and more muscular. Her voice may deepen, and her testes may descend into what she thought were her labia. Her clitoris will grow into something like a penis. Is she still a girl? Was she ever?

If a chromosomally male embryo has androgen-insensitivity syndrome, or AIS, the cells' receptors for testosterone, an androgen, are deaf to the testosterone's instructions, and will thus develop the default external sexual characteristics of a female. An individual with androgen-insensitivity syndrome has XY chromosomes, a vagina, and undescended testes, but her body develops without the ability to respond to the testosterone it produces. In fact, people with complete AIS are less able to process testosterone than average women. Consequently, they tend to have exceptionally "smooth-skinned bodies with rounded hips and breasts and long limbs," Dreger writes in *Hermaphrodites*.

People with incomplete AIS, on the other hand, could end up looking and sounding like Caster Semenya. Their bodies hear *some* of the instructions that the testosterone inside them is issuing. But that does not necessarily mean that they would have an athletic advantage.

For example, the Spanish hurdler Maria Patiño, who had AIS, went to the World University Games in Kobe, Japan, in 1985, and forgot to bring a letter from her doctor verifying that she was female. Until 1999, gender verification was compulsory for all female athletes. Officials scraped some cells from the inside of her cheek for chromatin testing. If visual inspection had still been the standard, Patiño's gender never would have been questioned. Her genitals, and the rest of her, looked female, but according to the test she was male. The story got out, and she was stripped of her past titles. Her boyfriend left her. Her scholarship was revoked, and she was evicted from the national athletic residence.

In 1991, the International Association of Athletics Federations abandoned this method as unreliable, and, nine years later, so did the International Olympic Committee. Patiño was requalified in 1988, when she was able to prove that her body could not make use of its testosterone, and that she had developed as a woman. "I knew I was a woman," Patiño said, "in the eyes of medicine, God, and most of all in my own eyes."

The approach that the IAAF appears to be taking in its review of Semenya's test results from Berlin is not unlike the British Gynaecological Society's muddled attempt to determine the sex of its living specimen. The IAAF's gender policy states that an athlete "can be asked to attend a medical evaluation before a panel comprising gynecologist, endocrinologist, psychologist, internal medicine specialist, expert on gender/transgender issues." It has not come up with a single litmus test for sex; its goal, like that of the IOC in such situations, is to reach consensus. The federation does not define the criteria that its group of experts must use to reach their determination, however. "It seems to be working with a kind of 'I know it when I see it' policy," Dreger, a professor of clinical medical humanities and bioethics at Northwestern University's Feinberg School of Medicine, told me. The policy does not indicate who should be tested and on what grounds. An athlete will be examined if "there is any 'suspicion' or if there is a 'challenge' " to her sex. Evidently, a blog post qualifies as a challenge.

In conjunction with other sports bodies, the IAAF will hold a special conference, in January 2010, to review the policy. On November 18, it sent out a press release stating that there would be "no discussion of Caster Semenya's case" at the November council meeting, despite its earlier promise to resolve the issue there.

Unfortunately for IAAF officials, they are faced with a question that no one has ever been able to answer: What is the ultimate difference between a man and a woman? "This is not a solvable problem," Alice Dreger said. "People always press me: 'Isn't there one marker we can use?' No. We couldn't then and we can't now, and science is making it more difficult and not less, because it ends up showing us how much blending there is and how many nuances, and it becomes impossible to point to one thing, or even a set of things, and say that's what it means to be male."

In 2000, Anne Fausto-Sterling, a professor of biology at Brown University, conducted what remains the study of record on the frequency of intersexuality, and concluded that 1.7 percent of the population develops in a way that deviates from the standard definition of male or female. (Some scholars have argued that Fausto-Sterling's categories are too broad, because they include individuals who show no noticeable expression of their chromosomal irregularity.) Based on this figure, intersexuality is much more common than Down syndrome or albinism, though it can be harder to keep track of: Every baby born in the United States is registered as "male" or "female."

The word "hermaphrodite" is as outdated and offensive to the people it once described as the word "mulatto." In one Greek myth, Hermes, the son of Zeus, and Aphrodite, the goddess of love, have a child endowed with all the attributes of both of them. "Hermaphrodite" implies a double-sexed creature, fully male and fully female, which is a physical impossibility for human beings. (You can be half and half, but you can't be all and all.)

In the 1990s, a movement spearheaded by an activist who used to call herself Cheryl Chase, and now goes by the name Bo Laurent, insisted that what was needed was a new identity. Chase founded the Intersex Society of North America (now defunct) to draw attention to the frequently tragic consequences of doctors' performing irreversible surgery on newborns to enforce a sex—one that the baby might just as easily as not grow up to reject. The society advocated assigning intersex children a gender at birth but leaving their bodies intact, so that upon adulthood they could make their own choices about whether they wished to undergo surgical modification.

Then something unexpected happened. "The intersex identity started getting inhabited by people who weren't really intersex," Dreger said. "The people who accumulated around the intersex identity tended to be queer and out and comfortable with this identity outside the gender binary." They felt that refraining from interfering with infants' ambiguous genitalia was the first step on a desirable path to dissolving gender altogether. To them, this idea was "as politically inspiring as it is utterly disconnected from the actual experience of intersex people or the heart-wrenching decisions their parents have to make when an intersex child is born," as Vernon A. Rosario, a professor of psychiatry at UCLA, put it in a recent issue of *The Gay and Lesbian Review*.

Semenya, whether she wants to be or not, has become a hero to many people who "don't fit the sex and gender boxes," as Jarvis, from Winnipeg, posted on the website casterrunsforme.com. A person named Megan Ewart wrote, "I'll bet you've got a lot more transgendered allies than just me that are feeling your pain."

Now there is an even newer term of art for people born with ambiguously sexed bodies who do not wish to be connected with the LGBTQI—lesbian, gay, bisexual, transgender, queer, intersex—camp: "disorders of sex development," or DSD. By naming the condition a medical "disorder," advocates of the DSD label hope to make the people it describes seem less aberrant. "Oddly enough, it does normalize it in a certain way," Fausto-Sterling said. "It's putting it on the same plane as other anomalous development—like congenital anomalies of the heart." Advocates of the DSD label are not seeking to create a third sex. Rather, they want disorders of sex development to be treated like any other physical abnormality: something for doctors to monitor but not to operate on, unless the patient is in physical discomfort or danger.

In science and medicine, categories are imperative, but they are also inflected by social concerns. "Mammals," for example, were so named by Linnaeus, in the eighteenth century, because their females produce milk to suckle their young. Was it irrelevant that scientists like Linnaeus sought to encourage mothers to breast-feed their own children, and to do away with the "unnatural" custom of wet-nursing? "There are philosophers of science who argue that when scientists make categories in the natural world—shapes, species—they are simply making a list of things that exist: natural kinds," Fausto-Sterling said. "It's scientist as discoverer. The phrase that people use is 'cutting nature at its joint.' There are other people, myself included, who think that, almost always, what we're doing in biology is creating categories that work pretty well for certain things that we want to do with them. But there is no joint."

If sex is not precisely definable, how else might sports be organized? Theoretically, athletes could be categorized by size, as they are in wrestling and boxing. But then women would usually lose to men. Or athletes could be categorized by skill level. Almost always, this would mean that the strongest élite female athletes would compete against the weakest élite male athletes, which would be pretty demoralizing all the way around.

Another option would be to divide athletes biochemically. Testosterone is, for an athlete, truly important stuff. Developmentally, testosterone spurs linear bone growth in adolescents. Fully grown people use testosterone in doping because it helps create muscle mass and increases red-blood-cell production, which, in turn, increases cellular oxygen-carrying capacity. The more oxygen an athlete has in her cells, the more efficiently her muscles operate and the longer it takes for her body to start producing lactic acid, the substance that causes cramps and pain. Testosterone makes a faster, better athlete, and enables a body to recover more quickly from exhaustion. Hypothetically, according to Eric Vilain, a professor of human genetics and pediatrics at UCLA, those with a certain level of functional testosterone (testosterone that the body can actually make use of) could be in one group, and those below it could be in another. Although the first group would be almost all male and the second group would be almost all female, the division would be determined not by gender but by actual physical advantages that gender supposedly, yet unreliably, supplies.

But, setting aside the issue of gender, there is still no such thing as a level playing field in sports. Different bodies have physical attributes, even abnormalities, that may provide a distinct advantage in one sport or another. The NBA, for instance, has had several players with acromegaly—the overproduction of growth hormone. Michael Phelps, who has won fourteen Olympic gold medals, has unusually long arms and is said to have double-jointed elbows, knees, and ankles. Is Caster Semenya's alleged extra testosterone really so different?

There is much more at stake in organizing sports by gender than just making things fair. If we were to admit that at some level we don't know the difference between men and women, we might start to wonder about the way we've organized our entire world. Who gets to use what bathroom? Who is allowed to get married? (Currently, the United States government recognizes the marriage of a woman to a female-to-male transsexual who has had a double mastectomy and takes testosterone tablets but still has a vagina, but not to a woman who hasn't done those things.) We depend on gender to make sense of sexuality, society, and ourselves. We do not wish to see it dissolve.

What the IAAF concludes about Caster Semenya could have ramifications for sports in general and for South Africa in particular. This is true not only because it is Semenya's place of origin. South Africa has an unusually high level of intersex births. Nobody knows why.

During apartheid, for every white town there was a black township. Only the white towns appeared on maps, though the townships were nearly always more populous. John Carlin, in his account of the 1995 rugby World Cup, *Playing the Enemy: Nelson Mandela and the Game That Made a Nation*, describes townships as "the black shadows of the towns." Khayelitsha is the black shadow of Cape Town. According to the most recent census, half a million people live there, but in reality the number is probably much higher. Many of their parents and grandparents settled in the Cape Flats, outside of Cape Town, after the Group Areas Acts of the 1950s made it illegal for them to live in the city. "Khayelitsha" is Xhosa for "New Home." Shacks made of corrugated tin, cardboard, and scrap wood, many without electricity or running water, sprawl for miles along mostly unmarked dirt roads, punctuated by beauty parlors and fruit stands in structures no bigger than British telephone booths.

By Khayelitsha standards, Funeka Soldaat's small home, with its solid brick walls and tiled floor, is very fine. Soldaat is an LGBQTI activist. Both she and a cousin—whom Soldaat, following local custom, referred to as her sister—were born with anomalous genitalia, and both underwent "corrective" partial clitoridectomies when they were young, which they now regret. This is the standard "treatment" for babies born with a clitoris longer than one centimetre but smaller than 2.5 centimetres, at which point it becomes a medically acceptable penis. The scar tissue that forms after such a procedure can impede sensation for the rest of a person's life.

"My sister, she look just like Caster," Soldaat said, smiling. "She don't have the breasts. She never get a period. Everybody thinks she's a guy, just like Caster. We call them, in Xhosa, italasi. It is not a new thing—everybody has a word for it." That there is a name for intersex does not mean it is a condition that is ever spoken about. "One thing that is so difficult for African people: there's no way that you can discuss about something that's happened below the belt," Soldaat said. "All the time you don't know what's happening in your body, and there's nobody that try to explain to you. Then it becomes a problem. If my mom would know that I'm intersex and there's nothing wrong about it, then there was nothing going to make me panic."

Particularly in remote areas, where babies tend to be born in the presence of a mother, a grandmother, and maybe a midwife, it is easy to keep a baby's genitalia a secret. People want to insulate their children from the shame of being different, so they simply pretend that they are not. "Limpopo and Eastern Cape are the high incidence of intersex people," Soldaat said. "And when you grow up in the rural areas it's a mess, because people don't even go to doctors." The determination of gender is made very simply. "It depends what they do when they go to the loo," Soldaat said. "That's what makes their children to be women. If they go to the loo and they sit, that's it."

On her coffee table, Soldaat had a photocopy of the South African magazine You, which featured a photo spread showing Caster Semenya dressed in high heels and a short skirt, her hair fluffed out and her face made up. Her expression was painfully uncomfortable, and the pictures were garish.

"My sister was crying when she saw this whole thing on paper," Soldaat said, flipping through the pages. "It's a disaster. She look like a drag queen! I can just imagine her at night when she's alone, looking at these pictures."

Soldaat tossed the papers on the floor. "When we are really, really poor sometimes, and we really, really want to protect ourselves, people take an advantage," she said. "That's why it was easy for people to force her to do this, for ASA to do this." Athletics South Africa received a payment from You in exchange for Semenya's appearance in its pages. "To say that she enjoyed doing this, that's a lie! There is no way. There is no way!"

Soldaat has a shaved head and was wearing big jeans and a baseball cap with the words "Mama Cash," the name of a Dutch women's-rights organization, on it. She is a lesbian, and she said that she suspected Semenya is, too.

"Everyone! Everyone who is like this likes women," Soldaat said, laughing. "Everyone!" ("Caster has never cared about men other than as friends," her father told a reporter. "Her sisters were always after boys in the way that I, too, was always after girls when I was younger. But Caster has never been interested in any of that.") If Soldaat is right, then Semenya's life may well get more difficult. Soldaat was going to court later that day to listen to the proceedings against several men accused of raping and murdering a lesbian in Khayelitsha. "They are raping lesbians to correct them," she said. "In order they can be a proper woman."

Soldaat said that Semenya should run with women. "It will never be like intersex women have their own Olympic Games—that's ridiculous!" she said. Soldaat has a big, raucous laugh, and the idea of that imaginary competition absolutely killed her. Soldaat was a runner herself when she was young. "If she can't run in the Olympics, Caster has to continue running with other girls in South Africa. Because, really, that's what she wants, that's what she is, that's what keeps her alive: that's running."

The only thing more slippery than the science in the Semenya case is the agendas of the men who have involved themselves in it. There is a bounty of political gain for whoever spins the story most successfully.

Julius Malema, the president of the ANC Youth League, has said that he does not believe in the existence of intersex people, and has tried to frame the concept as a suspect and unwelcome import from abroad. "Hermaphrodite, what is that?" Malema asked at a press conference in October. "Somebody tell me, what is 'hermaphrodite' in Pedi? There's no such thing. So don't impose your hermaphrodite concepts on us." (The word is *tarasi*, according to a professor of South African languages at Yale.) The Youth League issued a press release decrying a "racist attack on Semenya" orchestrated by the media in "Australia, which is the most lucrative destination for South Africa's racists and fascists who refused to live under a black democratic government."

Julius Malema is not known for being levelheaded. He won the presidency of the Youth League in a highly contested election in 2008. Just a few months later, while Jacob Zuma was fending off charges of racketeering and fraud (the charges have since been dropped), Malema became notorious for vowing, "We are prepared to die for Zuma. Not only that, we are prepared to take up arms and kill for Zuma." (Zuma also beat a rape charge, in 2006.) Zuma has called Malema "a leader in the making," worthy of "inheriting the ANC" one day. Malema has demonstrated an ability to mobilize people and an almost reckless willingness to use charges of racism to do so. He has been Leonard Chuene's most steadfast defender.

Chuene has, since the revelation of his deceit, become almost as controversial a figure in South Africa as Caster Semenya. Countless editorials have accused Chuene of sacrificing her in his quest for a gold medal and have demanded his ouster. In Dr. Harold Adams's report to Parliament, he calls Chuene's decision "short-sighted and grossly irresponsible." Though Chuene received a vote of confidence from Athletics South Africa's board after his admission, the ANC asked him to apologize; its rival party, the Democratic Alliance, demanded his resignation, and the Deputy Minister of Sport called him a liar. Minister Mayende-Sibiya told me that Chuene's behavior was "totally unacceptable."

Julius Malema has continued to paint any criticism of Chuene as racist. In early October, one of ASA's biggest sponsors, Nedbank, announced that it would withdraw its support pending a change in ASA's leadership. Malema retaliated by calling for a boycott of the bank. "We will teach them a lesson about the power of the masses," Malema said. "They may have money, but we can defeat them because we have the masses."

On three occasions, Leonard Chuene's personal assistant made an appointment for me to interview "the president," as she calls her boss. She always called or emailed at the last minute to cancel. We had several calls scheduled, but Chuene never picked up his phone at the appointed time. Then, one day, I got on an airplane going to Polokwane, a small northern city. Sitting in an empty row, in a navy blazer and pressed jeans, was Leonard Chuene.

Chuene wanted to know how I recognized him. Only minutes before, I had been looking at his photograph in a newspaper, alongside a story about Nedbank's withdrawal of funds from ASA and ASA's failing finances. "I have become more famous than Caster," he said, and chuckled. Chuene has a shiny bald head and a little gut. He was once a serious runner and has completed more than a hundred marathons, he told me. He said he had no choice but to get Semenya tested. "You cannot just argue like a fool and say no. This is not the law of the jungle!" He speaks very quickly. He explained why he had not heeded Adams's advice to withdraw Semenya from the race.

"I don't have the results in my hand!" he said. "How did you expect me to take an informed decision?"

Indeed, Adams had had word from the Pretoria clinic but no actual documentation of the test results. "Where is the evidence?" Chuene said. "Now I come back home and they will say, 'When this black child from the rural be No. 1, why do you deprive her?' "

Chuene shrugged. "They say I lied. That's what they are saying. I said no. There is confidentiality! IAAF is in trouble for breaching that. Who was going to be Leonard to say that?" The engines started roaring as the small plane took off. "It was 22-Catch situation!" Chuene shouted over the noise. "If I will do this, it's 'Why did you withdraw her?' If I did not, 'Why did you allow her to run?' Whatever way you look at it, I'm judged. I'm judged!"

There were around twenty people on the plane. We were airborne, and the engines quieted. Chuene did not. "The stupid leader is the one who says, 'I'm not sure; I don't know.' I had to take a decision! She must run. If Chuene didn't allow her, it meant she was going to stay in South Africa. This thing has given her more opportunity! Everybody knows her. The world is out there to say, 'Your problems are our problems.' Imagine if I had not let her win!" As we touched down in Polokwane, he said, "If there is to be help, it is because of the opportunity created by Leonard Chuene."

Recently, Semenya told the *Guardian*, "It's not so easy. The university is OK but there is not many other places I can go. People want to stare at me now. They want to touch me. I'm supposed to be famous." She added, "I don't think I like it so much."

The law firm Dewey & LeBoeuf announced in September that it was taking on Caster Semenya as a client. It is still sorting through what happened and deciding whom to sue. One afternoon, I drove with Benedict Phiri, an associate in the firm's Johannesburg office, across the Blood River from Polokwane to Ga-Masehlong to meet Semenya's mother. Ga-Masehlong is a small village dotted with jacaranda trees; goats graze on the garbage and the grass on the roadsides. The houses have tin roofs, and people put rocks on top of them to keep them from blowing away. There are satellite dishes in several yards, but most people have dug their own wells and collect firewood from the bush for cooking. Everyone knows everyone else in Ga-Masehlong, and it was easy to get directions to the house of the champion.

At the Semenya home, there was a flyer tacked to the front door promoting a lecture that Julius Malema was giving at the local elementary school. Phiri knocked. We heard shuffling and then the sound of locks turning and bolts sliding. Phiri called out that he was Caster's lawyer, but nobody came to the door.

A few minutes later, a pretty girl wearing an orange fleece jacket walked into the yard and introduced herself as Maphela. She said she was fourteen. "Do you want my story?" she asked in English. "I am Caster's sister! But I am not like her. I am different from Caster." I asked her what she meant, and Maphela replied emphatically, "I am not that way."

Maphela looked toward the window where her mother, Dorcus, was hiding her face behind the curtain and motioning vigorously for her daughter to stop speaking with us. We asked Maphela if she would tell her mother that Phiri was Caster's lawyer. Maphela ran off toward the back door.

We sat on the stoop of a cooking hut in the Semenyas' front yard, and waited with the chickens and the goats. An elderly neighbor named Ike came into the yard. "Caster has done a wonderful thing," he said. "This has brought to mind when the Philistines were persecuting the Israelites." Ike told us that he just wanted to check on the family and see how their visit from Julius Malema the previous evening had gone. This made Phiri nervous.

After a few minutes, Maphela returned. She told us that her mother would not meet with Phiri, because she did not agree that Caster should have a lawyer.

As we drove away through the bush, Phiri called his boss in Johannesburg, a white former rugby player named Greg Nott. I could hear Nott yelling through the phone. "We knew this would happen all along," Phiri said, trying to calm him. "Julius Malema is Chuene's ally, and Julius is giving Caster money."

On the occasion of the ANC Youth League's sixty-fifth anniversary, in October, Julius Malema presented Caster Semenya with a hundred and twenty thousand rand (about $16,000) at a gala dinner in Johannesburg. "I can even see it," Phiri said on the phone. "They probably told the mom, 'People will come and say they're her lawyer. Don't believe it.' " Phiri was afraid that Malema would step in and persuade the family to side with Chuene, who comes from the same region, and whose interests might not be served by lawyers poking around. One of the first things that Dewey & LeBoeuf did when the firm took the case was to ask both ASA and the IAAF to provide documentation of the tests and any other pertinent paperwork; neither organization has fully complied.

The firm is representing Semenya pro bono, so good publicity will be its only reward. "And that," Phiri said, "could blow up in our faces."

Nobody wants Chuene out of office more than an old friend and colleague named Wilfred Daniels, who started at ASA with him, sixteen years ago. "From day one we connected, in the struggle days, you know?" Daniels said.

"We were like, we belong together." Both Daniels, fifty-eight, and Chuene, fifty-seven, grew up as promising athletes who could never compete internationally because of apartheid. They understood each other then, but not anymore.

Daniels—whom everyone calls Wilfie—is the unofficial mayor of Stellenbosch, a leafy college town in the wine country. He likes to hold court at the Jan Cats restaurant, in front of the elegant Stellenbosch Hotel. As he sat at his street-front table on a sunny afternoon in a green Izod jacket and track pants, drinking a bottle of Chenin blanc, every other person who passed by stopped to pay his respects, or at least waved at him driving by. Daniels was a famous athlete in his youth, and he is even more famous now. In early September, he resigned from ASA in protest over its handling of Caster Semenya, and had since been in the papers constantly. "We allowed it," he said. "If we as management were on our game, we would've objected. We accompanied her to the slaughter. And that is my dilemma."

Daniels was not directly involved in the testing or the cover-up. During the first training session in Berlin, "while she was warming up and stretching, putting on her spikes, she told me they had done tests on her. I said, 'What tests?' " Semenya told him that she didn't know what they were for, but she described what had happened. "They put her feet in straps and 'they work down there,' she said. They told her it was dope tests." Semenya had undergone routine doping tests many times before. She knew that this was something very different.

"If you and me who come from the big cities, if we find it repulsive, I mean, what about a rural girl," Daniels said. "She doesn't know what's happening around her. She's seven, eight months in the city now, in Pretoria, a new life altogether, and nobody takes the time to explain to her?" He shook his head in disgust. "It was unprovoked talk, and she's not somebody who talks, normally. And she spoke to me as a Colored guy, as a man, about intimate, female things. That to me was like a cry for help."

The sins of ASA, as Daniels sees it, are, first, not giving Semenya adequate information about the Pretoria tests—including her right to refuse them—and, second, not pulling her out of the competition in Berlin.

"It's the day before the championships," Daniels said. "Eighteen years old, your first World Championships, the greatest race of your life. You can't focus, because you have to go for gender testing. And you come back and you have to watch on TV: They are explaining the possibilities. I found her in her room, sitting in front of the TV like this," Daniels put his hand up to his face to show how close she was to the screen. "And they're talking about her and she's trying to understand what they're saying. Because nobody has spoken to her, to tell her, Look, this is what these tests might mean. I felt so ashamed."

Daniels has worked in various capacities at ASA over the years, first in management, then as a coach, and, most recently, as ASA's coördinator with the High Performance Centre, the program at the University of Pretoria where Semenya is now. Daniels does not agree with the IAAF's assessment that Semenya's seven-and-a-half-second improvement was "supernatural." She went from training on the dirt roads of Limpopo to a world-class facility. She is also an extraordinarily hard worker. "Understand: Maria Mutola is her hero," Daniels said. "So she had wonderful goals and ideals for herself; she was really trying to emulate her hero one day." Maria Mutola is a runner from Mozambique whose event, like Semenya's, was the eight hundred metres. Mutola also happened to have a strikingly masculine appearance.

Daniels believes that the best that can happen for Semenya at this point is to have a career like his. He has travelled the world and met many of his heroes. He has a cellar with more than two thousand bottles of red wine. He eats his grilled springbok at Jan Cats and clearly enjoys being a local eminence. But it is probably not the life he would have led if apartheid hadn't prevented him from competing internationally; and it is not the life that was in front of Caster Semenya before she went to Germany. "I understand that her running days are over," Daniels said.

There's another scenario, in which Semenya's story could become one of against-all-odds victory. The IAAF could apologize and decree Semenya female. Kobus Van der Walt, the director of sport at the High Performance Centre, pointed out that though Semenya has beaten the South African record for her event, she hasn't come anywhere near Kratochvílová's world record, which means that there are plenty of women with a chance of besting Semenya. Conceivably, one day we will see Caster Semenya at the Olympics with a medal hanging from her neck. She could be the poster child for triumphant transgression.

But that is not what Daniels thinks will happen. "Now her life is over," he said. "Not only as an athlete but as a human being. Even if the IAAF says there's nothing wrong with her, people will always look at her twice. There should be hell to pay for those responsible." He pounded his fist on the table. "I've got a daughter. If that was my daughter, what would I have done as a father? Somebody might have been dead by now."

On November 5, Chuene and the entire board of ASA were suspended by the South African Sports Confederation and Olympic Committee, pending an investigation into how they handled Caster Semenya.

One afternoon at the High Performance Centre, I sat up in the bleachers, killing time before a meeting with Kobus Van der Walt. I was surrounded by a spread of neatly partitioned fields, like a Brueghel painting: There are twenty-four cricket nets, six rugby fields, twenty-two outdoor tennis courts, nine soccer fields, seven squash courts, and a track surrounded by a three-thousand-seat stadium, all kept in impeccable condition. Runners in little packs zoomed around the fields and into the distance. Spring sunlight flicked along the blue of the swimming pool.

A figure in a black sweatshirt with the hood up walked along the path about thirty yards in front of me. There was something about this person's build and movements that drew my attention. I got up and followed along the path, until I caught up to the person where he or she was stopped behind the cafeteria, talking to a waiter and a cook, both of whom were much shorter than she was. It was Caster Semenya.

She wore sandals and track pants and kept her hood up. When she shook my hand, I noticed that she had long nails. She didn't look like an eighteen-year-old girl, or an eighteen-year-old boy. She looked like something else, something magnificent.

I told her I had come from New York City to write about her, and she asked me why.

"Because you're the champion," I said.

She snorted and said, "You make me laugh."

I asked her if she would talk to me, not about the tests or Chuene but about her evolution as an athlete, her progression from Limpopo to the world stage. She shook her head vigorously. "No," she said. "I can't talk to you. I can't talk to anyone. I can't say to anyone how I feel or what's in my mind."

I said I thought that must suck.

"No," she said, very firmly. Her voice was strong and low. "That doesn't suck. It sucks when I was running and they were writing those things. That sucked. That is when it sucks. Now I just have to walk away. That's all I can do." She smiled a small, bemused smile. "Walk away from all of this, maybe forever. Now I just walk away." Then she took a few steps backward, turned around, and did.

AUTHOR'S AFTERWORDS...

This was the most exciting reporting experience of my career. I was obsessed with the story and when I got on the plane to Johannesburg, that was really all I had—passion. I had never been to Africa before, I had no contacts there, and, frankly, I knew very little about sports. But if you care enough about a story, somehow you figure it out.

I knew Caster Semenya went to the University of Pretoria, so that's where I went. I started going to the campus and talking to anyone I could get to meet with me: student organization representatives, other athletes, whoever. To some extent, reporting always works in concentric circles: you start by calling or meeting with people who you happen to have access to who may have only a passing connection to your subject, and then they lead you to people who are one circle closer in, and you keep doing that until you are at the center of the target.

When I was at my hotel at night I called her lawyers, I called Athletics South Africa, and I tried to reach someone at the IAAF. Meanwhile I was struggling to get some sense of life in contemporary South Africa: The people at my hotel kept telling me not to go out on the street by myself because crime had become so rampant. During the day I ignored their warnings and zoomed all over Pretoria and Johannesburg without any trouble. One evening, I went out at 6 as the sun was setting and the street was crowded with people coming home from work, mothers with children. I felt sure the people at my hotel were being overprotective and absurd. I ate dinner at a little restaurant inside a strip mall where men were playing music and I chatted with the proprietor. When I got up to leave at 8, he asked if I had a driver and I said no, I was going to walk the five blocks to my hotel. He insisted on driving me back himself—he said there was no doubt in his mind I would get hurt if I left unaccompanied and he didn't want that on his conscience. I thought he was being ridiculous but I got in his car. We did not pass a single human being out on the street. "You see?" He said. "We are all prisoners in our homes after dark."

When I got back to my room that night, I happened to see an report on TV about the various scandals within Athletics South Africa by a reporter named Deborah Pattah. I emailed the station and to my surprise, Pattah called me back the next day and took me to lunch. She did the most generous thing one reporter can do for another and gave me direct phone numbers for half the people I was trying to find. I will never forget that.

Things were starting to work. Semenya's lawyers had agreed to meet with me, the head of athletics at the University of Pretoria was going to see me, and my colleague at the *New Yorker*, Michael Specter, had arranged for someone he knew from his reporting on HIV and infectious diseases to drive with me from the airport in Limpopo up to the village where Semenya grew up so I could meet with her childhood coach. All of that was sort of normal, but there were a few surreal incidents during my trip that just felt like outrageous fortune. I remember getting dressed in my hotel the morning I was going to see the head of athletics and having this image in my head of Caster Semenya on the track at her University: I had this weird sense that I would see her there that day. And that's what happened. I got there early and had to kill time and I sat on the bleachers looking around and then there she was, just walking along. That's when I first met her. It was bananas. It was as if you'd decided to write a story about The Beatles and you just went to Abbey Road and waited for the four of them to cross the street and then suddenly there they were.

Along those same lines, as the days passed and people started returning my calls, the one guy I could not get ahold of was Leonard Chuene, the head of Athletics South Africa, who was at the center of the "gender testing" scandal. His secretary kept making appointments for me and then canceling them at the last minute. And then one day, he was standing right next to me, about to get on the same tiny plane to Limpopo that I was. Not only that, the seat next to him was empty. It was the kind of thing that happens to reporters in movies.

Other than Deborah Pattah, Semenya's coaches, and Semenya herself, it seemed that everyone I met on that trip misled me in some way—it seemed as if everyone had screwed up to some extent and was trying to cover themselves. So I was trying to navigate the country, I was trying to track down the players, and then, ultimately, I was trying to sift through a lot of bullshit to get to the truth of the story. When I got home, there was one final hurdle: the science. The more I learned about the biology of gender, the more I realized that what seemed like a given—that there are men and there are women, and that it's pretty clear who is which—was actually another warren of uncertainty and dishonesty.

This was a once-in-a-decade story for me. For one thing, it had everything to do with the issues I'm most obsessed with—things I've thought and written about a lot. But it was set in a country and a field about which I knew nothing, so it was an enormous opportunity for me to learn and to bring my readers along with me on a process of discovery. But most importantly it had what you most want from any story: complexity at every turn.

Brian Mockenhaupt

B rian Mockenhaupt is a contributing editor at *Reader's Digest* and *Esquire*, and is the nonfiction editor at the *Journal of Military Experience*. He writes regularly for The *Atlantic* and *Outside*. His work has also appeared in *Pacific Standard*, *Backpacker*, the *New York Times Magazine*, and *Chicago*. He served two tours in Iraq as an infantryman with the U.S. Army's 10th Mountain Division. Since leaving the service in 2005, he has written extensively on military and veterans affairs, reporting from Afghanistan and Iraq, home-towns and hospitals, and Mt. Kilimanjaro, which he climbed with a former soldier blinded by a bomb in Baghdad.

Prior to joining the Army, Mockenhaupt worked as a newspaper reporter in the United States and in Phnom Penh, Cambodia, at the *Cambodia Daily*, an English-language newspaper, and as a contributing reporter for the *Far Eastern Economic Review*, reporting from Cambodia, Burma and South Korea.

Sgt. Wells's New Skull

He goes to war and wonders what it will be like if he gets hit. Will he be tough, maybe heroic? Will he piss himself? How bad will it hurt? He isn't sure when, but at some point the thought shifts from the possible to the inevitable. *When* he gets hit. Because now he's sure it's going to happen.

This is how it goes.

The dreams come first. Every night he huddles on the rooftop with his squad and the grenades rain down. They aren't wearing their body armor, just T-shirts. He tries to cover his men with his arms, but he can't protect them. He's helpless. And the grenades keep falling.

After he's sent out to pick up what's left of the suicide bomber, still smoking and too hot to put in the body bag, that dream is joined by this one: He lies in bed, waiting for sleep, and hears something down on the floor, scratching, sliding. There's the bomber, a head and a torso, just as they'd found him, crawling toward him in the darkness.

Staff Sergeant Brian Wells has been in Iraq ten months. This is getting old. Time to go home.

But he stays, we all stay, because that's the Army and that's war.

On April 23, 2005, First Lieutenant Dan Hurd, Wells, and his squad are preparing for a foot patrol in a village just west of Baghdad, searching for weapons caches. With a cockeyed smile, Hurd tells Wells he might want to keep his distance from him today. "I dreamt last night I blew up on a dismounted patrol," he says. "I saw my wife speaking at the funeral."

Wells laughs. "I have horrible dreams every night," he tells Hurd. One bad dream is no big deal.

A few hours later, just before sunset, they're outside a metal shop, near an artillery round they've just found. That's a win for the day, one less roadside bomb. Hurd and Wells are standing with Captain Scott Shaw, the company commander, talking about finding some cover. No sense staying out in the open. And now Hurd is watching Wells fall. He didn't hear the bullet snap past his right shoulder, but a second later, with Wells already unconscious and halfway to the dirt, he hears the shot.

Crack.

Now he's yelling.

"Medic!"

The soundtrack of war would probably bore you. Mostly you'd hear bullshitting and bitching. But sometimes you'd hear long rips of machine-gun fire and explosions so loud, they box your ears and rumble in your chest. That's exhilarating. So that's war, you'd say with a greedy, giddy smirk. And sometimes you'd hear something that shoves your guts into your throat. A sharp, short, desperate cry.

"Medic!"

Shaw is yelling, too.

"He's dead! He's dead!"

Now all sound is drowned out by gunfire as the platoon rakes an apartment building four hundred meters to the northeast, which everyone figures is the origin of the shot. If there's a sniper in the building, this should keep him from firing again. The racket builds in coughs and spurts. Every four rounds, the rifles and machine guns spit out tracer rounds that glow red as they zip through the air at a half mile a second.

Dust is rising around the apartment building as bullets pulverize the concrete. Someone calls out a target. Brown car. The gunmen are leaving in a brown car. Across the canal to our front, maybe two hundred meters away, a gray sedan comes into view and the gunner on my Humvee starts firing, throwing rounds across the canal, blowing out the back windows of the car, which stops. I'm standing outside the truck, using the open armored door as cover, with my rifle raised to my eye. My ears ring from the machine gun barking beside me. Through my scope I track the driver. Easy shot. He's getting out of his car now, hesitating, terrified. He's back in and speeding away, clearly not the gunman. I lower my rifle. But I could have killed him, and no one much would have cared.

The platoon's medic is off that day, so the job falls on Specialist Scott McCarthy, an infantryman trained as an EMT. Every day that he's the assigned medic, he prays no one is hurt on patrol. He joined the Army to shoot guns and kick in doors, not to be responsible for saving his friends' lives. He's eating Tostitos and salsa on the hood of a Humvee when Wells is shot. He hears the call and sprints around the corner with the aid bag, a mobile ER packed with thirty pounds of IVs, morphine, splints, airway tubes, and bandages.

Panic crowds his thoughts. *Oh shit. Oh shit. Oh shit.* There's Wells, lying on his back, eyes closed. Shaw is kneeling beside him, shielding his body. "Get down," he tells McCarthy, not wanting another soldier dropped by the sniper. "He's dead." McCarthy hears him, but not really. He doesn't hear much at all.

Everything's foggy, quiet, far away. *Oh shit. Oh shit. Oh shit.* He lowers his ear to Wells's mouth and feels breath. "No he's not!" he yells. "He's alive!"

The bullet struck the edge of his helmet, just above his left ear, punched through the layers of Kevlar, split the top of his ear, and drove into his skull, shooting fragments of bullet and bone into his brain. Blood seeps from the wound and congeals in a pool in the dust. McCarthy slides his fingers to the back of Wells's head, feeling for an exit wound, but there isn't one. Thank the helmet for that. Without something to slow down a tiny cone of metal traveling at nearly two thousand miles an hour, Wells wouldn't need a medic, might not have a brain left in his skull. As it is, the bullet has done plenty of damage. Before putting a piece of gauze over the entrance wound, McCarthy sees bits of brain mixed in with the blood. It looks like greasy sausage.

There's a half dozen people working on him now. Cutting off his web gear and body armor. Loosening his boots. Sticking his arms with IVs. McCarthy kneels behind Wells, cradling his head, squeezing it, really, with his left hand clamped over the wound. Our interpreter, Sala, who must be sixty-five but walks with us in the heat every day, is crouched by McCarthy. "Wells! Wake up!" There's pain in his voice. "Wake up, Wells!" And soon he does. His body shifts. He moans and mumbles.

The Black Hawk is fifty feet overhead and thwacking madly, covering us in a wave of dust. The pilot sets down on a soccer field and a knot of soldiers shuffle to the bird, taking turns as stretcher bearers. McCarthy trips and falls to his knees but is up again, his blood-soaked hands never leaving Wells's head. They load the stretcher, shut the door, and the bird rises. We watch it disappear, headed for the Green Zone, and we wonder if Wells is dead.

At the Combat Support Hospital, a ten-minute flight away, the ER team drives a six-wheel John Deere Gator to meet the helicopter, the sides of its small bed folded down to receive the stretcher. For a moment no one is holding Wells down, and his left arm flails and snatches the bandage from his head.

Neurosurgeon Major Michael Rosner is the realist on call at the hospital. Before he starts the four-hour operation, he gives his initial assessment: Wells is going to die. Rosner has been doing surgery in Baghdad for the past three months. He is always busy. And when a neurosurgeon is needed, the patient usually isn't doing too well.

The bullet caused a massive skull fracture, but what's killing Wells right now are the bone fragments and shrapnel that tore through the torcula, the cluster of vessels at the base of the brain that drains blood from the head. In wars past, doctors wouldn't have bothered. Battlefield triage necessitates putting resources and manpower where they'll save lives. Even in the Baghdad CASH in 2005, with an operating room better equipped than those at Walter Reed hospital in Washington, Rosner is expecting death. And if Wells does live, he'll be a vegetable. "We're going to operate, but I'm not too optimistic," Rosner tells Alpha Company's First Sergeant, Terry Sutton, who's just arrived at the CASH. "I'm not sure he's going to make it off the table."

If you're lucky, the wispy thread that's your life goes on for a while. If you're not, then this is how your story ends. Twenty-five years old with a wife, a little boy, a little girl, and a bullet in your brain. You don't figure it'd be like this. Maybe you'd take a hit and grit your teeth and curse as they patch up your bloody arm. Or there'd be a flash and the lights would go out for good. But not like this, not in between.

Yet here he is, a million miles from East Wenatchee, in Washington's Cascade Mountains. He joined the Army so he wouldn't spend his days making pizzas and smoking pot. After seven years he's hung on to his irreverence and his playfulness, but he's also grown into a military asset, a fast-thinking, self-aware, tactically sound leader who's respected and trusted by his men. And he loves it. He loves this job. It's so much fun. Back at Fort Drum in upstate New York, where we were training for Iraq, we watched his combat acrobatics. He would jog forward with his M4 and dive into a somersault, pop up and fire three rounds into a target, barrel-roll to the left and fire three more, roll again, and stop on his back, firing upside down. Just like the video games. God knows he plays enough of those. Sometimes when he's on patrol, or moving in to raid a house, he sees an image of himself, as though he's at the controls in a first-person shooter.

But in video games, you respawn when you're shot in the head.

Rosner posts Sutton outside the operating room so he can watch through a window near the door and relay updates to the guys in the waiting room. There's Wells, stretched out on a table four feet away. The doctors quickly shave his head, mark incision lines with a Sharpie, slice into his skin, and peel back the flaps. The cranial saw is whining now as they lower the blade into bone. They pull the piece off and there's his brain. The nurse comes to the door. They're in the occipital lobe now and the damage is extensive. This could affect speech, balance, sight, and hearing. Again Sutton is told it doesn't look good.

The surgical team cuts out a softball-sized chunk of skull to give Wells's brain room to swell, cleans out the shrapnel and bone fragments, and puts a tube in his head to drain the blood. Sutton expects delicate, subtle movements. Instead he watches Rosner probe the cavity with metal instruments, and at times with his fingers. "He's a little rough with his brain," Sutton thinks. "I hope he doesn't do any more damage."

Somehow, Rosner keeps Wells's brain and body from shutting down on the table. Colleagues will later speak of the surgery with awe, saying it's the most difficult case of its kind. With his head sewn up, he's wheeled upstairs to a room he'll share for the night with two Iraqis, a baby and a man who seems to be held together by stitches, hundreds of stitches. Iraqis don't often end up in American hospitals, so chances are we had something to do with their wounds.

The entourage of brass troops in, and our brigade commander, Colonel Mark Milley, says a prayer over Wells and pins on his Purple Heart while he's still alive. When they've gone, McCarthy and Staff Sergeant Carlos Santos, who has worked with Wells for four years, are alone with him. His eyes are black. His head's wrapped in a turban of gauze. On a blanket pulled up around his bare chest, a large note urges caution with the patient; his brain is unprotected. What the hell do I say to him? McCarthy wonders. He spent so much of the night worrying. Now the worry shifts to anger. He leans in close. "We're going to get that motherfucker for you," he says. "We're going to find him."

We don't.

As McCarthy is pledging vengeance, we're surrounding the apartments, a cluster of four three-story buildings. The whole company is out tonight. The breaching squads move through the shadows and into the stairwells. They stack in four-man teams outside the doors. My watch shows midnight. All of the apartments are quiet. One glows with the flicker of a TV. In the hallway, whispered commands. "Go." The racket starts at once. Pounding on the sheet-metal doors. If there's not a hasty answer, the breach man kicks in the door. Flashlight beams bounce around inside the apartments. "Get down! Get down!" Children wake and scream. Women wail and men plead. Mister, mister, please. The cries start anew with each floor the teams ascend. The answer is mostly the same. Get the fuck down. Shut the fuck up.

Soon all the apartments are cleared and searched, the men hustled outside to be interviewed. There are no gunmen here, no rifles. But there is a story: In the late afternoon, two masked men came to the apartments and roughed up some residents, ordered them to keep quiet and out of sight, then broke into an empty third-floor flat. A short while later, residents heard a single shot and saw the men speed away.

Tit for tat. That's the way the insurgency goes. You kill them one day, they kill you the next.

Back at camp, after the raid, I stand in the darkness outside our rooms smoking cigarettes with a friend, Staff Sergeant Raul Davila, one of Wells's fellow squad leaders in 1st Platoon. "Our luck ran out today," he says. "Ten months of good luck and it ran out." He's right. Our luck has been absurd. IEDs that blow up late or not at all. Bullets and shrapnel that miss by inches. A car bomb that detonates against a Humvee but no one is seriously hurt. We knew this day was coming.

I lie in bed, staring into the dark, at an image of Wells on a table, doctors crowded around. He was riding in my truck today, telling me about his daughter's birthday party the night before, how his son threw up in the movie theater. I want to pray for him, to give him something, but I don't know what. You can't end this here. You're too good for this. I want to talk to my wife, because I still can.

In the morning we find out he's lived through the night. He did better than some. Kevin Prince, from Plain City, Ohio. Anthony Davis Jr., from Long Beach, California. Aaron Kent, from Portland, Oregon. They all died in Iraq on April 23. Who knows how many were wounded. Throughout the war the average has been about sixteen a day. Deaths run just over two a day.

The communications blackout, prohibiting calls or emails home, has been lifted. So his wife now knows. Michelle knows.

When it comes, you're not expecting the call, or the knock on the door. But really, you are. When my wife heard cars pull in late at night as she lay in the dark, when the neighbors were supposed to be gone, she knew. They're here. And the day the UPS deliveryman knocked on the door, that time she was sure.

Michelle is at her sister's in Toronto. She expected a call from Brian by now. The worry is always in ebb and flow, and right now it's rising. When her phone does ring, it's a 315 number, the Fort Drum area code. The caller is from Casualty Affairs. Here it comes. He says her husband's been injured, and the crushing weight lifts a little. Maybe he hurt his back or bumped his head. Then he tells her he's been shot, in the head, and she crumbles.

Linda Wells, Brian's mom, knows before she even knows. Her migraine starts on Friday, around the time Rosner is pulling off her son's skull, eleven time zones away. This is her first migraine in eight months, and the worst ever. As the Army is calling the house, leaving messages, she's at the hospital with Brian Sr. getting a shot of Demerol. When they get home, before they can punch play on the machine, a family friend calls with a message from Michelle.

Brian Sr. stands up straight, rigid. "What? Shot?"

The drugs are gone, as though she hadn't had the shot. The headache gnaws and the room spins. Brian Sr. phones family. Linda collapses.

Wells leaves Baghdad for Germany hours after his surgery, but once he's airborne, his cranial pressure spikes. The plane lands in Balad, Iraq, and doctors cut out another big chunk of his skull. Now he's missing most of the left side of his head. But the bone isn't thrown away. Instead, after both operations, doctors slit open his belly and slide the pieces in above his abdominal muscles, where they'll stay clean and nurtured by blood, until it's time to rebuild his skull.

Three days after the shooting, Wells arrives at the National Naval Medical Center in Bethesda, Maryland, the heat and dust and sewage stink replaced by polished floors and the whiff of antiseptic. Lieutenant Colonel Rocco Armonda, the hospital's vascular neurosurgeon, ups Wells's sedation, putting him into a coma, and wraps his chest in a cooling vest that chills his blood. This slows the metabolic rate of his brain, reducing swelling and giving the blood vessels time to reroute themselves around the disrupted area. Armonda operated on troops for a year in Iraq and has handled dozens of cases at Bethesda. He's never seen a head-trauma patient survive an injury this severe.

Michelle is there within hours. When the doctor gives her the rundown of his injuries, just before letting her in to see him, she nearly vomits. There are bullet fragments still in his brain, and the swelling has bent and crunched his brain stem. He may not be able to see or speak. He may not know who she is. That's if he wakes up. Right now there's no activity on the left side of his brain and very little on the right.

And then she's with him, for the first time since his two weeks of leave in December, she's with her husband and she barely recognizes him. It's him, yes. That's his face. That's his flame tattoo, rising up his right forearm. But he's so swollen. His hands, his arms, his face—they're all fat and puffy. At least he's not alone anymore. She reaches for him and caresses his skin.

"I'm here," she says.

Linda and Brian Sr. arrive later that day. So begins the hospital vigil.

They touch him and play music and read him the celebrity news from trashy magazines. They tell him how the guys are doing in Iraq. They sing to him. They pray and they weep. And he does nothing. He doesn't smile or moan or twitch.

They learn the language of the monitors, the reassuring beeps and dings that say everything's fine, and the beeps and dings that signal alarm. Within days, they're fluent. Their eyes fix on the tiny screens, making quick note of the numbers every time they enter the room. Heart rate. Blood pressure. Core temperature. Oxygen levels. Intracranial pressure—that's an important one. They watch the monitors as they speak to him. Maybe the sensors will say what his body cannot, that he really does hear them.

Being in his room, even though he's lying there limp, can be a refuge from the rest of the hospital. That's a horror show. It's all wrong. Those people shouldn't be here. They're young, they're strong, they're healthy. At least they were. Now they're missing arms, legs, and eyes. They're burned and broken. And what's going on inside their heads, that's a whole other mess. Michelle and Linda had read about the wounded, they followed the news. But they had no idea it was this bad. Some of them don't even have family coming to visit. At night, as Linda listens to the beeps and dings that say her son is still alive, she hears screams down the hallway. This time it's a boy missing half of his face. He wakes not knowing where he is or why his face is gone.

During the days there's a different sort of shouting as the neuro team moves from room to room, checking on the head cases. Eventually it's Wells's turn. The team comes in and Michelle leaves. She can't bear watching this. But Linda stays because she needs to see something, anything, a sign her boy's still in there. The doctors pound his chest, jab his sternum, and yell. Brian, wake up! Sergeant Wells! They bend his fingers back, scrape the bottoms of his feet, and poke under his fingernails. Nothing.

The doctors have been asking Michelle if she's thought about the future. They don't have to ask. That's all she thinks about. What if he's not who he was? What if he doesn't know me or the kids? What if he can't walk or speak? What if he never comes back? They ask if she and Brian have talked about situations like this, what he would want. Yes. He would never want to live like this.

To counter the doctors' prognosis, there are the other families. They migrate to one another for support. And the ones who have been at the hospital for a while, who know the routine of hope and despair, they can read the faces of the new arrivals, the newly despondent. Listen, doctors told me my son had two days to live, the mother of a marine sniper tells Michelle. And now look at him. He's out of his coma and starting to talk.

On Wells's fifth day in the ICU, his left arm jerks. Doctors tell his family that's nothing to get too excited about because the movement wasn't prompted by a command. On a scale of 3 to 15, the Glasgow Coma Scale rates a patient's ability to open his eyes, obey commands, and speak understandable words. Wells is a 3. He can do nothing. But this offers no indication of how badly his brain is damaged. The coma was induced with drugs to regulate his body functions and prevent more swelling. Until he wakes up, it's anyone's guess.

They're weaning him off the sedation now, and his eyes flutter and open, just barely. Somewhere in the second week, Michelle puts a video recorder to Wells's ear and plays a scene of him with his four-year-old son, Terje, at a park. Terje is climbing a rope to the top of a wooden jungle gym. Wells hovers close by, waiting to catch him. "I'm going to do it, Dad. I'm going to do it on my own," Terje yells, and hauls his little body over the top. "I did it, Daddy. I did it by myself."

Bam. Wells opens his eyes, nearly all the way.

"That's your little boy," Michelle says, sobbing. "You have to be here for him. You have to come back and show all these doctors they're wrong."

Wells doesn't come back yet. His eyes are open more often now, but he looks at nothing in particular. The family keeps the same routine, telling stories, showing pictures, and reading emails from family and guys in Iraq.

The brain isn't resting; it's figuring out how to work again. Imagine a circuit breaker deep in the base of the head. Trip that breaker and your brain's power grid needs time to come back online. If you're knocked out briefly, say, by a punch, your brain might flip the power back on in seconds. But the more severe the trauma, the longer it takes to reestablish the connections. If some of the transmission lines are damaged beyond repair, the brain searches out alternate routes for its messages. So the mind emerges from a fog that becomes less patchy, revealing more pieces of the world it knows—faces, sounds, smells, pain. The process can take weeks, months, or years. Some never come back. For Wells, the emerging begins with an arm jerking, his eyes fluttering. He sleeps less each day. He shrugs his shoulders and moves his head. He flinches when poked. He squeezes Michelle's hand randomly. She holds up his thumb and pleads with him, coaches him. "You need to do this. Do you hear me?"

And then, in the middle of May, after he is moved from Bethesda to Walter Reed, Wells gives a thumbs-up when prompted by doctors, so they know his brain can understand a command and send a message to his hand to execute the prescribed action. Once, after a nurse readjusts his catheter and leaves the room, Michelle asks him if that hurt. He raises his middle finger. And a few days later, when Michelle asks if he wants her to read him a letter from our battalion commander, he holds his hand near his crotch and tosses it back and forth, mimicking masturbation. Wells is alive.

On May 24, a month after he is shot, doctors discover that Wells can see, and nurses are now using pictures to ask him questions. This one shows a human body. Are you in pain now? He nods. Yes. Where? Stomach and head. How much pain? Seven out of ten. What can I do to help you? Do you want meds? No. Wells points to a picture of a family. Your wife and mother are here. No. He shakes his head slowly, side to side. Now Michelle understands. You want to see the kids, don't you? Michelle asks. Wells nods yes and tries not to cry. She has been worrying about this. It needs to happen. He needs it and the kids need it. But their invincible father will be lying here, tubes stuck in him everywhere, unable to talk. Are you sure? she asks. Yes.

The kids come the next day, after a meeting with a child psychiatrist to prepare them for what they'll see. Wells wants a kiss from Terje, but his son balks, nervous he might hurt his dad. Instead he hands him a Hot Wheels car, pulls out another for himself, and the two play on the bed, rolling cars across the covers. "My dad's really sick, isn't he?" Terje asks Michelle. "Yes," Michelle says. "But he's getting better with our love and the doctors' help." Rachel, who's ten, stands beside the bed, holding Wells's hand, and smiles sweetly when she gets three squeezes, their sign for "I love you." Later, Michelle and Rachel walk through the hospital, surrounded as always by the wounded and the limbless. "Why couldn't he have been shot in the leg and lost his leg or something?" Rachel asks. Michelle wonders that all the time.

Wells doesn't even know why he's in the hospital. His stomach hurts so bad, it must have something to do with that. He doesn't know there are two pieces of skull in his belly, only that his gut aches like he can't believe. He knows his wife is Michelle. He knows he has two children. He knows his birthday is November 28, that he's from Washington State and Michelle is from Canada. And that's about all. The memories are scattered in tiny shards. Do you remember being deployed? Michelle asks. No. Do you remember what you do for a living? No. She tells him he was a soldier, one of the best there was. She shows him a picture of us from Iraq, on patrol on Halloween, wearing fake mustaches. He's crying now, nodding as she points to each of us. He knows us, but he doesn't know the picture. Where is he, and why is everyone holding weapons? Michelle tells him he injured his head in Iraq, and that's why he's having these problems. It will all come back, she says. This just takes time. Your mind is protecting you from things you don't need to remember yet.

He's trying to mouth something to her, but she can't understand. Can you write it down? He scrawls it on a board: "Please don't forget about me."

Michelle is crying again, for what must be the hundredth time this week. "I could never forget about you," she says. "You've had my heart in your back pocket since the day I met you, and it'll be there forever."

He's confused and teary for the rest of the day, and Michelle has no trouble reading his lips. "Don't leave me here," he says over and over. "I'm scared."

He dreams of Iraq without knowing why. There is violence and pain. People are dying and he can't save them. He dreams of explosions and awakens frantic, feeling for his legs. So many explosions. That must be why he's here, an IED. Every morning he mouths the same questions to Michelle, having forgotten the answers. Why am I here? What happened to me? She treads lightly, giving him little bits. She tells him he was shot, but not by a sniper. She doesn't want him to know it was so personal, that someone had tracked him in his sights and fired a single shot.

A few days later doctors insert a speaking valve into Wells's trachea tube, allowing air to brush against his vocal cords. In a quiet, raspy voice, he speaks: "This hurts," he says. His next words set Michelle to crying again. "I love you, my wife." Then he says he wants food, and he wants out of the hospital. And soon he wants to hear more about his life before, his life as a soldier. Michelle mentions his friends still in Iraq and now he's distressed. He's crying. "They all have to get out of there before they die," he says. "They have to get out of that shit. They don't want to be like me. I can't save them from here."

He's lost thirty-five pounds since he was shot, down to 135 by early June. He pukes a dozen times a day because the section of brain that controls equilibrium was damaged, making him constantly nauseous. When he sits up, he vomits. The injury tweaked his vision, so he sees everything in double. An eye patch helps but leaves him with no depth perception. He's eating soft foods now, but still has some food pumped directly into his body. The tube in his stomach has coiled, so it's been replaced with a tube inserted into his intestines. Doctors have put another tube through his nose and down into his stomach to suction off bile and gases, part of what's making his stomach hurt so much. He's already yanked out that tube once when no one was watching him. The skull pieces were hindering his movements and have been removed. Instead of bone, doctors will rebuild his head with plastic. Wells is fine with that. Anything to get rid of the pain in his gut. The trachea tube is out as well, so he's breathing on his own, and there are no more worries about him drowning from fluids slipping into his lungs. But there's still the risk of a brain infection or the shrapnel that's still in his head shifting and causing a seizure and further brain damage.

In late June, a few days after our platoon returns from Iraq, Wells is loaded into an ambulance for a four-hour ride to the Hunter Holmes McGuire VA Medical Center in Richmond. There he's reunited with some of his friends from the neuro unit at Walter Reed. Eddie, a marine sniper, shot in the head, and Joe, hit with an IED in Mosul while riding in a Stryker armored vehicle. A chunk of shrapnel hit his forehead and plowed a groove through his brain. They all floated for days in comas but survived. Now, at the rehabilitation hospital, they learn how to live again.

They're a sad-looking lot, heads caved in like deflated basketballs. Wells is the furthest along of the three, already talking and starting to walk. Joe can't do either and doesn't seem motivated to improve, so the therapists partner him with Wells, who, everyone agrees, is absurdly good-natured about his situation. This is the first time Wells has actually seen Joe's face. At Walter Reed, before Wells could lift his head, he'd seen only Joe's feet. On their second day of therapy, when Wells rolls into the room, Joe smiles for the first time. For a while, Wells is the only patient in the neuro ward who can talk, and he talks to Joe, all day long, rambling on about anything. Joe's first word, several days later, is *Brian.*

The nausea is under control now, so Wells throws up less, and the feeding tube is gone. When his stomach hurts, it's usually from eating too much, which he does often, whenever he can. He spends hours a day in therapy. He walks, supporting himself on parallel bars, and works with a speech therapist, stumbling over some words and going blank on others. In a mock apartment inside the hospital, he makes the bed, dresses himself, and uses the bathroom. He's sent down to the little store for ingredients and makes pizza and Caesar salad in the apartment's kitchen. He tries, and tries again, until he gets it. This is the soldier in Wells. He doesn't want to say he can't do it, doesn't want to disappoint the therapists. Someone tells you to do something, you do it.

He's healed enough now to be released on weekend passes, and Michelle takes him to see *Wedding Crashers*, pushing him in his wheelchair to a handicapped spot near the front. He's wearing his eye patch and his hockey helmet. He loves the movie and just being out of the hospital, doing something normal. But people stare, and he feels like a cripple. In the hospital, being damaged is the norm. Not out here.

And then the doctors tell Wells he's done being a patient, no more living with the damaged. The day they come home, on a warm August afternoon, we throw a little party at their house in Watertown, just outside Fort Drum. A red-white-and-blue banner hangs outside the house: WELCOME HOME BRIAN. YOU'RE OUR SUPERMAN. WE LOVE YOU AND WE MISS YOU. There's beer and cupcakes inside. He tells us he'll have to go back to Iraq someday, to find the piece of his head and ear that were shot off. If there's an upside to this, he says, it's that he can wear his favorite hat again, a fitted baseball cap that had shrunk a bit. Now that his skull is smaller, the cap fits just fine.

There is relief in being home, but this is matched by anxiety and uncertainty. Wells needs help with everything. He can't shower or use the toilet by himself. He can't get a snack or a glass of water. He can barely dress himself and can't tie his shoes. He teeters when he walks, and Michelle worries constantly that he'll fall and smack his head, or that Terje will throw a Hot Wheels and hit the soft spot.

In September they return to Walter Reed for the cranioplasty surgery to replace the missing section of skull. I'm alerted to this by a text message from Wells: "B gets his new head September 16!"

Humans have been drilling into skulls to relieve pressure for thousands of years, holes that doctors once covered with gold hammered flat and slipped under the scalp. But even in recent years, the process was a patchwork, with surgeons making a template on the operating table from the patient's exposed skull. The fit wasn't precise, the replacement pieces weren't strong, and patients were in significantly more danger, both from being under anesthetic for up to eighteen hours and from increased risk of infection.

Wells's implant is fashioned in a small lab, more *Star Trek* than hospital, on Walter Reed's ground floor. Stephen Rouse, director of the hospital's 3-D Medical Applications Center, starts with two-dimensional CAT scans of Wells's head, showing the exact outline of bone and the missing piece of skull. Rouse converts the scans into a three-dimensional image and pastes a mirror image of the right side of Wells's skull over the hole, giving him dimensions for the implant. The 3-D image serves as a blueprint for the stereolithography apparatus, a six-foot-tall metal box in which a laser etches models from liquid epoxy resin. Rouse uses the technology, originally developed for industrial applications, to crank out plastic skulls, femurs, and organs. In the machine's Plexiglas-walled chamber, a platform rests just below the surface of the pool of yellowish light-sensitive resin. Following the blueprint, the laser dances across the resin, which hardens when hit with the beam. With each pass, the platform drops .125 millimeters, another layer done. Again and again the laser passes over the resin.

A day later, the model is finished. The platform rises and an exact replica of Wells's skull—with the same huge hole stretching around the whole left side—emerges from the vat. In most other hospitals, surgeons don't really know what they're dealing with until they crack open a patient's chest or saw off his skull. At Walter Reed, they know exactly what they're getting into. Before Colonel Leon Moores opens Wells's skull, he holds his pseudo-skull in his hands, turning it upside down and sideways studying the hole and planning his attack. Rouse crafts another piece of resin matching the missing piece of skull. This is built up with modeling wax into the precise shape and checked against the skull model for final adjustments. The piece is used to make a plaster mold, which is filled with polymethyl methacrylate, a plastic mixed into a putty. Within several years, doctors hope to make these implants from hydroxyapatite, the building block of our bones. Over time, bone cells would invade and alter the bioactive implant, which would slowly become natural bone, leaving the skull whole again. But for now, the plastic is the best thing going, and harder than bone. Encased in the mold, the implant cures in a pressure cooker for twenty-four hours, and then Wells's new head is ready.

Nurses wheel him into the operating room on a Friday morning, and Michelle paces and fidgets and waits. Colonel Moores, a former infantry officer and now chief of neurosurgery at Walter Reed, slits open Wells's scalp and starts peeling back the flap. In the five months since the skull pieces were removed, the skin and scar tissue have fused to the dura, a millimeter-thick protective sac that envelops the brain. Moores runs his knife between dura and scalp, much as you might skin an animal or clean a fish. But this is much, much slower, a millimeter at a time. Delicate work, and the risks are severe. The dura is also fused to the brain, already injured and prone to bleeding. A wrong move with the scalpel can cause a hematoma, stroke, or seizure. And there's the ever-present threat of infection, a risk multiplied if Moores pierces the dura. For more than an hour, he works at Wells's scalp, gently tugging it back, exposing the rim of bone around the giant hole in his head. The skull model sits nearby for reference. Of more than a hundred cranioplasties the Army has performed since the beginning of combat in Afghanistan and Iraq, this is one of the biggest, so big it's done in two pieces.

Moores and his team set the sterilized implant pieces. Sometimes the skull has grown in the time between the scans and surgery, so the bone must be shaved. But here there's a perfect fit, just like the model. The implant won't actually touch the brain, and while there's always a danger of rejection, that hasn't been a problem in the operations performed thus far in the war.

Using a half dozen titanium plates a centimeter long and three millimeters wide, Moores joins skull to implant, fastening the bridges with titanium screws anchored in bone and plastic. He runs sutures through holes in the implant and into the dura, pulling up the sac. This will prevent blood clots from forming between the dura and the plastic. He pulls the sutures slowly, over many minutes, to keep from tearing the delicate brain tissue that clings to the dura. Moores also runs sutures through the temporalis, a fan-shaped muscle that normally runs from the cheekbone to the side of the skull. This is cosmetic. Wells's jaw would work fine without it, but the side of his head would look dented.

Three hours down and Moores is done. The scalp flaps are pulled up and stapled shut. Wells has his new head.

As he recovers in his room, a visitor stops by, someone he has never met. "I can't believe you're sitting here and you're talking," Dr. Rosner says. Finished with his time in Iraq, Rosner is now stationed at Walter Reed. "You weren't looking so good last time I saw you."

Being back at Walter Reed, now that his mind is fully awake, Wells sees what Michelle saw in those early days. So many wounded. The two walk through the hospital, and they know people are staring at them. Michelle remembers seeing wives taking their wounded husbands out to dinner and feeling so jealous because her husband was in a coma. It's not really jealousy, she says, but hunger. Wanting something so bad. And she can see it on their faces when she and Brian pass. Why can't that be my husband? Michelle knows. She knows how greedy you get. You just want him to wake up, and he does. So then you want him to see and speak and walk. And when he does all that, you want your life to be the way it was, before the war, or at least before that phone call.

Wells sees Joe before leaving for home, and he's sliding. Joe already had his cranioplasty. He was walking and talking. But a spinal-fluid infection moved to his brain, he contracted pneumonia, and a virus he brought back from Iraq is thriving in his weakened body. His eyes are closed. He's unresponsive and can no longer breathe on his own. He'd come so far, and now here he is, back in the ICU, where he was six months ago. In fact, he's in Wells's old room. Michelle looks at Joe and thinks how easily that could have been Brian. Still could be. What if he gets an infection or the shrapnel moves? Wells is wrecked. Helpless. He can't save Joe.

If they could just switch places. He'd do that in a second. He knows he could make himself better. Joe just doesn't have the same drive. But Wells could do it. Just look at him. He's already done it. He'd take it for Joe. He'd go through this again.

At home, one wall of his living room is devoted to the military. There's a picture of Alpha Company from its first Iraq deployment, and another of the ship Wells's great-grandfather served on in World War I. On a narrow shelf are nine twelve-inch action figures depicting soldiers through America's recent wars, an American flag folded into a neat triangle, and a half dozen coins he's received over the years in recognition of achievements. The two most recent additions to the shelf almost pass unnoticed. The first is an empty 7.62mm shell casing, given to Wells by one of our friends who worked as a sniper in Iraq. The casing, from one of his kills, is inscribed in black marker: *FOR THOSE WHO HAVE FALLEN, NOT FORGOTTEN. HAJI SUPPOSITORY.* Not far away on the shelf is a small misshapen wad of metal, the largest piece of bullet Rosner pulled out of Wells's brain.

There will be no more additions to the shelf. Wells will be medically retired from the Army this month. When he was barely out of his coma, the Army started the paperwork for his medical-evaluation board, which decides whether soldiers are still fit for duty. By the end of last summer, the Army's decision was made. He can no longer perform his duties as an infantryman. This has been his life. He was a soldier. He planned on making it to Special Forces and retiring as a sergeant major. For a while after his injury, he thought about staying in and maybe working as a physical therapist. At least he could wear the uniform every day. But now he's done with the Army. He feels chewed up and cheated, abandoned by this Army he loves. His unit at Fort Drum has been great. Checking in on the family, calling Washington to unsnarl red tape, finagling an extension for their government housing. But the Army, he never figured it'd be like this. He starts talking about life after the military and stops, already tearing up.

"I got kind of patriotic," he says. "I kind of got suckered into that, brainwashed a little bit."

He has his moods now. People think he's doing great when they see him chasing his kids around or drinking a beer at a party. But he calls himself mildly retarded, and that angers Michelle. He's joking, but he means it, too. Now he's disabled. He feels disabled. Once he has his eye surgery and the patch can come off, he'll at least look normal. And that's what he really wants. Michelle's response is immediate and always the same. "What does normal mean, anyway?" she says.

Wells knows. Along with being able to tie your shoes and remember what someone told you five minutes ago, normal means people not noticing him when he walks through the mall. Kids ask why he wears an eye patch. He tells them his eyes are too strong. If he didn't wear it, he could see right through them. A woman at the hospital asks if he was shot in a hunting accident. So he wears hats when he's out. He says he's not embarrassed; he just doesn't want people to be nervous around him.

He used to support the war all the way, before he saw how many were getting wounded, what it meant to be wounded. Being in the Army is dangerous business. He knew he might die. His uncle Michael, Linda's older brother, died in Vietnam. So he knew. But still.

"If I had the choice to go back or have never been there, I'd fucking have never been there, because I'd be normal," he says. "You get to know all these people because they're hurt, and that's the only reason you know each other. So it sucks."

A few days after his cranioplasty, Wells visited Arlington National Cemetery with a group of wounded soldiers from Walter Reed, the friends he never wanted. Guys like Bobby, who lost a leg to an IED, who always says

Wells has it so much worse than him. Wells says the same about Bobby. There's always someone in more pain. He and Bobby sat in wheelchairs at the Tomb of the Unknown Soldier and watched the lone guard walk back and forth, twenty-one steps each way, back and forth. A few visitors came to shake their hands, thanking them for what they've done and wishing them speed in their recoveries.

Wells and Bobby couldn't see it from their wheelchairs, but down the hill and through a thicket of trees, the dead are making a final assault on the virgin land of Arlington. The rest of the cemetery feels quiet, tranquil, with tourists walking the rolling hills, through stands of mature trees. But in Section 60, where most of the new arrivals are sent, there is work to do. Three separate crews dig in the mud, lowering concrete vaults into the ground, ready to receive bodies now en route. The Iraq and Afghanistan vets are clustered together in a few rows of headstones. Before them a grassy field, waiting to be filled, stretches east, toward the Pentagon, the Potomac, and beyond.

AUTHOR'S AFTERWORDS...

On Christmas Day, 2004, I was resting on my sleeping bag in a small room crowded with slumbering bodies and assault rifles. Our nine-man infantry squad had been stuck with a week-long temporary duty guarding the power station just across the highway from the Abu Ghraib prison in western Baghdad.

I still had hours before my next shift—pacing the roof and watching for insurgents who might sneak in to sabotage the area's already fickle power supply. I opened a copy of *Esquire* and found a Christmas present: a wonderful piece about fishing for striped bass by Chris Chivers, my former colleague in a suburban bureau at the *Providence Journal*. I had left the paper, my first job out of college, five years earlier, after a three-year stint. I moved to Phnom Penh, Cambodia, and worked for the English-language *Cambodia Daily* for two years, then moved to Seoul, South Korea, where I freelanced for several months before enlisting in the U.S. Army, which started a several-year stretch as a journalism outsider, solely a consumer instead of practitioner.

Munching on snacks my parents had sent in a care package, I immersed myself in the story, a rejuvenating mental break from the stress and monotony of the war zone. I emailed Chris several days later to tell him how I'd spent my

Christmas and he said I should talk to the folks at *Esquire* once I'd come home; they'd like to hear my thoughts on the war, and what I'd been doing in Iraq.

Ten months later and once again a civilian, I asked Chris if that offer of an introduction was still good, and was soon sitting at *Esquire* with Mark Warren, the magazine's executive editor. I sketched out a few thoughts, just topics, really. I didn't yet understand the difference between a story idea and an actual story.

Mark asked what brought me to New York City, and I told him about Brian Wells, my former squad leader, who had been shot in the head while we were on patrol in western Baghdad. I'd been visiting him at Fort Drum, upstate; I'd driven Brian and his wife, Michelle, down to the city, where they were guests at a special dinner, along with the neurosurgeon who performed one of Brian's reconstructive surgeries.

That's the piece Mark wanted—the terrible, remarkable story about how my friend had very nearly died, brain matter leaking into the dust, and was saved by the wonders of today's battlefield medicine.

Until that moment, I hadn't considered writing about Brian. That was just something that happened to a friend; reporting for me had always been an outsider-looking-in experience. But Mark had been at this a very long time, and immediately saw what I did not, that such an intimate story about the wounding and recovery of a soldier would have the power to reach people deeply, even those who had become desensitized by years of war coverage.

I'd kept a journal while I was in Iraq—which was a great asset for this piece, taking me back to those days, the images and fears, and even chunks of conversation—but I hadn't written a story in three years. And I'd never written a story like this, so personal and raw.

For this piece, more than any other reporting project, I worried what the subject would think once it was published. Brian and Michelle trusted me to tell the story, and after all he'd been through, after all *we'd* been through *together*, I felt a heavy burden to get it right. He was my friend. He'd been to parties at my house. And for many months we'd been responsible for each other's lives. This moved beyond the typical journalistic tenets of fairness and objectivity into murkier territory.

And what about keeping a professional distance from sources and subjects? How could I keep distance when I'd been talking to him about his daughter's birthday party minutes before a sniper's bullet smashed into his skull? When we went out later that night hunting the men who had shot him? When we read daily emails from Michelle about the agonizing wait for Brian to wake from the coma, and then his slow struggle to speak, to walk, to remember?

The best I could do, all I could do, was tell the story as I understood it to be true.

I had my journals. And the dozens of emails Michelle wrote to friends and family documenting Brian's slow progress, heavy on both emotion and the details of medical procedures, were an invaluable resource for reporting the tick-tock of his recovery. But I also interviewed many of my former co-workers—bosses, peers and subordinates. They hadn't known me in my previous reporter life; they knew me only as a soldier, a fire team leader in 1st Platoon. And they certainly hadn't known me like this, asking them to remember moments in grainy detail, to tell me exactly what they had been doing and thinking. But they wanted a true document of what had happened to their friend, just as I did, and because they had known me in such precarious times, they trusted me.

In the years to come I would travel repeatedly to Iraq and Afghanistan as a reporter to spend time with soldiers and marines, a few times in situations more harrowing than those I faced as a soldier in Iraq. But this was the beginning of my re-entry back into journalism, and the blending of these two worlds: I cut a stack of printer paper into smaller pieces and on each wrote a scene, a detail, a scrap of dialogue, then arranged them on my living room floor and watched Brian's story take shape.

Maximillian Potter

M aximillian Potter is the executive editor of *5280*, Denver's magazine. Under his editorial guidance, *5280* has earned many of the most prestigious honors in journalism, including its five print National Magazine Award nominations. When not editing, Potter writes for *5280*, *Vanity Fair*, and other publications.

As a writer, Potter has twice been a finalist for the National Magazine Award. He's been a finalist for the GLAAD award, the IRE prize, and the Michael Kelly Award. Kelly judges commented that his articles are "beautifully written, ambitious in intent, and most of all—fearless in their pursuit of truth." He has won the Military Reporters and Editors prize, and the Silver Gavel, which is the American Bar Association's highest recognition for legal reporting. His work has been recognized and anthologized in several volumes. "The Assassin in the Vineyard" won the 2012 New York Deadline Club Award for Magazine Feature; Potter is working on a nonfiction book based on the piece.

Potter's work has appeared in *Philadelphia*, *Premiere*, *Details*, *Outside*, and *GQ*. He has served as a contributing editor to *Rodale* and *Details*. *Folio* has dubbed him a "Publishing Innovator to Watch" and a "Top Talent." A native of Philadelphia, with a master's degree in journalism from Northwestern University's Medill School, he lives in Denver with his wife and two sons.

The Assassin in the Vineyard

The winter-night sky above the Côte d'Or countryside of Burgundy, in eastern France, is cloudless, with just enough moon to illuminate the snow-covered ground and silhouettes. From dense woods atop a hill, a man emerges. He moves from the trees and starts down the gently sloping hillside—and almost immediately he is surrounded by vineyard. The vines are frost-dusted and barren, twisted and vulnerable, like the skeletons of arthritic hands reaching for spring.

The vineyard is within a sea of vineyards that stretches seemingly without end to the man's left and right: row after row after row they unfurl, barely separated from one another by ribbons of fallow land or narrow road. In the direction he walks, easterly, the vines flow with him down the hill, continuing as the ground flattens, until off in the distance they end at a small village. The hamlet, Vosne-Romanée, is constructed of ancient stone and topped with shake shingles, its humble, storybook skyline marked by a church steeple. At this late hour, in early January 2010, shutters are closed, and no one stirs.

As the man descends the hill, navigating the vines, he exudes the purpose of someone who knows precisely where he's headed and what must be done when he gets there. All around him the vine rows are so uniformly straight it's evident they have been meticulously arranged, painstakingly cultivated. At one particular vineyard, the man stops. Unlike the vineyards around it, this one is marked by a monument: a tall, gray, stone cross that towers over the vines like a sacred scarecrow. In the base of the cross are engravings; there's a date: 1723. The cross is perched atop a section of a low stone wall, and affixed to the wall is a sign in both French and English. It reads:

MANY PEOPLE COME TO VISIT THIS SITE AND WE UNDERSTAND. WE ASK YOU NEVERTHELESS TO REMAIN ON THE ROAD AND REQUEST THAT UNDER NO CONDITION YOU ENTER THE VINEYARD. THANK YOU FOR YOUR COMPREHENSION.

Here, in the vineyard called La Romanée-Conti, the man drops to his knees. For a moment, it appears that he might pray, that he might be one of the thousands of devotees who every year for decades now have come from around the world to see this patch of earth that oenophiles regard as a kind of mecca-Xanadu.

"A fabulous thing"—so begins one of the books about this vineyard. "Mysterious, sensuous, transcendental, the greatest wine in the dukedom of Burgundy, once reserved for the table of princes, its origins blurred in the mists of time—cannot help but spawn fabulists. For two centuries, no wine—no vineyard—has so deeply and so consistently motivated man's mythologizing instinct as La Romanée-Conti."

But the man has come for other reasons entirely. His breath puffing into the frigid night air, he reaches to his forehead, and a headlamp flicks on. From his shadow of a shape, he produces a cordless drill and a syringe. He begins to drill into the *pied de vigne*—the foot of the vine—the low whir of the drill's motor lost in the cold, smothered by the overwhelming quiet. He moves to a neighboring vine, less than a yard away, and does the same.

He takes up the syringe. He plunges it into the hole he has drilled in one of the vines and injects some of the syringe's contents. He performs the same procedure on the other vine. The man collects his drill and syringe, turns off his headlamp, and makes his way up the hill. He steps from the sea of vineyard and disappears back into the trees.

Burgundy's Côte d'Or is arguably the world's most enigmatic wine-growing region. About a three-hour drive southeast of Paris, it is a thirty-mile-long-by-two-mile-wide slice of countryside between Dijon in the north and Beaune to the south. Within Burgundy—or Bourgogne—there are dozens of subregions, and within those, numerous towns and villages. Vosne-Romanée is a village in the Côte d'Or. And in this relatively tiny sliver of Burgundy there are literally hundreds of vineyards, or *climats*.

Although the region cultivates almost exclusively one type of red grape, the Pinot Noir, the wines of each *climat* are distinctive. This is not the hype of wine marketers or the sales pitch of French wine brokers—*négociants*—but rather a geological fact. Abrupt, dramatic changes in fault lines and other natural phenomena unique to the Côte mean the characteristics—the *terroir*—of individual *climats*, even ones side by side, can be wildly different. So, too, then are their Pinot grapes. Along with the hundreds of *climats*, there are almost as many wine-making *domaines*, and most every *domaine* has its own viticulture techniques. Therefore, to refer to a wine from this area as a "Pinot Noir" means nothing and discounts everything.

All of these same factors are what draw discerning oenophiles and savvy collectors to Burgundy. The diversity, the complexity, the romantic alchemy of it all, when done well, when uncorked and dancing over the palate, are what make Burgundies ... well, so divine. As the writer Matt Kramer put it in his critically acclaimed guide to the region, *Making Sense of Burgundy*, "Even the most skeptical are willing, after savoring a genuinely great Burgundy, to concede that there may well be—dare one say it?—a Presence in the universe beyond our own."

The fact that Burgundy has such a small wine-growing region and produces, comparatively speaking—in relation, say, to the expansive French Bordeaux region—so few bottles only makes the quest for the finest Burgundies all the more worthwhile. One would be hard-pressed to find an educated wine-lover who would disagree with Robert Sleigh, one of Sotheby's leading wine experts, when he says, "Romanée-Conti is hands down the best and rarest Burgundy in the world—the Holy Grail." The legendary vineyard is a postage stamp of soil at 4.46 acres, producing roughly 500 cases annually, which is less than one-fiftieth the production of Bordeaux's Château Lafite Rothschild.

Indeed, whatever superlatives can be ascribed to a wine apply to the eponymous wine from the Romanée-Conti vineyard. It ranks among the very top of the most highly coveted, most expensive wines in the world. According to the Domaine de la Romanée-Conti's exclusive American distributor, Wilson Daniels, acquiring or purchasing a bottle is as simple as calling your local "fine-wine retailer." However, because DRC is produced in such limited quantities, and because the high-end wine market is such an intricate and virtually impenetrable Web of advance orders—futures—and aftermarket wheeling and dealing, it's not as simple as the distributor suggests. Wilson Daniels's own website points would-be DRC buyers to wine-searcher.com, which is a worldwide marketplace for wine sales and online auctions. There, the average price for a single bottle from 2007 (excluding tax and the buyer's premium) is $6,455—and that's the most recent vintage available.

A bottle of 1945 Romanée-Conti would be a steal at $38,000. Last October, in Hong Kong, Sotheby's Sleigh staged a record-setting sale of Romanée-Conti. The seventy-seven bottles, which included three magnums, were divided among eighteen lots, spanned relatively recent vintages between 1990 and 2007, and fetched a total hammer price of $750,609. A single bottle of 1990 Romanée-Conti went for $10,953—which was a few hundred dollars more than the sale price that day for an entire twelve-bottle lot of 1990 Château Lafite.

Only a few months before that Hong Kong auction, word of the attack on the vines of Romanée-Conti began seeping into the world beyond Burgundy. Very little news of the incident—what in reality was an unprecedented and remarkable crime—had been reported in the French media. In the United

States, there was nothing other than small blurbs in the wine press. Clearly, no one in Burgundy—including the patriarch in charge of the family-owned-and-operated Domaine de la Romanée-Conti—wanted to talk about it publicly. By way of explaining the silence, a former mayor from the Côte and a wine-maker there, Jeanine Gros, summed it up succinctly: "'Wine' and 'poison,' these two words do not belong in the same sentence."

"There are no great vineyards produced by predestination, by divine providence," the French observer Pierre Veilletet wrote. "There is only the obstinacy of civilization." The obstinate one in charge of the great Romanée-Conti today is seventy-one-year-old Aubert de Villaine. Over two rainy days this past fall, he allowed me into his Domaine de la Romanée-Conti and discussed, albeit most reluctantly, the plot against his wine. However, as de Villaine pointed out, he does not feel that the vineyard is his family's per se; rather, it belongs to Burgundy, to history—and to fully appreciate the crime, the sacrilege, one must understand all of the holiness and hedonism that flow through Romanée-Conti.

The Benedictine monks of the medieval Catholic Church were the original obstinate ones who civilized Burgundy's Côte. They were the *défricheurs*, or "ground clearers," who married the fickle Pinot Noir grape to the ostensibly inhospitable terrain. They discovered that a narrow strip of land about halfway down the gently sloping hillside produces the very best wines—the *grands crus*. "The Slope of Gold," it was called. While the monks first cultivated the vineyard that would become Romanée-Conti, it was the Prince de Conti, centuries later, who gave the wine its name and infused it with nobility and naughty.

The worthless forest and fallow land that the Duke of Burgundy had deeded to the monks in the 1100s were by the late 1500s profitable *climats*, and the monarchy wanted in. Taxation compelled the priory to sell a "perpetual lease" on their finest *climat*, the first incarnation of Romanée-Conti: Cros des Cloux. Between 1584 and 1631, Cros des Cloux had three owners, before it was transferred to the Croonembourg family. Under this owner, Cros des Cloux blossomed in the marketplace. As it did, for reasons historians can't fully explain, the family changed the name to La Romanée. By 1733 the Croonembourgs' La Romanée was going for prices as much as six times those of most other reputable growths of the Côte. Still, when the Croonembourg patriarch died, in 1745, the family over the next fifteen years slipped into debt and La Romanée was sold to Louis-François de Bourbon—the Prince de Conti.

A noble, and a magnet for intrigue, drama, and a good party, Louis-François was married and had a mistress by the time he was sixteen. His mother-in-law caught wind of the affair and to punish him persuaded the monarchy that her young son-in-law ought to serve in King Louis XV's army. During France's 1733 war with Austria, Louis-François earned the rank lieutenant general and the king's admiration.

The king came to cherish the prince. He not only gave de Conti his own army but knighted him into the Order of Malta, one of the highest honors of the time (which excused him from the otherwise required vow of celibacy). The king grew so close to the prince that the king's mistress, Madame de Pompadour, came to despise de Conti. It so happened that when the Croonembourg estate offered La Romanée for sale in July 1760, she, too, desired it. Perhaps knowing that if Madame de Pompadour learned of his interest in the vineyard she would surely outbid him, the prince hired a proxy who successfully represented him in the sale.

The Order of Malta appointment gave Louis-François claim to the Palais du Temple, in Paris. He and his mistress turned the palace into something of a party compound for intellectuals and artists—Mozart was a regular guest. Immediately upon purchasing La Romanée, the prince removed the wine from the market and kept it for himself, for entertaining at the palace. The La Romanée that had been first cultivated as God's work, and that was then sold for six times more than other *grands crus*, was now exclusively for nobles and their VIP dinner parties, out of reach for mere mortals.

The Prince de Conti died as America was born, in 1776. His son, Louis-François Joseph, the next prince, carried on his father's partying and aristocratic ways. And this did not serve him well in the wake of the French Revolution. "His house is filled with plotters and conspirators" is how one historical record describes the prince in 1790. "It is easy to see ... that it is he and he alone who conceives and guides aristocratic plots." The prince was arrested, and the government auctioned his vineyard, which for the first time was billed at sale as La Romanée-Conti.

The vineyard passed through three families between 1794 and 1869, the year that Aubert de Villaine's ancestor Jacques-Marie Duvault-Blochet took over. Upon Blochet's death, shares of Romanée-Conti splintered among his heirs, and no one thought much about the vines until 1910, when Aubert's grandfather Edmond Gaudin de Villaine, who had married into the family, took on the role of managing the DRC.

Edmond was the architect of the modern DRC. He unified the parcels of Romanée-Conti that had fractured among the heirs. In 1912 he trademarked "Domaine de la Romanée-Conti," and in 1933, Edmond acquired all of the La Tâche vineyard, which is but a few yards from Romanée-Conti. Acquiring sole ownership of Romanée-Conti and La Tâche gave the DRC *monopoles* over the two best vineyards in Burgundy, and for that matter two of the best vineyards in the world.

Of course no success is without struggle. World War I destabilized Europe's wine market. America, with its Prohibition and Great Depression, was not yet a market that could be counted on. Fortunately, Edmond found a like-minded partner in a local *négociant*, Henri Leroy, who bought a fifty percent share in the Domaine. Thanks to their collective leadership and financial resilience the Domaine's *monopoles* of La Tâche and Romanée-Conti remained whole and strong. What's more, even as other *domaines* had to sell and divide their *climats*, Leroy and de Villaine maintained parcels of other top-tier vineyards—Échézeaux, Romanée-St.-Vivant, Richebourg, and Grands Échézeaux—all very near one another, under the banner of the Domaine de la Romanée-Conti. These *climats*—along with the lone DRC Chardonnay Montrachet, which the Domaine acquired between 1964 and 1980—produce grands crus that are second in quality, reputation, and price only to La Tâche and Romanée-Conti.

Growing up and watching his grandfather, and then his own father, Henri, give so much of themselves to the DRC, young Aubert was not sure wine-making would be for him. One of six children, he went to Paris, the big city, where he studied political science. In the early 1960s he moved to America and hung out for a year in Northern California, wine country of all places. He wrote a couple of articles about California wines for *La Revue du Vin de France*. He fell in love with an American girl from Santa Barbara with a *Gatsby*-esque name, Pamela Fairbanks, who would become his wife.

It was after moving about, leaving the DRC, that a twenty-six-year-old de Villaine came to realize that his life, his soul, was indeed rooted in the Domaine, and in 1965 he asked his father if he could begin working at the vineyard. Ever since, de Villaine's reverence for the DRC has been absolute. He and Pamela do not have children, so in the fall of 2010, he turned over his shares in the Domaine to his nieces and nephews. He tried to make them understand that the shares were not gifts from him and were much more than shares in a company. He impressed upon his young relatives that the shares derived from people they had loved dearly: one of de Villaine's two brothers, who died very young, and his own father, who died years ago. He told his nieces and nephews, too, that the shares were fruits from vines cultivated by people they never knew, who gave the best of themselves for many generations.

On the top of Aubert de Villaine's otherwise tan, bald head there is a doily-size pinkish splotch. When he takes a moment to give something consideration, he scratches this spot, just as he does when he has to decide when the harvest ought to begin—and just as he did on that day in early January 2010 when he found himself reading an unsigned note informing him that the DRC must prepare to pay a ransom or Romanée-Conti would be destroyed.

It was not so much a note as it was a package, delivered to his private residence. (A similar package arrived at the home of Henry-Frédéric Roch, who holds the title of co-director of the DRC and represents the Leroy family's interest in the Domaine.) Inside the cylindrical container, the type an architect might use for blueprints, was a large parchment. Unrolled, the document was a detailed drawing of Romanée-Conti. While the 4.46-acre vineyard is essentially a rectangle, there are nuances to its shape. De Villaine noticed that whoever had sent this letter and sketched the vineyard knew its every contour, and what's more, the author had noted every single one of its roughly 20,000 vine stocks. In the center of the vineyard sketch this person, or persons, had drawn a circle. There was a note, too, which conveyed that the vineyard would be destroyed unless certain demands were met; the note stated that another letter with further instructions would be coming in ten to fifteen days.

De Villaine viewed the letter as a hoax, some kind of sick joke. Really, if he has to admit it, he chose to see it that way. That was easier, *much* easier, than to think it was real. Then, in mid-January 2010, he received another package at his home. It was in the same type of cylindrical container, and inside was the same sketch of the vineyard. Only this time there were two circles. In addition to the circle in the center, there was another, much smaller circle in the upper left corner of the vineyard.

The correspondence instructed de Villaine to leave one million euros in a suitcase in the corner of the Romanée-Conti vineyard, right near the area represented by the small circle on the drawing. By way of proof that he—she, they, whoever they were—meant business, the letter informed de Villaine that some eighty-two vines of Romanée-Conti had already been poisoned. According to the note, the two vines in the area marked on the sketch by two Xs in the small circle had been killed by poison. The other eighty vines were marked by X's in the much larger, center circle; however, those could be spared with an antidote—that is, provided de Villaine paid up.

This time, de Villaine called the authorities. He did not call the local police. Burgundy is too small, too full of gossips and competitors who might use this fact or fiction against his Domaine. True or not, if the world thought the DRC vineyards had been compromised ... Well, de Villaine could not begin to imagine, or, rather, he *could* imagine what that might mean. He could not afford for this to be mishandled, and so he called a police official he'd met in Dijon who was now a senior official with the police based in Paris. Investigators arrived at the DRC. The two vines supposedly poisoned were removed. Quickly, it was determined they had been poisoned, and were dying. The other eighty or so vines in the large circle—while they had been drilled—in reality had not been poisoned. That part, at least so far, was a bluff.

Whoever was responsible, de Villaine was convinced, knew exactly what he was doing by targeting the DRC. It was clearly someone who had been sneaking around in his vineyard, and for quite some time, to produce such a detailed sketch. What's more, it appeared to de Villaine that whoever it was likely knew a great deal about wine. The second letter included sophisticated wine-making terms, like *décavaillonnage* and *démontage*.

And there was this fact: From what the police had discovered, the criminal, or criminals, used a syringe to inject the poison. This was especially significant—over the centuries, *vignerons* had used such a *pal* or syringe-like technique to inject liquid carbon disulfide into the soil and save the vineyards from devastating infestations by the phylloxera insect. Meaning, the very methodology that had been used to preserve the vines was now being employed in an attempt to kill the vineyards of Romanée-Conti.

On the advice of investigators, de Villaine did not drop off the money as directed. Instead, a trusted employee, in the dark of night, left a note in the vineyard on the specified day, February 4. In the note, de Villaine relayed that he would pay as demanded, but it would take time to muster the euros; he'd have to call an emergency meeting of the shareholders from the Leroy and de Villaine families. Within a matter of days, de Villaine received another mailing—what would be the third and final piece of correspondence. The tone of this letter was polite, even grateful that payment would be made. It instructed de Villaine to *please* deliver the money in a valise to the cemetery in the neighboring town of Chambolle-Musigny. The suitcase was to be left inside the cemetery gates at 11 p.m. on February 12, 2010.

The week of the arranged drop-off, de Villaine was scheduled to be out of the country, in America, on a promotional tour for the DRC's 2007 vintages. The investigators assigned to the case encouraged de Villaine to go about his normal business. They told him it was important to act as if nothing unusual were afoot. They reminded him, too, that the same DRC employee who had left the note at the vineyard could serve as the drop-off man. Jean-Charles Cuvelier, the deputy manager of the DRC, the police said, appears to "be capable and cold-blooded." The latter part of the description was wry cop humor, for Cuvelier is about as cold and hard as a freshly baked croissant.

Cuvelier has been de Villaine's indispensable lieutenant since 1993. The two met at a party in Dijon. Cuvelier, then in his early thirties, had mentioned that he was a schoolteacher who worked with at-risk kids and that the job was wearing on him. De Villaine mentioned he was looking for an assistant. Ever since, Cuvelier has been at de Villaine's side, or, rather, quietly anticipating his needs. As Étienne Grivot, himself a respected wine-maker in the Côte, puts it, Cuvelier is considered "the guardian of the Temple."

Cuvelier is a stocky man, now in his late fifties, with bifocals perched on the end of his nose, which he tends to wrinkle. He has a gap-toothed smile and fidgets a great deal, but with a nervousness that's endearing. Evidently he easily perspires through a dress shirt and a wool sweater on a cold day, but only because, it seems, he is sweating the details of the DRC.

Not all that long ago, Cuvelier became a widower. After a prolonged battle against cancer his wife of thirty years died in June 2008. And so, who would have blamed Cuvelier if, on that night of February 12, 2010, he had allowed himself to wonder what his wife would have said if she could see him now, walking into a cemetery in the black of night, carrying a suitcase filled with one million in fake euros. Not knowing who or what was behind this plot and what might be in store, he could only hope she would watch over him and keep him safe.

The ancient village of Chambolle-Musigny is only about two miles north of Vosne-Romanée, if you take the right dirt road through the vineyards of the Côte. Like Vosne-Romanée, Chambolle-Musigny has no more than 600 full-time residents. The cemetery is on the outskirts of the town. You pass it on the way in and out; it's square, surrounded by a stone wall, and not much bigger than a public pool. The entrance is an arching, green wrought-iron fence. Just as the criminal had directed, it was 11 p.m. when Cuvelier pushed through the squeaking gates.

Earlier in the day, Cuvelier had traveled to the police station in Dijon, where he was briefed on the night's plan. There would be about a dozen armed police officers hidden about the cemetery, with their eyes on him and everything around him. In the bag, along with the fake euros, there'd be a transmitter—a tracking device—that would be activated when the bag passed by a sensor embedded in the threshold of the cemetery archway. Cuvelier was instructed to keep the earpiece for his cellular phone in his ear and activated, as a police officer would be in constant communication with him. Cuvelier, breathing heavily, trembling, perspiring, his heart pounding, entered the cemetery. It was cold and dark, with frost on the tombstones. He dropped the bag in the flower box just inside the gate and exited. He got into his car and drove off. No more than thirty minutes later, he received a call from the police: *We got him.*

Cuvelier immediately phoned de Villaine in the United States and passed along the information police had thus far. The man's name was Jacques Soltys; he was in his late 50s. Stunningly, catching him had been a snap. After Cuvelier left the bag, police spotted Soltys coming down a hillside on foot, then heading toward the cemetery. He retrieved the bag and walked off. He was caught less than 200 meters from the cemetery, on his way to a nearby train station. In the days that followed, as police learned more, so did Cuvelier and de Villaine.

The DRC had not been Soltys's only mark. He had simultaneously orchestrated a similar plot against another very highly regarded vineyard, Domaine Comte Georges de Vogüé, in Chambolle-Musigny. Police discovered this because the first package mailed to de Villaine had a Paris postmark. Footage from the surveillance cameras at that Paris post office revealed that another package, very similar to the ones mailed to de Villaine, had been mailed to the owners of de Vogüé. That vineyard, too, had lost two of its vines to poison.

As deVillaine and Jean-Luc Pépin, the director of de Vogüé, suspected, based on the extortion notes and sketches, Soltys indeed knew about winemaking. When Soltys had been about twelve or thirteen years old, his parents sent him to the Lycée Viticole de Beaune, a boarding trade school that specializes in wine-making. According to the current principal, Pierre Enjuanès, who still has Soltys's file, Soltys was raised in the Épernay area, a region known for champagne. His parents were wine-makers there, overseeing a modest vineyard. And, Enjuanès says, Soltys was trouble from the start. He was at the school for only a few months before he was expelled, for offenses including smoking, cursing, and staying up all night. In the file at the school, there's a black-and-white picture of young Soltys: dark hair, starched white collar, furrowed brow. A headshot for a boy that would have a life of mug shots.

Soltys went from delinquent to career criminal. He'd committed a string of armed robberies and even attempted a kidnapping. During one of the crimes, shots were exchanged with the police, and Soltys ended up hit in the chest. In all he'd been sentenced to at least twenty years. Though he served only a portion of that time, he'd spent most of his adult life behind bars. Soltys figured that there were easier jobs to pull off, like extorting wine-makers.

Soltys had done a considerable amount of planning and preparation. He'd built a makeshift shack deep in the woods atop the hills overlooking the vineyards. In the shack, among other things, police found a sleeping bag, a couch, a hot plate, a change of clothes—the clothes of a vineyard laborer—batteries, a headlamp, a cordless-drill kit, syringes, many bottles of the weed killer Roundup, and a handgun.

Soltys had not been operating alone. He'd been able to mail the package to de Villaine's home because, according to what the police told de Villaine, Soltys had his son, Cédric, follow the wine-maker and learn his address. Unlike his father, Cédric, who according to sources is in his late twenties or early thirties, didn't have a record but, according to several sources, is mentally fragile. Perhaps because of the way his father had raised him, or, rather, didn't raise him. Regardless, the portrait of the son that emerges is one who relied heavily on his father. Soltys Sr. may have treated his son poorly, but he also looked after him. It was an *Of Mice and Men* George-and-Lennie bond. According to a central character in the investigation, Soltys's life of crime had left his wife, Cédric's mother, struggling to get by. If anything, it seems, she too was a victim.

To show his thanks to the investigators, when de Villaine returned from his trip to America he invited them to the Domaine and uncorked a few bottles of 2006 Vosne-Romanée Premier Cru—along with a tasting of a 1961 Romanée-Conti—to toast their work. In the weeks following the arrest, as word of the crime leaked into the French press, de Villaine began hoping that the whole matter could be bottled up quietly, that whatever criminal proceedings there needed to be would be resolved without trial.

De Villaine was concerned that a trial would generate media attention, which in turn might inspire copycat crimes. Also, why would he want the world to think about the fact that weed killer had been injected into vines of Romanée-Conti? Five months after the arrests, the prosecution's case against Jacques and Cédric Soltys became extremely difficult to pursue, because in July 2010, Jacques turned up dead in a Dijon prison. According to prison officials, he'd hung himself in a bathroom.

The French legal system is unlike America's. Among the many differences, once a suspect is in custody, the matter is turned over to a *juge d'instruction*. Akin to a one-person grand jury, this judge takes over the investigation, overseeing both the defense and the prosecution, *and* the police, and decides whether official charges—"formal accusations"—should be filed. Until a trial begins, there are no public records of the case. No police reports are made public, not even mug shots. Defense attorneys can be fined or worse for speaking to the media. Officially, the only officer of the court empowered to discuss the Soltys matter is Éric Lallement, the equivalent of the district attorney of Dijon.

On an afternoon late last year, Lallement showed me into his office and through an interpreter fielded questions about the matter. A man in his early fifties, dressed in a blue suit, he sat with his legs crossed and fiddled with his cuff links while he spoke. On the coffee table between us was a file filled with information about the Soltys case. He kept this file to himself but referred to it periodically throughout our conversation. Soltys, he said, left behind a suicide note, but in it he did not, as a father might do, attempt to absolve his son of responsibility. Cédric, he said, had been released from prison, but not cleared of charges.

Lallement suspected the judge would determine formal accusations were warranted against the son. After all, he said, Romanée-Conti is not only a Burgundian treasure but a national one, and it is important for the government to send the message that such crimes will not be tolerated.

Of particular interest to Lallement is that the Soltys plot to poison the most storied vineyard in the world is unprecedented. While there have been crimes of vandalism, agriculture terrorism, and extortion on vineyards in France and elsewhere, never before has there been a poisoning of the vines. The top wine-makers of the most storied domaines and families in Vosne-Romanée—Étienne Grivot, Louis-Michel Liger-Belair, Jean-Nicolas Méo-Camuzet, Jeanine and Michel Gros—all say that they have never seen a crime like this before.

Yes, they are concerned. Quite frankly, they all would rather not discuss such a vulnerability. Like de Villaine, they are concerned about the possibility of copycat attempts. They quietly support his wish that there be no trial, that there be no further talk of the Soltyses and poison in the vines, as there is nothing anyone could do, or at least wants to do, to prevent such crimes. "A Burgundy with fences and lights and patrolled by German shepherds," says Cécile Mathiaud, press director for the association of Burgundy wine-makers. "This is something I cannot imagine. This would not be Burgundy."

According to a law-enforcement official, when Cédric found out about his father's suicide, he sat in a chair, staring into space, looking lost. This same source said that while the judge may determine formal accusations may be warranted against Cédric Soltys, experts hired to determine his mental competency would likely declare he is not fit to stand trial, and the matter would never reach a public trial. Thus far, Lallement's prediction for the legal proceeding is the correct one. Early this year, according to Jean-Luc Chemin, a prosecutor colleague of Lallement's, the French courts had determined that Cédric will face trial. Chemin says he has been assigned to prosecute the case, which he suspects will begin "sometime after September."

Such a trial might solve a lingering mystery: on the surveillance tape the police obtained from the Paris post office, the person mailing the Soltys packages was not Jacques or Cédric, though it was unclear who exactly the person was. Perhaps whoever it was was an ignorant pawn, simply someone asked to mail a few parcels. Or perhaps not. According to Jean-Luc Pépin, the director of the Domaine Comte Georges de Vogüé, the police found evidence of plans to carry out similar plots against other vineyards. "Oh, yes," he says, "it appeared there would be more vineyards targeted."

Outwardly, at least, Aubert de Villaine seems to have moved on. After all, the two tainted vines have been removed, and all traces of the Roundup are gone. Ultimately, no other vines were harmed—the *terroir* has been preserved, there will be no impact on future harvests. In addition to producing the world's finest Burgundy, de Villaine is at the forefront of a campaign to have the United Nations Educational, Scientific and Cultural Organization recognize all of the Côte as a World Heritage site. Currently there are 911 sites around the world that have received this rare distinction. World Heritage status means that, among other criteria met, the site has "outstanding universal value." The Great Barrier Reef, the Great Wall of China, the Tower of London, the Statue of Liberty, and the banks of the Seine in Paris are but a few on the list. It would, undoubtedly, be a fitting tribute for the DRC, the de Villaine family, the larger Burgundian family, and France. Such an honor, Aubert de Villaine understandably hopes, would make it easier for everyone to forget all of this talk of wine and poison.

AUTHOR'S AFTERWORDS...

Reporting and writing "The Assassin in the Vineyard" reminded me of many things that I love about magazine journalism. Most notably, perhaps, that it really is an asset to be clueless.

So, the summer of 2010, my wife and I are on a weekend getaway to Napa. We're not oenophiles. We don't know the difference between the wines of Napa and Sonoma, never mind France's Bordeaux and Burgundy. The concept of *terroir*? You've got to be kidding. I don't know how to pronounce it, never mind understanding what it would mean if someone were to poison the most sacred *terroir* of Burgundy. We're in California wine country because it's our anniversary and my wife spotted a great internet-only deal to the Russian River Valley. An old college friend and his wife, who live in Napa and are themselves winemakers, give us a tour of the area. By late morning, we're sun-kissed and after a few glasses of Riesling served by a guy who looks like Santa Claus in a shed of a tasting room wall-papered with dollar bills, we're pleasantly tipsy. My friend, who's telling fantastic stories about Napa, says, "But the story everyone out here is talking about is the one about a crime in France—a crime against the DRC." Me being me, I ask: What's the DRC? And my buddy gives me a look of pity (*You're such a Neanderthal, Potter*) and he explains.

This was how I first learned of Domaine de la Romanee-Conti, and that this DRC is the world's most storied domain. The wines made there, or rather grown there, in the *terroir* of Burgundy, are the rarest and very best, and, surprise, the most expensive in the world. This was the first time I heard the name Aubert de Villaine. It's when I learned that someone had poisoned—or maybe not, as folks weren't sure—the most-prized of all of the DRC vineyards, Romanee-Conti. Within a day or two, I did a little Googling and learned, just as my friend had said, that the only coverage of this crime were a very few blogs in the wine press. I wrote an email pitching the idea to Graydon Carter, the editor of *Vanity Fair*. In no time, Graydon wrote back telling me to head to Burgundy and, oh, how's this for pressure, "write one for the ages."

Naturally, first thing, I contacted Monsieur De Villaine, who politely conveyed he did not want to cooperate. Not knowing any better, I boarded a plane to France, figuring that De Villaine was just another potential source among sources, and that this was just another story among stories. Once in the tiny town of Vosne-Romanee, I knocked on the door of the domain, just like that. Never realizing that this is something one simply doesn't do, and that the odds of De Villaine being there and that he would make himself available were slim to none. Yet, De Villaine happened to be in and agreed to give me an audience. He explained to me why he did not want to cooperate. Among his sound reasons, he did not want to inspire copycat criminals. Also, he was concerned that the history of his domain, which is a family owned, national treasure, would become a victim a second-time—this time to a crass presentation in the media (you know, by me). I asked him to consider that worldwide ignorance of the details of the crime against his domain had, as my friend in California had said, fostered a fear: Winegrowers worried that if whatever happened at the DRC could happen there, then maybe it could happen here.

De Villaine asked if I was going to report the story regardless of his cooperation. Not knowing any better, I said, Yes. He was quiet for a moment and then said he would cooperate, but only if I incorporated the history of the domain, and that he not be quoted. The history was integral to the story, so of course. And De Villaine didn't need to explain why he did not want to be quoted. Even then it was clear to me this was a humble man who did not like the spotlight of any kind, let alone one highlighting an atrocious and an unprecedented crime against his family's vines, and in turn, his community's vines—their *enfants*, as he called them. I agreed not to quote him.

I interviewed, De Villaine, among others, over a period of days. I began to research Burgundy and *terroir*, the Burgundian appellations and wines, and the extraordinarily unique Burgundian culture, French criminal law, and so much else. As I became more familiar with the work of wine writers who have spent much of their lives trying to convey what is contained in Burgundy, both the wine and the place, I discovered the subject matter was vast and complicated, yet seemed to remain elusive. I wondered just what the hell I'd gotten myself into. If I'd known all of what I didn't know when I first heard my friend talk about it, I would have never dreamed of attempting to report the piece. As I became more and more aware of who De Villaine is, I realized that without his cooperation I would have been at a severe disadvantage. I might have been able to write a piece, but I would not have gotten as close to the truth—not just the truth of the crime, but also to the truth of all that was at stake. The crime was an attack on the *domaine*, yes, but it also was an assault on a history and a culture. You might even call it sacrilegious attack on a religion.

I often hear that the new common wisdom in our changing media environment holds that aspiring journalists need to develop a specific area of expertise in order to survive. And I guess I totally disagree. I'm an expert on absolutely nothing. As anyone who knows me can attest, I know very little, often nothing, about a whole lot. However, I am curious about many things. In fact, I'm not so sure I want to be an expert on anything, especially when it comes to the things I enjoy. The mystery, the act of discovering the story, is precisely the part that intrigues me. And I believe that's what intrigues the reader, too. Anyhow, I've come to think of my universal non-expertise as a kind of constructive ignorance, and I've found it to be a fantastically useful trait as a magazine journalist. If I wasn't this way I don't know that I would have taken on most, or perhaps any, of the topics I've written about. Certainly, if I'd known then what I know now, "The Assassin in the Vineyard" wouldn't exist.

Tony Rehagen

Tony Rehagen started over in 2003 when, after eighteen months of recovering from J-school burnout behind a library circulation desk and singing Michael Jackson covers to the back walls of empty bars, he realized that the only thing his journalism degree from the University of Missouri was good for was a career in journalism. (This made it infinitely more valuable than the undergraduate degree he'd earned in history.) As the lone reporter at the weekly Centralia, MO, *Fireside Guard*, Rehagen took photos of car wrecks and freakishly large tomatoes, laid out the front page, and wrote about city council meetings, farming, and small-town life. As business and health editor at the daily *Southeast Missourian*, the poor and overweight young man focused on his weekly centerpieces, fighting with copy editors about style, managing editors about length, and longing for the day his job would give him time to really immerse himself in the reporting and writing, to go beyond one sit-down interview and a couple of follow-up phoners for a few hundred words and really live and tell the story in full.

That day finally came in January, 2005 when Rehagen was hired to write long-form features for *Indianapolis Monthly*. Since then, his work has also appeared in *Men's Health* and *Atlanta*, where he is currently a senior editor. He has won the Society of Professional Journalists' Sigma Delta Chi award for contributions to journalism and has been a finalist for the City and Regional Magazine Association's Writer of the Year award for his body of work in 2009, 2010 and 2011.

The Last Trawlers

M ichael Boone can find the sea with his eyes closed. He peers into the black of 3 a.m. from the helm of the *Little Man*, hands on the pegs at ten and two, guiding the seventy-five-foot fiberglass trawler slowly down the narrow Darien River toward the Atlantic. The only light is a half moon and an electronic depth finder that throws the young captain's reflection onto the pilothouse window. Michael barely looks at the instrument. He knows by heart every rock, every coil and curve of the grassy shore, every jut in the shallows and hunk of debris that lurks just beneath the calm, dark surface. He has run these eleven winding miles, in blinding rain and fog, since he was twelve and had to stand on a milk crate his daddy bolted to the floor so he could see over the wheel.

Michael's feel for these waters reaches beyond his own experience. He inherited this path from his father, who learned it from his father, who learned it from his. Four generations of Boones, one of several families puttering out from Darien, a small town sixty miles down the coast from Savannah, to scour the ocean floor for shrimp. And other than a few tweaks in navigational technology and creature comforts like an air-conditioned cabin, the shorted-out TV in the back, and the clunky flip-phone that does little more than take calls and tell time in his pocket, Michael operates pretty much in a clearer snapshot of how his grandpa, Sinkey Boone, fished, the way so many men have shrimped off Georgia for more than sixty years. There aren't as many of those men as there used to be. The *Little Man* slips past several boats, tow arms up, paint-chipped hulls barnacled, bobbing idly at dock along the river. More than 200 boats once trolled here. Now there are maybe half that. Buildings are shuttered, piers in disrepair. Darien is quiet. Some families, like the Skippers, have sold off their fleets and their docks. Others cling to the helm only because they have nowhere else to go. Michael started skipping school at age eleven to join his father on the boat. Today, at twenty-three, he is easily one of the youngest boat captains—perhaps the youngest—in these parts, an exception to a new Darien generation that has been steered away, if not discouraged by the old guard, from the sea, Michael's two older brothers included. These waters, after all, are troubled. The price of gas is too high, the price of shrimp too low. The market has been flooded by competition from shrimp farmers, foreign and domestic. Wild Georgia shrimp are scarce at the neighborhood restaurant and grocery store. Worse, nobody seems to know enough about the homegrown variety to ask. And meanwhile the nets' harvest is not as bountiful as it once was.

Michael Boone stares ahead, piloting the *Little Man* out of Doughboy Sound and into the ocean, choppy waters slapping against the hull. He gently opens the throttle, revving the ancient engine in the belly of the boat to life. Course charted, speed leveled at just over eight knots, Michael leans back in his captain's chair. He holds the giant wooden wheel with an outstretched foot and rests his hands behind his head. Outside, the unseen sun traces the horizon with a thin white line as night lifts over a boundless sea.

In the distance, he counts one, two, three starlike specks scattered on the water—lights from the decks of other shrimping boats, working through the night. Michael can envision a much different scene from not so long ago, lights almost innumerable, a skyline at sea. "There used to be twenty, thirty, forty boats out there," he says flatly. "Twenty years ago, this was a city."

Back on the mainland, the city of Darien—population 1,900, seat of McIntosh County—is little more than a few streetlights whizzing by on a night-time drive down I-95. But its position along a natural tributary, at the mouth of the Altamaha River, made it a boomtown in the 1800s and early 1900s. The river rafted large loads of longleaf pine and cypress from the Georgia interior into Darien to be milled and shipped around the world. In the 1940s, one of those log bundles floated a man named Tessie Boone from Tattnall County, two counties inland, to town.

By that time, more than a century of unfettered cutting had decimated Georgia's timber industry. But Darien had already begun reinventing itself as a fishing town. The proliferation of gas-run trawlers empowered small fishermen to venture farther off the coast and reel in a commercial-sized catch, while refrigeration enabled them to ship it all over the country. The big ticket was wild brown and white shrimp that bred and fed on the bottoms just a few miles offshore. Tessie was hired as a crewman on local shrimp boats, and in 1946 he built his own, *Altamaha I*, cutting many of the planks by hand. All four of Tessie's sons came aboard at a young age, and by the late 1950s, when the Boone boys were old enough to operate their own vessels, the patriarch started Boone's Seafood, one of dozens of family-owned wholesale shrimp companies that popped up along the Georgia coast.

Unlike the family farms of the Midwest, where every hand was needed in the field or the farmhouse, shrimping tended to be a smaller enterprise, with just two or three men per boat—a captain, who decided when and where to fish, and one or two strikers to tend the nets—and a handful of men and women off-loading and processing the hauls back at the dock. As a result, shrimpers' sons generally weren't conscripted into service. But they went out anyway, kids ten and eleven ditching school to hop into the departing trawlers, eventually dropping out to work on the water. "If you don't get into it young, you don't get into it," says Greg Boone, Michael's dad and one of Tessie's eight shrimping grandsons. "When the kids start insisting on going out and they don't get sick, you know they're going to get into it."

When Greg was getting into it in the 1970s and early 1980s, big shrimp were fetching $6, sometimes even $7 per pound, and Georgia shrimpers were pulling in up to 6 million pounds each year. Gas cost fifty cents to a dollar per gallon, and after expenses shrimpers were easily netting $50,000 to $60,000 (about $130,000 to $160,000 today) fishing four months out of the year. Greg says he once cleared $18,000 in one day, the equivalent of around $40,000 in today's dollars. "And we didn't even get up until the sun was off the water," he says.

The dull 7 a.m. sunlight seeps into the pilothouse, revealing Michael, lean and muscular in a dirty white undershirt and jeans. The console before him is cluttered with charts, half-empty water bottles, a blackened tobacco spittoon, a crinkled bag of SunChips, and, pinned above the windshield, a washed out Polaroid of his mother. Long divorced from his father, she owns a meat market back in Darien.

Below his mother's picture is a recent photo of Michael and a young blonde holding a chubby baby boy. The woman's name is April. Michael has never gotten around to marrying her, but "we might as well be," he says. "I've been with her for six years." The couple recently learned that they are pregnant again—a girl—one of several reasons Michael is impatient to stop working for his father and buy his own boat, the only real way to make money in this business. But even with so many shrimpers dry-docking their dreams, a working trawler still runs anywhere from $35,000 to $70,000, to say nothing of the cost of running it on diesel at $3.20 per gallon. Those $40,000 days are maritime myth now.

What's more, as a captain, Michael sees only fifteen percent of the daily take, compared to the sixty-five percent that goes to the owner—Michael's father, in this case. Michael wants his father to cut him a deal on the *Little Man*, but Greg Boone won't hear of it. He's been saying for years that Michael should scrape together what he can and buy a $10,000 clunker to fix up and make his own, just as Greg did thirty years ago. He's told Michael over and over: *If you want something bad enough …*

Michael calms the throttle to a hum at Blackbeard Hole, a stretch of water between the Georgia coastline and Blackbeard Island, a couple of miles from the mainland, eleven miles northeast of the dock. Federal-controlled seas (those beyond three miles from shore) are open to shrimping year-round, but coastal waters are typically closed until late April, until the shrimp have laid their eggs and the larvae have begun moving in to feed on spring plants that grow in the shallows and estuaries. However, because of last year's long winter, Georgia didn't open season until the end of June. Boatmen didn't mind—the delay allowed their quarry more time to breed, feed, and grow. July was a strong month, but due to engine troubles, the *Little Man* was docked for all of August and September. Michael needs to play catch-up. "Left some shrimp here the other day," he says, stretching and standing to rouse the crew.

He walks through the bridge, past his quarters and the bathroom and into the mess hall, outfitted with oven range, a sink, and a fridge full of sweet tea, hot dogs, eggs, and sliced ham—anything to avoid frying meat in the pot of stale oil sliding around on the rack in the oven. Built in 1975, the *Little Man* is wired and piped, although the crew flushes the toilet with a tin pot full of water. In Tessie's day, these amenities were unnecessary, as small-town shrimpers left at dawn and returned before dark. But with radar for guidance and electronic chart plotters that can log what areas have been fished, Tessie's descendants can stay out for days. Michael is often at sea more than a week, stuffing the cargo hold as full as he can.

Behind the kitchen are the crew's quarters—a narrow cell with low wooden bunks. At Michael's *woo-hoo*, twenty-two-year-old Tommie Hurst springs from his top bed. He's new—a high-school friend of Michael's who came aboard last July after a second DUI cost him his job with the Department of Corrections. Behind him is Tracy "Tray" Palmer, forty-seven, a divorced father of two who's been a striker since he joined Michael's grandfather on his boat thirty years ago. Tray takes his time, carefully leaving his Bible and a notebook on the bottom bunk.

On deck, Michael switches on an old winch, reeling in a steel cable on the starboard side attached to a sample sack—a net about the size of Santa's bag, the contents of which will give the crew an indication of what to expect from the larger nets that they dropped at 5 a.m. Tommie and Tray guide the sack to the open deck and spill the contents: a pile of small fish, cannonball jellyfish or "jelly balls," and sixty-six brown shrimp, most between six and ten inches long—a good sign. "It's pretty," Tommie says, picking out an eight-incher. "This one, you just want to arr...," as he bites the head off.

The winch grinds as it winds thick steel cables that stretch to the end of twin sixty-four-foot tow arms, pulling the nets from the shallow sea. On each side emerge two quarter-ton steel doors, nine-by-four-foot plates chained together at an angle to form a kind of plow. For the past two hours, the boat has been dragging the doors along the sea bottom, some five to seven feet down, dredging shrimp that dwell there up and into the nets towed behind them.

The nets, bursting with the day's first catch, are hoisted out of the water and emptied over the deck, forming a writhing, two-foot mountain of white fish, sunfish, blowfish, jellyfish, jelly balls, rays, eels, and crabs. The strikers pick out the light brown, almost translucent shrimp, separate the heads with a quick pinch of thumb and forefinger, and throw the meaty torso and tail in a basket. Shrimp are actually worth five cents more head-on, but they'll keep that way for only three days, and Michael is hoping for a weeklong haul. The strikers work with honed efficiency, but still not fast enough for the other fish, the bycatch, which are picked off by the dozens of gulls and pelicans or are left to flop and slowly suffocate. The waste would be worse if not for Michael's grandfather, Sinkey, who developed the TED (Turtle Excluder Device) or "Georgia Jumper"—a chute attached at the tail-end of each trawl that diverts larger fish, horseshoe crabs, and sea turtles before they get caught in the net. In the 1980s, the government made TEDs mandatory on every vessel.

When the baskets are full, the bycatch is swept into the sea, and the shrimp are lowered into the hold, rinsed in water and the preservative ammonia bisulfate, and packed in ice. Meanwhile, the doors and empty nets return to the ocean bottom and the process starts anew, over and again until dark—unless the captain deems the daylight pickings too slim and resolves to keep at it through the night.

As the sun sets on the *Little Man*, after sixteen hours of shrimping in Blackbeard Hole, Michael estimates that they've pulled in a bumper crop of more than a thousand pounds of shrimp. Even at just $5 a pound (barely two-thirds the price of thirty years ago, not factoring for inflation), that's more than $5,000 for one day. To celebrate, the crew dines on a boxed Thai noodle mix spruced up with a couple dozen ocean-fresh Georgia shrimp.

In the late 1970s, while everyone with a boat seemed to be trawling a small fortune from the sea, landlubbers cut into the game. Arizona, Texas, and Florida started cultivating their own shrimp in ponds year-round. Without the overhead of boats, nets, and gasoline, farmers could sell their shrimp at a lower price. And when equatorial countries like Thailand and Ecuador got into the shrimp-farm business—penny-paid labor and lack of government regulation making their product still cheaper—the U.S. market began to flood. Prices tumbled. In 1980 farm-raised shrimp constituted two percent of the world's shrimp production.

By 1991 that number was twenty-five percent. Today ninety percent of all shrimp eaten in the U.S. are imported, and nearly half of that are raised in ponds.

Meanwhile, the local shrimpers' struggle to compete has been exacerbated by the rising cost of gasoline. In a weeklong trip, *Little Man*'s engine will gulp down about 1,500 gallons. At $3.20 per gallon, that's almost $5,000, which means it will take 1,250 pounds of shrimp just to cover fuel, to say nothing of the other equipment, from the $40 rubber boots to the $1,200 nylon nets. Throw in ten percent of the take for each striker and another fifteen percent for the skipper, and it's easy to see why the boat owner sweats as much as the crewmen. And what happens when something goes out on one of these old boats, like an engine blows or, God forbid, the nets just don't find the shrimp? "Things are tight, it's easy to fall behind," says Greg. "And with a little bad luck, you can't catch up."

With far fewer boats trolling these waters than thirty years ago, one might think there'd be more shrimp for the taking. But even though scientists say the brown and white shrimp populations have held steady, average annual hauls are down by more than a third, sometimes half, of what they were in the 1980s. Shrimpers acknowledge the practical explanations: fewer boats going out, therefore fewer bringing in, and fuel costs limiting the area covered. The weights of the harvest are mostly self-reported to the state by the shrimpers, anyway. But something about being at sea for days at a time tends to make these men superstitious. They don't throw back debris caught in the trawl for fear they might run into it later. To avoid tempting fate, they don't harm the gulls that squawk incessantly and coat the boat with droppings. And they often pick their dragging spots by following a feeling in their gut. So when the nets come up light or empty, shrimpers may wonder what they've done to anger the gods.

But for the moment, the luck of Darien shrimpers is holding. Even though the harsh 2010 winter killed off too many shrimp to enable South Atlantic shrimpers to take advantage of Gulf Coast competition idled by the BP oil spill, 2011 was warmer, leaving a larger crop and more time in the fall to harvest it. Local wholesalers like the Boones, who sell almost all of their catch to outside distributors, found a new buyer out of Tampa who was steadying his price for jumbo shrimp at right around $5 a pound. That, combined with a temporary leveling-off of gas prices, made for a good year. Still, Darien shrimpers will tell you that if they hit another snag like the early 2000s, when fuel prices soared and shrimp prices dove, it may put them all out of business for good.

In his ledger, Michael crunches the numbers: He figures *Little Man*'s haul from the first day of this voyage will fetch $4,850 back at the dock. That's $485 for each striker and $727.50 for Captain Michael. A good day.

But then, on the day's final haul, one of the nets gets torn, snagging on a submerged rock formation that Michael didn't have on his charts. This earns a cell phone chewing-out from his father and a chance for the young captain to practice his sewing skills, hand-patching the hole with a spool of black thread—one of the many money-saving skills every true shrimper needs. In the name of budget-streamlining, Michael has shimmied out on the trawling arm over heaving seas to save a $150 set of doors, nearly sliced open his hand rethreading a $400 steel cable, even wrestled a $5 fish from the gullet of a stowaway pelican (although, admittedly, the latter was on the principle of the thing). Greg says that his son knows "about two-thirds of what I knew when I was his age. Two-thirds of what Michael needs to know to own his own boat."

The torn trawl is an omen. The next morning, the crew oversleeps. The sample sack is little more than a few dozen shrimp among a mass of jelly balls, and the first catch, not hauled in until 9 a.m., is correspondingly light. Michael collapses in his captain's chair and offers an off-key chorus: "Mama said there'd be days like this..."

Tommie plops down on his stool, shades on, earphones in, hovering over his pile like a poker player. Across from him, Tray sits, legs straight out, popping shrimp heads with practiced repetition. "I like being out here," he says, looking out at the broad blue sky, fingers snapping heads all the while. "It gives me peace of mind. Clarity."

But up in the pilothouse, Michael finds anything but. He is poring over charts and maps, scouring his memory for where the shrimp might be waiting. The only "science" he has to go on is the knowledge that during low tide like this, shrimp tend to cluster, and that the later it is in the year, the farther out they are likely to be. He has a map marked with the places he has tried before. Beyond that, the hunt is pure intuition. And Michael can pick any patch of blue on the map—there is no such thing as territory among shrimpers. No one owns the sea. Besides, because of the way shrimp gather on the uneven ocean floor, rippled with little trenches and holes where bottom-dwellers can hide, one trawler can drag right beside another and catch three times as many shrimp.

By 2:30 in the afternoon, the *Little Man* has pulled in only 300 pounds of shrimp. Tommie and Tray, who have both worked with Greg, joke openly about the elder Boone's unpredictability, about how he will often abort a bad drag on a whim, pull up his nets, and motor to another spot. They laugh that he would've quit Blackbeard Hole a long time ago. But the crew knows that the son is the photo negative of his father. They know Michael intends to drag this spot until he hits pay dirt, even if it takes all night.

And indeed, as the distant shore swallows the sun, the bright fluorescent lamp atop the mast of the *Little Man* joins the three or four others scattered across the black sea. The winch grinds, the doors dive, dragging the trawls again across an invisible floor. Tommie hits the mess for a snack, while Tray remains on the empty deck, savoring the disappearing horizon. And as night reclaims the unlit pilothouse, Michael waits, staring into nothingness, groping for a clue as to what may lie in the darkness beneath.

AUTHOR'S AFTERWORDS...

Befriend a photographer. That's the best original advice I can offer any reporter. Ideas are what separate successful writers from merely talented ones. And while hanging out with other journos is great for drinking and commiserating about the process, we are by nature a competitive breed—particularly possessive of our ideas. Over bourbons, my compatriots and I have divulged things we wouldn't tell our wives, but we won't drop a hint as to what we're working on.

But while we scribes are in our dark home offices, hoarding our pitches and writing, photographers are out in the world, stopping at every roadside flea market or abandoned gas station, shooting, filling their portfolios between assignments and, most importantly, collecting stories. Nearly all of them are thrilled to have someone to put words to their images, to help score an extra paycheck and some glossy exposure.

Such was the case with my pal Jamey Guy. The freelance lens man was driving up the Georgia coast on his way home from a paying gig when he spotted the Boone trawlers bobbing in the Darien River. He found his way down to the docks and asked if he could tag along for a couple days and take some pictures. The Boone crew shanghaied the shutterbug for a week. But when he finally got back to land, Jamey had megabytes of images and a story about a fourth generation Georgia shrimping family. He also had names, cell numbers, even some basic background info, and, more importantly, he had a rapport with the family. All I needed to do was call and drop his name.

A ready-made story, right? It would have been easy. Just brush up on Melville, wax romantic about the broad pastel horizon and the grit of men bracing against the heave and sway of the ancient sea. But that wouldn't have been a story—it would've been flashy captioning for a wonderfully evocative photo essay. If I was going to add anything to these images, I was going to have to dive past the novelty of being on a boat in the middle of the ocean and get at what the hell these people were actually doing out there.

This is the danger of chasing a topic rather than a specific narrative. Just because it's interesting doesn't mean it's relevant or that it will resonate with your readers. It is one thing to say you're going out on a boat to do a story about shrimping, but you have to find that undercurrent, that universal reality that will reach the reader who has never, and probably would have never, given the subject a first thought. We had a pretty good lead with the fourth-generation shrimper angle. But now my job was a lot like that of a shrimp boat captain: Head out to sea for a few days, fill my notebooks with as much as they could carry, and hope that after all the bycatch is sifted out, I'll have something that made the trip worthwhile.

During the reporting of every subject, there is usually one interview or experience that contains the one line that is the heart of your story. Sometimes you recognize it immediately, but most of the time, I find it only after hours of scouring my notes. In this case it was on the fifteenth page of my notebook, my shorthand barely legible--I'd been scribbling blindly in the wee hours as Captain Michael Boone pointed out three lights, other boats, on the horizon, and told me there once was ten times more. Then his key quote:"20 years ago, this was a city."

This last line pointed to two central themes for my piece: First, it was a plain illustration of a dying industry. At its foundation, this was a business story, a readily relatable tale of an economic crisis accelerating the demise of another age old American occupation, not unlike farming or manufacturing. Second, the statement was made by a twenty-four-year-old who was clearly drawing on experience beyond his years. He had no personal memory of twenty years ago—it was passed down, just like the route he could navigate in the dark, just like the profession itself, from three generations of Boone men. Michael was born into that pilot house, into the ceaseless and increasingly hopeless search for treasure in the depths—and fulfillment in the eyes of his forbearers. In some ways it seemed he never had any other choice.

These two themes provided the nets through which I could now sort the material I had gathered. The economic side was easy enough to see once my love affair with the sea had been beaten out of me by the monotony of routine. The innocent anticipation that built as the grinding old winch hoisted the day's first catch dripping from the depths was hard to suppress. This is partially because the crew was putting on a show, running up and down the deck, swinging on ropes, decapitating brown shrimp with their teeth. But the repetition and the rising summer sun wore the actors down, too. The nets went back out and came back in, periods between long monotonous sentences of waiting, loading, and sorting through bycatch. Their reaction had nothing to do with the intrinsic joy of the catch. They saw size and weight and dollar signs—made apparent by their celebratory glee after a bountiful first day ebbing to despair on the sparse haul on the second. Meanwhile, as he scoured the seafloor for pay dirt, Captain Michael was constantly working the math up in the pilothouse.

The family angle was a bit more subtle. I made use of the long lulls by interviewing the captain from the co-pilot's seat. But much of what he related was factual, historical. The pressures of following and living up to the names of his forbearers surfaced in the details: The turtle guards on the nets invented by his grandfather that revolutionized the industry and established the Boone name. Striker Tray having worked for three generations of Boones, laughing about and contrasting what Michael's father would do when the catch dried up. And then there was the invisible father, Greg Boone, reduced in scene to a critical father's voice on a cell phone and in the back of Michael's mind.

As the sun set on the second day, I wasn't yet positive that my story was in my notebooks, but I was reasonably sure that if it wasn't, staying out another day or two wasn't going to help. I was also certain that if the ride I had chartered to rescue me didn't show before dark, the story would have to be written by someone else from the notes found floating in the Ziplock bag around the spot where I drowned trying to swim for shore. But just as evening's long shadows started to fade into the dusk, my single, outboard-motor chariot skipped into view. And as we sped away toward the Darien docks, the light of the *Little Man* slowly shrank into a star-like dot, joining three other lights across the horizon, the sparse remnants of a once-thriving city on the sea.

Robert Sanchez

Robert Sanchez specializes in long-form features for *5280*, in Denver. A former writer for *The Philadelphia Inquirer*, *The Associated Press*, *The Denver Post* and the *Rocky Mountain News*, Sanchez has won or has been nominated for multiple state and national awards, including the Livingston Awards for Young Journalists, for which he has been a finalist three times. The City and Regional Magazine Association twice named Sanchez as a finalist for its writer-of-the-year award, and CRMA has named him as a finalist in its feature writing, profile writing and civic journalism categories. Two of Sanchez's stories for *5280* have been included in *Best American Sports Writing*. Sanchez graduated with honors from the University of Missouri School of Journalism in 1999. He is married to his high school sweetheart, Kristen. The two have a daughter, Alexandra, and a son, Michael.

The Education of Ms. Barsallo

C igarette butts dot the asphalt and a beer bottle lies smashed on the side-walk outside Cole Arts & Science Academy on Denver's northeast side. A haze climbs from a grass-and-dirt field where children play soccer; nearby, young women in tight jeans push baby strollers past the dated American sedans that line the streets. A worn Ford truck is parked on Franklin Street, with signs asking for scrap metal lashed to the sides. Millie Barsallo, a twenty-two-year-old, first-year teacher at Cole, a preschool-through-eighth-grade public school, rolls past the Ford and turns into the school's near-empty parking lot on this mid-August morning. The engine of her father's 1998 Toyota Camry whines to a stop. Barsallo steps onto the asphalt. Ribbons of sunlight cut through the maple and pine trees that surround the school. She shields her eyes. It's a few days before school begins for the 615 students here, and Barsallo has a sick look on her face. "I think I'm about to freak out," she says.

She heads for the school's side entrance. In the shadows, the area looks like a dead-end, open-air alley. Three stories of red brick and glass rise around her. A security camera the size of a baseball looms over the metal doorway. Barsallo pushes a button on the intercom.

"It's Ms. Barsallo," she says.

She waits a few seconds.

"*Hello?*" she says again.

She pushes the button again.

"It's Ms. Barsallo," she repeats, this time a bit louder.

The doors click open.

Seventeen of Cole's forty-seven teachers are new for the 2009–2010 school year. Principal Julie Murgel's corps of teachers is comprised, in part, by rookies like Barsallo, who were recruited from the Teach for America program, a national Peace Corps–like organization. Of all Murgel's hires this year, the principal's certain Barsallo, a recent Cornell University graduate, is special. A bilingual, minority woman with an Ivy League education would be coveted anywhere, but Barsallo landed at Cole, perhaps the most unlikely gift Murgel could have gotten. "She'll be our superstar," the principal guarantees before the start of the school year. "I just know it."

Barsallo—pronounced *Bar-SY-oh*—was assigned to the school's English Language Acquisition-Spanish (ELA-S) program as a literacy teacher for third- and fourth-grade students. It would be a daunting task. Not only would Barsallo have to navigate the bureaucracy of a chronically underperforming school, but she'd also have to teach forty Spanish-speaking children, all of whom were expected to be able to read and write fluently in English.

Those already at Cole knew the Colorado Department of Education and Denver Public Schools were paying close attention this year. According to the 2008–2009 school year's statewide standardized tests, seventy-eight percent of the school's third- through eighth-grade students couldn't read at grade-level. For the Hispanic third- and fourth-graders, the figure jumped to eighty-nine percent. Without significant improvement, Cole could find itself on the academic chopping block. If that happened, it'd be the third time in the past five years that a school in this building had closed. "There's a lot to be done, but we're going to give these parents something to be proud of," Murgel, a roundfaced, thirty-nine-year-old former math teacher, promised at the start of the school year. "People will come in here and know we're serious about education."

Barsallo's second-floor classroom is at the end of a long hallway bathed in fluorescent lights and lined with lockers—none of which have actual locks. Room 208 is small, a fact Barsallo becomes acutely aware of when she opens the door and a blast of heat hits her. Her new room is stifling.

Rectangular tables are bunched together and take up a majority of the room. Barsallo flips on the overhead lights, sets down the box, and fans herself with a folder. On her right is a small library with pillows, a beanbag chair, and *National Geographic* magazines from the 1960s. There are chalkboards on each side of the room, a dry-erase board at the front, and a bank of windows along the back.

As Barsallo pops open a window, the neighborhood is splayed before her. She can see the soccer field, a bodega, a Mexican restaurant, and a few homes. A maple tree—its green leaves shimmering—stands directly outside the room. Wooden branches stretch at odd angles toward the open window. "You can see everything from here," Barsallo marvels.

After a few moments, she starts to cut blue butcher paper. Eventually, some of the lessons she will teach will be memorialized and taped on walls and on windows: reminders on how to draft a story, on subject-verb agreement, on recognizing and capitalizing proper nouns. Barsallo cuts a white piece of paper into the shape of a cloud and places it on the blue sheet. On the cloud, she writes a goal: Her students will improve one-and-a-half years in reading by the schoolyear's end. "I'm so excited to watch them grow," Barsallo says. She's giddy: "Of course, they're also going to write complete sentences, paragraphs, all that. I hope they're coming here ready to learn."

A few days before school starts, outside Barsallo's classroom and next to a broken water fountain with a yellow note above it that reads, "Don't work," a line of parents and children forms at her door. Barsallo sits at a table in the middle of her room with a girl and her mother, a mountain of papers and books between them. The fourth-grader, with an upturned nose and a blue, heart-shaped ring on one finger, looks away. Her wet hair runs down her back, and the water darkens her shirt.

"I'm so sorry," the girl's mother says in Spanish, pointing to her daughter's head. "Sometimes I can't brush her hair because I have to work in the morning."

Barsallo flashes a crooked smile. "That's fine," she says in Spanish. "She's a very beautiful young woman."

To help guide her through the year, Barsallo will use a tool called the Developmental Reading Assessment (DRA), a one-on-one test that allows teachers to observe and score children's reading levels. During her first week at Cole, Barsallo would test at least two dozen children. With few exceptions, their scores would be startlingly low.

Barsallo gives the girl a book and immediately sees that she's struggling. Barsallo finds another book, this one about a boy who loses a hat. While the girl reads, Barsallo uses a pencil to mark words the girl doesn't understand or mispronounces. When the girl finishes, Barsallo forces a smile. "We have some work to do, but we'll get there," she says. "Good job."

Later, a third-grader named Ricardo (all the students' names have been changed) sits with his father, who tells Barsallo that English isn't spoken at his house. "If you send something home," the man says in Spanish, "I won't know how to correct it." After Ricardo, it's Ronaldo, one of Barsallo's six special-education students. As the boy reads, he gulps for breath between words that sound meek and scared. "That's OK," Barsallo reassures him. "Take your time."

Next comes Jorge, a cute third-grader with chubby cheeks and spiky, gelled hair. He plops down in a chair.

"Did you read a lot this summer?" Barsallo asks.

Jorge looks out the door and sees two friends watching him. "No," he says, loud enough for the boys to hear. "I didn't read at all." The friends nod in approval.

"What would you like to read about?"

"I like video games."

"If I find books on video games, you'll read those?"

Barsallo passes Jorge a book, and the boy starts to read. Barsallo soon sees his score has improved from last year—a jump from a high-kindergarten to an early-first-grade level. Barsallo offers a high five and takes the boy out to the hallway.

"He spent the entire summer reading," Jorge's mother tells Barsallo excitedly. Jorge looks at his shoes, and his face turns bright red while his friends giggle.

One by one, the parents and their children come into the room for the assessment. Eventually, the line outside disappears, and soon the classroom is quiet. A fan spins lazily overhead. Barsallo stares at the pile of marked papers: Nearly half of the children she's tested today—all third- or fourth-graders—read at a kindergarten or first-grade level. Only a few are close to where they should be.

"My babies," she says in disbelief. "They can't read."

Barsallo never imagined herself worrying about children's reading scores. A 2009 graduate of Cornell's Department of Government, she has a friendly face, black hair, and warm, brown eyes. When she smiles—which is often—it's followed with a giggle. Though Barsallo went to college in New York, she grew up in Aurora, where she was raised middle class, the middle child of a mother and father who left Panama to seek educations in the United States. Her parents returned to their native country in the 1980s, then immigrated back to the United States when Barsallo was an infant. The family lived in a two-story home near Buckley Air Force Base. While her dad went to work as a manufacturing engineer, Barsallo taught herself English by watching cartoons on her parents' only television. She became a top student: Her early academic career culminated with a scholarship to St. Mary's Academy, a Catholic school in Cherry Hills Village. There, she earned a 3.9 grade point average, was on the dance team, and was one of the school's only students from the class of 2005 to attend an Ivy League school.

"I always thought I'd go to law school, then go to Capitol Hill, and then change the world," Barsallo says. But at the beginning of her senior year, she got a recruiting email from Teach for America, an organization that takes high-achieving college graduates and places them in some of the nation's poorest urban and rural public schools. The concept intrigued Barsallo, whose life as a minority student in mostly privileged, white schools gave her a unique perspective. "Everyone wants to pat you on the back for the stupidest things, like, 'Congratulations for not having a baby at sixteen,'" she says. "The expectations are pretty low." Barsallo wrote two essays, interviewed twice, and was accepted by TFA. She then applied for jobs in Colorado and eventually was offered a job at Cole.

The chance to teach in Denver was a blessing. Not only would it give Barsallo a way to be close to her family—she loves her mother's fried plantains—but the job would also give Barsallo an opportunity to work with children who reminded her of people she grew up with. While friends planned high profile, post-graduation gigs—at Harvard University, at Sotheby's, at the State Department—Barsallo accepted a $34,000-a-year job at Cole, packed her belongings, and moved home.

Many of her students also took a circuitous route to get to Cole. Barsallo knew her students were either immigrants—from Mexico, mostly—or children of immigrant parents. Nearly all of them lived in poverty. Some children had only recently started attending school regularly. One boy had been homeless a year earlier.

For the teachers who worked at Cole the previous year, like veteran teacher Paula Lopez-Crespin, the school calendar became a series of battles— over discipline, homework, parental involvement, and self-doubt. Teachers who imagined themselves changing the neighborhood would quickly find resistance among students and parents. "The more you persevere, regardless of your limitations, the better you can serve your kids," Lopez-Crespin says. "If you let it, school can seem like a major challenge every second of the day. You could second-guess yourself to death here." It would not take much for someone young and idealistic, like Barsallo, to soon be overwhelmed.

Barsallo knew her classroom inexperience would hinder her first months at Cole. There were complaints of out-of-control parents, of a lack of direction from the administration, of a lack of support for struggling teachers. If the veterans felt pressure, what would happen to her?

On a bright October morning, Barsallo's mother, Gilda, visits her daughter's classroom. She chats with Barsallo's students, shows old photos, and tells stories of growing up in Panama.

"What was Miss Barsallo like when she was our age?" a girl asks.

"Oh," Gilda says, "she was very silly."

The boys and girls giggle. They beg Barsallo's mother to speak with them in Spanish, and she does.

After sending the children to lunch, Barsallo and her mother steal away to an empty teacher's lounge near the first-floor stairwell. Barsallo pulls out a plate with a small pizza on it and quietly heats the meal as her mother watches.

"What's wrong?" Gilda asks.

"Nothing," Barsallo says.

"Millie, what's wrong?"

Barsallo hesitates and looks to see if anyone is outside. She shakes her head. "I can't say," she says. "I just can't say."

The truth was that just a few months into the year, things were getting more difficult for Barsallo. She spent hours after school brainstorming ways to engage each student, then took the lesson plans home and stayed up late working on them. She'd foregone a boyfriend and any semblance of a regular social life to focus her time on Cole and her students. Every morning, though, her plans evaporated. Every day, by the day's end, it seemed as if she'd ceded more control of her classroom to children who didn't seem to respect her. The list of infractions was never-ending: One day, two girls threw punches over a boy. Another day, Barsallo learned that some of her students were using the word "nigger" when referring to black students. And an argument between Barsallo's fourth-graders ended with one yelling at the other in Spanish: "Oh, yeah, your family is a bunch of wetbacks!"

At least three boys in her class hadn't turned in any homework yet, and whatever interventions Barsallo had tried with them—phone calls to mothers, private meetings at her desk—resulted only in shrugged shoulders and promises to do better. She wanted to be angry, but in some ways, she understood.

Barsallo had her own challenges: For weeks at the beginning of the year, the school didn't issue her a computer; later, she realized that she hadn't been given a password to access a school database. When she met Zachary Rahn, the school's twenty-five-year-old administrative intern, for a "formal observation," he told Barsallo that her classroom was "messy." The notes she'd written on butcher paper and hung on the walls made her room look disorganized; her desk—with stacks of papers and books and pencils—was a distraction.

Barsallo was hurt and upset; the room was her handiwork, and she thought it was an inviting place for her students. "I'm trying," she says, tears welling in her eyes. "I really am." She spoke to her TFA program director, Scott Wolf. "Millie's got to get past this," he says later. "She can be a great teacher, but she's got to realize that it isn't going to happen overnight."

Even more of a problem was the fact that her most troubled students—the children goose-stepping across the floor during independent reading time, those leaving the room without Barsallo's permission—were becoming a constant distraction. "I'm losing the kids who actually want to be here," she says. She considered punishing students by writing referrals to the administration's office, but the infractions didn't seem to warrant that. And, inevitably, the kids who would get sent away potentially needed the most attention in the classroom.

Barsallo had come to Cole expecting adversity, but not this. She went out of her way to follow school directives religiously, but nothing seemed to improve. Her class was among Cole's worst when it came to writing ability, but the school was stressing reading this year. "It's never-ending," Barsallo says. The contradictions of her new life—the seriousness of her charge and the absurdities about the way it was all coming apart just a few months into the school year—confounded her.

Across the hall, things were worse. There, twenty-four-year-old Emily Brown and Lopez-Crespin had no qualms about issuing referrals, but their classes showed only marginal improvement. After one flurry of write-ups, a fourth-grader made a prank call from Brown's class phone. None of her students would give up the culprit, though the teacher was certain everyone knew who it was. "Ninety percent of what goes on around here is really positive, but it's that ten percent that grinds you down," says Ben Cooper, a Cole administrator. "You've got to pick yourself up every day and make a decision. Are you going to rise to the occasion, or are you going to lie down?"

Barsallo asks herself that question with regularity. At home, inside the terrace-level apartment she shares with her sister and a friend, Barsallo walks into her bedroom, which is covered with clothes and ungraded papers. She tells the story of her own third-grade teacher, whom she last saw a few months before leaving for college in 2005. "I told her I was going to Cornell, and tears started streaming down her face," Barsallo says. Now that Barsallo's the teacher, she wants to know that she's doing what's right for her students.

"I want to be that teacher who sees one of my kids ten years from now, and they're telling me how they're kicking the world's ass," she says. "But how can I get there when it feels like my ass is the one that's being kicked?"

Cole Arts & Science Academy is a tired sprawl of 1920s-era brick and limestone that rises from a modest northeast Denver neighborhood. Statistically, the 400 Hispanic students who attend Cole are already lost. As minority children, many of whom live in poverty, they are more likely to drop out of school, and, when they're older, to have a child out of wedlock or find themselves in jail. In their immediate future, they're more likely to get "unsatisfactory" scores on the Colorado Student Assessment Program, the standardized exam, known as CSAP, used to measure core knowledge among third- through tenth-grade students in the state's 1,769 public schools.

Colorado closely monitors the test scores and rewards districts, schools, principals, and staffs that excel—and disciplines those that don't. It's a dance Cole's families know well. In 2005, the state's Department of Education closed the then-Cole Middle School after four years of failing results. The school was replaced with a 6–8 charter school named KIPP Cole College Prep, which closed in 2007 after going through four principals in two years. That same year, DPS transformed the school into a storage facility for things such as theater costumes, an insult the families here still haven't gotten over. "The district's hurt us bad," one parent says. "Our neighborhood has become a dumping ground."

When DPS announced that Cole Arts & Science Academy would open in 2008, there was little reaction. "We're asked to trust one more school," a parent of several Cole students says. "How many times do we have to hear that things are fixed, that everything is going to be better?"

To lead the rebuilding effort, DPS chose Murgel, the former principal at Denver's Whiteman Elementary School. Murgel is a bilingual math teacher by trade and a fifteen-year DPS veteran with a can-do attitude. She looked at Cole's challenges through the eyes of her mother, a Montana native with a son who has Down syndrome. Nearly forty years ago, she started that state's largest work program for disabled adults. "She refused to let my brother fall through the cracks at a time when almost everyone would have given up on him," Murgel says. Just as her mother had done, Murgel was determined to give these children a shot.

The summer of 2008 saw a flurry of activity. Murgel had an office on Cole's third floor and used a borrowed ten-year-old computer. She kept murals of successful minority leaders—Martin Luther King Jr., Cesar Chavez—in the hallways and had colors, like tangerine and yellow, painted on the walls to brighten things up. Graffiti was blasted from the brick outside. "I was going to wipe away all the years of negativity," Murgel says now. She devised plans—expectations regarding when students and staff would be in classrooms; parent contracts; a school uniform with a green shirt—and solidified her staff. In the midst of her preparations, someone burglarized her office.

Murgel pushed on. From the beginning, she envisioned Cole—known as CASA around the neighborhood—as a metaphorical home, a proving ground for a generation of academic castoffs, families who'd recently had their schools close and were searching for a viable option. "They needed hope," the principal says. "The kids needed someone to tell them that they were worthy of a college education and a better life."

A year after Cole opened, families noticed that much of Cole's equipment had been salvaged from shuttered schools— "Wyman" and "Mitchell," the names of two recently closed elementary schools, were written prominently in black marker on Barsallo's classroom computers and overhead projector. Outside the school, no one bothered to remove the old, cracked, weed-infested "Cole Junior High" sign on Martin Luther King Boulevard. And when gang members marked up the iconic columns of Cole's facade, the school simply put a coat of paint over the graffiti. For all the talk about making the school a place of hope, some parents felt their children were getting a hand-me-down education.

Despite the feelings around the neighborhood, the 2009 school year brought at least some opportunity. Not only had Murgel hired new teachers, but she'd also gotten Colorado's Department of Education to designate Cole as one of a handful of "innovation" schools within DPS. Under the Innovation Schools Act of 2008, select public schools are given wide latitude to waive state, district, and union rules when it comes to how money is spent, which curriculum is used, and how teachers are hired and fired. The designation was a coup for Murgel, who'd sought more autonomy to run her school.

As part of the rebuilding, Murgel wanted teachers who would think outside of the failed methodology, who were ambitious, familial, and resilient. Among the crew was Rene Panozzo—Barsallo's ELA-S counterpart on the second floor—a bilingual journalism major from Iowa who'd teach third- and fourth-grade math and science. And there was Emily Brown, the third-grade literacy and social studies teacher who'd recently earned degrees in anthropology and environmental studies from an elite, private college in Maine.

Around Cole, there was reason for optimism. One of Denver's other innovation schools—Manual High School, just down the street—closed in 2006 but was becoming the highest performing low-income school in DPS. "We don't have any time to waste," Murgel says. "The kids don't have any time to waste."

Ana, a nine-year-old Cole student, calls Barsallo "the best teacher in the world," and the "reason I come to school." Ana has deep-brown eyes, and an easy smile. Her full, dark hair cascades down her back, and, from a distance, it's as if you're looking at Barsallo from thirteen years ago. It's not just her physical appearance that draws the comparison. "I either want to be a teacher or a lawyer," the fourth-grader says. "When I grow up, I want to help people."

Barsallo has taken an interest in Ana, who is part of a group of students that stays after school. Barsallo recommends books for her and keeps in mind that Ana likes scary stories. Ana almost always finishes her homework, and Barsallo is sure to draw a smiling face in black pen on her quizzes and tests, and to pin them to a bulletin board outside the classroom door so everyone can see.

By November, Ana has gone from a fifth-grade reading level to an eighth-grade level. It's a jump that catches everyone's notice and has teachers dreaming about the girl's future. "She could really make it," Panozzo says. Ana's neighbors have noticed, too. On Saturdays, they stop by her home and ask her to translate letters from their landlords.

College is Ana's goal, but she's unsure if she'll ever get there. She's being raised by her grandmother and her grandmother's boyfriend—Mexican immigrants whom she refers to as "Mom" and "Dad"—and she and her siblings live in the couple's rented home. Money is tight, and Ana's "parents" make ends meet by selling candy and burritos on sidewalks outside city schools.

Ana is protective of her books and of a girl named Isabella, a slightly built fourth-grader who's one of Ana's closest friends. The two live near each other, and they spend their free time running in the park or looking through magazines that feature one of their favorite teen stars, Disney's Selena Gomez. Like most Hispanic children who grow up around here, Ana is Catholic. She carries her faith like a shield. "My mother said the first child is blessed by God," she says, "and that's me."

It's late autumn now and the brown leaves on the maple tree outside Room 208 rise and fall with the gentle breeze. The projector is on in Barsallo's classroom; third-graders are huddled on a checkered rug near the dry-erase board. Barsallo steps in front of the children.

"Why are we here? Why are we working hard?" she begins. "Let me put it a different way. Why do we need to learn how to read?"

"To get smart?" one girl says.

"Did you know that one in four kids grows up not knowing how to read?" Barsallo asks. She steps in the middle of her students. She points to the children: "One, two, three, four," she says. "You, number four: You won't know how to read."

The boy buries his face in his hands.

"Did you know 44 million adults can't read well enough to read a simple story? Did you know that future prison inmates read at a third-grade level?" Barsallo asks. "They're making a bed there for you right now."

"Is prison like jail?" one boy asks.

"You all want to get to fourth grade, right?" Barsallo continues. "And you want to get through elementary school, middle school, high school, and go to college, right? Because, I've got to tell you, people are looking at your reading level and making a bed in prison for you. They're betting half of you aren't finishing high school."

For the first time in weeks, the room is silent. The kids stare at the floor.

"How are you going to stop this?" Barsallo asks. "Because, you know, reading English is not something you can choose not to do. You will finish your homework. Stop looking for excuses. So, how many of you are going to work hard for yourselves, for your families, and for your futures?"

A bunch of tiny hands shoot into the air—every kid in the room.

"You *will* decide your future," she says. "You *will* change those statistics. You *will* make your parents proud. But you have to want to do it."

Another pause. More silence.

"How can we turn this class around to take charge of our future?" Barsallo asks. "I'll start: Quit talking during silent reading. What else?"

"Don't fight in the classroom," one student says.

"Don't talk while the teacher talks," another says.

"What I'm trying to tell you is that you must always do your work. Is that hard to understand?" Barsallo asks. Now she gets to her point, the reason she's been staying up nights, worried.

"This is the first year you take the CSAP," she says. "That's not the most important thing to me. The thing for me is that I want you to leave this classroom being good readers and writers. We need to know where we're at, compared to other kids, and the CSAP will help us. We have less than fifty days until that test.

"So are we all going to be at the third-grade level?" she asks. Heads nod. "No," Barsallo says, emphatically, "many of us are not. That's OK, though, because we're going to give this our best. Remember, when you come to class, it's not about today. It's about every other day after that."

More stares. More silence.

"How many of you are going to change those statistics?" Every hand goes up.

"If you see someone struggling today, what will you say?" Barsallo asks.

The kids answer back in unison: "I believe in you."

"Good," Barsallo says. "Now let's get to work."

Barsallo worries later that she was too harsh with her students. But, she says, "That was something they needed to hear. I have to be honest with them, even if the truth is hard to listen to."

By mid-December, about a month after her speech, there's no question about the words' effect on her students: The latest DRA results are in, and Barsallo's stunned to see the improvement. Almost every child bested their previous score, and they're on their way to reaching the individual objectives Barsallo had set at the beginning of the year. Some have already reached their goal. "I'm so proud of you!" Barsallo beams during class the day before winter vacation.

The children sit around tables and cut out paper snowflakes that they'll give to the teachers as Christmas gifts. "You're great!" one girl writes on her project. Outside, snow sticks to the maple tree, its bare branches covered in frozen clumps of white.

Although the reading work has paid off, Barsallo's still concerned about her students' writing proficiency—and writing is a major part of the statewide standardized exams. Heading into the winter break, Barsallo has never felt like this: simultaneously energized and defeated. She's certain that most of her children will perform poorly on the written portion of the exam, but when Barsallo raises the issue with Cole's curriculum adviser, she's given a recommendation to carve out more time for writing. When Barsallo asks what instruction can be cut to make room, she's met with a stare. If Barsallo was hoping to be rescued, help wasn't coming any time soon. "This is a roller coaster. You're up one day, and then you get test scores and you think you're the worst teacher ever," the administrative intern Rahn says. "Millie's going to doubt herself, because we all doubt ourselves."

In late January, weeks before third-graders start the CSAP, an air of anxiety permeates Cole. There's a rumor that a staffer was fired for drinking alcohol. A teacher stopped one of Barsallo's students in the hall recently, but when the teacher realized the boy didn't fully understand English, the teacher began to wave his arms furiously and bark like a dog.

Barsallo had to laugh about the incident, but privately the stress was suffocating. Today, nearly all of her third-graders failed a pop quiz in which Barsallo asked them to name five "tricks" to use when answering CSAP questions, advice such as re-reading questions and searching for key words. Barsallo looks worn. Ungraded essays sit on her desk. One reads: "...Fainali ai wuas riyi japi en dat wuas mai bes dei eber." *Finally, I was really happy, and that was my best day ever.*

Outside Barsallo's room, some of the teachers are prepping their students for the CSAP the same way cheerleaders might pump up a school for a football game with its archrival. Lopez-Crespin's students are dancing and chanting in the hallway: "Jump, beat the CSAP! Jump, jump! Beat the CSAP!"

"You got it, guys!" Lopez-Crespin encourages the children as they swish their hips. "You got it!"

It all felt false to Barsallo. More than halfway into the school year, she'd sunk her entire life into this class, this school. If she wasn't at Cole, she was attending required classes for Teach for America, or she was out with her colleague, Panozzo, which usually meant two hours of discussion on how to get a student to write a complete paragraph. And what had Barsallo gotten out of it? What had her kids gotten out of it?

The low hum of third-grade chatter fills Barsallo's room as Cristina, an eight-year-old with a black ponytail and hoop earrings, pulls a chair up to Barsallo's desk and prepares to take another reading test.

"You nervous?" Barsallo asks the girl. Cristina tugs at an earring.

"Kinda," she says. "Yeah, maybe."

`"OK, then. Shake it out. I believe in you."

Cristina's scores have been uneven—hardly a surprise for a student learning to master a new language. The girl showed promise earlier in the year; since then, she's bounced around, and, recently, fallen backward. Barsallo points to the scores in a blue binder, and Cristina cranes her neck. Her head drops.

"You're falling behind," Barsallo says softly. She moves her head close to the girl's. "That doesn't mean you're not growing; it just means we need to work on your reading fluency. I don't want you to get discouraged about this. It just means we need to work a little harder." She pauses for a moment. "You know, we could all work a little harder."

The morning of February 9 is the first CSAP day for Barsallo's third-graders. It's 7:30, and Barsallo's breath blows white in the air as she heads from her car to one of Cole's side entrances.

Inside the school, overhead lights cast a harsh glare on the freshly mopped tile. The walls are decorated with posters encouraging students to "Rock the CSAP!"

Barsallo carries paper towels and disinfectant wipes to her room and sets them on her desk. She silently starts to scrape tape from tabletops and spends the next half hour scratching away. She grabs a towel and wipes off a pencil mark.

One of the special-education teachers sticks her head into Barsallo's room.

"You ready for this?" she asks.

"There's nothing I can do about it now," Barsallo says, shrugging her shoulders.

The other woman laughs. "A test they can't read," she says, mockingly. "Woo hoo."

The posters and butcher-paper notes that decorated Barsallo's classroom walls—sentence diagrams, book genres—are now covered. Boxes of granola bars are stacked on Barsallo's desk. "Four kids told me they ate breakfast yesterday," Barsallo says. "That isn't gonna fly."

The loudspeaker crackles to life. Strains of Survivor's "Eye of the Tiger" begin to wail through the school's halls. "Good morning, Cole Arts & Science Academy!" Murgel says over the driving guitar riff.

Barsallo scrubs the desktops. She scrapes and wipes without speaking. She works her way across one line of tables, then another. Then she stops. Warm air blasts from the wall heater.

Less than two hours before the most important test of her third-graders' lives, Barsallo stares at a pencil sketch on a table in the last row. It's a boxy crucifix scribbled into the wood laminate. Barsallo studies it for a moment. She picks up a towel to wipe it away; then she sets down the towel. "Maybe I should leave it here," she says. "I'm not kidding."

By March, there was growing concern about gang activity in the neighborhood. There are stories of gang members attacking Cole students near the school. Graffiti covers the school's brick-and-stone exterior, and sharp-edged, black-marker scrawls dot playground equipment. On the school's front door are the scrubbed remnants of a vulgar greeting that had been removed: "Fuck Cole Frevr," it read.

A police cruiser is parked on a sidewalk a few feet from the school. An officer sits in the vehicle, but the teachers inside the school don't know why he's here. Police have been at the school three days this week. An ambulance was parked outside days earlier.

No one in the administration is talking about what happened, but the buzz is that a student was seriously injured, maybe on the playground, and that the mother of the hurt child vomited in Murgel's office because of shock. There's skepticism about the veracity of the story among teachers. "No one tells us shit around here," one teacher says.

Murgel's bunkered herself in her office for most of the week, but when the school bell rings on this Friday, she tells one of the secretaries to call up to the second floor and ask Barsallo, Panozzo, Brown, and Lopez-Crespin to come down for a meeting. The third-grade CSAP scores are in.

The principal stands behind her desk, next to Rahn. She waves a stack of papers in her hands. "This is it," Murgel says. "I haven't looked." Rahn passes out the papers.

"Don't flip them over until I say so," Murgel says. "We're going to see these together." The principal takes a deep breath, then counts aloud: "One, two, *three*."

There's a whoosh of paper and eyes instantly scan the numbers. No one speaks. Barsallo squints her eyes. Brown's forehead furrows.

"What does this say?" Brown asks. "I can't understand it."

"Me neither," Barsallo says.

They look to Murgel. She drops her paper. "It means—" she says, pausing for effect, "you guys did great!"

The room bursts into cheers. Brown rests her hands on the top of her head. "My God," she says, her voice cracking in disbelief. "My kids *learned* something."

Of course, it's a relative assessment, one that would confuse Barsallo for the rest of the year. According to the 2010 CSAP data, one of every four Cole third-graders can read at grade-level. For the non-English speakers like Barsallo's, it's closer to one out of ten—but those scores are still two percentage points higher than last year, and the school's overall performance is almost seven percentage points higher than 2009. Barsallo shrinks in the corner. "Millie!" Murgel calls out. "That's wonderful, and we're gonna keep improving. Great job!"

There are high fives and hugs in the room. Despite the teachers' and students' work, despite the incremental gains made throughout the year, Cole once again would be one of Denver's lowest achieving elementary schools. On this afternoon, though, Barsallo was witnessing a celebration.

By the spring, uneasiness was building at Cole. At an earlier faculty meeting, Murgel announced that the assistant principal would not return in the fall. There were rumors among staff that the assistant principal was not the only one who would be going: The librarian and up to eleven teachers could lose their jobs. By early May, a few had received their notices.

The uncertainty hadn't deterred some teachers from wondering whether they'd be receiving their end-of-year bonus. To prepare, they lowered their student-growth objectives they'd set nine months earlier to more closely match the smaller gains that their classes actually made during the year. They were cooking their academic books, essentially, but no one seemed to care; it was accepted practice around Cole, one that could mean an extra thousand dollars in teachers' pockets come year-end. Barsallo refused to play along.

With less than a month left in the school year, demands continued to grow: There were summer reading lists to prepare, tests to administer, and rooms to clean. Despite the challenges she'd encountered, Barsallo was determined to return to Cole the following August—better informed and better prepared to handle the burdens that undoubtedly would face her in her second year. If anything, she felt more confident to perform the job she'd signed up for. And more than ever, she was confident her students had something to offer—their DRA scores showed continued, across-the-board increases—and that each was better for their experiences at the school. "They know they can succeed if they put their minds to it," she says. "They're all geniuses to me."

From Barsallo's mouth, the words are not empty. As part of her end-of-year work, she'd spent time talking to Cole's gifted-and-talented program coordinator about whether some of Barsallo's students—like the gifted Ana—would qualify. Without Barsallo as an advocate, her high-achieving fourth-graders would have little chance of finding additional opportunities around Cole.

And yet, two weeks before the school year is to end, students are rolling on the floor, hanging from the door, and wandering the hallway. Barsallo approaches a table. The boy is supposed to be writing a topic sentence, but so far all he's written is: "The cobra."

"That's not a topic sentence, dude," Barsallo says, pointing her index finger at the words. She realizes quickly that this isn't the most incomplete work at the table. She looks at another boy's blank paper. "I see you've written so much," she says sarcastically. "You need to slow down because you're on fire."

Barsallo returns to her desk, calls a boy over, and asks him to read a book.

Another student begins to pull books out of the library. "I told you not to go in there," Barsallo says. "Sit down, now!"

A few minutes later: "No, you can't go to the bathroom."

Then: "Miss, can I have $10?"

The boy at Barsallo's desk is clearly frustrated. He starts to close the book. Barsallo wraps her arm around his shoulder. "Miss," the boy says, setting the book aside, "I'm dumb. I can't do this."

"No one thinks you're dumb," Barsallo says.

"I do."

The class battles swirl around them. Barsallo sees each one as if they're happening in slow motion.

"Stop fighting over a pencil. It's ridiculous."

"Sit in a chair and read a book."

Someone vomits in a trash can in Lopez-Crespin's room, and the news makes its way across the hall. Barsallo's students race out of her room. The school bell rings.

Later, Ana pulls Barsallo aside.

"Miss," she says, "there's something I need to tell you."

Her grandmother's boyfriend, the man she calls her father, had been arrested a few blocks from Cole—there was an issue with his license plates, and he didn't have identification. Now he's locked up, awaiting deportation.

Barsallo hugs the girl.

"Miss, I might have to move to Mexico."

Barsallo tightens her arms around the girl. Thoughts race through her mind. Ana was born here; she needs to complete her education in the United States. She can do great things. There's no way Ana can leave. She won't learn. She won't be challenged. Barsallo won't let it happen.

Then, just as quickly, she lets go. Barsallo knows she can't fix the situation, that she can't change the series of events that are already in motion.

"I'll see you later, OK?" Barsallo says quietly, and then Ana disappears out the door.

A fifteen-foot piece of limb broke off the big maple tree outside Barsallo's window the last week of school, and part of the tree fell into a chain-link fence. Slivers of wood and bark are spread across the sidewalk like broken glass. The limb, it turns out, was rotting from the inside.

Upstairs, on the final day of classes, Room 208 looks empty. The paper clouds are off the wall. The chalkboards are uncovered. The books are put away. The lights are off. A fan whirs in the background.

Barsallo and Ana stand in the late-afternoon shadows. In a few days, the soon-to-be fifth-grader will be on her way to Mexico to rejoin her family. Barsallo lifts a black fabric bag with the word "Love" written on it in pink and places it on a table between Ana and herself. The bag is stuffed with tissue paper, which Barsallo fluffs with the tips of her fingers.

"I wrote you a letter and put it in here," Barsallo says. "You have some books, too, so read those."

Barsallo pushes the bag toward Ana, and the girl stares at the gifts. She sweeps her black hair off her forehead, and there's a long, awkward silence. Ana has a pained look on her face. Her nose scrunches.

"I'm going to miss you, Miss," Ana finally says as she wraps her arms around Barsallo.

Barsallo engulfs the girl, resting her cheek on top of Ana's head. The two close their eyes and rock back and forth in the dimming light.

"Come back, OK?" Barsallo whispers in Ana's ear.

"I'll come, Miss, I'll come."

The two step away from each other and lock eyes. Barsallo purses her lips.

"What?"

Ana looks away.

"Nothing."

"What?"

"I don't know what to do next, Miss," she says.

"What do you mean?"

"I don't want to go," Ana whispers, holding back tears. "What do I do?"

Barsallo reaches out and holds Ana again. Seconds pass. Then a minute.

"I don't know, either," Barsallo says. "But you know I love you."

Her words hang in the air. "You're going to be a rock star at your new school. You know that, right? You're going to be so fly."

AUTHOR'S AFTERWORDS...

Find the right character.

If there's any advice that I can give to aspiring narrative non-fiction writers, it would be that. With a good character, anything becomes possible. Scenes are bountiful, dialogue is engaging, the story comes alive.

That's not to say my story, "The Education of Ms. Barsallo," was a cakewalk. I spent nine months—an entire school year—with twenty-two-year-old Millie Barsallo as she taught third- and fourth-grade students in a cramped English Language Acquisition classroom at a struggling Denver school. My early goal was to meet often with Barsallo, to get her to understand the kind of story I wanted to write and to have her become comfortable with having me around. I promised to be as unobtrusive as possible. I wanted to be around without it feeling to her like I was around all the time.

In return, my access would get me into her world. And I wanted to know everything. After a few visits with Barsallo at school, I eventually visited her at her apartment. I met one of her roommates and I met her mother and her father and her younger brother. Barsallo and I chatted over dinner several times. By late fall, she began to open up.

I picked Barsallo from three teachers recommended by the Teach for America program. That's not to say I'd simply found the first person who agreed to participate in this story. In fact, I had researched at least ten others in the previous three years—though none of those first-year teachers met the standards I'd set for my main character. If I was going to spend nearly a year reporting this story, I wanted to make sure I was telling the right story about the right person. I knew I had one chance to write this and I would never get an opportunity for a do-over.

For this piece, my teacher definitely needed to work at a struggling school. The school needed to be the second character in this story—a lively place with depth and weight to it. Cole Arts and Science Academy—a chronically underperforming school that served an almost-exclusively minority community—fit that description. As for my teacher, she needed to be young, well-spoken and thoughtful. I wanted someone who could self-analyze quickly and be critical if it was needed. I wanted someone who wasn't afraid to speak up. My teacher needed to be goal-oriented; partly because I knew a classroom of young children would be a challenge and that staying on task would be difficult. Finally, I wanted a teacher who thought teaching was the most important job in the world. In essence, I wanted someone who planned to change the world. And I found her.

I met with the school's principal to get the buy-in. I pitched the story as an honest look at the challenges and successes that teachers face in schools across America. In a way, I was looking at urban education, writ large. The principal readily agreed. I met many of the teachers on Barsallo's floor, and I talked to the school's parent-teacher group.

And then I watched. I visited the school at least three times a month and I met Barsallo outside the classroom. I saw her interact with her fellow teachers—many of whom were roughly her age—and I attended as many school events as possible. If there was a school play, I showed up—even if I knew it wouldn't make it into my story. Reporting is a two-way street, and I wanted to let her know that I cared about her mission and that I thought what she did was interesting. If I was going to ask her deeply personal questions, then I needed to let her know that I was willing to take this ride with her—the whole way.

I hope that doesn't come across as hokey, because I really believe it. I want to know as much as possible about my characters. If you want to be a narrative writer, you can't be in and out of someone's life and then disappear forever. You have to know what makes them who they are. When your sources start opening up, you'll see what I mean.

Because I'd spent time finding the right character, I knew my scenes would come. I had no idea the tree I'd been watching from Barsallo's classroom window—my metaphor for her own change as the school year went along—would collapse near the end of the school year. I had no idea that one moment at school—when Barsallo says goodbye to her best student, who had to return to Mexico—would be so intimate and so beautiful. But I can honestly say that finding these scenes wasn't a surprise. When you pay attention to your reporting universe—when you dive deeply into a story—good things happen. Suddenly, memorable scenes are everywhere.

This story has been among the most rewarding of my career. It taught me so many things, among them organization and dedication. It also taught me to trust my instincts—to wait for the right moment and for the right character. Anyone could have rushed out a story about a first-year teacher in a school. Very few could do it in a way that was meaningful and memorable. When people think of my story, I don't think they remember the actual writing; they remember the scenes and the dialogue I captured. They remember the feelings those moments evoke. I'm just the guy in the corner, watching it all unfold.

Eli Saslow

E li Saslow is a staff writer at the *Washington Post*, where he writes feature stories for the National desk. He is also a contributing writer for *ESPN The Magazine.*

A graduate of Syracuse University, he was a distinguished visiting professor of journalism at The University of Montana in 2010. His first book, *Ten Letters: The Stories Americans Tell Their President,* was published by Random House in 2011. He runs a nonprofit called Press Pass Mentors, for high school students interested in journalism. He lives in Washington, D.C. with his wife, Rachel, and their daughter, Sienna.

Three Minutes to Fort Totten

He heard the familiar whine of a Metro train approaching the platform, and Tom Baker decided to run for it. The next train was scheduled to arrive at Takoma Station in two minutes, another in six minutes and yet another in ten. But it was the first Monday of summer, and Baker had left work early with a weightlifting routine to complete and an overgrown garden to tend. A doctor at Walter Reed with an emergency pager affixed to his waist, Baker had learned to schedule and protect every minute of his free time. This was his train.

Baker, forty-seven, bounded up the escalator, two steps at once, until he reached the empty platform. The train idled on his left, its doors still open. The operator, a forty-two-year-old named Jeanice McMillan, stuck her head out the window and watched Baker run toward her. She was an hour into her final shift of the week, seven loops on the Red Line away from going home to a son who just had returned from college. But she smiled and held open the door, and that was how the final passenger made it onto Car 1079, the first car of Metro Train 112, headed south toward downtown Washington.

An automated voice greeted Baker as he slid into a seat directly behind the operator.

"Doors closing."

Train 112: a nondescript Metro train, six cars in all. Car 1079: at least sixteen people scattered across sixty-eight seats, lost in their own worlds late on a Monday afternoon. Baker stood up again. If he walked to the rear of the car, he would be closer to his exit at Fort Totten. He would shave nine seconds off his commute home. That seemed important.

Baker tossed his blue backpack over his shoulder and walked the full seventy-five feet to the back of the car, passing all the other passengers on his way. There was a dentist reading a book about golf; a college student closing his eyes after the fourth day of an internship; a young architect fiddling with his cellphone; a seventeen-year-old checking her makeup in a small mirror before applying extra lip gloss.

Near the front of the train, a twenty-three-year-old named LaVonda King was on her daily trip to pick up two young sons from day care. She had just finished a cellphone conversation with her mother, who suggested that King print advertising fliers for her new hair salon. A good idea, King agreed. She already had the keys to the shop and a name she had daydreamed about since high school: "LaVonda's House of Beauty."

In the far rear of the car, Dave Bottoms listened to an iPod. A chaplain who had just finished his first day on the pastoral staff at Walter Reed Army Medical Center, Bottoms, thirty-nine, felt scattered from the stress of a new job. Wasn't today his dog's seventh birthday? Did his new BlackBerry work? Were there any leftovers in the fridge for a quick dinner? Bottoms reached into his backpack and grabbed a photocopy of a homily by St. Irenaeus. Maybe, Bottoms thought, a little reading would quiet his mind.

Baker stopped walking when he reached the chaplain and stood near him, leaning against a wall by the rear exit of the first car. Baker had moved from Texas to Washington four years ago, bought a downtown condo and sold his car. So liberating. He loved the predictability of Metro. It was 4:57 p.m., and Train 112 lurched into motion, with Car 1079 at the lead. Baker grabbed a pole to steady himself and turned to face the door he planned to use to exit the train. He would make it to the gym by 5:45, probably home by 7:30. A good night ahead. Three minutes to Fort Totten.

As Baker looked out the window, Bottoms felt the train roll into motion but never bothered to look up from his reading. Ride the Metro long enough and it becomes like sleepwalking: Trees on the right, a blur of graffiti on the left, a subtle bump-bump-bump of the car so predictable that it somehow becomes relaxing. The operator came over the speaker system and said something about a delay, but his iPod muffled her announcement. The train slowed and accelerated, stopped and started, and all the while he kept reading.

But then, panicked shouts came from the front of the car.

"Oh no. Watch out!" one passenger shouted.

"Oh my God!" screamed another.

Bottoms instinctively grabbed the handrail of the seat in front of him, heard a shrieking crunch of metal, was thrown forward in his seat and saw something coming toward him that at first didn't make any sense. It was a jumble of dust, shoes, glass, seats, carpeting, Metro maps, metal poles and people. It was the front half of Car 1079. But in the first instant, it appeared as a rolling, roaring wave that was coming closer and closer. Carpeting near Bottoms's feet began to rise up and crumple like tissue paper. The wave swept within fifteen feet in front of Bottoms…ten feet…seven. A studied theologian and an experienced chaplain, he recited a simple prayer.

"God, make it stop."

"God, make it stop."

The wave crested against the seat directly in front of Bottoms, and a cloud of dust enveloped him as the train rocked to a halt. Bottoms stood up, scanned the car and tried to understand what had just happened. Had the train derailed? Had it fallen off a bridge? Had it hit something? He looked in front of him. Where was the floor? He looked up. Where was the roof? Why, as the cloud of dust settled, was he sitting at an incline, staring at a cloudless blue sky, and at another train stretching down the tracks, and at a man on the roof of that train covered in soot and dangling his legs over the side of the car as if perched on the edge of a swimming pool?

Chaos now, everywhere. Jamie Jiao, the man sitting on the roof of the train, who moments before had been the college intern lost in thought near the front of Car 1079, felt something wet under his chin and realized he was bleeding. Baker, the doctor, searched what was left of the floor for his glasses. Brianna Milstead, seventeen, frantically gathered the scattered contents of her makeup kit. A young woman looked down to see that the tattoo on her ankle was gone, along with most of the skin on her lower leg. A fifteen-year-old boy squirmed in his seat and froze suddenly when he realized that his legs were stuck between the buckled floor and jagged metal.

Bottoms sat back down in his seat, stunned. All at once, he heard the sounds. A wailing rush of hysteria.

"Mommy! Mommy! Ohmygod."

"Somebody help! Please. My foot's stuck."

"Baby, where are you? Are you okay? Baby? Baby?"

He understood now that he was in the only section of the car that remained intact. Six or seven other passengers were there, too, and in front of them was the pile of wreckage, from which a new sound emerged. It was a young woman's voice, quiet at first and then louder, until finally it eclipsed the rest of the noise and echoed off the walls, a chilling, panicky shriek.

"I'm here.

"I'm here.

"Please don't leave me."

Bottoms crawled up the pile toward the voice, scraping his knees against jagged glass and metal. He paused for a second, worried that his extra weight might cause the pile to shift, but what was an extra 150 pounds on a mountain of wreckage? Two tours as a chaplain in Iraq had instilled in him the instinct to comfort the injured and dying. Years ago, when he first joined the service, a mentor had told him: "You don't let anyone suffer alone."

Elsewhere in the car, passengers let their instincts take over. The seventeen-year-old, who was prone to panic attacks, curled into a fetal position on her seat. Baker scanned the car and assessed the injured: Some had head gashes and broken bones, and he thought they would need hospitalization. The fifteen-year-old boy pinned between seats probably had a broken femur, and moving him would risk causing a spinal fracture or a bleeding artery. The girl yelling beneath the rubble—she was the most worrisome of all.

Brandon Burgess, twenty-six, an architect, saw the remains of Car 1079 in hard lines and schematics. The pile of wreckage was probably five feet high and spanned the width of the car. The rear exit doors would not open because a bulkhead had collapsed. The side doors were all blocked or jammed. There was no way out.

Near what had once been the center of the car, a muscular nineteen-year-old named Daryl Smith Jr. glanced down, saw that his foot was trapped and felt a surge of adrenaline. He looked over at his girlfriend, who was bloody and crying. "Baby! Baby, we have to move," Smith said. He yanked his leg loose, picked up his girlfriend and carried her to the rear of the car. Smoke and dust filled his lungs. He needed air. He needed space. There was no choice. He would create a new exit.

Smith had boarded the train in black slacks and a tucked-in polo shirt, an ensemble inspired by his recent reading of a book called "Dress for Success." He had a new job as a recruiter for a financial planning firm and was en route to distribute company fliers at the zoo. He had wanted to look good. But now a shirt was just a shirt, and he pulled off the polo and wrapped it around the tattoo of the word "blessed" on his right forearm. He stepped up to the rear door of the car, cocked back his arm and swung.

Other passengers worried that Smith would break his arm before he would be able to break the window. Maybe, Smith thought, but so what? Maybe Car 1079 would catch fire and explode. Maybe another train, barreling obliviously down the tracks, would add another nightmare to this pileup. He would not wait to find out. His knuckles ached. Another passenger pointed out a fire extinguisher near his feet. He picked it up and hammered it against the glass.

Again.

Again.

A small crack appeared. The passengers saw it and cheered. Smith continued to swing. The crack spread across the window like a spider web. Burgess, the architect, ducked behind a barrier in case the fire extinguisher exploded from the force of the blows. He guessed that the window was probably made from tempered glass and covered by film coating, built to withstand collisions at up to 59 mph. But as Smith swung, Burgess started to yell like he was watching a football game. "Yeah, you've got it. You've got it. Keep going. You're the man!"

Finally, the crack reached the upper right corner of the window, and the glass popped out. Smith scooped up his girlfriend and lifted her through the open frame. The panic-stricken seventeen-year-old followed. Then the dentist, limping gingerly on a broken foot. And then Smith himself, bloody and shirtless, with a gash in his head that would take six staples to close. They were out. They were free.

Some of them.

"Help me!" the young woman in the pile cried.

Baker, the doctor, slumped against a wall near the rear of the car, feeling helpless. He had tried to dig through the pile of debris toward the woman, but he worried that one wrong shift in the pile would only make things worse.

Bottoms, meanwhile, knelt on top of the pile, looking through it, trying to spot the stranger underneath.

"Please don't go," she said.

"I'm staying," he said.

The chaplain leaned over, his face inches from the top of the debris, and spoke into the darkness. He said the first thing that came to his mind.

"We can pray," he said.

"Okay," she said.

Bottoms spoke the Lord's Prayer. He had recited it thousands of times, but its six simple sentences still resonated within him. "Our father, who art in heaven, hallowed be thy name," he said. "Thy Kingdom come, thy will be done, on earth as it is in heaven."

There was familiarity and comfort in those opening lines. Only an hour earlier, Bottoms had visited and prayed with about a dozen injured patients at Walter Reed, a part of his daily routine. He believed that prayer fortified the injured and pacified the dying. During a year in Iraq, he had watched over a three-bed medical clinic that sometimes overflowed with thirty patients, and those experiences returned to him in the train car: dying soldiers to whom he had administered last rites; a badly burned Iraqi man who died on the street in Bottoms's lap.

Bottoms was an Army brat from birth, trained for trauma. In Car 1079, his voice remained steady and calm.

The young woman's voice pitched and trembled. She had graduated from Largo High School in 2003, tried a few years of college in Ohio and then returned home to attend beauty school. Her mother did hair, so she decided to do hair. Fashionable and girlish, she had compiled so many outfits that she kept one closet filled with unworn garments that still bore their tags.

"Please," she said now. "I'm dying."

"You're not alone," Bottoms said. "What's your name?"

"LaVonda," she said.

"LaVonda," he said. He wanted to write it down. Another passenger handed him paper and a pen.

"Can you spell it?" he asked.

"L-a-v-o-n-d-a," she said.

"Okay. Great. And what's your last name?"

She moaned, so Bottoms repeated his question. On the second try, LaVonda King tried to spell out her last name, but her reply was sporadic, and her voice was quieter. Bottoms wrote down K-L-I-N-G on his piece of paper, adding an extra letter. "Okay," he said. "Good."

From his perch against the wall and on top of a pile of rubble, Bottoms looked out the window and spotted a police officer standing across the train tracks. Bottoms banged hard against the glass, quick jabs with the side of his fist, but the police officer walked in the opposite direction. Bottoms banged one final time in frustration. Why couldn't the officer hear him? LaVonda King was only moaning now.

"Hold on, LaVonda," Bottoms said.

He had been told once in Iraq that hearing was the last of the senses to fail before death, and he remembered that now. Maybe, somewhere beneath the chairs, carpeting and glass, LaVonda was still listening. Maybe she could hear him, even now.

"LaVonda, are you bleeding?"

No reply.

"Keep talking to me, LaVonda."

No reply.

"LaVonda."

Nothing.

Bottoms looked behind him at what remained of Car 1079. Baker was comforting the fifteen-year-old boy with a trapped leg while the young architect looked on. Everyone else had exited. Bottoms looked back down into the pile.

"LaVonda," he said. "I'm still right here."

The first rescuer entered Car 1079 at 5:20 p.m., climbing in through the makeshift window Daryl Smith had created. Lt. Tony Carroll approached the pile of debris and immediately evaluated the scene: a lifeless body with blood pooling near the head on the roof of the other train; two women visible in the wreckage beneath him, and other victims surely hidden underfoot.

"Okay," he called to the three firefighters rushing in behind him. "Let's get to it."

The rescuers moved quickly, casting away seats, wielding hacksaws and cutting away twisted pieces of metal. They started to free the fifteen-year-old boy, and Baker left his side and climbed out the exit. Only then did he think about how unfortunate he was to have made this train, and how fortunate he was to have moved from a seat in the front to the back.

A fireman sifted through a special Metro rescue bag, carried on every fire truck, which contained keys to unlock doors and specialized prying tools. One team of firefighters began working from the right side of the pile, another from the left. After ten minutes, they cleared enough debris to reveal LaVonda King, dressed in designer jeans and a blouse, lying motionless against a pair of seats.

You don't look at the faces, Carroll had warned his men.

Bottoms looked.

LaVonda King was slight and pretty, with her hair done up nicely in a bun, still styled from an evening of celebrating with friends at Wild Wings on Friday night. She had gone there after picking up the keys to LaVonda's House of Beauty and danced late into the night. This was more than a new business, she had told friends. This was the career that would earn her money to make a trip to Atlantic City, to buy a car, to rent an apartment for her two young sons, ages two and three. This was her beginning.

Bottoms knew he needed to leave, but he had to do one last thing. He reached toward LaVonda and touched his fingers to her arm. He thought he detected a pulse, but he was in the way of the firefighters now. They had twelve hours of digging ahead, a long night that would uncover a total of seven bodies under the pile. Those would be the hours in which Bottoms, Baker and the others would finally come to understand that they had crashed into another Metro train, that their car had climbed onto the back of that train as it disintegrated, that it was miraculous they had survived.

At that moment, though, what Bottoms knew was the firefighters needed him to clear out. He picked up his backpack and iPod and followed the architect through the window, and that was how the last living passenger exited Car 1079.

(*Washington Post* staff writers William Wan, Theola Labbé-DeBose, James Hohmann, Josh White and Allison Klein contributed to this report.)

AUTHOR'S AFTERWORDS...

As is often the case with newspaper narratives, the biggest challenge in putting together this piece was time. The crash happened on a Monday night, and my editors assigned me this story early Tuesday afternoon. They asked for a narrative reconstruction of the crash, and they wanted it to lead the following Sunday's paper. The *Washington Post* has a tradition of writing these types of reconstructions after big news events, and they are usually put together by people with more talent and experience than me. David Maraniss won a Pulitzer Prize for one a few days after the Virginia Tech shootings; he was also a finalist for a reconstruction of the terrorist attacks on September 11, 2001. You should read them both. I did several times while I wrestled with this story about the Metro crash. Those Maraniss pieces both inspired and scared the hell out of me.

I figured out quickly Tuesday afternoon that the key to pulling off a good narrative in the next four days was to minimize the target. The Metro crash involved two trains, hundreds of passengers and thirty years of governmental neglect in safety and maintenance. Trying to reconstruct all of that was too big. It didn't seem like a manageable reporting target in the time I had. More important, it did not seem suited to a streamlined, contained narrative story. I wanted to help readers understand what it felt like and sounded like on that train. I wanted to put them there. I decided to make the story about the people and circumstances contained within one car of that train, the one that suffered the most damage.

It was an obvious choice. Much less clear was what to do from there. Unlike planes where people have tickets and assigned seats, people move freely around the Metro. We had no idea who was in our car. Neither did the crash investigators. My first day and a half of reporting involved interviewing dozens of crash survivors simply to find out where they sat. I carried around printouts of the inside of a Metro car, and survivors sketched their location for me. These printouts eventually turned into a graphic for the story.

Once we knew who was inside the car, the real reporting began. I interviewed everyone in person. That is always best, because it is easier to push for specifics and details. I had beers with the pastor, walked around Walter Reed with the doctor and spent time at LaVonda King's house with her relatives. It took a few days and a dozen interviews before I pieced together that the doctor and the pastor had been trying to save LaVonda King. Once I realized that, it became clear that their exchanges would be the main narrative of the piece—the tension that drove it forward. They became my main characters. I spent the most time getting to know them—the details of their lives and their exchanges on the train. Details are always the key to narratives. They are what make the characters and the circumstances feel real. So I also searched out every bit of information about their Metro ride that I could find: the daily schedule, the riding time from Takoma to Fort Totten, and more.

Writing the piece involved one very long day. I eat cereal when I write—lots of cereal—and on that day the bowls piled up all over the house. It probably took me twelve hours of writing to put together a draft. I am a pretty methodical writer; I want to be happy with one sentence before I move onto the next. I don't usually outline too much. I knew where I wanted the story to begin and where I wanted it to end. I also had a broad idea for each section, and I knew what character would be introduced when. That is usually enough to get me started.

I spent another five or six hours refining bits of the story with my editor, David Finkel. He helped me think more about pacing: fast, simple sentences in spots where we wanted the action to move, and slower, more complex sentences to give the reader a breath.

The story ran in Sunday's paper. One of the highlights came the next day, when I got an email from Maraniss. "You pulled it off," he wrote.

Wright Thompson

W right Thompson is a senior writer for ESPN.com and *ESPN The Magazine*. He started his sports writing career while a student at the University of Missouri, covering sports and writing a column for the *Columbia Missourian*. Between his junior and senior years, he interned at the *Times-Picayune* in New Orleans and then covered sports as a beat writer for the paper. He moved to the *Kansas City Star*, where he covered a wide variety of sports events including Super Bowls, Final Fours, The Masters and The Kentucky Derby. He assumed full-time writing duties at ESPN.com in 2006. His work has been anthologized in seven editions of *The Best American Sports Writing*. He lives in Oxford, MS.

The Last Days of Tony Harris

Friday, Nov. 2, 2007, Brasilia, Brazil

The city outside the window of Room 1507 at the Carlton Hotel is a most unlikely place to go insane. Designed as living modern art, Brasilia is defined by its order. But Tony Harris doesn't see order. He sees danger. He knows how this must sound, to the locals he's confiding in, to the friends and family he's emailing and calling back in Seattle. He knows he sounds out of his mind. But something is after him. A familiar idea is forming deep in his subconscious: *Run.*

While the city outside is light, the hallway is darker than the bottom of a river. The halogens only come alive when a motion sensor detects life. The room itself is worn, a step or two down from the place he stayed the last time he played basketball here, more than two years ago. But then again, at thirty-six, he's worn, too, so worn he'd never planned on playing again. There are two narrow beds and tan bedspreads and brown carpet. The bedside table is cracked, the original wood grain visible beneath the varnish. A single page in the thick phonebook is creased: the page for funeral homes.

Wireless Internet is his best friend, the connection making him feel safe. He needs it. The emails coming to the United States from Tony Harris are scary. Just the other day, he wrote his mother-in-law: *I know that I can be paranoid at times but I know when I hear things. And when people stop talking when I come into the area, I just pray that I am wrong Connie I want to see my family again and I LOVE MY WIFE SO MUCH I WANT TO SEE OUR CHILD THAT LORI AND I ARE HAVING. I DIDN'T COME BACK HERE FOR THEM TO SET ME UP AND KILL ME.*

The phone next to the bed is his other lifeline. Dial 8-2 for a wakeup call. Dial 2 for room service, like he did yesterday, to have a little piece of home sent up: a steak and a Coca-Cola. Dial 0 for an outside line. Zero takes him home. Yesterday, he talked with his wife, Lori. He told her of the closing darkness, of the whispers in the locker room: *He had slept with someone's wife the last time he played here, or that he'd fled because he had AIDS.* That's why he brought proof of his negative AIDS test—to show the players and stop the whispers.

They didn't seem interested. He didn't understand. So last night, on the phone with Lori, confused and scared, he began settling his accounts. *Tell my mama I love her. Tell my son I love him and to finish school and make something of himself and that I'm proud of him.*

"You're scaring me," she said.

"I need to tell you this in case something happens to me," he said.

Last night, he thought he was dead for sure. This morning, a plan begins to form. He asks Brent Merritt, a friend from Seattle who played here, to call the team. He follows up with an email, asking Brent to call back if he doesn't hear from him. Ask to speak to me, he instructs. But then a thought enters his head: What if the team has someone pretend to be him? What would Brent do? He needs a test. Yes, a test. That's it. So he gives Brent a password of sorts. Ask the person claiming to be me what the name of my dog is. If he doesn't say Enya, then it ain't me.

Then he goes to play for his new team, Universo. Once, not that long ago, Tony was one of the best players in the Brazilian league. Tonight, he doesn't take a single shot. When the game is finally over, he rushes back to his hotel room, away from the tailing cars and lobby whispers.

The sun has gone down. If he could see this from above, like a god or an omniscient narrator, he'd see this city as an island of lights in a vast darkness. Out the window to the left is the famous television tower, the highest man-made point in Brazil, a raised fist of those who came out here into the bush five decades ago to hack out civilization. To the right, over the top of the Hotel Das Americas, is a highway climbing out toward a tiny village named Bezerra, toward the wilderness. He'll go in both directions before his running is finished.

He sends an email to his wife:.

To: Lori J Harris

From: T bone

Date: 11/02/2007

I am home now. I just feel like crying all night. Babe I am really paranoid I still think that they are going to try and do me harm. Why do I feel this way I am not sure. Forgive me please babe I am sorry. Tell me why when I got home into my apartment the TV was way up loud and when I left it was really low and the maids cleaned my room earlier.

Soon, Tony Harris falls asleep. It will be the last night of his old life.

Real Danger or Paranoia?

Our man in Brasilia orders a *caipirinha*. Gauchos around him carry skewers of meat. He wears a green shirt, and his head is crowned with a full crop of hair. His name is Simon Henshaw, a diplomat's name. His title is consul general, a diplomat's title. He has been around the world, to the banana republics of Latin America, the Pacific and Africa. He is a man who has heard truth and lies, who has seen light and dark, and learned there is but a thin line separating the two. He lives in the city but understands the wilderness. It surrounds him. A half-hour out of town in any direction, he says, there is desolation. For the past month, he has been investigating the strange case of Tony Harris: Seattle basketball prep star to Washington State Cougar to international professional to ... gone. He, too, wants to know what happened *out there*. It's so hard to make sense of it all.

He wants to know what you will be writing. Well, you tell him, there's a lot of Joseph Conrad in this tale. A man travels down his own personal Congo, a descent, until the jungle consumes him at journey's end. He learns there is danger and evil in the world and is unable to escape its fated pull.

Henshaw mulls this over. "Who's Kurtz?" he asks.

The darkness chasing Tony Harris, is it out in the world? Or is it inside of his mind?

Saturday, November 3, Fleeing Brasilia

Another game ends. Tony shows a flicker of the man who led the Cougars to the NCAA Tournament in 1994, helping to jump-start Kelvin Sampson's coaching career. He scores eight points and doesn't dribble the ball off his foot, as he did a few days ago. But the panic that started in his mind has now reached his legs: *Run! Run! Run!* It flashes on and off in his head like a neon sign.

He nervously changes into a gray track suit, ties his blue-and-white, size-thirteen Nikes and asks a teammate he trusts, Estevam Ferreira, to give him a ride to the Carlton. Estevam says sure, and they climb into his Renault. Back at the Carlton, Tony invites his friend upstairs. On the fifteenth floor, Tony begins packing. This isn't the first time he has done this.

"Tony, what's happening?" Estevam asks.

"I miss my wife" is all Tony has by way of explanation. "I want to get away from here."

Tony is in a hurry but not rushing. Methodically, as if following a well-practiced escape plan, he takes about fifteen minutes to get a backpack ready: laptop, a change of clothes, a few other essentials. The rest of his belongings he leaves behind. Tony and Estevam walk into the hall, the movement clicking on the light, down the elevator, toward the bar, left past the front desk. When Tony steps out of the hotel, there is no turning back.

The airport sits about ten miles south of the main urban corridor, on the road winding down toward the lake, past the zoo. Tony begins to lose control.

He has fought so hard for the past four days, trying to talk these feelings away or stuff them deep down inside and get through just one more season. But he can fight no longer. Now he must *run!* There is a cost for crossing the thin line between imaginary and real, between light and dark.

"I'm afraid," he sobs.

"What are you afraid of?" Estevam asks.

"There is someone trying to get me."

"Who?"

Tony doesn't answer. He weeps. He is silent. He weeps again. An elaborate drama is playing out in his head, behind a thick stage curtain, the tears muffled noises that let his audience of one know something is happening, something powerful and awful, even if Estevam cannot catch a glimpse of the action.

Finally, they arrive at the airport. Tony asks Estevam to wait, then goes inside alone. Only he does not buy a plane ticket home. Who knows why? Instead, he purchases a ticket to Natal, a beach town in the northeast of Brazil. He is planning to fly there, where his friend Erika lives, then figure out what to do next. Erika worked at the hotel where he stayed when he played here before. At security, though, he hits a wall: He doesn't have his passport. The team has it. With a game each day and the need to provide documents for each player before each game, it's easier if the team keeps them. It's standard practice, but Tony's sure the team is in on this plot to kill him. Can't ask the team. Now he doesn't know what to do.

Estevam, sitting in his car, watches his friend coming out of the airport. Tony looks scared. His plan has fallen apart. Without structure, the night becomes even more frightening.

"So tell me what you wanna do now," Estevam says.

"I don't know," Tony says. "Please help me."

To Estevam, who is also nervous now, this feels like a spy movie. He has known Tony for years, and if someone is trying to kill Tony, might they also try to kill him? He thinks. Thinks. Thinks. He and Tony call Lori, and a new plan is hatched. The bus station. Goiania is a city close to Brasilia. Buses leave every hour. Tony likes this. He has a friend in Goiania, an ex-girlfriend, Daniela. They drive back toward Brasilia, to the bus station, a half-hour trip.

Estevam still doesn't understand. "Let's go to the police," he says.

Tony says no. No cops. No U.S. Embassy. Only escape.

The bus station finally appears in front of them, and the two men go inside. Tony purchases a ticket, and Estevam walks him to the correct bus. Something is coming to an end. Both men sense it. Tony hugs his teammate and says, "You live in my heart."

Estevam searches for the words. "Go with God," he says.

The tears are gone, replaced by a lost look in Tony's eyes. What is going on behind those eyes? What do they see? Estevam searches his friend's face for clues, for some sort of road map of the journey to come. He sees sadness but also relief. Tony climbs the bus steps and finds his seat. The bus pulls away. Before it leaves the comforting glow of the station, Estevam sees Tony sitting by the window. The men lock eyes a final time. Tony gives him a thumbs up. In the last breath of the vanishing light, he takes his right hand and beats on his chest.

You live in my heart.

What Changes When a Man Has Seen the Evil of the World?

In Seattle, as word spreads of Tony's disappearance, his friends and family try to make sense of it. They know Tony is running. Some know Tony has a history of paranoid behavior. Some know it isn't the first time he has been scared.

The first time, eight years ago, he was in South Korea playing basketball. He was out with a teammate, Derrick Johnson, and two girls in the VIP section of a Seoul club. A group of Korean men, speaking Russian, attacked the woman with Tony, striking her in the face with a bottle. Later, after she had jumped in their cab to escape, a van chased them down, cut them off on a bridge and the woman was yanked from the car by the same men. Johnson laughed it off. Tony didn't. He started seeing danger in every shadow. He stopped going out. Something inside of him changed. "From there I saw the paranoia," Johnson says. "Tony made it through the rest of the season. It was toward the end of the season. The paranoia didn't happen to the point where he left." Tony eventually got home and everything was fine. He'd left the fear in Korea.

The second time was three years ago, in Brazil. That time, he could not control it. He'd been there for five seasons, a popular star, leading his team to titles. Kids rushed to him after games for hugs and autographs. Girls waited at every exit of the gym. Everybody loved Tony Harris. But on Feb. 11, 2005, soon after returning to the country after being in America for a few months, he said he had food poisoning and refused to play or go to the hospital or even leave the locker room until the game was over. Bad shrimp, he said. The next day, at 6 a.m., he called the team's general manager and asked for a ride to the airport. He had to get home immediately. Tony paid for his own ticket.

This time, different people got different stories. Tony told the team his son from a prior relationship had been in a horrific car accident. He described the accident, and the hospital procedures, in great detail, and would continue the elaborate lie when he returned in 2007. The general manager was very worried about his friend, not knowing there had been no car accident. Tony told two basketball friends he just didn't have it anymore. But the story he told his pastor was more frightening: After a dispute with the team over money, some men took him way out into the wilderness and left him, wanting to send a message. Message received. Only this time, he brought the fear home with him. "When Tony came back from Brazil last time, something was not right with him," family friend Glynis Harps says. "Something heavy was on his mind, and he was preoccupied. I don't know what happened. Tony was scared."

He believed people were following him. Once, he yelled "duck" to a friend. There was no one there. Once, he saw a man he'd fought with as a preteen walk into a gym. He ran from the gym, leaving his gear behind, explaining later that the guy was going to hurt him. A friend says the long-lost "enemy" never knew Tony was in the gym. He stopped going to gyms entirely, giving up basketball for the first time in his life.

What did all this mean? It didn't answer Henshaw's question. It just changed it slightly. Had he seen too much to look at the world as a civilized place again? Or was he beginning to lose his mind?

Sunday, November 4, Goiania to Bezerra

Tony Harris stands outside the green gate, next door to the motorcycle repair shop, waiting on a cab driver to let him in. Where is this guy? There he is. Jose Lindomar Jesus, called Baiano by his friends, steps into the light, eyeing the tall man before him. He's carrying a backpack and seems scared, looking around as if he's expecting someone. It's Sunday morning, and there is no one else on the street.

Baiano shows Tony a place against the turquoise walls of the house where he can sit. Baiano goes into the house. Tony slumps down. It had been a long night. He arrived at the bus station in Goiania at around 2 a.m. He called Erika and tried to get Daniela's number; they were all friends in Uberlandia. Erika didn't have it. The plan was not working. He asked how to get to Natal from Goiania. She told him to take a bus. No, he explained, that bus went through Brasilia, and he could not have that. Finally, they came up with a solution—a cab to Salvador, where he'd get a friend of Erika's to meet him and accompany him to Natal. OK. Good. Tony walked a few blocks to find a cab parked in front of a local hospital. That guy wouldn't do it, but he thought his friend might. Now it is 8:30 a.m., and Tony is here.

Soon, Baiano comes outside, dressed and cleaned up. Sliding across the black leather seats, Tony gets into the front of the white Chevy cab. Baiano takes a right out of his driveway, past the motorcycle repair shop, winds through the gears as they climb the hill toward the center of town. Tony wants to go to the Bank of Brazil, which accepts American ATM cards. The machine is in the far back right corner, and Tony slides his card, enters his PIN and ... is declined. The cab driver tries to read the screen over his shoulder. Tony is at his daily withdrawal limit. He'd taken out money already at the bus station. What to do? Harris gives the cab driver about $340, most of the money he has on him, and promises to pay the remaining $1,100 in Salvador. This means altering the plan yet again. Tony finds an Internet café, a dark, narrow shotgun building with low ceilings and green walls, buys a half-hour of Web time and a phone card, sits down at Terminal 3, a stark white cubicle, and sends an email. Back home in Seattle, Lori's computer is set to ding when she gets mail. It's before dawn in Seattle, which doesn't matter to Tony.

He sends the first email at 9:34 a.m. Ding! *Babe what are you doing this it tony i need to talk to you cause i have to put some money in some ones account so that i can get to erikas city please respond*

Less than a minute later, he writes again, virtually the same message. Ding! This time, Lori hears and answers. Tony gives her Baiano's cell-phone number and license number, tells her the plan and then logs off. Soon, Baiano's phone rings. It's Lori. She and Tony talk. It's a short call, just a few details. This is the last time they will ever hear each other's voices.

"Love you," Tony says.

"Love you, too," Lori says.

The errands finished, Tony and Baiano leave Goiania. Tony chain smokes, getting through three cigarettes until the rain comes and Baiano rolls up the window. After an hour and a half, they cross the border between Goias State and the Federal District. A big sign above the road marks the boundary. It also reads: BRASILIA 54 KM.

Without a word, Tony dives over the passenger seat, legs in the air, clawing for the back seat until he's lying down, curled up, and all that's visible from the window is the rainy-season sky overhead, clouds so big and nasty they seem to swallow you whole. When it's clear, the sky above Brazil looks like the front porch of heaven, all impossible blues and pillowy clouds. But when rainy season comes, and the storms roll in, the sky seems angry.

Baiano asks Tony what he's doing.

"I have a headache," Tony says.

They drive through Brasilia, past the television tower and the Carlton Hotel. Tony cowers, out of sight. Finally, outside the city, Tony is coaxed back up front and the journey continues toward Salvador, until about 2 p.m., when Baiano gets hungry.

A town appears on the horizon, a badlands outpost named Bezerra. The car rolls past a barren savanna, the road lined with concrete poles and barbed wire protecting a military artillery range. There is an opening in the wire just before the village, near a small shantytown hugging the road. The centerpiece of Bezerra is a Texaco station, with a little diner attached called Sabor Gaucho. Long-haul truckers fill the sprawling parking lot, fueling up on the run to the coast. Baiano parks. Tony refuses to go inside for lunch, so he waits in the car. After lunch, they pull up to the pump a few yards away. Tony hands Baiano his debit card and agrees to wait some more.

Something changes his mind. Tony gets out of the car, leaving his backpack inside the cab. He walks into the small convenience store, which is in between the diner and the office where you pay for gas. A young man named Warley Dyone is behind the register. Everything seems normal. Tony asks the price of a bottle of orange juice and a small package of cookies. Warley tells him.

Out of nowhere, a troubled expression crosses Tony's face. Is there some debate inside his head that's about to be settled?

"Where's the taxi driver?" he asks.

"He's in the office paying for the gas," Warley says.

Tony does not reply. Is the neon sign in his head flashing again? RUN! RUN! RUN! He wheels around, out the glass doors, past the pumps, running, making a hard left at the highway, past the restaurant next door, out of sight. Warley chases after him. So does Baiano, who was going to ask for the PIN. Without it, the charge will be declined, later showing up on Tony's credit card statement as a failed attempt.

When Warley and Baiano reach the street, they see nothing. Tony has left behind a past, a future, a city of fans, a fourteen-year-old son, a pregnant wife, a change of clothes, a backpack and the laptop computer that has kept him tethered these past few days.

He has disappeared into the woods.

Why Did He Return to Brazil?

Two weeks after the shocking details finally became public, Estevam Ferreira walks off the basketball court following a Universo practice. He knows how afraid Tony had been the last time he was here. Like everyone else, he has a question: "Why did he come back?"

You tell him the story. Life was hard for Tony after Brazil. He tried to do the right thing—whatever scared him also made him grow up. He married Lori, joined a church, volunteered at a local homeless shelter. For a while, he worked with children at a juvenile detention center named Echo Glen. His past followed him, though. When his job was about to become full-time, a background check found a report about child abuse. Years before, a teacher found Tony had spanked his son, leaving a mark, just before dropping him off for school. Never mind that the report absolved Tony of abuse. Almost two years to the day since he had left Brazil, he lost his job. That was nine months ago. Then Lori got pregnant, and he felt emasculated by his inability to support his family. Tony tried, applying for work at more than fifty places. But without a bachelor's degree, his fleeting fame did him no good. No one seemed to remember, or care, that he'd taken Washington State to the NCAA Tournament. He withdrew into himself, fighting with Lori, even briefly moving out. But he kept trying, moving back in the house, taking correspondence courses, applying for more jobs, even one at a grocery store, anything to feed his family. Then the phone rang. It was his old general manager from Brazil, desperately in need of a replacement player for an upcoming tournament. Tony was desperate, too. For his family, he would try to keep it together.

You look Estevam in the eyes. "He needed the money," you say.

This lays Estevam low. He turns away, crosses his arms, sighs, cannot speak. He thinks of his friend, a man terrified of this place but willing to risk it all to provide for his wife and child. The courage that must have taken. He thinks about his friend and when the words don't come, he touches his chest with his fist.

You live in my heart.

November 4-7, Bezerra

Tony Harris is hiding. What must he be thinking, crouching in the woods, counting the minutes and hours until it's safe to come out? Baiano drives up and down the street for a while, but after an hour and a half heads home, with Tony's backpack in his car. Some time Sunday evening, Tony comes out of the wilderness. He begs for food. Migrant workers and hobos frequent this road, stopping for work when they can find it, so people don't think this is strange.

No one sees Tony on Monday. There are no reports of him walking the road. But Monday afternoon, about 4:30, he finds a phone, according to team trainer Mario Saraiva. He dials a familiar number: Mario's. He was once a friend, but is now someone who Tony thinks might be part of the plot to kill him.

Tony says hello.

"Where are you?" Mario says. "I'm gonna pick you up."

Tony must make a decision. There is a struggle inside of him, these competing urges. Is Mario a friend? Is he an enemy? Tony shakes off the doubt. The sign is telling him to Run!

"No," Tony says. "I won't tell you. You'll tell the others, and they'll come to kill me."

Tony hangs up. He disappears again, and no one sees him Monday or Tuesday. Police will later assume he was hiding in the bush, burning up during the day, freezing at night. The U.S. Embassy will say it had no more confirmed sightings, but the Brazilian police, along with a resident in the town, say he made one more walk into the light.

On Wednesday morning, according to police records, a man looking like Tony knocked on a woman's door, begging for coffee and bread. On Wednesday afternoon, a few wandering hobos talked to him briefly. He was covered in dirt and grime and asked them for a clean shirt. They would say later they gave him one, but it was never found.

That night, around 7 o'clock, Harris stumbled toward the gas station, where this all began, past the pumps, back through the glass doors. Maria Paula Gonçalves, wearing her red uniform, stood behind the counter. The man was nervous, she would say later, barely looking at her, looking over his shoulders instead. He asked for a pack of Derby cigarettes and paid in the Brazilian equivalent of dimes.

Three and a half hours later, he returned. Maria had finished giving her husband his nightly medicine and making a plate of leftovers for a beggar when Tony appeared in the diner. For a moment, she thought he was the same person she just fed.

"I'm hungry," he said.

"I already gave you food," she said.

Then she looked down. The other man wore flip-flops. This man was wearing gigantic basketball shoes. It was the same guy who bought cigarettes. A few days later, after seeing his picture on television, she would say it was Tony Harris. Right now, he was just a man who needed food. She fixed him a plate, some leftover meat, rice and beans, wrapped it up to go. This time he was calm, not looking over his shoulder. He took the food and headed back out into the night. It's about four miles to where he would complete this final walk. Maybe he went down the highway a quarter of a mile, left through the gap in the barbed wire near the mini shantytown. Poor people often fish at a lake through there, which is why the fence was down. Was that where he went? No one knows for sure.

No known person would ever again see Tony Harris alive.

What Really Happened Out There?

Pedromar Augusto de Souza is the chief of police in the nearest city. The Formosa station house has six bullet holes in the door; police work is serious business here in Brazil, where cops and gangsters have running gun battles.

Eye for an eye, tooth for a tooth, and, as if to prove it, Pedromar pulls a big hog-leg .45 automatic from his waistband, ejects the magazine from the butt, jacks the chambered round, which bounces three times and settles. He hands over the shiny gun for inspection. The bullet? A hollow point. Goes in little, comes out big.

He has been working hard investigating the bizarre death of Tony Lee Harris, American citizen. It's the only case assigned directly to him. From afar, he has heard the conspiracy theories from the folks back in the States: that Universo lured Tony down to Brazil to kill him; that the police are covering up a crime, or worse; or even that the Brazilian Army killed him. Most of the theories are rooted in misinformation: Some media reports in Seattle included errors, which aroused suspicion; the cremation of the body was viewed as suspicious, though family members back home didn't know there was really nothing left but skin, bones and worms. He knows people think he's not being thorough. "It would be easy to say it's a suicide and close the case," he says. "I want to make really sure it was not homicide. To be one hundred percent sure."

There are a few questions left. The decomposition of the body prohibited an accurate toxicology report. The cause of death is still officially undetermined, and lab officials cannot say with complete certainty that it was a death by hanging. They are virtually certain, but the state of the corpse has hindered the detective work. And there are other stray facts: Two cigarette butts were found near the body. Lab technicians are working to determine whether these were smoked by Tony, though no lighter was found near his body. Tony's wedding ring was missing. His wallet was missing. His sweatpants were missing. There was likely money missing, though how much is unknown.

And then there's the biggest mystery of all: the curious extra shoelace.

De Souza needs answers before closing the case. Right now, there is a sliver of doubt. A heartbreaking possibility exists: Could Tony Harris have been losing his mind, running from people who were not chasing him, only to end up surrounded by actual danger? "The most likely is suicide," de Souza says. "But some people walking around the street asking for money, maybe they saw him and thought this guy has money and they killed him. That's another question."

Will it ever be possible to conclusively prove what happened?

De Souza considers the question. The body had no bullet holes or stab wounds, no broken bones or tissue under the fingernails. But the rain and the wilderness erased any other forensic clues.

"No," he says.

The Final Days, Outside Bezerra

The walk to the monkey pepper tree is long and difficult, no matter the route. Tony Harris leaves the gas station, and disappears into the *Cerrado*, a sprawling Brazilian savanna that surrounds the town. *Cerrado* means "inaccessible" in Portuguese.

The land is frightening and foreign, quilts of open field dotted with termite mounds and tall, tropical trees. There are long runs of covered forest. The greens are psychedelic. Jaguars roam the forests and grasslands, their roar like a loud cough. Water flows, maybe a stream, maybe runoff from a recent shower. Large birds circle the tops of the trees, their shrieks breaking the peaceful gurgle of the water. Songbirds sing a sweet melody in the background. During the day, the sun bakes down, steaming all living things with alternating flurries of sun, rain, then more sun. At night, the chill comes and with it a darkness unlike anything a man from a civilized world has ever seen. At night, it's like God himself forgot the *Cerrado*.

How long was Tony lost out here? A day? Two? Three? The soldiers say you could live for a month, if you knew what you were doing. The place is covered with edible fruit and fresh water. No one knows where Tony Harris walked, or what he thought or felt as he wove deeper and deeper into the maze-like wilderness. Was he scared? Did something finally turn off that neon sign in his mind? Did he stop running? Did someone stop him from running? Somehow he ended up at the monkey pepper tree. It's clearly visible, atop the crown of a small mound, in a clearing, a few smaller trees setting a perimeter. Though there is deeper forest around it, from the tree, a man can look up and see heaven.

No one knows exactly what happened to Tony Harris in his last minutes, but they do know where he was found. Police estimate he died on or about Friday, November 9. An anonymous call came in on Sunday, November 18, his birthday. About twenty feet from the monkey pepper tree is a fishing hole, though you can't see it without crawling through dense vegetation. A walking path to it, if you know where to dip into the forest, goes past the tree. Police believe the tipster is an illegal fisherman without permission to be on military property. That's yet another heartbreaking detail: Tony Harris loved to fish and some investigators believe he might have been out of his mind from dehydration. But if he had walked more or less straight here from town, he ended up only twenty yards shy of life-saving water and more fish than he could have eaten in a month.

Police and soldiers arrive on the scene. They smell it before they see it, a grotesque, barely human form, bleached white in spots and warped by the sun and rain, skin losing to gravity in big folds, those big basketball shoes just a foot off the ground. Bugs swarm and body fluids stain the trunk of the tree black. The corpse, no longer Tony Harris, hangs from a sturdy branch by a black shoelace. They notice that both of the shoelaces are in place. So he brought an extra shoelace with him from Brasilia, managed to keep it despite losing his computer, pants, wallet and ring? Could have happened.

The location of the pepper tree leads everyone who sees it to think suicide. This place seems too remote for anyone to have carried a body so far, and forensic evidence suggests Tony's life ended in this clearing, hanging from a monkey pepper tree, four miles from Bezerra, 6,000 miles from Seattle, totally and utterly alone.

It's the perfect tree. A short step up onto a low branch, an easy reach to tie the shoelace around a higher branch, then a quick step off. Death would have begun quickly, air cut off, the pressure on the spinal column beginning a domino effect, motor ability lessened or lost. Did his life flash before his eyes? Did he see a lost job and rejected applications? Did he see people chasing him and shadows and whispers? Or did he see other, happier things? Maybe a boy in Seattle pointing so many years ago and telling his mom: That's Tony Harris. He plays for Garfield. Maybe a bear hug with Kelvin Sampson after making it to the NCAA Tournament. Or did he see his fourteen-year-old son, who looks just like him, or his wife, or his mother, or his friends? Did he see his future?

No one knows. But the police do believe this: The very last act of Tony Harris on planet earth was to fight for his life. As he hung from that shoelace, his time now down to seconds, unable to use his arms and legs, he bit down on the tree, sinking his teeth into the trunk, as if to buy one inch of life-saving air. He failed, and he died there, hanging from the monkey pepper tree.

The day after cutting his body down, police found a hole burrowed deep into the bark of the tree. Laying on the ground below was a tooth, the last will and testament of a man struggling for light in a place consumed by darkness.

Epilogue

The two letters addressed to Tony Harris made it real. The first was from the state of Washington, absolving him of any further child support. There was a space for "reason" and one box had been checked: deceased. The next letter hurt even more. It was from a grocery store. Sorry, it began, we cannot extend you an offer. His application had been denied. Lori wept, for the man Tony wanted to be, and for the man she'd lost. "He was always well intentioned," she says. "He really had a heart of gold. It just broke my heart, because I could see the potential and the goodness in him, and nobody would give him a break."

She replays the last months. She's a mental health worker and yet she never saw signs of a serious problem. Sure, he was really down, refusing to talk about his pain, finding solace alone on a lake, fishing. But the contract in Brazil seemed to make him whole again. Why kill himself now, with a child on the way, with so much to live for? She doesn't believe it. It doesn't make sense. "Tony was a pretty boy," she says. "It's very hard to even imagine how awful his last days must have been in order for him to end up like that. All I have is the image of how he was found and his body was decomposed and that last phone conversation. It just makes it almost impossible to feel like you can move on. It's so hard."

On the day of the funeral, a butterfly lands at the foot of the monkey pepper tree, flapping its wings slowly, refusing to fly away. Soon, another joins it. A continent away, his family spreads Tony's ashes on the Green River in Washington, where he had so often found peace, the water slowly taking him away forever. At the service, they mourn the end of Tony Harris' life, and begin the rest of their own lives without him. His son, D'Nique, goes to a gymnasium. He's on the JV team, and his first high school game is that night. No way he's going to miss that. Basketball is his connection with his father.

In the locker room, D'Nique quietly asks if he can switch jerseys with a teammate for the game. He wants to take that court with No. 4 on his back, the number Tony wore during happier times, when he was a star in Brazil. D'Nique doesn't talk about that, though he also writes a "4" on his own sneakers. He will offer tribute to his father in the only way he knows how: with a game. He walks onto the court, already six foot three and growing, looking so much like his father, wearing his father's number. He can't miss that night from three-point range, and in the stands, next to his mom, sits a man who'd seen Tony play. The hairs on the back of the man's neck stand up. It is as if he has seen a ghost.

AUTHOR'S AFTERWORDS...

This story came together quickly. The news of Tony's disappearance broke, and I immediately got in touch with his family, who didn't believe the information they were getting from Brazil. Very early, I realized that his wife and the people close to him were extraordinarily open with me, and more than anything, they wanted someone down there looking for the truth. In a matter of days, the decision was made to make this happen: Go to Brazil. I remember the excitement. Fixers were located, drivers and translators found. We bought plane tickets, booked hotel rooms, figured out the best way to retrace the steps of Tony Harris. All my editors seemed to know we had something great out in front of us, and we focused mainly on logistics and process. That's what the final days before getting on a plane for something like this are often like. Everyone was giddy.

Everyone except for Jay Lovinger.

Jay is my editor, although that term doesn't begin to sum up his importance. We talk every day, about my writing, about other people's writing, about the other people he'd edited—from Gary Smith to Hunter S. Thompson—and what made them great. Sometimes, the stories feel like an accidental byproduct of the process. Jay's great talent lies in his lack of ego, and how his only goal is to help you shepherd the story you want to tell through all the stages of its growth. He's at his best when I call and just dump all my thoughts out in a rush, and then listen, and answer, as he helps me arrange them. We both have remarkably similar ideas about what makes a story interesting. There's a shorthand that has developed; he can tell me what is wrong with an idea, or a draft, and I know exactly what he means and what he wants. Now I anticipate his questions before I even start. Those are just a few reasons why I was confused over his reaction to Tony Harris.

He seemed lukewarm.

To be honest, I got kind of angry. At this point, I believed Harris had been killed, and I worried what would happen if I started asking questions down in Brazil. We were going to some shady places, and I was trying to marshal all my confidence and keep it at the level needed to do this right. I remember, distinctly, saying to him, "This isn't what I need from you right now."

What could be better, I asked? There's a guy who disappeared. We're gonna track his steps. Talk to people. Recreate it. It's straightforward. Simple. And he said, well, that's not interesting to me. Either he got murdered or he didn't. Then what? How is that about the larger human condition? I sort of sputtered. Then the real conversation started. What is this really about? What's happening on a deeper level? What are the forces battling each other? How is this universal? He asked lots of questions and as I answered them, a new idea formed: It's about someone hanging onto sanity, about civilization and the wilderness, about light to dark, city to jungle, sane to crazy. Jay and I talked some more and, on his suggestion, I took a copy of Joseph Conrad's *Heart of Darkness* on the plane with me.

That's what I read on the long flight south. The themes resonated with me: a man confronting something inside of himself that even he didn't understand, a window in the elemental framework behind the façade of civilization. It allowed me to see the Tony Harris story for what it was, and seize what it presented: a chance, in a tight, powerful, muscular arc to show something important about the world. That's what great nonfiction does, and when it sniffs the possibilities of something greater, even lasting. We get to address the big questions, to try and understand important ideas and conflicts.

My first night in Brazil, I sat with the U.S. consul general at a steakhouse, having a long dinner and rum drinks. We talked about all the facts at play here, about the long road into the jungle I'd retrace, and he also talked about going into the darkness.

"Who's Kurtz?" he asked.

That's one of the many questions that can never be answered, only explored. What was Tony Harris chasing? What was chasing him? More than I'd ever done before, I really thought about those larger human conditions Jay was always talking about. His advice not only helped me on this story, but it changed the way I approached all stories. Look at the facts and try to think deeply about them, to really see the connections. Don't superimpose psychobabble on things, but make sure you're engaged completely in the most important and often overlooked part of the writing process: thinking.

This was an important trip for me in my development as a writer. I evolved as a thinker. At night in the hotels, I outlined, setting up the right questions and moving with muscle and intent toward the answers, showing how the imagery and sentence structure would change along with the characters, progressing with the story. I saw the tight narrative arc, and I understood how and why this story could be structured—in terms of architecture and intent—as a short story, which should be the goal of all nonfiction. When the reporting ended—I had a late night flight back home—my translator and I had a few beers at a bar near his house, a Brazilian neighborhood place. Then I threw my bags in a cab and headed toward the airport, listening to the stereo in the cab—the moment is so vivid that I remember the song, Bon Jovi's one about making a memory—and I really felt like I'd turned a corner. There was a great story in the notebooks at my feet and I knew exactly what to do with it.

Seth Wickersham

S eth Wickersham is a senior writer at *ESPN The Magazine*, where he's written since graduating from the University of Missouri in 2000. He writes frequently for ESPN.com and contributes to Outside the Lines and E:60. Although he primarily covers the NFL—profiling the likes of Peyton and Eli Manning, Tom Brady, Bill Belichick, Eric Mangini, Albert Haynesworth, Tank Johnson, Michael Vick, and Deion Sanders—Wickersham has also written about gay rugby, the plight of a fired college basketball coach, suicidal Kenyan runners in Alaska, and NCAA compliance officers. He also suffered the laborious task of traveling to London to interview legendary Queen guitarist Brian May about "We Will Rock You," the most-played stadium anthem ever.

The Final Furlong

D eath is delivered pink. The lethal liquid that's injected into the jugular of broken-down racehorses is always colored. That way, a vet can find it quickly. That way, it can't be mistaken for any other drug. There's no time for fumbling when a 1,200-pound animal has suffered a catastrophic injury—a broken leg or a fractured ankle. There's no time for indecision when you're staring at a shattered jag of bone piercing the skin as if it were tinfoil. Today, a muggy New Year's Day in New Orleans, death sits in the backseat of a white Toyota Tundra parked by the grass track at Fair Grounds Race Course. Two pink bottles glow like flashlights inside a black leather medical bag. In one bottle is succinylcholine; in another, pentobarbital. The former is a paralytic, the latter a barbiturate. Thicker than syrup, each is dispensed through a three-inch, fourteen-gauge needle from a syringe as fat as a corn dog. Once injected, the barbiturate puts the horse into a deep sleep; then the paralytic attacks the cardiovascular system and the brain. The bigger the needle, the faster the transport, the quicker the death. On most days, these drugs stay in the backseat, unused. On most days.

On most days, Lauren Canady goes unnoticed. She spends a lot of her time behind the wheel of the white Tundra with the "track vet" sticker on its side, following the horses as they run. It's her job to aid them when they are injured and to euthanize them on the spot when necessary—and it was necessary sixteen times at Fair Grounds last season. Today's first race hasn't yet begun, so Canady leaves her truck idling near the starting line and walks under the grandstands toward the paddock. Wearing a blue windbreaker and khakis, the forty-two-year-old veterinarian blends in easily with the fans: race card in one hand, coffee and lit Marlboro in the other.

In the paddock, ten horses circle, models strutting on a runway, on display one last time for the gamblers to ogle before they place their bets. Shiny and sculpted, the thoroughbreds revel in the attention. They are born to compete, and they show it in how they flatten their ears when behind by a length or bite a challenger who gets too close or stretch their necks to win by a nose and then pose for the cameras afterward. At the moment, Canady is judging them for the final time too, searching for a limp or bob or any sign of injury. This is her second inspection of the day, the hands-off kind. Hours earlier, she administered a more rigorous exam, feeling legs and joints for signs of injury. Now she must catch anything she might have missed. She watches the animals closely as they're led out to the track, then climbs into her truck, giving each a final look as the grooms cram them, one by one, into the green starting gates ...

And they're off.

So is Canady, crouched in the driver's seat, hands at ten and two, seatbelt undone, the Tundra trailing the horses from the dirt as they run on the turf. Her blue eyes flip between the stampede and the road, the truck fishtailing as it accelerates. Next to her in the front seat is Waverly Parsons, the track chaplain, who, minutes earlier, administered a prayer for the owners, trainers, jockeys, grooms and horses. On the floor behind them is a blackmetal equine leg splint, big as a ski boot. On the backseat, the black medical bag.

Rounding the first corner, Canady is silent and tense, as she is during every one of the ten races she works each day. She can't usually drive faster than thirty miles-per-hour without tearing up the road, so most of the horses have far outpaced her. A quarter mile ahead, jockey Francisco Torres is saddled on Heelbolt, winner of his previous three races.

Suddenly, Torres feels a jolt and hears a pop, like a bat hitting a softball. He will later say Heelbolt "took a bad step"—jockeys always say the horse took a bad step. Heelbolt pulls up, hobbling as he slows from forty-miles-per-hour to a stop. A scared Torres leaps off, landing several yards away.

As Canady rounds the second corner in her truck, the radio attached to her belt, labeled Vet 1, screams, "A horse is down! A rider is down!" She hits the gas.

Every eye is on her.

They don't shoot horses anymore. They used to, back when horse racing mattered, back when it grabbed America like football does now, when a day at the track meant dressing for church, with men in suits and women in hats, back when it was more about horses and less about money—and less about us. In 1973, when Secretariat won the Triple Crown, about $4.5 billion was wagered annually on horse racing. That number has since grown to nearly $14 billion. And yet the sport flashes on and off our radar now, briefly catching our attention when a Funny Cide or Smarty Jones threatens to make history, or, more tragically, when death comes to the track—as it did for Eight Belles at last year's Kentucky Derby—and we're reminded that one of our country's oldest sports is one in which the athletes sometimes die during competition.

Left to do the killing are the track vets, the people who pride themselves on being the strongest advocates for the horses, the people who don't give a damn about the money. "We police the sport," Canady says. It's often a thankless job. The starting salary for a regulatory vet is about $55,000, with ten-hour days the norm. There is constant, unspoken pressure not to scratch horses from competition; some owners yell at trainers who ask vets to look for injuries. While Canady is warm to most owners, she is pals with few. "You have to be friendly," she says, "but not friends."

Euthanizing horses is a small part of the job—nationally, 1.5 out of every 1,000 must be put down because of injuries sustained on the track, according to the Association of Racing Commissioners International—but it's the worst part. Dean Richardson "cried for days" after euthanizing his most famous patient, Barbaro. David Fitzpatrick, chief vet for the Illinois Racing Board, tears up as he talks about horses he has put down. Celeste Kunz, the emergency vet at the Meadowlands in New Jersey, cried when Eight Belles suffered that fatal injury—and she was watching the Derby from home. "It felt like every horse I've ever lost died that day," Kunz says. After Canady put down a foal with terminal birth defects, she "didn't talk to anyone for days."

Death can be spooky. In 1993, Kunz was working at Jersey's Monmouth Park, where mist and fog blow off the Atlantic Ocean onto the beachside track. Visibility was awful, but competition rarely stopped. After one race, Kunz counted nine horses at the finish; ten had started. She took off on foot, walking the track with her medical tool kit, squinting through the mist until she saw a shadowy figure, already a ghost: It was a gray and white horse with a fractured ankle, waiting for someone to end his misery.

Death can be mystifying. In 2004, when Canady was working at Finger Lakes Race Track in upstate New York, she got word that a horse had been injured on a hot walker, a carousel that slowly leads the animals in circles to cool them down. When she arrived, the vet saw one of the horse's hind legs had snapped in half, but she couldn't figure out how. There were no other horses nearby, no holes in the ground, no rails that might have been kicked. "The leg just broke," Canady says with a sad shrug.

Death can be contagious. Earlier this year, seven horses had to be euthanized in two weeks at Santa Anita. Critics blamed the synthetic surface, which the California Horse Racing Board had mandated for all major tracks to improve safety. By and large, the new surface had worked, reducing deaths from catastrophic injuries statewide from 3.01 per 1,000 in 2007 to 2.29 last year. But all of a sudden horses were dropping at an alarming rate, the public was wondering why, and Santa Anita officials didn't have an answer. Then, as inexplicably as the breakdowns started, they stopped. Only two horses in the next sixty-eight days were euthanized.

More than anything, death can be hard to shake. Most veterinary schools don't teach students how to cope with it. The American Association of Equine Practitioners doesn't have a support line to call. Vets just suck it up and go, using medical necessity as a shield. Kunz has learned to hide her feelings in those hectic moments. Still, a "nervous, energetic fear" courses through her body as she injects a horse with that toxic solution. "The decision to euthanize is scary," she says. "You're really isolated on the track. There are no other vets with you. But you can't go to pieces because you have to be there for the horse."

That's why these vets picked this career—because they love horses enough to suffer for them, because they understand that death is sometimes better than life. They know that a broken bone is often a death sentence for an animal whose internal organs, including digestive and circulatory systems, are dependent on continued mobility. Casts and slings restrict movement and prevent those organs from functioning properly, leading to life-threatening diseases. As a result, Kunz says, "the cases where we euthanize a horse are black and white."

Death by lethal injection comes in about a minute, which seems very peaceful, very quick. So it's stunning to hear many vets say that this method isn't in the best interests of the horse. They would rather ditch the pink and do the killing in the way they deem most humane.

With a gun.

The truck slides to a stop. Canady sees Heelbolt, standing fifteen yards away. He's a gorgeous horse: glistening brown coat that darkens into black legs, speckles of white surrounding his eyes, a cowlick topping the crest of his head. He's exactly four months shy of his fifth birthday, April 1. He loves apples and carrots. He's so gentle, owner Ray Guarisco and trainer Sturges Ducoing can't recall his ever kicking anyone. But Heelbolt is competitive. He has done well over the past few months, prompting Guarisco, an equipment contractor in nearby Morgan City, to visit the track today. It's the first time the owner has seen his prize horse run in person.

Canady grabs the splint and the black bag, ducks under the railing and runs up the five-foot hill to the track. Two ambulances, one for the rider, one for the horse, are en route. Chaplain Parsons runs toward Torres, who is crumpled on the ground.

"Are you okay?" Parsons asks.

"I'm fine," Torres says. "Check on the horse."

Canady is almost there. This is the job she was born to do. She loved horse racing as a kid in New Castle, PA. Although her parents insisted her middle name, Kelso, was shared coincidentally with the Hall of Fame thoroughbred, she prefers to think it was fate. She graduated from Cornell vet school in 1997 and worked at tracks in the Northeast before moving to New Orleans. "All my life I've wanted to be around horse racing," says Canady, a single mom with a seven-year-old daughter. "You have to be a dreamer to work at a track. This is a dream for me."

As she nears Heelbolt, he is facing away from her. He's calm, but she can see he's standing on only three legs. His left front ankle is dangling and shattered, attached only by skin. Two arteries are split. Blood is everywhere—on his leg, his hoof, the grass. *Wow, this is a bad one.* Canady has seen this type of injury before, and she's seen how horses react to it. Some grunt and snort and thrash. Others, seemingly unbothered, try to run. But in her twelve years as a vet, she has never seen a critically injured horse do what Heelbolt is doing now. Eating grass.

For hundreds of years, there was no argument about the best way to kill a horse. Those injured in the chariot races of ancient Greece and Rome were presumably stabbed. With the introduction of the musket around the fifteenth century, and with European armies spreading firearms and horses all over the world, killing an injured horse with a gun became accepted practice. It was quick, cheap and easy—never mind that bullets often ricocheted out of the horse's head or that men might make the mistake of shooting the animal between the eyes. (A horse's brain is located toward the back of the head. To find it, draw a line from the outside of one eye to the opposite ear, then do the same from the other eye; where the lines intersect is the brain.)

In 1930, vets started using the Bell Gun, one of the first tools designed to kill livestock in a clean, safe, precise way. It weighed five pounds, spit .32-caliber bullets and had a bell-shape protective cover over its muzzle. To use it, vets simply fit it onto a horse's forehead, unscrewed a slot, inserted a bullet and tapped a lever. No kickback and no mess, only a sharp pop from point-blank range.

Manuel Gilman used the Bell Gun. Now eighty-eight years old, the former vet at Jamaica, Belmont and Saratoga helped put down "a couple hundred" horses during his career, including Ruffian, the legendary filly, and Air Lift, the brother of Triple Crown winner Assault, depicted famously in W.C. Heinz's story "Death of a Racehorse." Gilman occasionally made light of the darkest aspect of his job. If his daughter, Jane, complained about having a cold, he'd say, "Maybe I should get out the gun." When he actually did use it, on horses, he thought it was the most humane form of euthanasia. "The quicker, the better," he says. "I always thought that. Still do."

Most vets of Gilman's era shared that sentiment, as did fans. Then the television age dawned in the early 1950s, and opinions changed. Horse racing suddenly became a brand, and as a brand, it couldn't afford bloody drama, especially once its popularity began to dip. "Shooting a horse was too traumatic for people to see," says Bob Copeland, a protégé of Gilman's who has worked in New York, Miami and Cleveland and is now is in Kentucky. "We had to say farewell to the Bell Gun."

The transition from guns to drugs was clumsy and cruel. The first solution employed was strychnine, the poison Native Americans once used to tip arrows. Vets dissolved the pills into two ounces of water and injected it. But strychnine didn't work quickly; it suffocated horses over five minutes, sometimes longer. They often died of panic-induced cardiac arrest. "It wasn't very humane or effective," Copeland says.

John S. Lundy of the Mayo Clinic came up with the current pentobarbital mix in 1930, but Gilman says it wasn't until the late 1950s that racetrack vets began to carry bottles of it in their bags. By then, it was being used off the track, too. Pentobarbital was rumored to be the cause of Marilyn Monroe's death, and the Clash wrote a lyric about its trade name: "Nembutal numbs it all, but I prefer alcohol." In 1973, no less a horseman than Ronald Reagan, who once said he knew "what it's like to try to eliminate an injured horse by shooting him," floated lethal injection as a form of capital punishment. Today, the pentobarbital mix costs about $50 a dose, and a DEA license is required for purchase. It's illegal for nonmedical purposes in most countries and in every state except Oregon. *The International Herald Tribune* wrote last year about the flocks of suicidal people who visit Tijuana to buy it on the black market. Stacy Katler of the Oregon Racing Commission says that 120 ccs shot into a horse's jugular "works nine out of ten times."

For some vets, though, that isn't good enough. Truth is, they could shoot horses if they wanted. The American Veterinary Medical Association permits it, citing a primary advantage: "Loss of consciousness is instantaneous." A box of .32-caliber bullets costs about $15, much cheaper than a dose of poison. A silencer could kill the noise, and a tarp could block the crowd's view. "The gunshot is very humane," says Larry Bramlage, who put down Eight Belles. According to Bernard Rollin, an animal-rights activist and professor at Colorado State, it's the most humane way.

But it doesn't matter if it's legal or faster or if it's the method of choice by vets who put a horse's interests first. It's not going to happen, not on racetracks, not now. Most of today's vets aren't from Gilman's era. They're from a generation that, frankly, doesn't want to shoot any animal, especially not when cameras are rolling. "If you can have a quiet, peaceful death," Kunz says of lethal injection, "I don't know if we can do better."

There he is, standing on three legs, bleeding from a fourth, calm as a marsh, snacking on grass. Heelbolt has no idea he's injured. Not yet, anyway. Ten minutes from now, his nerve endings will begin to send excruciating signals to his brain. As serene as he seems, he is already exhibiting signs of shock. His eyes, once coldly fixed on the track, are teary and dilated. His breathing, once quick, has quickened even more. His coat, once shiny from the pumping of oil and sweat glands, has dulled. Parsons, the preacher, gently strokes Heelbolt's nose as the horse nibbles on the turf. "It's going to be okay," he says, knowing it won't.

Canady doesn't hear a thing in situations like this. Heelbolt's nonchalance shook her initially, but now she's focused. She typically looks for every reason to save a horse, but this is an easy diagnosis. Back in the trailer that serves as her office, she has a computer program that classifies injuries by severity: 0 to 3, the horse is salvageable; 4, it's iffy; 5, it's over. This is a 5. Canady removes Heelbolt's saddle and unclips the radio from her belt. "This horse requires euthanasia," she says into it.

Out comes the pink. Canady draws 10 ccs of succinylcholine mixed with 50 ccs of pentobarbital into a syringe, then fills another with an extra 50 ccs of pentobarbital. She moves to Heelbolt's left side, where it's easier for a right-handed person to administer an injection. She strokes his neck to say good-bye—as she does with every horse she puts down—then puts her left index finger on his jugular and presses down, swelling the vein. She drives the needle straight into his jugular, piercing his sweaty, leathery skin, and depresses the large plunger with her thumb, pushing in the poison, darkening the pink as it mixes with blood. After it empties, she draws out the needle and repeats the motion with the second syringe. The whole process takes just a few seconds. Heelbolt doesn't flinch.

Moments after a lethal injection, a horse will feel a warming sensation, then unfold, as if stretching. But Heelbolt, maybe for the only time in his life, kicks. His broken ankle whips into Canady's chest—*thwap!*—smearing blood on her jacket, knocking her back. Parsons moves to make sure she's OK. As he does, Heelbolt falls under the railing, landing shoulder first, his nose in the dirt. He blinks rapidly for ten seconds or so until his eyes, once beautifully alert, are blank. As his fellow horses, having just finished the race, jog by, his life is measured in shallow breaths—until he is no longer breathing, until he is just 1,200 pounds of expired muscle, his bloody, shattered leg hooked on a railing. It's hard to know what a peaceful death looks like, but this isn't it.

Canady tosses her bloody jacket onto the track. Two men place a rubber mat next to Heelbolt. With Canady's help, they use it as a sled to pull the horse into the ambulance. Afterward, Canady sits in her truck, shaken and quiet. Now is not the time to reflect, so she turns the key and slowly circles the track. The image of Heelbolt standing on three legs and munching grass tumbles through her head. It will later, too, in the dark after she puts her daughter, Jayne, to bed. She wonders if a death in the year's first race is a harbinger. Sure enough, she'll put down seven more horses at Fair Grounds over the next three weeks.

But now another race is minutes away. Canady parks the truck at the starting line, grabs her race card and pen and opens the door, ready to go back to work. After a few steps, she stops. She's cold, in only a short-sleeved shirt. Parsons offers his jacket. "Thanks," she says. "I'll get it back to you tonight." Canady puts on the coat, blue and tan and bearing a crucifix, then disappears into the paddock, where ten shiny thoroughbreds strut like models on a runway. The white truck idles behind her, a dusty black bag sitting on the backseat.

AUTHOR'S AFTERWORDS…

I learned the power of recreating scenes over a calzone. It was July of 1999, the summer before my senior year at the University of Missouri, and I was an intern at *The Washington Post*. Every week on the top floor of its 15th Street offices, *The Post* hosted intern lunches with various writers and editors— informal, instructive Q&A's about our craft. Up to that point, assignments had carried me around the country and away from every lunch. But this one, I wouldn't miss. This was the big one.

Bob Woodward.

I wore a tie, dressing up to mask my Woodward ignorance. I hadn't read any of his books, not even *All the President's Men*. (After the fashion of *Seinfeld's* George Costanza, I'd watched the movie.) I recognized him upon his entrance only because of the picture on the back of his latest book, *Shadow*, which I'd brought for him to sign—for my dad. Chatter ceased as he sat at the head of the table, which was scattered with catered *calzones*. Woodward made some small talk, and—sensing that the inevitable and repetitive Watergate questions were imminent—leaned forward and in his Midwestern accent said, "I want to help all of you. What kind of reporting problems have you experienced?"

In my case? Most of them.

I had arrived in D.C. feeling pretty cocky, but my confidence was drowning under daily—often twice- or thrice-daily—deadlines. My ass was being served, and I needed a reportorial lifeline, something that I could carry back to school and into my career, something beyond, "Put the fucking score higher!"

That arrived when Woodward—resigned that his audience, like all, wanted to hear about only his reporting—described how he recreates scenes. He discussed how he interrupts subjects for details; how he crosschecks information; how he compiles documents and notes and transcripts and every piece of reportage to illustrate a moment. His questions—his tools—are not magical. They are basic—who, what, when, where, why, and how. Methodically applied to each revelation in a constant cycle, the details begin to emerge in a cogent picture.

Of course, Woodward's advice was elemental and unoriginal. But to hear it from a legend gave it a sermonic weight, like John Elway reminding young quarterbacks to step into their throws. Years of practice since that day culminated in "The Final Furlong."

After Eight Belles had to be euthanized during the 2008 Kentucky Derby, my boss, Gary Belsky, assigned me to look into the conflicted culture of racetrack veterinarians. More than that, he wanted me to witness a death. So three nights a week for a month, I rode alongside Dr. Celeste Kunz, vet at the Meadowlands track. But no horses broke down. I researched tracks where horses were falling like rain, as if I were trying to find the deadliest corner in Fallujah. I arranged to hang with a vet at Santa Anita, northwest of L.A., site of seven horse deaths in less than a month. But once I arrived, the vet basically told me to stick that pink syringe where the sun doesn't shine. A few months later, I found myself beside Dr. Lauren Canady at Fairgrounds track in New Orleans, where sixteen horses had been euthanized during the previous season. I sat next to her for ten hours a day, every day for a week, following the horses through the dirt, contending with a looming deadline and my perverted rooting interest.

But no horses died during my time in New Orleans, either. So I turned to the power of recreation. I asked Canady about the recent death that had affected her most. Without hesitation, she mentioned Heelbolt, who had broken his leg a few weeks earlier, on New Year's Day. And it was on: I asked every question I could think of, interrupting her as she reenacted each step, for many hours over several days, then more phone calls after I'd returned home. I watched video of Heelbolt's fatal run, and spoke to everyone in the final frames—the jockey, the trainer, the owner, other Fairground employees—employing Woodward's prosaic but elemental five Ws and the H. In the end, I felt like I had witnessed Heelbolt's death. Not many of my stories make people cry—perhaps that's because few stories make me cry—but that one did, including its star, Lauren Canady.

Magazine writing is like carpentry: the grind precedes the art. Like Woodward, this story above all others taught me to stick to the basics. It worked pretty well for him. And it will work for you, even when editors and deadlines are breathing down your neck and horses that are supposed to die, don't.

Jason Zengerle

J ason Zengerle is a contributing editor at *New York* and at *GQ*. Prior to joining those magazines, he worked at *The New Republic*.

During the dozen years he was employed at *TNR*, known as a political magazine, Zengerle wrote mostly about non-political subjects, like the story that follows. Now that he works for general interest magazines, he writes primarily about politics. Over the years, his work has also appeared in *The Atlantic*, the *New York Times Magazine*, and other publications. He has been anthologized in *The Best American Political Writing*, *The Best American Medical Writing*, and others. He graduated from Swarthmore College with a major in political science and a minor in art history.

He lives with his wife, son, and daughter in Chapel Hill, North Carolina.

Going Under

In December 2003, Brent Cambron gave himself his first injection of morphine. Save for the fact that he was sticking the needle into his own skin, the motion was familiar—almost rote. Over the course of the previous 17 months, as an anesthesia resident at Boston's Beth Israel Deaconess Medical Center, Cambron had given hundreds of injections. He would stick a syringe into a glass ampule of fentanyl or morphine or Dilaudid, pulling up the plunger to draw his dose. Then he'd inject the dose into his patient. If the patient had been in a panic before her surgery, Cambron would watch her drift into a pleasant, happy daze; if she had been moaning in pain after surgery, he'd watch the relief spread across her face as the pain went away. It was understandable, perhaps, that Cambron was curious to experience these sensations himself, to feel what his patients felt once the drugs began coursing through their bodies. It could even be considered a clinical experiment of sorts. "I had thought about it for a long time," he later confessed.

The way in which Cambron handled his own injection reflected that intense curiosity, but also a degree of caution. Although Cambron had been a physician for less than two of his 30 years, in that brief time he'd acquired a fund of knowledge that left him certain he knew what he was doing. With his patients, he typically delivered drugs intravenously, so that the medicine went directly into their bloodstreams and its effects were immediate. Now that he was administering the drug to himself, he injected it into his muscle; that way, the morphine would have to seep through layers of fat and tissue before it began to circulate through his system, resulting in a slower, less intense, and presumably safer high. An intravenous injection, as one of Cambron's fellow residents would say, is like "putting fuel on a fire," but an intramuscular injection "is like putting a cookie in your mouth and letting it soak, so that you're not really chewing it and it's not getting into your stomach."

Cambron initially told no one of his decision to use morphine, not his colleagues, not even his live-in girlfriend, from whom he hid his syringes. What he was doing was illegal, and he knew others would disapprove. But his shame was leavened by a certain amount of confidence, even arrogance. During the 80-hour weeks he put in at Beth Israel, a Harvard teaching hospital considered one of the best in the world, he practiced medicine at its highest level. People could quibble with other choices Cambron might make, but if he chose to do something medical, even to himself, then it was, by definition, the right choice.

That first injection of morphine, however, would quite possibly be the last time Cambron actually chose to do drugs. As the needle broke the skin and the morphine slowly seeped into his system that December day, Cambron began to cede control over his own medical powers. Before long, his career and much more would be in jeopardy.

The common conception of anesthesiologists is that they do little more than put people to sleep while surgeons perform the true medical miracles. The reality of their job is more complicated, not to mention harrowing. In the course of putting a patient under, the anesthesiologist must maintain the patient's delicate physiological balance. Because the drugs he uses to put a patient to sleep often lower the person's heart rate and blood pressure, the anesthesiologist must administer other drugs to raise them. If the surgery requires silencing the patient's brain and paralyzing his muscles, then the anesthesiologist must control the patient's breathing, since the patient can no longer do so himself. During a surgery, in short, the anesthesiologist essentially takes over the patient's basic life-preservation functions.

As frightening as this process sounds, it routinely enables patients to undergo complex surgical procedures safely and without physical pain. Before the mid-nineteenth century, when anesthesia began to emerge as a medical specialty, this was rarely the case. Limbs were amputated and teeth extracted while patients were sentient and awake. Typical is a story recounted by a nineteenth-century Boston surgeon who helped treat a young man with tongue cancer: "The cancerous end ... was cut off by a sudden, swift stroke of the knife, and then a red-hot iron was placed on the wound to cauterize it. Driven frantic by the pain and the sizzle of searing flesh inside his mouth, the young man escaped his restraints in an explosive effort and had to be pursued until the cauterization was complete, with his lower lip burned in the process."

Among the doctors troubled by the pain and suffering he caused his patients was a young Connecticut dentist named Horace Wells. In December 1844, Wells attended a performance by Gardner Quincy Colton, a one-time medical student who had become a sort of scientific showman. Colton invited a volunteer from the audience to place in his mouth a wooden faucet connected to a rubber bag of nitrous oxide. After inhaling the gas, Colton's volunteer ran around the theater like a wild man, gashing his leg in the process. What intrigued Wells, according to Henry W. Erving's *The Discoverer of Anesthesia:*

Dr. Horace Wells of Hartford, was that the volunteer seemed impervious to pain. As it happened, Wells needed to have his wisdom tooth removed. The next day, he had Colton give him a dose of nitrous oxide, after which one of Wells's colleagues performed the extraction. "I didn't feel it so much as the prick of a pin!" Wells reported. He went on to give nitrous oxide to more than a dozen patients, storing the gas in an animal bladder and then asking them to suck it into their mouths via a wooden tube while he held their nostrils shut.

A few years later, after some setbacks with nitrous oxide, Wells began to experiment with chloroform as an anesthetic. As with nitrous oxide, he experimented on himself. This time, though, Wells developed an addiction to it, which sent him into a downward spiral. At the age of 33, after being arrested, he inhaled some chloroform and then with a razor severed his femoral artery, bleeding to death.

Today, anesthesiology has obviously come a long way from Wells's animal bladder of laughing gas. But, for all its technological advances, the specialty is still plagued by an addiction problem among its practitioners. In 1987, the addiction medicine doctor G. Douglas Talbott reviewed the files of 1,000 M.D.s who had enrolled in the Medical Association of Georgia's Impaired Physicians Program. He wanted to know how the drug-addicted physicians broke down by age, gender, and, most importantly, medical specialty. What Talbott discovered, and subsequently published in the *Journal of the American Medical Association*, was disturbing: Although anesthesiologists made up only 5 percent of the physician population, they accounted for 13 percent of those physicians being treated for drug addiction. The numbers Talbott found for younger physicians were even worse: While anesthesia residents constituted 4.6 percent of all resident physicians, they accounted for 33.7 percent of residents in treatment for drug addiction.

No studies have found a correlation between the addiction rate and medical error (although in 2002, a 31-year-old Washington State woman suffered severe brain damage after her anesthesiologist, who was addicted to Demerol, allegedly mismanaged her care during a routine surgical procedure). But Talbott's article served as a wake-up call to the specialty nonetheless. In the 20 years since its publication, anesthesia departments have worked to educate their members about the risk of addiction; they've become more vigilant about monitoring access and use of drugs by members; and some have even instituted mandatory urine tests for practitioners.

And yet, the problem has persisted. A 2005 study that surveyed more than 100 anesthesiology residency programs found that, between 1991 and 2001, 80 percent of them had physicians who became addicted to drugs during their training, and nearly 20 percent reported one death due to overdose or suicide. "We've gone through lots of steps to try to make it harder and harder, and that hasn't seemed to have had a lot of impact," says Keith Berge, an anesthesiologist at the Mayo Clinic in Minnesota who sits on the American Society of Anesthesiologists (ASA) Committee on Occupational Health. "Addiction," a recent article in the ASA's journal *Anesthesiology* concluded, "is still considered by many to be an occupational hazard for those involved in the practice of anesthesia."

When Brent Cambron arrived in Boston in the summer of 2002 to start his residency at Beth Israel Deaconess Medical Center, he could legitimately claim to be one of the top young anesthesia doctors in the country, and that was before he'd even handled his first case. Anesthesia is considered one of the most competitive specialties, and the program at Beth Israel, with its Harvard affiliation, was even more rarefied. It selected just twelve residents that year, and those it chose were invariably at or near the top of their med school classes.

That was certainly true of Cambron, a handsome young doctor with close-cut brown hair, gentle green eyes, and a thin, athletic build. But in other ways he didn't fit the typical Beth Israel anesthesia resident profile. Unlike many of his colleagues, who hailed from major metropolitan areas on the coasts, Cambron had grown up in the no-stoplight town of Sperry, Oklahoma, about 15 miles north of Tulsa, the son of a data processor and a homemaker. After scoring off the charts on his ACT test and graduating as his high school class's valedictorian, he attended the University of Oklahoma on a scholarship, matriculating to the University of Oklahoma College of Medicine. From his days in Sperry to his time in med school, Cambron had always sailed to the head of the class with ease. "There were some people who had to put in fourteen hours or so to learn the material, but it always seemed like Brent could do it in about seven," recalls Matthew Paden, a medical school classmate. "People would be incredibly stressed out and sleep-deprived and pepped up on coffee, and then he'd come walking down the hall with a smile on his face on his way to ride his bike."

Despite his whiz-kid status, Cambron seemed happiest when he came off as ordinary. "You kind of had to know him for a while to know how smart he was," says his college roommate John E. Thomas. "He didn't flaunt it." Although he was a gifted musician, the outlet he chose for his musical talents was a college party cover band called Hummer. Even in that, he preferred to stay in the background, playing rhythm guitar and singing backup. "Brent was very much a behind-the-scenes, below-the-radar kind of guy," says James Suliburk, one of Cambron's bandmates who also went to college and med school with him.

When it came time to do his residency, Cambron chose anesthesia, which would provide him with good pay, reasonable hours, and plenty of intellectual and emotional challenges. In their need for constant vigilance, anesthesiologists are frequently likened to airline pilots: Both jobs entail long periods of boredom punctuated by moments of extreme terror. "From the moment you walk in the hospital until the moment you leave, you're waiting for disaster to happen," says Ethan Bryson, an anesthesiologist at Mount Sinai hospital in New York. "And [when it does], you have to be ready to immediately intervene, recognize what's going on, and fix it, because someone's life depends on it."

As low-key as he liked to appear, Cambron craved this type of pressure. "If something was going to be difficult," says Thomas, "Brent always took it on." While most of his medical school classmates chose to do their residencies in Oklahoma, he decided to travel the great geographic and mental distance to Beth Israel.

Cambron immediately took to Boston. He rented an apartment on bustling Newbury Street, right in the heart of the ritzy Back Bay neighborhood, and attended concerts and Red Sox games. At the same time, he proved to be an excellent fit for Beth Israel. Even among the first-year residents, who typically work slavish hours, Cambron stood out for his penchant to get to the hospital early and leave late, something one fellow resident attributed to his "Midwestern work ethic." More importantly, during the long hours he spent at the hospital, he impressed his colleagues with his clinical skills. "Sometimes a resident isn't born with what we call the 'oh shit gene' to recognize that something with a patient is quickly deteriorating," says Anthony Hapgood, a former Beth Israel anesthesia resident who was in the class ahead of Cambron's. "Brent wasn't like that. He could recognize when something was going wrong. He treated it early, and he treated it appropriately."

Cambron soon developed a reputation for level-headedness during those moments of extreme terror, a level-headedness that was rare not only in residents but in more senior anesthesiologists, as well. Vivian Jung Tanaka, another of Cambron's co-residents, remembers the masterful way Cambron "ran codes", medical jargon for leading the effort to resuscitate someone who has stopped breathing. "He was one of those unusual people that, no matter what happened, he kept his cool," she says. His placid demeanor was matched with a burning intelligence. "I think the first two years, he got the highest score on the practice board exam," says Suzanne Harrison, who was in Cambron's resident class.

In July 2004, Cambron's fellow residents and senior colleagues selected him to serve as a chief resident, one of the highest honors a junior physician can receive. By the time he received that honor, Cambron had been giving himself injections of morphine, fentanyl, and Dilaudid for nearly eight months.

The drugs most frequently used in anesthesia today, such as the opioids fentanyl and Dilaudid, as well as the sedative propofol, are among the most potent in the history of medicine. Dilaudid and fentanyl, for instance, are eight and 100 times more potent than morphine, respectively. These drugs aren't only powerful, they're also extremely addictive. Because they are chemically engineered to have short half-lives, so that their effects do not linger and patients can be safely discharged sooner after their surgeries, recreational users of such drugs quickly develop heightened tolerances to them, meaning that they have to use more and more of the drugs in order to achieve their desired highs. "There's a crash-and-burn phenomenon with these drugs," says Paul Earley, the medical director of the Talbott Recovery Campus in Atlanta, which specializes in treating impaired physicians. "Whereas an alcoholic physician or one who's abusing oral narcotics might not manifest obvious signs of addiction for years or even decades, it's common for anesthesiologists to show up in treatment six months or nine months or a year after their first time taking one of these drugs."

Cambron was no stranger to recreational drug use. According to a journal he kept, he was a heavy drinker in college and in medical school; he also occasionally smoked marijuana. But maintaining a hard-partying lifestyle in the midst of an ambitious academic career seemed like the type of challenge that Cambron thrived on. "We would go out and party all night and do the things college kids do," recalls one of Cambron's college friends, "and then he'd get up the next day and study for an hour and go take a midterm and ace it." When Cambron arrived in Boston for his residency, he cut back on his alcohol consumption. Soon, though, Cambron began to go out drinking on weekends with some of the people in his program. In December 2002, he found a resident who did cocaine and the two began using together. When his co-resident couldn't get cocaine, they would snort powdered Ritalin. In the year before he began injecting himself with opioids, Cambron was drinking three or four nights a week and using cocaine once or twice a month. Ironically, once he tried the morphine, he liked it in part because it allowed him to drink less.

When Cambron was appointed chief resident, it seemed to strengthen his conviction that, when it came to his drug use, he knew what he was doing. "I felt that things must be going well since everyone thought I was doing well," he later wrote in his journal. Not long after becoming chief, when Cambron began having trouble with his girlfriend (who had moved with him to Boston from Oklahoma), he increased the doses, along with the frequency, of his opioid injections. And the frequency increased even further after Cambron and his girlfriend broke up about halfway through his one-year term as chief. He started spending more time socially with the residents he supervised, including one, he discovered, who also took intramuscular injections of morphine. They began doing the drugs together. In January 2006, the resident revealed to Cambron that she had started taking the drugs intravenously. Soon he was giving himself regular i.v. injections of morphine, fentanyl, and Dilaudid and occasional injections of propofol.

For a time, Cambron was able to manage his drug use as he had in the past. Indeed, in July 2006, after he completed a fellowship in pain medicine, Beth Israel hired him as an attending physician and he became a clinical instructor of anesthesiology at Harvard Medical School. But, before long, the i.v. injections left him with cravings that he could only satisfy with ever larger and ever more frequent doses. It became harder for him to conceal what he was doing, and his work began to suffer. On one occasion, he fell after giving himself an injection of propofol, splitting open his forehead and leaving him with a black eye. The doctor who once got to work early and left late was now getting to work late and leaving early. Some of his colleagues told him he looked "disheveled."

In December, a senior physician approached Cambron and asked if he would meet with her after grand rounds the next day. When Cambron looked at the schedule, he realized that the grand rounds speaker was the director of the Massachusetts Medical Society's Physician Health Services, a group that assists physicians struggling with drug addiction. Cambron knew what was coming, but he came up with a plan. His resident friend, who had recently returned from an unsuccessful three-month stay at the Betty Ford clinic, had obtained clean urine for her own regular drug tests. He took some of her supply to work with him the next day. And when, after grand rounds, he was confronted with suspicions that he was using drugs, he agreed to produce a urine sample.

But Cambron could only avoid getting caught for so long. He continued to use more and more frequently, injecting himself before work and then taking syringes to use at the hospital. By the end of January, he was giving himself i.v. injections of Dilaudid throughout his days at the hospital and slurring his words for the five or so minutes after each hit. Officials at Beth Israel wouldn't comment on exactly how or when they discovered Cambron was using drugs, citing hospital policy not to discuss personnel matters, but, in early February,

Cambron took a leave from the hospital to enter a rehabilitation facility in Virginia that specializes in treating impaired physicians.

On the night before the Fourth of July in 2007, Cambron put on blue hospital scrubs, rented a Zipcar, and drove 20 miles from the Back Bay to a hospital in the suburban town of Norwood, where he'd once done some part-time work. Four weeks earlier, he'd returned to Boston from the Virginia rehab facility. He was sober and committed to recovery, and to going back to his old job at Beth Israel. Although this would seem akin to, as one anesthesiologist friend of Cambron's put it, "sending an alcoholic to work in a bar," it is actually not uncommon. Anesthesiology residents who become addicted and successfully complete recovery are often then redirected toward lower-risk medical specialties. But those anesthesiologists who have finished their training (as Cambron had) are more typically permitted to return to the specialty, so long as they are monitored by an impaired-physicians program, something Cambron had agreed to.

But, not long after getting back to Boston, Cambron was summoned to a meeting at Beth Israel with the hospital vice president and the chair of the anesthesia department, during which they asked him to resign from the hospital staff and agree to a voluntary suspension of his license. (Cambron's resident friend had earlier agreed to these same conditions, although her medical license was ultimately revoked.) Cambron acquiesced, but he was devastated. "I felt betrayed by the people who were to have supported me," he wrote in his journal. A week or so later, Cambron snuck into Beth Israel, stole some propofol, and returned to his apartment, where he injected himself.

Now, as Cambron walked into the mostly empty Norwood hospital, his scrubs concealing the fact that he was, at that moment, prohibited from practicing medicine, he was once again determined to get sober. He carried with him used needles and some of his old supplies. He was going to throw them away. Even in the throes of addiction, he was still a physician and was a stickler when it came to the disposal of hazardous materials. "He was worried someone would get hurt going through the garbage," says Margaret Yoh, a Boston woman who was Cambron's girlfriend. But Cambron couldn't resist temptation. He swiped some propofol from an operating room, locked himself in a bathroom near the endoscopy unit, and injected the drug into his femoral artery. Before long a cleaning woman tried to gain entrance to the bathroom, but Cambron wouldn't come out. When he finally emerged over an hour later, hospital security officers were waiting for him. They noticed the blood on his hand, on his scrubs, and on the bathroom floor; they also noticed that Cambron was acting like, as one of them later put it, he was "on something." The security officers called the police. Cambron told them that he'd come to Norwood to pick up a bag for an anesthesiologist friend; the blood stains on his scrubs, he explained, were old. "I don't know why you keep questioning me," he protested. "This is no big deal." When they asked to search his backpack he refused. He was placed under arrest for trespassing and the officers then went through his bag, discovering a veritable pharmacy. He was charged with larceny and drug possession. At the police station, one of the officers asked Cambron if he was sick or injured. He told them he had the "disease of addiction." "To what?" the officer asked. "To everything," Cambron replied.

Cambron's father and his sister Kelly flew from Oklahoma to Boston to bail him out of jail. Kelly stayed at Cambron's apartment over the next several weeks to look after him. With a c.v. that now included a failed stint in rehab and an arrest record, Cambron seemed to have lost everything. But his medical license was still only suspended, not revoked, and he continued to hold out hope he could eventually return to anesthesia. He begged his sister to help him understand why he felt the need to use drugs in the first place. "He'd ask me if something went wrong in his childhood that he felt he'd need them," Kelly recalls. "I tried to help him figure that out and I couldn't. He was looking for any kind of reason for why he'd feel he needed them, because he couldn't figure it out, and it really bothered him."

The anesthesia specialty has been struggling with this question itself: Why do so many of its members suffer from addiction? The simplest and most popular explanation is access. Anesthesia is the only medical specialty in which physicians draw up, label, and account for their own drugs. As such, they have more opportunities than other physicians to abuse those drugs. "Anesthesiologists are left alone with open ampules of highly potent narcotics, " explains the Mayo Clinic's Berge, "and it's easy to divert for their own use." Cambron was proof of that. Beth Israel Deaconess Medical Center, according to its vice president for education Richard Schwartzstein, has multiple policies and procedures in place to prevent such diversion, including the requirement that anesthesiologists "waste" whatever drugs they don't use on a patient in front of a witness or that they return the unused drugs to the pharmacy, which are then verified through random tests. But these safeguards proved no match for a determined addict like Cambron. "Addicts are smart, we're smart; they're desperate, we're not desperate," says Berge. "So they're going to outsmart us every time."

In recent years, however, the access hypothesis has started to be questioned. Its leading critic is Mark Gold, a psychiatrist and the former chief of addiction medicine at the University of Florida's McKnight Brain Institute. "If it's just holding the drugs," says Gold, "the pharmacists have the drugs, so do drug-abuse researchers, and not many of them become drug abusers or drug dependent." In 2004, Gold presented an alternative hypothesis to explain anesthesiology's addiction problem: exposure. Using gas chromatography-mass spectroscopy equipment, Gold had researchers scour several working operating rooms for traces of anesthetic agents. Sure enough, even though the anesthetics were administered intravenously, the researchers found throughout the operating rooms trace amounts of fentanyl and propofol, which the patients had exhaled. The highest concentrations were found around the patients' heads, which is where the anesthesiologists typically sit during surgeries. Gold, who did some of the pioneering work on secondhand cigarette addiction during the 1990s, had his new hypothesis. "It wasn't a great leap," he explains, "to say, possibly, that some number of anesthesiologists who become drug abusers and drug-addicted may have as an important contributory factor exposure to secondhand drugs in the O.R. Their brains changed in response to the secondhand drugs, and they developed cravings as if they were taking the drugs themselves."

Most anesthesiologists and other addiction experts doubt exposure can explain the problem, since the amounts of anesthetics found in the operating room are so miniscule. "I think it's invoking an incredibly complex explanation for something that has a much more simple explanation," says Berge. And yet, even many of those who subscribe to the access hypothesis concede that it's unsatisfying. "I agree that access has something to do with it," says one anesthesiologist, "but people have to want to take advantage of that access. There has to be some other explanation."

Cambron's arrest started him on a vicious cycle of recovery and relapse. Over the next year, he would make numerous, serial attempts to get sober again at the treatment facility in Virginia, at McLean Hospital outside Boston, and at a retreat in rural Connecticut that was started by Alcoholics Anonymous co-founder Bill Wilson. In each instance (including after he was arrested a second time, at Beth Israel), he would become sober for a while, before eventually, inevitably relapsing. In this, he was hardly unique. One 1990 study found that two-thirds of opioid-addicted anesthesiology residents who returned to their programs relapsed. Their continued access to drugs was surely a contributing factor, but there was something else that seemed to prevent their recovery.

The first of the twelve steps to sobriety is for the addict to admit that he is powerless over his addiction. The second step is to believe that a power greater than himself could restore him to sanity. But admitting this sort of powerlessness flies in the face of what makes someone a good anesthesiologist to begin with. Some anesthesiologists and addiction medicine specialists like to talk about what they call the "AOA disease", referring to the Alpha Omega Alpha medical society, a sort of Phi Beta Kappa for med school students. Because only the top medical students are able to enter anesthesia residencies, it's a specialty stocked with overachievers. "They're driven and they don't know how to take care of themselves well, they're too compulsive about their work, they can't let cases go, they're almost wound too tight," Talbott Recovery's Earley says of anesthesiologists. "And then, when the drug comes along, they just feel like, ahhhhhhhhh, I can finally relax. And it's in that experience that the setup for continued use occurs. If you've been wound tight all your life, the first time you use narcotics, you say to yourself, this is how normal people must feel." Raymond Roy, the chair of the anesthesiology department at Wake Forest University School of Medicine, relates some black humor that has made the rounds in anesthesia circles: "How can you avoid having any substance abusers in your residency? Recruit from the bottom of your med school class."

Compounding the problem is the fact that anesthesiology doesn't only draw overachievers but overachievers who, in order to succeed in the specialty, must also be control freaks and, in particular, control freaks about drugs and the human body. "So much of what we do as a physician and as a specialist is control someone else's physiology," says Mount Sinai's Bryson. "We give what would be equivalent to a lethal injection on a daily basis if we didn't intervene. A lot of what we do is controlling the body's reaction to drugs. And I think that creates a false sense that, if we can control what's going on with somebody else, we should be able to control this in ourselves."

Cambron certainly seemed to suffer from that delusion. "He always told me that when he was taking these drugs, he knew exactly what he was doing," says his sister Kelly, "that whenever he messed around with stuff, because of his medical knowledge, he knew how much to do without going overboard."

Sometime in the night on October 13 or in the early morning hours of October 14, 2008, Cambron returned to the surgical suite on the third floor of the Beth Israel Deaconess Medical Center's Shapiro building. Once, the nine operating rooms there had been his professional home, where he'd work on knee repairs and breast biopsies and cataract surgeries. Now, they were simply a place where he could get drugs. Because the surgical suite in the Shapiro building was reserved for outpatient procedures, Cambron knew it would be empty at night. As he walked through the maze of hallways and through a series of imposing double doors, no one challenged his presence.

Cambron assembled his stash: It included five syringes, a 50-milligram vial of Demerol, four ten-milligram bottles of morphine, four ten-milligram bottles of Dilaudid, and a ten-milligram bottle of vecuronium, a muscle relaxant that, taken at high doses, will cause respiratory arrest in a matter of minutes. He brought all of it into a small room that bore the label "soiled utility" and was used to clean anesthesia equipment, closed the door, and began to inject himself.

At about 7:30 a.m., an anesthesia technician, who was making her morning rounds before the day's first surgery, opened the door. Cambron was sprawled on the floor between two stainless steel wash basins, his body surrounded by needles and empty vials, including, most ominously, the ten-milligram bottle of vecuronium. The technician ran for help and a team of doctors crowded into the small room. There was nothing they could do. At 7:47 a.m., a Beth Israel Deaconess anesthesiologist pronounced his former colleague dead. Cambron was 35 years old.

Two months later, with his death still under investigation by the police department, Cambron's friends and family don't know whether he meant to kill himself or whether his overdose was accidental. He left no suicide note, and he gave no signs that he was contemplating such an act. Indeed, he had recently arranged his apartment so that his girlfriend could move some of her things in. But the empty bottle of vecuronium is a haunting goodbye. After all, in spite of everything else that had gone wrong in his life, Cambron was an excellent doctor. Some of those who knew him have a hard time believing that he could have made such an elementary and catastrophic medical mistake.

AUTHOR'S AFTERWORDS...

How do you bring a dead man back to life? That was the fundamental challenge posed by this story. By the time I first learned of the existence of Brent Cambron—from a short article in the *Boston Globe*'s Metro section headlined "Body of doctor found at Beth Israel; death may have been suicide"—he was already gone.

I was intrigued by Cambron not only because of the circumstances of his death, but because he was an anesthesiologist. Ever since my wife was in medical school and came home one night with the information that anesthesiologists disproportionately suffer from drug addiction, the factoid had been lodged in my brain as a potentially interesting story idea. And reporting and writing that part of the story was straightforward: read the relevant literature; interview the relevant experts; and then translate a complex and oftentimes esoteric scientific discussion ("gas chromatography-mass spectroscopy equipment," anyone?) into language lay readers can understand. Actually, that part of the story is fun. Any time you discover a high-stakes, and perhaps insoluble, taking place among extremely smart people that's unbeknownst to 99.9 percent of the public—as is often the case with scientific debates—it's a great thing to write about. That's why, even though my high school physics teacher once told me that I may one day do great things "but they won't be in science," I like to write about scientific topics.

Writing about dead people? Not so much. Part of my problem is squeamishness. I just have a difficult time approaching the family and friends of someone who's just died and asking them to talk about that person, even though I've now done it enough times that I know that, quite often, these people are grateful for the opportunity. (And if they're not, they simply, and usually politely, tell me they don't want to talk and I leave them alone.) But the bigger difficulty is that, no matter how many people you talk to about the dead person, their grief often occludes their memories in such a way that the dead person's life becomes so uncomplicated and unnuanced that it no longer feels true. And so as I talked to the friends and family of Cambron, many of whom were unstintingly generous with their time and patience, I felt that I understood parts of his life but that vast swaths of it, particularly as they related to his addiction, remained unknown to me. When you profile someone, it's always helpful to see how other people's perceptions of your subject square with your subject's self-perception. But I couldn't do that with Cambron. I didn't have a firm grasp on how he viewed himself.

And I never would have were it not for two documents. One was a police report pertaining to one of Cambron's arrests. It was written by a cop who apparently aspired to be James Ellroy, as it contained the sort of emotional detail you don't often find in a government document. Most crucially for my purposes, it contained Cambron's actual words—including the quote that, to me, is the most haunting of the entire story. Having told the cop that he had the "disease of addiction," the cop asks Cambron what he's addicted to. "To everything," Cambron replies—those two words laying bare his shame and desperation in a way that a thousand interviews with his friends and family never could.

The other, more important document was Cambron's journal. I knew that he'd kept one, but my knowledge of its contents was only secondhand. Finally, a person offered to share it with me. This person, for understandable reasons, would not let me borrow the journal. I wasn't even allowed to photocopy it. Instead, this person agreed to be the journal's chaperone and we would look at it together. So on one very cold and gray November afternoon, I met this person and for several hours we sat on the floor of a cluttered room and, taking turns, read the contents of the journal into my digital recorder. It was the journal that revealed Cambron's thoughts when he gave himself his first injection of morphine, as I describe in the beginning of my story; that attested to the supreme and false confidence he felt after being appointed chief resident despite his drug use; and that described the profound sense of betrayal he felt when Beth Israel fired him. And it was Cambron's journal, and the thoughts and feelings it contained, that ultimately allowed me to envision Cambron as he lived.

That afternoon I spent with Cambron's journal and this person who so clearly loved him, reading and hearing a dead man's words, is my indelible memory from reporting and writing this story. And it serves as a reminder to me about what's most important when I try to write this sort of piece. That as much as I, as a journalist, want to bring the dead person back to life, there are others who want that even more.

NOTABLES: More great young writers from the Next Wave

●●●

Katie Baker

Chris Ballard

Victoria Bekiempis

Justin Berton

Frank Bures

Monte Burke

Jeanne Emery

David Epstein

Jason Fagone

Wes Ferguson

Reid Forgrave

Pete Freedman

Natasha Gardner

Christopher Goffard

David Grann

Nicholas Hune-Brown

Michael Idov

Sasha Issenberg

Colleen Jenkins

Eric Konigsberg

Matt Labash

Joon Oluchi Lee

Ben Montgomery

Richard Morgan

Robb Murray

Michelle Nijhuis

Nathaniel Rich

Kelefa Sanneh

Mattathias Schwartz

John Jeremiah Sullivan

Jamie Thompson

Erik Vance

Jose Antonio Vargas

Inara Verzemnieks

Michael Weinreb

Paige Williams

Lisa Taddeo

Walt Harrington's Suggested Readings

●●●

Intimate Journalism, Walt Harrington
The Literature of Journalism, R. Thomas Berner
Literary Nonfiction, Patsy Sims
Telling True Stories, Mark Kramer and Wendy Call
Literary Journalism, Norman Sims and Mark Kramer
Writing for Story, Jon Franklin
The Art of Fact, Kevin Kerrane and Ben Yagoda
Writing Literary Features, Thomas Berner
Storycraft, Jack Hart
The New Journalism, Tom Wolfe
Telling Stories, Taking Risks, Alice Klement and Carolyn Matalene
The Sierra Club Nature Writing Handbook, John Murray
ASNE Best Newspaper Writing, annual collections
ASME Best Magazine Writing, annual collections.
*The Best...*series, annual collections of essays, sportswriting, and more
Reporting, Lillian Ross
The Call of Stories, Robert Coles
Pulitzer Prize Feature Stories, David Garlock
Follow the Story, James B. Stewart
Literary Journalism, Jean Chance and William McKeen
The Art of the Personal Essay, Phillip Lopate
Let Us Now Praise Famous Men, James Agee
Hiroshima, John Hersey
The Power Broker, Robert Caro
The Right Stuff, Tom Wolfe
Radical Chic & Mau-Mauing the Flak Catchers, Tom Wolfe
In Cold Blood, Truman Capote
The Bullfighter Checks Her Makeup, Susan Orlean
Random Family, Adrian Nicole LeBlanc
Revenge of the Donut Boys, Mike Sager
Wounded Warriors, Mike Sager

Scary Monsters and Super Freaks, Mike Sager
The Immortal Life of Henrietta Lacks, Rebecca Skloot
The Good Soldiers, David Finkel
The Warmth of Other Suns, Isabel Wilkerson
Blue Highways, William Least Heat Moon ·
The Snow Leopard, Peter Matthiessen
Fame and Obscurity, Gay Talese
The Kingdom and the Power, Gay Talese
The Final Days, Bob Woodward and Carl Bernstein
The Soul of a New Machine, Tracy Kidder ·
House, Tracy Kidder
Oranges, John McPhee
The John McPhee Reader, John McPhee ·
The World According the Jimmy Breslin, Jimmy Breslin ·
Desert Solitaire, Edward Abbey ·
Up in the Old Hotel, Joseph Mitchell ·
The Last Cowboy, Jane Kramer
A Bright Shining Lie, Neil Sheehan
The Best and the Brightest, David Halberstam
Beautiful Swimmers, William Warner
The Sweet Science, A.J. Liebling
Down and Out in Paris and London, George Orwell
Remembering Denny, Calvin Trillin
Hell's Angels, Hunter Thompson ·
The Executioner's Song, Norman Mailer
Armies of the Night, Norman Mailer
Great Plains, Ian Frazier
Essays of E.B. White, E.B. White ·
The Deer Pasture, Rick Bass
The Outermost House, Henry Beston
How the Weather Was, Roger Kahn
Arctic Dreams, Barry Lopez ·
Dispatches, Michael Herr
The Everlasting Stream, Walt Harrington
Crossings, Walt Harrington
American Profiles, Walt Harrington ·
At the Heart of It, Walt Harrington ·
The Beholder's Eye, Walt Harrington
In These Girls, Hope is a Muscle, Madeleine Blais

The Heart is an Instrument, Madeleine Blais
Ernie's War, Ernie Pyle
Homicide, David Simon
Common Ground, J. Anthony Lukas
Growing Up, Russell Baker
Slouching Towards Bethlehem, Joan Didion
The White Album, Joan Didion
Kate Quinton's Days, Susan Sheehan
There Are No Children Here, Alex Kotlowitz
The Last Farmer, Howard Kohn
The Story of a Shipwrecked Sailor, Gabriel Garcia Marquez
Hemingway's Boat, Paul Hendrickson
Looking for the Light, Paul Hendrickson
The Living and the Dead, Paul Hendrickson
The Hot House, Pete Earley
Beyond the Game, Gary Smith
The Spirit Catches You and You Fall Down, Anne Fadiman
The Promised Land, Nicholas Lemann
A Sand County Almanac, Aldo Leopold
The Orchid Thief, Susan Orlean
The Bullfighter Checks Her Makeup, Susan Orlean
Praying for Sheetrock, Melissa Fay Greene
A Turn in the South, V.S. Naipaul

Acknowledgments

●●●

Researchers: Samantha Bakall, Angelina Chapin, Ramzi Dreessen, Emily Stanford, Tanya Huang, Sohrob Nikzad, Ryan Schuler.

Contractors and benefactors: Phil Adams, Sara Adams, Edwin Lap, Martjin Lap, Milan Ajdinovic, SF AppWorks, Andrew Greenstein, Darius Zăgrean, Siori Kitajima, Andrew Mayer, Art Harris, Bruce Kluger, Marvin M. Sager, M.D.

Permissions

●●●

About the Editors

●●●

WALT HARRINGTON, a former long-time staff writer for the *Washington Post Magazine*, is the author or editor of six books and the winner of numerous print and broadcast journalism awards, including the Gustavus Myers Center Award for the Study of Human Rights in the United States for his book *Crossings: A White Man's Journey Into Black America*. His book, *The Everlasting Stream: A True Story of Rabbits, Guns, Friendship, and Family*, was made into an Emmy Award-winning documentary broadcast nationally on PBS. His book, *Intimate Journalism: The Art and Craft of Reporting Everyday Life*, has been widely used in journalism writing classes nationwide. He is a journalism professor at the University of Illinois at Urbana-Champaign. An archive of student work published from his feature writing classes is at www.intimatejournalism.com. His professional website is at www.waltharrington.com.

MIKE SAGER is a bestselling author and award winning reporter. A former *Washington Post* staff writer under Watergate investigator Bob Woodward, he worked closely with gonzo journalist Hunter S. Thompson during his years as a contributing editor to *Rolling Stone*. Sager is the author of four collections of non-fiction, two novels, and one biography. He has served for more than fifteen years as a writer at large for *Esquire*. In 2010 he won the American Society of Magazine Editors' National Magazine Award for profile writing for his article "The Man Who Never Was." Many of his stories have been optioned for film. For more information, please see www.MikeSager.com.

About the Publisher

●●●

The Sager Group was founded in 1984. In 2012 it was chartered as a multi-media artists' and writers' consortium, with the intent of empowering those who make art—an umbrella beneath which artists can pursue, and profit from, their craft directly, without gatekeepers. TSG publishes eBooks; manages musical acts and produces live shows; ministers to artists and provides modest grants; and produces documentary, feature and web-based films. By harnessing the means of production, The Sager Group helps artists help themselves, *artifex te adiuva*. For more information, please see http://www.TheSagerGroup.net.

CPSIA information can be obtained at www.ICGtesting.com
Printed in the USA
BVOW07s0639181213

339413BV00002B/110/P

9 781481 160896